THOMAS AQUINAS ON
THE CARDINAL VIRTUES

THOMAS AQUINAS ON
THE CARDINAL VIRTUES

*Edited and Explained
for Everyone*

CHRISTOPHER KACZOR
&
THOMAS SHERMAN, S.J.

FOREWORD BY
RALPH MCINERNY

Sapientia Press
of Ave Maria University

Sapientia Press
of Ave Maria University
5050 Ave Maria Blvd.
Ave Maria, FL 34142
888-343-8607

Cover Design: Eloise Anagnost

Cover Image: St. Dominic with four musical angels, from a gradual from San
Marco e Cenacoli (vellum) (detail of 88937 & 79797) by Fra Angelico (Guido
di Pietro) (c.1387–1455). Museo di San Marco dell'Angelico, Florence,
Italy/The Bridgeman Art Library

Printed in the United States of America.

Library of Congress Control Number: 2008941958

ISBN: 978-1-932589-51-1

In Honor of and in Thanksgiving to:

Norbert and Imy Ann Sherman &
Dennis Philander and Eileen McKee

TABLE OF
CONTENTS

Justice Toward God: The Virtue of Religion

Other Connected Virtues

Vices Opposed to Courage

Parts of Courage

The Gift of Courage

FOREWORD

HUMAN ACTS can be performed well or badly. They are performed well when our choices are directed to a good that truly fulfills us. To call something good is to say that it is desirable, and every action presumes a judgment as to what is good for us. It is because we are sometimes mistaken in our judgments about the good that we need to learn how to distinguish between real and apparent goods. But just getting the judgment right is not enough: our will must be attuned to the true good. It must be *my good*. Knowing the good is to be related to it as something true; in order to be related to the good as good, the will must come into play.

These are things we all already know. Simply to have correct information about the good does not entail that one will pursue it. However necessary knowledge of the good is, it is not the whole story. Such a book as this contains precious information about the moral life. The reader can come into possession of lots of truths about human action. But the most important truth of all is that such knowledge alone cannot make us what we ought to be.

Call this the paradox of moral philosophy as well as of moral theology. They are the pursuit of a knowledge that is incommensurate with the ultimate reason for the pursuit, meaning that you can get an A in Ethics and, in the enigmatic phrase, still be no better than you should be.

Virtue is, so to speak, adverbial: it modifies action. When the action is done well we derive from that "well" our conception of virtue as the excellence or perfection of an activity. A vice is the opposite. This presupposes, of course, that we are free to act or not to act, and to act in this way rather than that. Only free acts, those done deliberately and voluntarily, count as human acts. But there are other activities going on in us, and it is their presence that makes for the drama of human life.

The things we sense attract or repel us; they promise pleasure or pain. Like animals we have instinctive reactions to the pleasurable or the menacing, and there is a level of response to them for which we get neither credit nor blame. We feel fear; the desire for the pleasant is an immediate response. For animals this seems to be the whole story. It cannot be for us. Our emotions or passions—those instinctive reactions to what we sense—are the material of human acts. It is how we act when we feel fear or when we are drawn by the promise of pleasure that makes us what we morally are. We cannot not feel hunger and thirst, but how we eat and drink is up to us. We must act well, and that means, again, that we must both correctly assess where our good lies and seek it. Food and drink are undeniably good, but we must pursue them in the light of our comprehensive good.

This book lays before you what St. Thomas Aquinas had to say about the great categories of doing well, of the virtues. The schema of the cardinal virtues enables us to cover the whole spectrum of moral action in such a way that we begin with sweeping generalities and move progressively toward more specific matters. I think the authors of this book, Christopher Kaczor and Father Thomas Sherman, were inspired when they hit upon the idea of providing such a summary as this. There has been much talk of virtue ethics of late and of that one might say what the metaphysics professor on Second City said of his topic, "The Universe:" "Wot else is der?"

Here you will find a discussion of the virtue needed to make right judgments about the good, the virtue of prudence. You will find discussions of the two virtues that enable us to act well despite the tug of our emotions, the virtues of temperance and courage. Finally, the virtue of justice deals with the fact that we are *ab ovo* members of communities, the family, the city, and not isolated and autonomous individuals. If we were the latter, justice might seem simply a matter of trade-offs between agents who hope to lose as little as possible in their dealings with others. Because we are by nature members of families and cities, our good necessarily involves our relations with others. The good we share with others, the common good, broods over all the cardinal virtues.

Christopher Kaczor and Father Tom Sherman have put us all in their debt. The idea for this book was a great one; its execution is marvelous. The rest is up to the reader.

—Dr. Ralph McInerny
Michael P. Grace Professor of Medieval Studies
University of Notre Dame

General Introduction

ONE of the best-selling books of recent memory is Stephen Covey's *Seven Habits of Highly Effective People*. About seven centuries previously, Thomas Aquinas also wrote about the seven habits of highly successful people, successful not necessarily in the sense of having power, pay, or prestige, but in terms of fulfillment, meaning, and contentment. Practical wisdom, justice, courage, and temperance are the four cardinal, or "hinge," virtues of the moral life. Added to them are faith, hope, and love, the theological virtues that round out the moral life. For Thomas, these seven virtues, habits of the heart and mind, enable a person to lead a fulfilling and satisfying life. Without these seven habits, our relationship with God, each other, and ourselves will be jeopardized. For Thomas, God created us to love Him and serve Him and to be happy with Him and others in this life and the next. It is precisely by means of the virtues that God helps us and we help ourselves to achieve this noble goal.

In order to understand properly St. Thomas Aquinas on the cardinal virtues of practical wisdom, justice, courage, and temperance; first, we need to place his treatment of these virtues within the overall context of what constitutes a truly happy human life. For Thomas, a human person becomes truly happy in living heroically the Christian way of life. Part of the great achievement of Aquinas consists in organizing and putting into context all the various elements of the Christian way of life—virtues, laws, grace, sacraments, biblical teaching, and philosophical wisdom as well. The fundamental basis for his ethical teaching, as reflected in revealed wisdom and philosophical insight, is the deep human desire for happiness.

Happiness

St. Thomas devotes a large part of his masterpiece, the *Summa theologiae*, to an exposition of the moral life. As happiness for him is the point and goal of the moral life, Aquinas begins his exposition with an extensive examination of human happiness. Although the desire for happiness is natural for human beings, historically human beings have had widely different views on what constitutes happiness. Some believe that happiness is to be found in great wealth, others think that happiness consists in bodily pleasures, and still others think power, fame, or honors make up "the good life." While Aquinas acknowledges these different views by taking into consideration what is of value in each, he argues that true human happiness ultimately consists in the universal good of a loving contemplation of God Himself; any other view of happiness will, in the end, only frustrate our natural desire.

True human happiness is twofold: there is a human happiness in this life proportionate to human nature and an eternal life of supernatural happiness obtainable by and through God's power alone. The moral life, as St. Thomas describes it in the *Summa* has this twofold happiness as the goal and point of all human action.

Human Action

Morality is concerned with human actions as these actions lead toward or away from true human happiness. St. Thomas makes a distinction between "human action" and mere "acts of a human being." "Acts of a human being" are involuntary; that is, they are kinds of behavior over which we have no rational control, for example, the functions of our autonomic nervous system, digestive processes, reflex actions, or other unconscious acts like sleep-walking or snoring. Human action, on the other hand, is voluntary in character. A voluntary act is a willed act following some rational awareness of a good to be done or an evil to be avoided. For example, reading a book, calling a friend, or taking a walk are all human acts—acts arising from our knowing what we are doing and wanting to do it. Human action is therefore a knowing willing. If we do not realize what we are doing due to some involuntary ignorance or compulsion, then our action will not be a human action but an act of a human being.

A human act is morally good when three conditions are met. First, the act itself (the object) must be morally good or indifferent in kind; second, it must be done out of a good intention (motive); and finally it must be morally appropriate given the situation (circumstances). All three aspects of the act must be good for the act to be good. When one or more of these conditions are not met, the action is morally bad. For example, a benefactor might give some money to a person in need—a morally good or indifferent act in itself—but if the benefactor gives the money not in order to help the person but rather with the intention of bribing her, then the action is wrong. Or the benefactor might give money to the needy person with the intention of helping that person, but the money given is not the benefactor's money to give. In these examples the action is not morally good because at least one of the three conditions for moral goodness is not being met. Just as a good airplane pilot must be sober, clear-sighted, and experienced in flying (two of the three is not enough), so too for a human action to be morally good, the act itself, the intention, and the circumstances must all be good.

Intellect

As noted, for an action to be a human action, we first need to know what we are doing. The intellect is a power of the human soul and the origin of knowledge in human action. By our intellect we are able to know what is of universal significance in our experience. St. Thomas understands the intellect as either speculative or practical depending on the goal or end to which this knowledge is ordered. If the end in view is the consideration of truth itself, as in scientific knowledge, the intellect is speculative in its way of knowing. If, however, the end in view is a product or action of some kind, the intellect is practical. Examples of practical knowledge can be found in the artist's production of a piece of art or the human being's decision to act in a certain way. But besides the difference in goals, speculative and practical knowledge also differ in their respective objects. Speculative knowledge is knowledge of what is permanent and unchanging. Theological knowledge of God in faith, philosophical knowledge of human nature, and our modern scientific grasp of what is statistically relevant in natural phenomena—all are examples of speculative knowledge of what is permanent and unchanging. Practical knowledge, on the other hand, is knowledge of impermanent and variable sensible particulars. Practical productive knowledge renders impermanent and variable particular things into useful or beautiful human products, and practical ethical knowledge renders impermanent and variable individual actions in given situations morally good.

Will and Sense Appetite

Human action requires not just understanding but also *will.* Will is the human power of wanting. Wanting, or what St. Thomas calls "appetite," can be described as a response moving us toward something we in some way know as good, or moving us away from what we know as bad. Will is a rational want, or appetite, in response to what we rationally apprehend under the universal or common notion of good. For example, if I am thirsty, I can understand (by my intellect) that I am thirsty and that what I want is anything that will satisfy my thirst. "Anything that will satisfy my thirst" is a good rationally apprehended as something universal, that is, a good that I understand can include any number of particular things, like water, soda, iced tea, or beer.

If the will is a rational want, or appetite, our sense appetites are rather movements in response to particular sensible objects that pertain to specific physical needs we have. If I am thirsty, let's say, I immediately will want to drink that tall glass of iced lemonade you set before me. This desire for the glass of lemonade is an example of a sense appetite: a response to a particular sensed object that pertains to a specific physical need I have. St. Thomas distinguishes two kinds of sense appetites: the one he calls the concupiscible appetite; the other, the irascible appetite. The concupiscible appetite is concerned with what we may sense as pleasing, the irascible appetite with overcoming or resisting what we may sense as preventing us from attaining something we sense as pleasing. In this way the irascible appetites and their objects presuppose the concupiscible appetites for what we sense is pleasant. Love is the most basic of the concupiscible appetites, and all other sense appetites can be understood in relation to it.

Sense appetites are limited to particular sensible goods. For example, I want to drink that cold lemonade in front of me. The will as rational appetite, on the other hand, is not limited to any particular sensible good since it is a response to good understood universally. When I recognize that I am thirsty and understand that anything that will satisfy my thirst is what I want, I can choose either to drink that lemonade or not because I understand that while the lemonade can satisfy my thirst, there are many other particular things I could choose to satisfy that thirst—iced tea, soda water, or just plain water, to name just a few. In other words, because I understand and desire the good as universal I am free with respect to any one of the particular instances of that good. The basis of human voluntariness and freedom, then, is the will as the desire for what is rationally apprehended as good (or the desire to reject what is rationally apprehended as bad).

Our sense appetites can all too easily be in conflict with our rational appetite. We can rationally desire to eat only healthy foods but be drawn by sense appetite to those foods we sense as pleasant (tasty or sweet), which we know are not healthy for us. As free, each one of us bears the responsibility for directing all our choices to the universal good of true human happiness and resisting being driven by the impulse of sense appetite, social pressure, or any other extraneous influence.

Habits and Virtues

The powers of intellect and will are the origins or principles of human action, and those powers can be used well or poorly. Intellect can be used well, for example, when I learn to do my math homework correctly but poorly when I fail to learn that same assignment correctly. I can use my will well when I want to do what I know is good for me to do, but I can misuse that same power when I either do not do what I know I ought to do or when I do not do it as well as I know I ought.

What I need to do is to practice using my powers well so that I can acquire habits that enable me to do this. By repeated practice of doing math problems correctly or by repeatedly doing what I know I ought to do, I acquire a habit or facility with these intellectual or voluntary tasks so that I can perform them well and easily. Habit can be understood initially as a disposing of powers like intellect and will to act in a determinate way. Good habits dispose the power to act well; bad habits, on the other hand, dispose the power to act poorly. In addition to the internal principles of intellect and the rational and sense appetites, then, habits are also important internal principles of human action.

In the moral life good habits are known as virtues, bad habits as vices. The distinction between virtue as a good habit and vice as a bad habit turns on whether the habit produces acts that lead us toward or away from true human happiness. Virtuous acts are those that lead to true human happiness as acts suitable to human nature; that is, they are acts habitually performed according to the rule of right reason. Right reason is reason perfected by practical wisdom enabling us to discern well what action truly leads to true human happiness. Acts of vice, on the other hand, are acts that lead us away from our true happiness. These are acts opposed to human nature inasmuch as they are not performed according to the rule of right reason.

Just as intellect and will and the sense appetites are internal principles of human action, so the virtues can be divided into the intellectual and moral virtues. You might say that the intellectual virtues are perfections of the mind, whereas the moral virtues are perfections of the heart. Any virtue, then, perfects one of these two powers. Good intellectual habits such as science, understanding, and wisdom perfect the human intellect in speculative activities like theology, philosophy, or science, while the intellectual virtues of art and practical wisdom (prudentia) perfect the intellect in the practical activities of art and morally good action. Practical wisdom also requires appetitive virtue to the extent that it requires the virtuous use of the will and sense appetites for its good operation. This unity of the intellectual virtues of practical wisdom and appetitive virtue is what is known as the "unity of the virtues;" that is, in order to be practically wise, we must also have virtuous desires; yet in order to have virtuous desires, we must also have at least something of the intellectual virtue of practical wisdom.

The chief moral virtues include justice, fortitude, and temperance, which, along with practical wisdom, are called the "cardinal virtues." We will say more about each virtue when we examine the text of Thomas himself on each virtue.

Because Thomas believes that true human happiness is primarily a supernatural life with God, the natural human virtues of intellect and appetite are not enough for us to achieve supernatural happiness. Human beings have need of additional principles of action in order to be directed to attaining this perfect happiness ordained for us by God. These principles are known as theological virtues because they are virtues that enable us to act for the sake of God Himself. These theological virtues are faith, hope, and charity. These theological virtues are divinely infused rather than simply acquired by the gradual process of habituation through our own practice.

External Principles of Human Action: Law and Grace

The extrinsic principle of virtuous human action is God, who instructs human beings through law and supplies the ability to adhere to this instruction through grace. By law God teaches us how to act well, and by grace he gives us the power to do so.

Law

Morality for Thomas is not simply a rulebook of prohibitions, but rather an invitation to pursue true human happiness. We are made for happiness, not made simply to obey rules. The "rules" of morality (such as natural law) are not unimportant for Thomas, but the point and purpose of any moral rule is to secure human flourishing. Although St. Thomas says relatively little about law in comparison with how much he writes about the virtues, law nevertheless does play an important role in his ethics. St. Thomas understands law as a rule and measure of acts whereby we human beings are encouraged to act or discouraged from acting in certain ways. He defines law as an ordinance of reason for the common good, promulgated by one who has care of the community. What Aquinas means by "the common good" can be understood to be the sum total of conditions that allow us, either as groups or as individuals, to attain our ultimate goal of true human happiness more fully and easily. This good consists in a respect for and love of neighbor and requires the social well-being of the human community as a whole as well as the peace of a stable and secure just political order.

Eternal, Natural, Divine, and Civil Law

Eternal Law

Eternal law is the plan of God's wisdom by which all action and motion of the universe are directed. God governs all creation through ordering all creatures to their proper good and directs the whole universe according to Divine Wisdom. All other creatures move toward their proper good by acting spontaneously from their divinely bestowed natural inclinations, but we human beings as rational creatures can reflect on our natural inclinations, freely act in accordance with those inclinations, and so partake in a share of Divine providence by responsibly providing for ourselves and for others.

Natural Law

Natural law is said by St. Thomas to be "man's participation in the eternal law of God" (I–II, 91, 2). More specifically, natural law is the participation of human beings in the eternal law by our rightly living out the natural desire we have for happiness. This natural desire can be analyzed into certain fundamental natural inclinations. These natural inclinations include the desire for our self-preservation, the reproduction and care of offspring, life with others, and knowledge of truth, ultimately the knowledge of God. By reflecting on these basic natural desires we come to understand certain basic imperatives that we must follow if we are to be happy. Reflection on the basic inclination we have for our own self-preservation yields the imperative or precept to preserve our own life. Reflection on the natural inclination for the reproduction and care of offspring similarly generates precepts concerning appropriate acts of sexual intercourse, the necessity of marriage, and the promotion of family. Finally, the natural inclinations we have to live with others and to know the truth about God prompt us to formulate appropriate precepts for community and religious life. Natural law is "law" in that these basic inclinations are received from God our creator to lead us to happiness, and natural law is "natural" in that these God-given human inclinations are naturally human. The moral obligation to follow these precepts of natural law is thus not arbitrarily imposed from without but arises from within—from our rational reflection on our basic natural human inclinations and the goods that satisfy them. Thus, our following of natural law is not "a succumbing to" or "a yielding to" an unnatural exterior imposition upon us but rather a rational response to the natural drive within us toward happiness. Often, we think of "temptation" as an inner impulse to things that are bad and forbidden, but we need to recognize that we have an even deeper inner impulse to what is good, that is, to what leads to our true human happiness.

This deeper inner impulse we can call natural law. Natural law is our own participation in God's own providential care for our happiness. However, the natural law, which includes this moral reasoning from first principles to practical conclusions, is not sufficient as a guide for us in daily life. The limitations of human reason and the impediments of sin necessitate a divine law to direct us properly to true human happiness, which is ultimately supernatural. This divine law instructs us on contingent and particular matters about which it is particularly difficult to judge, helps us to understand better interior matters essential for complete virtue, and, finally, makes clear to us that all evil deeds, interior as well as exterior, are forbidden and punished (I–II, q. 91, a. 4). Like Scripture, the *Summa theologiae* is cited in a particular form so that passages can be found in various editions and translations. The citation here, I–II, q. 91, a. 4, means that the passage is found in the first part of the second part question 91, article 4. The *Summa* is divided into the first part (treating theology, God, angels, and human beings), the first part of the second part (treating human actions, passions, habits, sin, and grace), the second part of the second part (treating the theological and cardinal virtues), and the third unfinished part (treating the incarnation, life of Christ, and the sacraments). Each part is divided into various questions. Each question is divided into articles—the smallest self-standing unit of the *Summa theologiae*.

So God not only guides us by the natural law but also reveals to us what is to be done and what is to be avoided by divine law. The natural law is made more explicit and particularized by the divine law given to the Hebrew people in the Old Testament (the Old Law) and to the Christian people in the New Testament (the New Law). It is by means of this law that our conscience is ultimately guided.

Divine Law

St. Thomas distinguishes two aspects of the divine law: the Old Law and the New. The Old Law commands ceremonial precepts governing worship, judicial precepts establishing justice within the community, and moral precepts required by natural law (I–II, q. 99, a. 4). Whereas moral and judicial precepts receive their moral authority from natural reason, the ceremonial precepts receive their authority from divine institution alone. The New Law thus replaces the historically contingent judicial regulations and ceremonial requirements of the Old Law while retaining the moral requirements based on the natural law. Drawing from St. Paul, St. Thomas holds that the New Law is fundamentally the grace of the Holy Spirit dwelling in the hearts of believers and only secondarily a written law (I–II, q. 106, a. 1).

The New Law fulfills the Old in two ways. First, it justifies those who believe, thereby enabling us to obtain our ultimate end, supernatural happiness. Without the indwelling of the Holy Spirit, the commands and precepts of the New Testament would be inefficacious regulations. Second, the New Law fulfills the precepts of the Old Law through explaining the deeper sense of the Law, showing the safest way of fulfilling its requirements (that is, through intention and not simply conduct) and by adding to the Law the counsels of perfection. The New Law establishes the sacraments so that believers might receive more explicit assistance in their growth in grace and love.

Civil Law

St. Thomas understands civil law to be an ordinance of reason by one who has authority to direct the political society and its members to the common civil good of peace and order. Civil law directly concerns our external acts that dispose us to become virtuous, and forbids other acts that lead to vice and tend to make life in society impossible. Every civil law, in so far as it aims at the common good and is accordingly a just law, carries an obligation to be obeyed. Yet this obligation derives from a law more fundamental. This is the "unwritten law" or natural law, which in its most common precepts, is fundamentally the same for all of us as human beings.

Grace

Grace is an effect of God's love for us and is the means by which God leads us back to Himself (I–II, q. 111, a. 1). As a principle of human action, grace differs from virtue not only as an external principle differs from an internal one, but also in that grace is infused directly into our souls, whereas virtue is realized in some power of the soul. Grace differs from law in that, though both are external principles, law directs us by instruction and command, whereas grace supernaturally elevates us so that we can participate in God's own life, receive assistance in doing so, and attain the happiness that is eternal life. Weakened by sin, we tend to love ourselves more than God and our neighbor, and prefer our own private good to the common good. Grace heals this fundamental disorder, enabling us to love God more than ourselves and to love our neighbor as we love ourselves. Sanctifying or habitual grace is a supernatural quality of the soul by which we participate in the divine nature thereby enabling us to perform acts meriting supernatural happiness. Grace, then, is absolutely necessary for all of us if we are to obtain supernatural happiness.

The Theological Virtues, the Gifts of the Holy Spirit, and the Cardinal Virtues

St. Thomas understands the Christian life as essentially one of growth in faith, hope, and charity. He discusses the cardinal virtues of prudence, justice, temperance, and fortitude only after the theological virtues because he understands these four virtues as being retained and perfected within the Christian life. Because our human nature is perfected by grace, our will by charity and hope, our intellect by faith, the cardinal virtues we acquire are ultimately perfected by the infused theological

virtues. In addition to the God-given theological virtues, the gifts of the
Holy Spirit are special graces God bestows on us that dispose our intellectual and appetitive powers to be more readily open to the inspiration
of the Holy Spirit. St. Thomas coordinates the theological and cardinal
virtues of the Christian life with the gifts of the Holy Spirit. Faith is
complemented by the gifts of understanding and of knowledge. The gift
of understanding perfects the apprehension of truth and the gift of
knowledge perfects good judgment in speculative reasoning. Hope is
complemented by the gift of fear of the Lord; charity by the gift of wisdom; prudence by the gift of counsel; justice by the gift of piety; and
courage by the gift of fear. Thus while St. Thomas's full vision of human
flourishing is profoundly philosophical, it is fundamentally informed by
faith and the whole of the Christian theological tradition. Yet this theological tradition itself is informed and, in some sense, based upon a
vision of the human person that is also accessible to those without faith.

For Aquinas, virtues may be either acquired by human effort or
infused by God. Virtues that are acquired by human effort are called
"acquired virtues" and are similar to skills like playing a musical instrument or becoming excellent at a sport. It is only through repeated practice, characteristically done under the guidance of a teacher or coach,
that a person masters the ability to do the task well. Hearing lectures of
swimming alone will not make anyone a champion swimmer, only
working out in the pool can do that. Similarly, in music, a person must
actually play the piano, for hours and hours, month after month, in
order to become a musician, a person with the acquired habit of making music. Anyone with fingers can hit the keys, but only one with the
habit of playing can make beautiful music. Directed practice is the
only way to becoming a pianist.

In the same way, acquired virtue can only be attained by repeated
acts of the virtue. Most helpful is "coaching" from a parent, mentor, or
spiritual director, but absolutely necessary is repeated practice. To gain
the habit of toughness with respect to overcoming challenges, a person
must face the difficult and preserve in the fight to succeed. To gain the
habit of self-mastery with respect to enjoying food, a person must
choose to eat the right amount of food meal after meal after meal.

Only by repeatedly *doing* what virtue requires can a non-virtuous person slowly over time become a virtuous person who actually enjoys and easily accomplishes what virtue requires. Gaining acquired virtue could be likened to getting into terrific shape, a feat that is not accomplished by exercising only once in a while but by months of intense training.

By contrast, "infused virtue" is gained not through human effort but rather by divine gift. Gaining infused virtue is not like loosing weight by exercising day after day, but is more akin to a divine surgery that removes the weight by God's power. Via infused virtue, God provides the power to be able to do what virtue demands easily and joyfully. God grants these infused virtues often in response to prayer, individual prayer and especially the communal prayer of the sacraments of the Church. In baptism, God infused not only the theological virtues of faith, hope, and love but also the *infused* cardinal virtues of justice, temperance, courage, and practical wisdom. Since grace completes nature, the infused virtues given by God's grace and the acquired virtues attained through repeated practice work together for the good of the person seeking happiness. The infused virtues of justice, temperance, courage, and practical wisdom are extremely important; but still more important are the infused virtues more closely connected to God, namely faith, hope, and love.

The Theological Virtue of Faith

Our ultimate happiness consists in seeing God face to face, what St. Thomas calls the "beatific vision." But without the gift of faith by which we accept the revelation of God and His providential plan for us in the teaching and life, death, and resurrection of Jesus Christ, we could not come to know this happiness and make it the goal of our lives and our every action. The theological gift of faith, according to St. Thomas, is an assent of the mind, commanded by the will, to propositions on the basis of God's authority. Faith generates within us a firm conviction of the truth of what we believe. Faith is not simply an intellectual assent to propositions but involves the whole of us: our mind in belief and our heart in the conviction of the truth of what we believe based on our trust in God. There is an inner and outer dimension to this gift of faith. The inner dimension, or "inner act of faith," by which we firmly believe in what God reveals to us, is complemented by an exterior dimension, or "outer act of faith," by which we are enabled to make public confession of what we believe.

The Theological Virtue of Hope

Hope is a gift of God that enables Christians to believe that we will be granted the supreme good of eternal happiness that lies in the vision of God. Hope gives us the confidence we need toward the future to overcome anything that gets in the way of that supreme good. The gift of hope steers us clear of the apparently opposite temptations of despair and presumption. That is, without hope we might be so overwhelmed by God's holiness and the demands of justice that we might be tempted to despair of ever being able to share in a relationship with Him; on the other hand, we might take God's mercy for granted and be tempted to presume that our salvation is assured and neglect sincere repentance and constant prayer in our lives. The theological virtue of hope also instills in us the kind of trust in God appropriate to children of God and frees us from the slavish desire to obey merely to avoid punishment.

The Theological Virtue of Charity

God's gift of the theological virtue of charity enables us to enter into a friendship with God. This relationship is marked by benevolence, mutuality, and communication. In this friendship the presence and direct action of the Holy Spirit create within us a love of God for who God is and a love for ourselves, our neighbor, and everything else in and for God. By the theological virtue of charity we are able to rest in God as our ultimate and principle good, and for this reason charity is the greatest of all the virtues and the only theological virtue that will remain in our eternal enjoyment of the supernatural happiness of the beatific vision. We will not need faith, for we will see God face to face, and we will not need to hope to have an eternal relationship with God, for we will be enjoying that relationship. In that eternal relationship, however, we will continue to love and be loved by God—forever.

The Present Volume

Although this brief introduction to the ethics of St. Thomas Aquinas cannot capture the full breadth and detail of his achievement, it should provide some context and overview for the pages that follow. Needless to say, even the pages do not capture the whole picture, being as they are selections of the original text as translated from Latin. Still, we hope that they will be useful for understanding the teaching of St. Thomas on a matter of central importance for all of us, the pursuit of happiness via activity in accordance with excellence of character.

In *Aquinas on Faith, Hope, and Love*, Christopher Kaczor (co-author of this volume) wrote:

> In the fourth grade, I remember searching through the attic in our house (a favorite trick of mine in unsupervised moments) and running across an old box from my mother's college years. In the dusty cardboard box were mementos, class notes, and old books. I picked up one, called *The Basic Writings of Thomas Aquinas*. Basic, I thought, I'll give it a read. Although each word on the page was perfectly understandable, the meaning of virtually every sentence was completely beyond me. I'd read books with big words that I could not understand, but a book with more manageable words that still remained a mystery—this was something new. I tried reading this book again in high school and again in college, with not much more success. Perhaps there are some who can immediately comprehend the great philosophical and theological achievement of Thomas Aquinas on their first read, but I was certainly not among them. This book is the one I wish I had discovered.

This book also is meant to help alleviate some of the initial difficulties of reading St. Thomas in order to allow non-experts, either in a classroom setting or on their own, to begin to appreciate the wisdom and insight of one of the most influential minds of all time. Approaching Thomas Aquinas for the first time can be a daunting task—so many distinctions, so many references, so many unfamiliar terms. This book is geared to overcoming as many of these difficulties as possible.

Ideally, the *Summa theologiae* of Thomas Aquinas should be read in the original Latin. If we had sufficient linguistic training, we could sit down with the Latin text in the authoritative "Leonine" edition and fully understand (if not fully comprehend the depths of) each line. If we also had extensive training in the study of ancient handwriting (paleography), we might even be able to read the manuscripts that went into creating the critical edition.

In a similar way, in an ideal world, we would fly to Paris to study great works of art in the Louvre, but these impediments should not stop us from appreciating, in so far as we can, great works of art translated through the media of documentaries, art books, or the internet. Works of wisdom and beauty should not be the private property of the experts alone. In this book, the English text of the *Summa theologiae* comes from the classic Second and Revised Edition of the translation by Fathers of the English Dominican Province, published in 1920, courtesy of the kind permission of Kevin Knight at Newadvent.net. This translation has been modified in places and updated in order to remove archaic language, e.g. each instance of "Thou" and "Art" has been replaced with "you" and "are."

Not only has the translation been updated to facilitate understanding by non-experts, but in the interest of making this book as accessible as possible it contains only a selection of the complete treatment of the cardinal virtues found in the *Summa*. Passages of greatest historical or contemporary interest have been selected, and the order of the text recast for easier understanding.

The smallest complete division of text in the Summa is the "article" which forms a kind of mini-debate. Originally, an article would have the following structure. First, Thomas poses a question that can be answered with a 'yes' or a 'no,' such as "Does God exist?" Next he raises two or more objections to the view that he holds, such as "It seems that God does not exists because. . . ." Then he says, "On the contrary, God does exist. . . ." and he cites an authority that reflects his view, such as Scripture, Aristotle, or St. Augustine. Next, in the "body" or "corpus" of the article, Thomas provides his reasons for holding the position that he does. So, for example, in the body of the article about God's existence, he provides his famous "five ways" for demonstrating that there is a God. Finally, he returns and answers each of the objections he had previously raised to his view.

Thomas's original structuring of an article has been revised in this book to facilitate ease of understanding for the contemporary reader. Following Thomas's yes/no question, the next section eases into the authority Thomas cites for his view and his reasons for holding his position. Then one objection is introduced, and this objection answered. Then the next objection is introduced, and the next objection is answered, and so on. Although Thomas did not originally structure an article in this fashion, unless you have an extremely keen memory, you may find yourself forgetting the first or second objection by the time you read through the 'body' or 'corpus' of the text, and thus find yourself needing to return again to the objection in order to understand the response. The re-ordering of the text is meant therefore to require less effort from the reader.

Even with the reordering, Thomas's many distinctions, references, and unfamiliar terms challenge the typical contemporary reader. In order to help, many footnotes help clarify the text and should answer many of the questions that confront a non-specialist reader of the *Summa theologiae*. The notes are similar to the sorts of clarifications, interpretations, and additional information that would be given in a classroom to help students reading St. Thomas for the first time. They answer questions about the identity of important authorities cited by Thomas, such as Boethius, Aristotle, Augustine, and Cicero. They suggest further readings on the topics in question, elsewhere within the works of Thomas himself or by important predecessors or successors. They clarify the meaning of important words used in a very precise and technical sense. Finally, they are written to help make the understanding of the text as easy as possible for everyone.

PRACTICAL
WISDOM
(PRUDENCE)

<div align="center">~~~~~~~~~~~~~~</div>

PRACTICAL WISDOM (PRUDENCE)

ST. THOMAS examines first the virtue of practical wisdom in itself (q. 47) and then its "parts"—those traits that must exist for the complete act of this virtue. Among the parts of practical wisdom are those that are "integral," that is, those necessary for its exercise—like memory and docility (q. 49); those he calls "subjective," such as political and domestic practical wisdom (q. 50); and finally dispositions connected with practical wisdom, like the ability to identify exceptions to the law (q. 51). St. Thomas goes on to discuss the gift of counsel as that gift of the Holy Spirit corresponding to practical wisdom (q. 52). He then looks at the vices contrary to practical wisdom (qq. 53–55) and concludes by examining the precepts as enumerated in the Old Law (q. 56).

The virtue of practical wisdom is unique among the cardinal virtues as a virtue of the intellect in practical reasoning rather than of the will or the sense appetites (q. 47, a. 1). Practical wisdom is the virtue of practical reasoning that enables us to reason rightly about what we ought to do in any given situation and to do it. There are a number of important aspects of this cardinal virtue.

Practical Wisdom Requires the Theological Virtues for Knowledge and Desire of Happiness as Our End

The Christian life consists in the happiness of a lifetime of virtuous activity with the perfect happiness of an eternal direct vision of God as our ultimate goal. By the theological virtue of faith we know this true happiness and by the theological virtues of hope and charity we effectively desire this happiness as our goal. But to have true happiness as our goal is not enough. We need to make the right choices of action in our lives so as to reach that goal. We need an intellectual virtue of practical reasoning to help us discern and the character to choose effectively what is morally right to do, that is, what is the right means to live happily. Practical wisdom is the intellectual virtue by which we are characteristically able to discern what actions are the right means to happiness as our end.

Practical Wisdom Requires *Synderesis* and Conscience

If practical wisdom enables us to discern what action is conducive to happiness as our end, its effective exercise requires not only the theological virtues for a knowledge and desire of the end, but also the natural habit of what St. Thomas calls *synderesis*.

If the first practical principle of natural law is the precept "do good and avoid evil" and what is good or evil is determined by careful reflection on the basic goods that answer to our fundamental desires for life, family, and truth, *synderesis* is the habit of the human intellect disposing us to grasp immediately and infallibly these basic goods as the first principles of our practical ethical reasoning about what is morally good to do.

As a natural or innate habit, *synderesis* is possessed in equal degree by all human beings. Nevertheless, some may have a greater insight into the first principles of practical reasoning than others depending on differing natural intellectual capacities.

Besides *synderesis*, practical wisdom also makes use of conscience. While *synderesis* is a natural habit by which we possess the first principles of the moral order, conscience is an act of judgment concerned with particular applications, that is, with the practical reasoning that provides answers to particular moral problems.

Moral reasoning is practical reasoning about how to live well. According to St. Thomas, in this kind of reasoning we explicitly or implicitly begin with one or more universal principles as practical premises and from these conclude to a practical conclusion, the thing to be done. In this reasoning process, *synderesis* provides us with our most universal principles, presupposing the first principle, "good is to be done; evil is to be avoided." Reason supplies us with more specific and less universal precepts, directing us to the cause of a command or prohibition, such as "theft is evil because it is against the commandment of God, or because it is unjust." By our conscience, then, we reach the conclusion: "Theft should be, or should have been avoided." This judgment of conscience then becomes a proximate principle for human action. Both *synderesis* and conscience, then, furnish us norms for action: *synderesis* by providing us with the most general and universal principles, conscience by providing the immediate and particular reasoned judgment about the moral goodness or evil of the act. While *synderesis* is infallible, conscience can err in the process of reasoning. The natural law *(synderesis)* guides all of us, but our individual ethical judgments (conscience) about particular matters can be mistaken. For this reason, it is essential to form our conscience properly. Without the theological virtues and the requisite moral virtues, we may well have a poorly formed or simply incorrect conscience or even a well-formed conscience but without the will to act according to that conscience.

Practical Wisdom Requires and Governs the Moral Virtues

In addition to knowing and desiring true happiness by the theological virtues, and knowing the basic human goods as practical principles by the natural habit of *synderesis*, and the correct formation of conscience, if practical wisdom is to be effectively exercised in our choices of action, we also need a character transformed by the moral virtues so that we have the characteristic will to do what we by practical wisdom determine is morally good to do. As an intellectual virtue practically concerned with morally good action, practical wisdom requires the exercise of the moral virtues and at the same time governs those virtues. Virtuous inclinations may actually pull us in different directions in certain situations (e.g., friendliness and sobriety at a party, say, or justice and mercy in making a legal decision), and it is up to practical wisdom to determine which inclination is correct. In this way practical wisdom is a special virtue that commands the exercise of all the moral virtues.

Practical Wisdom Concerns the Particular

With the requisite theological and moral virtues of character and the natural habit of *synderesis* and a well-formed conscience we can, by exercising practical wisdom, examine any given situation from the right perspective, discern what is the morally good thing to do in that situation in light of that perspective, and do it. As each situation is individual, practical wisdom is concerned with what is individual: the morally good thing to do in *this* situation. Practical wisdom arrives at a practical judgment, which is the morally good action itself. In this way the judgment of practical wisdom is practical; it states not what is good in a merely speculative way but determines what is to be done by doing it!

Within the context of the complete Christian life as St. Thomas understands this, practical wisdom is a cardinal virtue working in cooperation with grace; living by grace exceeds living merely according to reason and ultimately includes living according to the mind of Christ; its purpose is not to be respectable but to be a fellow citizen of the saints and familiar with God. It springs from and lives only in charity, without which one may be shrewd but cannot be prudent. Furthermore, it is touched by the Spirit to act with heroism in the gift of counsel.

QUESTION 47

THE VIRTUE OF PRACTICAL WISDOM

ARTICLE 1 ⁓ Is prudence in the faculty of reason?

Yes, despite objections the contrary, Augustine says (QQ. lxxxiii, qu. 61): "Prudence is the knowledge of what to seek and what to avoid."[1]

I answer that, As Isidore says (*Etym.* x):[2] "A prudent man is one who sees as it were from afar, for his sight is keen, and he foresees the

---

[1] Reason directs many kinds of actions, not all of which are properly the subject of prudence. Earlier in the *Summa*, Thomas distinguishes practical wisdom from the fabrication of things in the external world, understood under the term "art." "[A]rt confers the mere aptness for good work, since it does not regard the appetite, whereas prudence confers not only aptness for a good work, but also the use: for it regards the appetite, since it presupposes the rectitude thereof. The reason for this difference is that *art is the 'right reason of things to be made'*, whereas *prudence is the 'right reason of things to be done.'* Now 'making' and 'doing' differ, as stated in Metaph. ix, text. 16, in that 'making' is an action passing into outward matter, e.g. 'to build,' 'to saw,' and so forth, whereas 'doing' is an action abiding in the agent, e.g. 'to see,' 'to will,' and the like. Accordingly prudence stands in the same relation to such like human actions, consisting in the use of powers and habits, as art does to outward making: since each is the perfect reason about the things with which it is concerned" (I–II, q. 57, a. 4). Practical wisdom does not, then, focus so much on the "results," as is typical of consequentialism. Rather, practical wisdom is a perfection of an aspect of the agent, directing the agent to the appropriate means to an end that accords with perfect happiness. We can assess a product of art (an automobile say) without knowledge of the ultimate purpose for which the car was made (to help or to harm others). Prudence, on the other hand, presupposes that the end in mind is good.

[2] St. Isidore of Seville (c. 560–636), a Latin father of the Church, was an author of tremendous learning, famous especially for his encyclopedic book, *The*

event of uncertainties." Now sight[3] belongs not to the appetitive but to the cognitive faculty. Therefore it is manifest that prudence belongs directly to the cognitive, and not to the sensitive faculty, because by the latter we know nothing but what is within reach and offers itself to the senses: while to obtain knowledge of the future from knowledge of the present or past, which pertains to prudence, belongs properly to the reason, because this is done by a process of comparison. It follows, therefore, that prudence, properly speaking, is in the reason.[4]

Article 4 ~~ Is practical wisdom a virtue?

Yes, despite objections to the contrary, Gregory states (*Moral.* ii, 49) that practical wisdom, temperance, courage and justice are four virtues.[5]

I answer that, As stated above (I–II, q. 55, a. 3; I–II, q. 56, a. 1) when we were treating of virtues in general, "virtue is that which makes its possessor good, and his work good likewise." Now good may be understood in a twofold sense: first, materially, for the thing that is good; secondly, formally, under the aspect of good. Good, under the aspect of good, is the object of the appetitive power.[6] Hence if any

---

Etymologies, used as a textbook throughout the Middle Ages for information about ancient culture and learning. He was also known as a man of great holiness who gave all his possessions away to the poor and defended the full divinity of Christ against the Arians.

[3] "Sight" in this passage refers not to the power of a person's physical eyes, but to his intellectual "insight" into the practical situation.

[4] Each of the virtues perfects an aspect of the human person. Prudence perfects the practical reasoning of the person. Practical reasoning involves acting in the world, rather than, for example, contemplating various truths, such as the nature of the planets (theoretical reasoning).

[5] Pope St. Gregory the Great's work, *Magna Moralia,* also known as *Lectures on the Book of Job,* was throughout the Middle Ages a classic text for understanding the moral life more deeply. The first monk to become pope, Gregory (b. ca. A.D. 540, d. A.D. 604) is also known, according to tradition, for originating Gregorian chant.

[6] The will seeks good as good, just as the eye sees a visible object as visible. A visible object may also have other characteristics under which it could be considered, for example, in terms of its weight or its density, but for the object *as seen* these other characteristics are not relevant. The will only wills that which appears under the aspect of the good and never seeks evil for the sake of evil. This teaching of Thomas, arising from Aristotle, also underscores the goodness

habits rectify the consideration of reason, without regarding the rectitude of the appetite, they have less of the nature of a virtue since they
direct man to good materially, that is to say, to the thing which is good,
but without considering it under the aspect of good. On the other
hand, those virtues which regard the rectitude of the appetite have
more of the nature of virtue because they consider the good not only
materially, but also formally; in other words, they consider that which
is good under the aspect of good.[7]

Now it belongs to practical wisdom, as stated above (a. 1, ad 3; a. 3),
to apply right reason to action, and this is not done without a right
appetite. Hence practical wisdom has the nature of virtue not only as
the other intellectual virtues have it, but also as the moral virtues have
it, among which virtues it is enumerated.

Objection 1. It would seem that practical wisdom is not a virtue. For
Augustine says (*De Lib. Arb.* i, 13) that "practical wisdom is the science of what to desire and what to avoid." Now science is condivided
with virtue, as appears in the Predicaments (vi). Therefore practical
wisdom is not a virtue.

Reply to Objection 1. Augustine there takes science in the broad
sense for any kind of right reason.

Objection 2. Further, there is no virtue of a virtue: but "there is a virtue
of art," as the Philosopher states (*Ethic.* vi, 5).[8] Therefore art is not a

---

of creation; in particular, human beings who are naturally ordered and cannot
help but choose what is (or at least appears) in some respect good.

7 Good may be understood in two very different senses. Good, materially but
not formally, pertains to that which is in fact good but is not apprehended
by the agent as good. In fact, it is good for children to eat vegetables, but
many children would not agree that it is good to eat vegetables. In other
words, something can be good objectively speaking but not appreciated as
good subjectively. The virtues enable a person not merely to recognize objectively (materially) that such and such an action would be good to do, but
also to appreciate it subjectively (formally).

8 "The Philosopher" for Thomas refers always to Aristotle. During Thomas's
youth, the writings of Aristotle were rediscovered and studied again in the West.
This rediscovery prompted an intellectual crisis because on several key teachings
Aristotle appeared to contradict Christian faith. The prestige of Aristotle's

virtue. Now there is practical wisdom in art, for it is written (2 Paralip. ii, 14) concerning Hiram, that he knew "to grave all sort of graving, and to devise ingeniously [*prudenter*] all that there may be need of in the work." Therefore practical wisdom is not a virtue.

Reply to Objection 2. The Philosopher[9] says that there is a virtue of art, because art does not require rectitude of the appetite; Wherefore in order that a man may make right use of his art, he needs to have a virtue which will rectify his appetite. Practical wisdom, however, has nothing to do with the matter of art, because art is both directed to a particular end and has fixed means of obtaining that end. And yet, by a kind of comparison, a man may be said to act prudently in matters of art. Moreover in certain arts, on account of the uncertainty of the means for obtaining the end, there is need for counsel as, for instance, in the arts of medicine and navigation, as stated in *Ethic.* iii, 3.

Objection 3. Further, no virtue can be immoderate. But practical wisdom is immoderate, else it would be useless to say (Prov 23:4): "Set

---

thought and the desire to preserve the faith led some to distrust reason, suppressing openness to new understandings that might be thought to threaten the faith. Others succumbed to a kind of rationalism that tended toward a repudiation of faith and a supposed sufficiency of reason without faith. Thomas forged a "middle path" between these extremes, a path that included a new synthesis of faith and reason, a harmonious interplay of Augustinian theology and Aristotelian philosophy.

9 For Aristotle—and following him, Aquinas—art, craft, or skill *(techne)* are similar to virtue *(areté)* in some ways but differ in other ways. Skill and virtue are similar in that both are habits (*Nicomachean Ethics* [*NE*] 1103b), concerning matters that are difficult (*NE* 1105a 10), requiring knowledge (*NE* 1105a), and having to do with the mean between extremes (*NE* 1106b 15). Craft, or art, and virtue differ, however, in that virtue, but not craft, requires decision for the sake of virtue (*NE* 1105a). Virtue, but not craft, requires a firm and unchanging character (*NE* 1105a). Finally, while craft, skill, or art aims at production, virtue aims at action (*NE* 1140b5). In other words, art is primarily concerned with changes made in the external world; virtue is primarily concerned with the "inner changes" brought about by moral (or immoral) action. In this article, Thomas makes the point that art does not require rectitude of appetite but virtue does require that desire be in conformity with right reason. One can be a greedy doctor (greed does not impede proper surgical technique), but one cannot be a greedy person of practical wisdom for greed inhibits a person from being truly practically wise.

bounds to your practical wisdom." Therefore practical wisdom is not a virtue.

Reply to Objection 3. This saying of the wise man does not mean that practical wisdom itself should be moderate, but that moderation must be imposed on other things according to practical wisdom.

ARTICLE 6 ⟿ **Does practical wisdom appoint the end to moral virtues?**

No, despite objections to the contrary, The Philosopher says (*Ethic.* vi, 12) that "moral virtue ensures the rectitude of the intention of the end, while practical wisdom ensures the rectitude of the means." Therefore it does not belong to practical wisdom to appoint the end to moral virtues, but only to regulate the means.[10]

I answer that, The end of moral virtues is the human good. Now the good of the human soul is to be in accord with reason, as Dionysius declares (*Div. Nom.* iv). Hence it is necessary that the ends of moral virtue pre-exist in the reason.[11]

---

[10] Practical wisdom governs the means by three distinct phases. First, practical wisdom "takes counsel," i.e., searches for the various suitable candidates for action, sundry means suitable to reach the end of a moral virtue. Secondly, an "act of judgment" is made to choose the single means to be used from among the various possible options that counsel brought forward. Finally, the "act of command" moves the agent to fully practical reason, where the chosen means is put into action. Practical wisdom can fail at any of these three stages. An agent may not take sufficient counsel and so fail to consider all the viable options. Or, a person may consider the viable options but then choose from among these a means that is less than fully apt for realizing the end. Or, finally, an agent may consider all the options, make a correct judgment about the best option, but then fail to carry out the choice. Full practical wisdom involves all three aspects.

[11] Here Thomas connects the virtues, especially practical wisdom, with the natural law, the preexisting ends of moral virtues existing in reason. The exact characteristics specifically of the natural habit of the moral virtues, sometimes called *synderesis*, were the subject of lively debate in the Middle Ages. Although "natural law" and "virtue ethics" are sometimes characterized by contemporary authors as two distinct and opposed approaches to the moral life, in Thomas these two ways of thinking are not only complementary but mutually interdependent. Without virtue, a knowledge of the natural law does not lead to right action. Without natural law, virtue lacks objective guidance toward the truly

For just as in the speculative reason there are certain things naturally known, about which is "understanding," and certain things of which we obtain knowledge through them, viz. conclusions, about which is "science," so in the practical reason, certain things pre-exist, as naturally known principles, and such are the ends of the moral virtues, since the end is in practical matters what principles are in speculative matters,[12] as stated above (q. 23, a. 7, ad 2; I–II, q. 13, a. 3), while certain things are in the practical reason by way of conclusions, and such are the means which we gather from the ends themselves. About these is practical wisdom, which applies universal principles to the particular conclusions of practical matters. Consequently it does not belong to practical wisdom to appoint the end to moral virtues, but only to regulate the means.

Objection 1. It would seem that practical wisdom appoints the end to moral virtues. Since prudence is in the reason, while moral virtue is in the appetite, it seems that prudence stands in relation to moral virtue as reason to the appetite. Now reason appoints the end to the appetitive power. Therefore practical wisdom appoints the end to the moral virtues.

Reply to Objection 1. Natural reason known by the name of *synderesis* appoints the end to moral virtues, as stated above (I, q. 79, a. 12),[13] but prudence does not do this for the reason given above.

---

   good. We might say that natural law without virtue is impotent to achieve the good, virtue without natural law is blind to the good.

12 For Thomas, theoretical reasoning begins with an intellectual insight into the formal structure of things we sense. This intellectual insight yields principles, or starting points, for demonstrative reasoning to conclusions about the necessary properties of things. These starting points for demonstrative reasoning do not change. Theoretical reasoning from understood principles to demonstrated conclusions presupposes the first principle of such reasoning, the so-called principle of non-contradiction: that a thing cannot be and not be at the same time in the same respect. Practical reasoning, on the other hand, begins with the good as end known in *synderesis*. This good as end rationally desired is the starting point of practical reasoning toward action as its conclusion. The first principle of practical reasoning is: good is to be done, evil avoided.

13 Here Thomas writes that "the first practical principles, bestowed on us by nature, do not belong to a special power, but to a special natural habit, which we call 'synderesis.' Whence 'synderesis' is said to incite to good, and to murmur at evil, inasmuch as through first principles we proceed to discover and judge of what we have discovered."

Objection 3. Further, it belongs to the virtue, art, or power that is concerned about the end to command the virtues or arts that are concerned about the means. Now practical wisdom disposes of the other moral virtues, and commands them. Therefore it appoints their end to them.

Reply to Objection 3. The end concerns the moral virtues, not as though they appointed the end, but because they tend to the end which is appointed by natural reason. On this they are helped by practical wisdom, which prepares the way for them, by disposing the means. Hence it follows that practical wisdom is more excellent than the moral virtues, and moves them: yet *synderesis* moves practical wisdom, just as the understanding of principles moves science.[14]

ARTICLE 13 ~~ Can practical wisdom be in sinners?[15]

No, despite objections to the contrary, The Philosopher declares (*Ethic.* vi, 12) that "it is impossible for a man to be prudent unless he be good." Now no sinner is a good man. Therefore no sinner is prudent.

I answer that, Prudence is threefold. There is a false practical wisdom, which takes its name from its likeness to true practical wisdom. For since a person with practical wisdom is one who disposes well of the things that have to be done for a good end, whoever disposes well of such things as are fitting for an evil end has false practical wisdom, in so far as that which he takes for an end is good, not in truth but in appearance. Thus man is called "a good robber," and in this way we may speak of "a prudent robber," by way of similarity, because he devises fitting ways of committing robbery. This is the prudence of which the Apostle

---

[14] The first principle of practical reasoning, belonging to *synderesis*, directs all human action, in so far as whatever we do is chosen under the notion or formality of the good *(sub ratione boni)*. Although we are often mistaken in pursuing illusionary goods, rather than authentic goods, we are "hard wired," so to speak, to seek good and avoid evil. Practical wisdom presupposes this inclination toward the good and then helps a person to find and employ suitable means to attaining the good.

[15] By "sinners" Thomas does not mean merely human beings who have sinned before and need God's grace for salvation. Rather he means a habitual sinner, someone who sins and remains in that state of alienation from God.

says (Rom 8:6): "The practical wisdom of the flesh is death," because, to wit, it places its ultimate end in the pleasures of the flesh.[16]

The second prudence is indeed true practical wisdom, because it devises fitting ways of obtaining a good end; and yet it is imperfect, from a twofold source: first, because the good which it takes for an end is not the common end of all human life, but of some particular affair; thus when a man devises fitting ways of conducting business or of sailing a ship, he is called a prudent businessman, or a prudent sailor; secondly, because he fails in the chief act of practical wisdom, as when a man takes counsel aright, and forms a good judgment, even about things concerning life as a whole, but fails to make an effective command.[17]

The third practical wisdom is both true and perfect, for it takes counsel, judges, and commands aright in respect of the good end of man's whole life, and this alone is prudence simply so-called, and cannot be in sinners, whereas the first prudence is in sinners alone, while imperfect practical wisdom is common to good and wicked men, especially that which is imperfect through being directed to a particular end, since that which is imperfect on account of a failing in the chief act, is only in the wicked.

Objection 1. It would seem that there can be practical wisdom in sinners. For our Lord said (Lk 16:8): "The children of this world are more prudent in their generation than the children of light." Now the children of this world are sinners. Therefore there is practical wisdom in sinners.

Reply to Objection 1. This saying of our Lord is to be understood of the first practical wisdom;[18] therefore it is not said that they are prudent absolutely, but that they are prudent in "their generation."

---

[16] Thomas here refers to false prudence, which might also be called cleverness, craftiness, or cunning, an ability that can be used for evil ends.

[17] In addition to taking counsel and sound choice of means, a chief act of prudence involves *acting* on good counsel and sound choice of means, not merely thinking about it. So someone who knows what is right but does not do it cannot be said to be truly a person of practical wisdom.

[18] Thomas speaks here of the first kind of practical wisdom that he discussed above, namely false prudence, which disposes cleverly to ends that are not good. Hence, the "good" robber or the "good" hit man knows how most effectively to reach an evil end.

Objection 2. Further, faith is a more excellent virtue than practical wisdom. But there can be faith in sinners. Therefore there can be practical wisdom also.

Reply to Objection 2. The nature of faith consists not in conformity with the appetite for certain right actions, but in knowledge alone. On the other hand practical wisdom implies a relation to a right appetite: first, because its principles are the ends in matters of action; and of such ends one forms a right estimate through the habits of moral virtue, which rectify the appetite: therefore, without the moral virtues there is no practical wisdom, as shown above (I–II, q. 58, a. 5);[19] secondly, because practical wisdom commands right actions, which does not happen unless the appetite be right. Therefore, though faith on account of its object is more excellent than practical wisdom, yet

---

[19] In this passage, Thomas says: "Other intellectual virtues can, but prudence cannot, be without moral virtue. The reason for this is that prudence is the right reason about things to be done (and this, not merely in general, but also in particular), about which things actions are. Now right reason demands principles from which reason proceeds to argue. And when reason argues about particular cases, it needs not only universal but also particular principles. As to universal principles of action, man is rightly disposed by the natural understanding of principles, whereby he understands that he should do no evil, or again by some practical science. But this is not enough in order that man may reason aright about particular cases. For it happens sometimes that the aforesaid universal principle, known by means of understanding or science, is destroyed in a particular case by a passion: thus to one who is swayed by concupiscence, when he is overcome thereby, the object of his desire seems good, although it is opposed to the universal judgment of his reason. Consequently, as by the habit of natural understanding or of science, man is made to be rightly disposed in regard to the universal principles of action, so, in order that he be rightly disposed with regard to the particular principles of action, viz. the ends, he needs to be perfected by certain habits, whereby it becomes connatural, as it were, to man to judge aright to the end. This is done by moral virtue: for the virtuous man judges aright of the end of virtue, because 'such as a man is, such does the end seem to him' (*Ethic.* iii, 5). Consequently the right reason about things to be done, viz. prudence, requires man to have moral virtue." In order for a person to be wise practically, the person must have the virtues. Likewise, in order to have the moral virtues, a person must be practically wise. There is, therefore, a unity of the virtues, an interdependence in the various forms of human excellence with respect to achieving the final end.

practical wisdom, by its very nature, is more opposed to sin, which arises from a disorder of the appetite.

Objection 3. Further, according to *Ethic.* vi, 7, "we say that to be of good counsel is the work of a person with practical wisdom especially." Now many sinners can take good counsel. Therefore sinners can have practical wisdom.

Reply to Objection 3. Sinners can take good counsel for an evil end, or for some particular good, but they do not perfectly take good counsel for the end of their whole life, since they do not carry that counsel into effect.[20] Hence they lack practical wisdom that is directed to the good only; and yet in them, according to the Philosopher (*Ethic.* vi, 12) there is "cleverness" [*deinotike*], i.e., natural diligence, which may be directed to both good and evil, or "cunning," [*panourgia*] which is directed only to evil, and which we have stated above to be "false practical wisdom" or "prudence of the flesh."

ARTICLE 14 ⤙ Is practical wisdom in all who have grace?

Yes, despite objections to the contrary, No man has grace unless he be virtuous.[21] Now no man can be virtuous without practical wisdom, for Gregory says (*Moral.* ii, 46) that "the other virtues cannot be virtues at all unless they effect prudently what they desire to accomplish." Therefore all who have grace have practical wisdom.

I answer that, The virtues must be connected together, so that whoever has one has all, as stated above (I–II, q. 65, a. 1).[22] Now

---

20 Practical wisdom as *practical* must be actually carried out and lived. It is not merely a theory about doing good or the knowledge that such and such an action would be good to do, but includes the command and carrying out of the action.

21 To have grace or to be in a state of grace is another way of speaking about a person who has friendship with God. Such people, were they to die, would continue to enjoy this friendship in heavenly bliss. A person who deprives himself of this friendship, and who dies, is irrevocably deprived of this friendship. Since the loving vision of God alone completely satisfies our natural human desire for happiness, the deprivation of this friendship is the experience of hell.

22 Here Thomas speaks of the "unity of the virtues," a theme also found in many of Thomas's predecessors. In question 65, article one of the First Part

whoever has grace has charity, so that he must needs have all the other virtues, and hence, since practical wisdom is a virtue, as shown above (a. 4), he must, of necessity, have prudence also.

Objection 1. It would seem that prudence is not in all who have grace. Practical wisdom requires diligence, that one may foresee aright what has to be done. But many who have grace have not this diligence. Therefore not all who have grace have prudence.

Reply to Objection 1. Diligence is twofold: one is merely sufficient with regard to things necessary for salvation; and such diligence is given to all who have grace, whom "His unction teaches of all things" (1 Jn 2:27). There is also another diligence which is more than sufficient, whereby a man is able to make provision both for himself and for others, not only in matters necessary for salvation, but also in all

---

of the Second Part *(Prima secundae pars)* of the *Summa theologiae,* Thomas writes: "Moral virtue may be considered either as perfect or as imperfect. An imperfect moral virtue . . . is nothing but an inclination in us to do some kind of good deed, whether such inclination be in us by nature or by habituation. If we take the moral virtues in this way, they are not connected, since we find men who, by natural temperament or by being accustomed, are prompt in doing deeds of liberality, but are not prompt in doing deeds of chastity. But the perfect moral virtue is a habit that inclines us to do a good deed well; and if we take moral virtues in this way, we must say that they are connected, as nearly all are agreed in saying." Why does Thomas believe that to have truly any one virtue one must have *all* the virtues? Thomas summarizes this view in the same article: "right choice requires not only the inclination to a due end, which inclination is the direct outcome of moral virtue, but also correct choice of things conducive to the end, which choice is made by prudence, which counsels, judges, and commands in those things that are directed to the end. In like manner one cannot have prudence unless one has the moral virtues, since prudence is 'right reason about things to be done,' and the starting point of reason is the end of the thing to be done, to which end man is rightly disposed by moral virtue." A virtuous person does the right act in the right way. Prudence is required in order to know the right way to do an act. Knowing what ought to be done requires being rightly disposed by virtue, for lacking virtue a person misapprehends what is unchoiceworthy as an end that should be pursued and fails to appreciate the goodness of doing the right thing. The prudent agent needs the moral virtues for a right desire for the true end; and the exercise of the moral virtues requires prudence in order to choose the right action as a means to that end. There is, therefore, a unity to the virtues.

things relating to human life; and such diligence as this is not in all who have grace.[23]

Objection 2. Further, a person with practical wisdom is one who takes good counsel, as stated above (a. 8, obj. 2; a. 13, obj. 3). Yet many have grace who do not take good counsel, and need to be guided by the counsel of others. Therefore not all who have grace have practical wisdom.

Reply to Objection 2. Those who require to be guided by the counsel of others are able, if they have grace, to take counsel for themselves in this point at least: that they require the counsel of others and can discern good from evil counsel.

Objection 3. Further, the Philosopher says (*Topic.* iii, 2) that "young people are not obviously prudent." Yet many young people have grace. Therefore prudence is not to be found in all who have grace.

Reply to Objection 3. Acquired practical wisdom is caused by the exercise of acts; therefore "its acquisition demands experience and time" (*Ethic.* ii, 1); hence it cannot be in the young, neither in habit nor in act. On the other hand graced prudence is caused by divine infusion. Therefore, in children who have been baptized but have not come to the use of reason, there is practical wisdom as to habit but not as to act, even as in the mentally retarded, whereas in those who have come to the use of reason, it is also as to act, with regard to things necessary for salvation. This by practice merits increase, until it becomes perfect, even as the other virtues. Hence the Apostle says (Heb 5:14) that "strong meat is for the perfect, for them who by custom have their senses exercised to the discerning of good and evil."[24]

---

[23] One could distinguish therefore between "supernatural" or "graced" prudence given to all who are in a state of grace and "natural prudence," which may or may not be had by a person in a state of grace. The person with charity has supernatural practical wisdom sufficient to achieve salvation, but the same person may lack practical wisdom in terms of achieving other goals. A holy person may not be entirely reasonable in all matters.

[24] Infused virtues are given by divine power; acquired virtues arise through repeated action.

ARTICLE 15 ~~ Is practical wisdom in us by nature?[25]

No, despite objections to the contrary, The Philosopher says (*Ethic.* ii, 1) that "intellectual virtue is both originated and fostered by teaching; it therefore demands experience and time." Now practical wisdom is an intellectual virtue, as stated above (a. 4). Therefore prudence is in us, not by nature, but by teaching and experience.[26]

I answer that, As shown above (a. 3), practical wisdom includes knowledge both of universals[27] and of the singular matters of action to which prudence applies the universal principles.[28] Accordingly, as regards the knowledge of universals, the same is to be said of practical wisdom as of speculative science, because the primary universal principles of either are known naturally, as shown above (a. 6),[29] except that

---

[25] In other words, is practical wisdom an innate characteristic in a human being, such as circulation of blood, sensitivity to pain, or the ability to breathe? Or, on the other hand, is practical wisdom something that must be developed in time through practice, such as the ability to read?

[26] Although prudence is not in humans by nature, as, say, eyesight or blood circulation, prudence, as well as the other virtues gained either through human action (acquired virtues) or through God's action (infused virtues), does not undermine or ruin human nature but completes and perfects it. Similarly, language is not in us at birth, but yet use of language is an aspect of human flourishing, perfecting what is given by nature.

[27] For example, theft is not to be done.

[28] For example, taking this wallet here and now would be theft.

[29] In speculative knowledge, certain things are known naturally by human beings, implicit as it were, in whatever it is that is known first. Although the child does not say to himself, "A thing cannot be and not be at the same time and in the same respect," he nevertheless knows this principle in the sense of making use of it when playing games, looking for lost toys, and interacting with others. The question "Is mommy here?" implies the first principle of speculative reasoning, the law of non-contradiction. Similarly, the first principles of practical reasoning are natural to human beings, implicit in their actions. Agents, in every action, act on the first principle of practical reasoning, that good is to be done and evil to be avoided, even though they may not articulate it. We seek out that which, at least to us at the moment, appears in some way good, and we avoid the opposite. Of course, our inclinations and judgments about what is good or evil in a particular matter may be mistaken. The good that we seek may be illusory. Secondary universal principles, such as certain concrete rules of the moral life, take more discernment and experience to come to know.

the common principles of prudence are more connatural to man; for, as the Philosopher remarks (*Ethic.* x, 7), "the life which is according to the speculative reason is better than that which is according to man", whereas the secondary universal principles, whether of the speculative or of the practical reason, are not inherited from nature, but are acquired by discovery through experience, or through teaching.

On the other hand, as regards the knowledge of particulars which are the matter of action, we must make a further distinction, because this matter of action is either an end or the means to an end. Now the right ends of human life are fixed; therefore, there can be a natural inclination in respect of these ends; thus it has been stated above (I–II, q. 51, a. 1; I–II, q. 63, a. 1) that some, from a natural inclination, have certain virtues whereby they are inclined to right ends; and consequently they also have naturally a right judgment about such like ends.[30]

But the means to the end, in human concerns, far from being fixed, are of manifold variety according to the variety of persons and affairs. Therefore, since the inclination of nature is ever to something fixed, the knowledge of those means cannot be in man naturally, although, by reason of his natural disposition, one man has a greater aptitude than another in discerning them, just as it happens with regard to the conclusions of speculative sciences. Since, then, practical wisdom is not about the ends, but about the means, as stated above (a. 6; I–II, q. 57, a. 5), it follows that prudence is not from nature.

Objection 2. Further, the changes of age are according to nature. Now practical wisdom results from age, according to Job 12:12: "In the ancient is wisdom, and in length of days prudence." Therefore practical wisdom is natural.

---

[30] Some interpreters of Thomas, for instance, Germain Grisez, have understood these natural inclinations as ordered to "basic goods" that human beings throughout the world seek as fulfilling in some way of human nature, among them life, family, friendship, wisdom, work, play, and integrity. There is a lively debate about Grisez's reading of Aquinas as well as whether Grisez's approach to ethics is sound. A good place to explore this debate is the book *St. Thomas Aquinas and the Natural Law Tradition* edited by John Goyette, Mark S. Latkovic, and Richard Myers (Washington, DC: The Catholic University of America Press, 2004).

Reply to Objection 2. Prudence is rather in the old, not only because their natural disposition calms the movement of the sensitive passions, but also because of their long experience.[31]

Objection 3. Further, practical wisdom is more consistent with human nature than with that of dumb animals. Now there are instances of a certain natural prudence in dumb animals, according to the Philosopher (*De Hist. Anim.* viii, 1). Therefore practical wisdom is natural.

Reply to Objection 3. Even in dumb animals there are fixed ways of obtaining an end; therefore we observe that all the animals of a same species act in like manner. But this is impossible in man, on account of his reason, which takes cognizance of universals, and consequently extends to an infinity of singulars.

---

[31] Nevertheless, it is also true that although age may dispose a person to having practical wisdom, the mere passing of years does not of itself *guarantee* that a person has the singular virtue of prudence of either an acquired or infused kind.

QUESTION **48**

THE PARTS OF PRACTICAL WISDOM

ARTICLE 1 ~~ **Is practical wisdom fittingly divided into three parts?**

Yes, I answer that, Parts are of three kinds, namely, "integral," as wall, roof, and foundations are parts of a house; "subjective," as ox and lion are parts of animal; and "potential," as the nutritive and sensitive powers are parts of the soul.[1] Accordingly, parts can be assigned to a virtue in three ways. First, in likeness to integral parts,[2] so that the things which must be operative for the perfect act of a virtue are called the parts of that virtue. In this way, out of all the things mentioned above, eight may be taken as parts of prudence, namely, the six [namely, "reasoning," "understanding," "circumspection," "foresight," "teachableness" and "caution"] assigned by Macrobius,[3] with the addition of a

---

[1] In discussing the parts of temperance, Thomas writes more explicitly about the nature of integral, subjective, and potential parts of a virtue, explaining that "a cardinal virtue may have three kinds of parts, namely integral, subjective, and potential. The integral parts of a virtue are the conditions the concurrence of which are necessary for virtue. . . . The subjective parts of a virtue are its species, and the species of a virtue have to be differentiated according to the difference of matter or object. . . . The potential parts of a principal virtue are called secondary virtues: for while the principal virtue observes the mode in some principal matter, these observe the mode in some other matter wherein moderation is not so difficult" (II–II, q. 143, a. 1).

[2] The "integral parts" of the virtue are those aspects that must be present for the virtue in question to exist. Sides would be "integral parts" of triangles, since a triangle cannot exist without its three sides.

[3] Ambrosius Theodosius Macrobius (d. 423) was a Roman philosopher and grammarian well known in the Middle Ages to theologians and poets alike

seventh, viz. "memory," mentioned by Tully, and *eustochia,* or "shrewd-ness," mentioned by Aristotle. For the "sense" of practical wisdom is also called "understanding": therefore the Philosopher says (*Ethic.* vi, 11): "Of such things one needs to have the sense, and this is under-standing." Of these eight, five belong to prudence as a cognitive virtue, namely, "memory," "reasoning," "understanding," "teachableness," and "shrewdness," while the three others belong thereto, as commanding and applying knowledge to action, namely, "foresight," "circumspec-tion," and "caution." The reason of their difference is seen from the fact that three things may be observed in reference to knowledge. In the first place, knowledge itself, which, if it be of the past, is called "mem-ory," if of the present, whether contingent or necessary, is called "understanding" or "intelligence." Secondly, the acquiring of knowl-edge, which is caused either by teaching, to which pertains "teachable-ness," or by "discovery," and to this belongs *eustochia,* i.e., "a happy conjecture," of which "shrewdness" is a part, which is a "quick conjec-ture of the middle term," as stated in *Poster.* i, 9. Thirdly, the use of knowledge, in as much as we proceed from things known to knowledge or judgment of other things, and this belongs to "reasoning." And the reason, in order to command aright, requires to have three conditions. First, to order that which is befitting the end, and this belongs to "fore-sight;" secondly, to attend to the circumstances of the matter in hand, and this belongs to "circumspection;" thirdly, to avoid obstacles, and this belongs to "caution."

The subjective parts of a virtue are its various species.[4] In this way the parts of practical wisdom, if we take them properly, are the prudence whereby a man rules himself, and the practical wisdom whereby a man governs a multitude, which differ specifically as stated above (q. 47,

---

(including Chaucer) through his influential commentary on Cicero's *Dream of Scipio.*

[4] The "subjective parts" of virtue are its "species" or sub-classifications. In the genus of "animal," the subjective parts of this genus would include various species such as human beings, dogs, and cats. In the genus of temperance, for example, are included the subjective parts, or species, of moderation with respect to the pleasures of food; moderation with respect to drink; chastity, having to do with the act of sexual intercourse; and purity, having to do with acts giving rise to the desire for sexual intercourse.

a. 11). Again, the prudence whereby a multitude is governed is divided
into various species according to the various kinds of multitude. There is
the multitude which is united together for some particular purpose;
thus an army is gathered together to fight, and the practical wisdom that
governs this is called "military." There is also the multitude that is
united together for the whole of life; such is the multitude of a home or
family, and this is ruled by "domestic prudence;"and such again is the
multitude of a city or kingdom, the ruling principle of which is "regna-
tive practical wisdom" in the ruler, and "political practical wisdom,"
simply so called, in the subjects.

If, however, practical wisdom be taken in a wide sense, as including also speculative knowledge, as stated above (q. 47, a. 2, ad 2) then
its parts include "dialectics," "rhetoric," and "physics," according to
three methods of practical wisdom in the sciences. The first of these is
the attaining of science by demonstration, which belongs to "physics"
(if physics be understood to comprise all demonstrative sciences).[5]
The second method is to arrive at an opinion through probable premises, and this belongs to "dialectics." The third method is to employ
conjectures in order to induce a certain suspicion, or to persuade
somewhat, and this belongs to "rhetoric." It may be said, however,
that these three belong also to practical wisdom properly so called,
since it argues sometimes from necessary premises, sometimes from
probabilities, and sometimes from conjectures.

The potential parts of a virtue are the virtues connected with it
that are directed to certain secondary acts or matters, not having, as it
were, the whole power of the principal virtue.[6] In this way the parts of

---

[5] Physics in the medieval sense used here differs from physics in a contemporary sense. Physics for Thomas includes an understanding of natures, not
merely the laws of physical bodies. "Nature properly speaking is the essence
(or substance) of things that have in themselves as such a principle of activity" (Aristotle, *Metaphysics,* 1015a, 13).

[6] "Potential parts" of a principal virtue, or "secondary virtues," have to do with
the general mode of a virtue (not being overcome by fear in the case of secondary virtues related to courage, not being overcome by desire in the case of
potential parts of temperance) but treat different "material" than the principle
virtue. Courage as a principle virtue primarily has to do with not just any
kind of fear, but fear of death. Temperance has to do with not just any kind of

practical wisdom are "good counsel," which concerns counsel, *synesis*, which concerns judgment in matters of ordinary occurrence, and *gnome*, which concerns judgment in matters of exception to the law, while "practical wisdom" is about the chief act, viz. that of commanding.

Objection 1. It would seem that the parts of practical wisdom are assigned unfittingly. Tully[7] (*De Invent. Rhet.* ii, 53) assigns three parts of practical wisdom, namely, "memory," "understanding," and "foresight." Macrobius (*In Somn. Scip.* i), following the opinion of Plotinus,[8] ascribes to prudence six parts, namely, "reasoning," "understanding," "circumspection," "foresight," "teachableness," and "caution." Aristotle says (*Ethic.* vi, 9, 10, 11) that "good counsel," "*synesis,*" and "*gnome*" belong to practical wisdom. Again, under the head of practical wisdom he mentions "conjecture," "shrewdness," "sense," and "understanding." And another Greek philosopher [Andronicus] says that ten things are connected with practical wisdom, namely, "good counsel," "shrewdness," "foresight," "governing," "military," "political" and "domestic practical wisdom," "dialectics," "rhetoric," and "physics." Therefore it seems that one or the other enumeration is either excessive or deficient.

Reply to Objection 1. The various enumerations differ, either because different kinds of parts are assigned, or because that which is mentioned in one enumeration includes several mentioned in another enumeration. Thus Tully includes "caution" and "circumspection" under "foresight," and "reasoning," "teachableness," and "shrewdness" under "understanding."

---

desire for pleasure, but desire for pleasures of touch. However, there are many other things one may fear or desire, and proper moral conduct with respect to these matters is in a certain way like courage or temperance, properly speaking (hence they are potential parts of a principle virtue), but the secondary virtues differ from the principle virtues because they treat less difficult matters. The fear of death and the desire for bodily pleasure are characteristically very strong passions, and the person who has integrated these strong passions with reason will, on account of that very self-mastery, have an easier time with fears or desires of a lesser degree.

7 Tully is another name for the Roman orator Cicero.
8 The writings of Plotinus (d. 270), considered a founder of Neo-Platonism, played a role in the conversion of St. Augustine. See *Confessions* Book VII.

Objection 2. Further, prudence is specifically distinct from science. But politics, economics, logic, rhetoric, and physics are sciences. Therefore they are not parts of practical wisdom.

Reply to Objection 2. Here domestic and civic practical wisdom are not to be taken as sciences, but as kinds of practical wisdom. As to the other three, the reply may be gathered from what has been said.

Objection 3. Further, the parts do not exceed the whole. Now the intellective memory, or intelligence, reason, sense, and teachableness, belong not only to practical wisdom but also to all the cognitive habits. Therefore they should not be set down as parts of prudence.

Reply to Objection 3. All these things are reckoned parts of practical wisdom, not by taking them altogether, but in so far as they are connected with things pertaining to practical wisdom.

Objection 4. Further, just as counseling, judging, and commanding are acts of the practical reason, so also is using, as stated above (I–II, q. 16, a. 1). Therefore, just as *euboulia*, which refers to counsel, is connected with practical wisdom, and *synesis* and *gnome*, which refer to judgment, so also ought something to have been assigned corresponding to use.

Reply to Objection 4. Right command and right use always go together, because the reason's command is followed by obedience on the part of the lower powers, which pertain to use.

Objection 5. Further, solicitude pertains to practical wisdom, as stated above (q. 47, a. 9). Therefore solicitude also should have been mentioned among the parts of prudence.

Reply to Objection 5. Solicitude is included under foresight.

QUESTION 49

QUASI-INTEGRAL PARTS OF PRACTICAL WISDOM[1]

ARTICLE 3 ~~ **Is teachableness a part of practical wisdom?**

Yes, despite objections to the contrary, Macrobius [*In Somn. Scip.* i, 8] following the opinion of Plotinus places teachableness among the parts of practical wisdom.

   I answer that, As stated above (a. 2, ad 1; q. 47, a. 3) practical wisdom is concerned with particular matters of action, and since such matters are of infinite variety, no one man can consider them all sufficiently; nor can this be done quickly, for it requires length of time. Hence in matters of practical wisdom man stands in very great need of being

---

[1] As Thomas says in II–II, q.49, a.5: "[T]he things required for the perfection of prudence are called requisite or quasi-integral parts of prudence." In q. 48, a. 1, he offers a taxonomy of all the different aspects, or "parts," of practical wisdom.
  (I) Integral parts or necessary components of prudence
   1. Prudence considered as a cognitive virtue includes:
      a. knowledge itself
         i. of the past: memory
         ii. of the present: understanding
      b. acquiring knowledge
         i. from another: teachableness
         ii. on one's own: shrewdness
   2. Prudence considered as a moral virtue, commanding and applying knowledge to action, includes:
      a. ordering a means to an end: foresight
      b. taking circumstances into account: circumspection
      c. avoiding obstacles: caution

taught, especially by the elderly who have acquired a sane understanding of the ends in practical matters.[2] Therefore the Philosopher says (*Ethic.* vi, 11): "It is right to pay no less attention to the undemonstrated assertions and opinions of such persons as are experienced, older than we are, and prudent, than to their demonstrations, for their experience gives them an insight into principles." Thus it is written (Prov 3:5): "Lean not on your own practical wisdom," and (Sir 6:35): "Stand in the multitude of the ancients," (i.e., the elderly), "that are wise, and join yourself from your heart to their wisdom." Now it is a mark of openness to the experience of others to be ready to be taught, and consequently teachableness is fittingly reckoned a part of practical wisdom.[3]

    (II) Subjective parts of prudence, the species or various kinds of prudence, include:
        1. Prudence taken in a narrow sense
           a. prudence pertaining to oneself
           b. prudence pertaining to others
               i. gathered together for a particular end, such as fighting—military prudence
              ii. gathered together for the whole of life in a family—domestic prudence
             iii. gathered together as a community
                  (a) for the ruler—regnative prudence
                  (b) for subjects—political prudence
        2. Prudence taken in a wider sense as including speculative knowledge has the following parts:
           a. physics/science: most certain premises
           b. dialectic: less certain premises
           c. rhetoric: least certain premises
   (III) Potential parts of prudence, secondary virtues connected with prudence concerned with less principle matter, include:
        1. Good counsel: a perfected inquiry before deciding on the objects of choice
        2. *Synesis:* judgment in ordinary matters, pertaining to common law
        3. *Gnome:* judgment in extraordinary matters, pertaining to natural law

[2] In the same vein, Mark Twain allegedly quipped: "When I was a boy of 14, my father was so ignorant I could hardly stand to have the old man around. But when I got to be 21, I was astonished at how much the old man had learned in seven years."

[3] This insight can also apply to being "docile" to what the Church, a teacher with 2000 years experience, has to teach us. The Latin of *docilitas* does not mean a mere passivity, submissiveness, or resignation, as does the English "docile."

Objection 2. Further, that which pertains to a human virtue is in our power, since it is for things that are in our power that we are praised or blamed. Now it is not in our power to be docile, for this is befitting to some through their natural disposition. Therefore it is not a part of prudence.

Reply to Objection 2. Man has a natural aptitude for being taught even as for other things connected with practical wisdom. Yet his own efforts count for much towards the attainment of perfect teachableness, and he must carefully, frequently, and reverently apply his mind to the teachings of the learned, neither neglecting them through laziness, nor despising them through pride.

Objection 3. Further, teachableness is in the disciple, whereas practical wisdom, since it makes precepts, seems rather to belong to teachers, who are also called "preceptors." Therefore teachableness is not a part of practical wisdom.

Reply to Objection 3. By practical wisdom man makes precepts not only for others, but also for himself, as stated above (q. 47, a. 12, ad 3). Hence as stated (*Ethic.* vi, 11), even in subjects, there is place for practical wisdom, to which teachableness pertains. And yet even the learned should be docile in some respects, since no man is altogether self-sufficient in matters of practical wisdom, as stated above.

ARTICLE 6 ~~ Is foresight a part of practical wisdom?

Yes, despite objections to the contrary, Stands the authority of Tully and Macrobius, who number foresight among the parts of practical wisdom, as stated above (q. 48).

I answer that, As stated above (q. 47, a. 1, ad 2; aa 6, 13), practical wisdom is properly about the means to an end, and its proper work is to set them in due order to the end. And although certain things are necessary for an end, which are subject to divine providence, yet nothing is subject to human providence except the contingent matters of actions

---

Rather *docilitas* means "aptness for being taught," which includes an active inward appropriation, an ardor for wisdom, and an intelligent amenability.

that can be done by man for an end. Now the past has become a kind of necessity, since what has been done cannot be undone. In like manner, the present as such has a kind of necessity, since it is necessary that Socrates sit, so long as he sits.

Consequently, future contingents, in so far as they can be directed by man to the end of human life, are the matter of prudence, and each of these things is implied in the word *foresight*, for it implies the notion of something distant, to which that which occurs in the present has to be directed. Therefore foresight is part of practical wisdom.

Objection 1. It would seem that foresight should not be accounted a part of practical wisdom. For nothing is part of itself. Now foresight seems to be the same as practical wisdom, because according to Isidore (*Etym.* x), "a person with practical wisdom is one who sees from afar [*porro videns*]": and this is also the derivation of "foresight" [*providentia*], according to Boethius (*De Consol.* v).[4] Therefore foresight is not a part of practical wisdom.

Reply to Objection 1. Whenever many things are requisite for a unity, one of them must be the principal to which all the others are subordinate. Hence in every whole one part must be formal and predominant, whence the whole has unity. Accordingly foresight is the principal of all the parts of practical wisdom, since whatever else is required for practical wisdom is necessary precisely that some particular thing may be rightly directed to its end. Hence it is that the very name of practical wisdom [*prudentia*] is taken from foresight [*providentia*] as from its principal part.

Objection 2. Further, practical wisdom is only practical, whereas foresight may be also speculative, because "seeing," whence we have the word "to foresee," has more to do with speculation than operation. Therefore foresight is not a part of practical wisdom.

---

4 Anicius Manlius Severinus Boethius (480–525) died a Christian martyr. As he awaited execution, Boethius wrote his famous *Consolation of Philosophy*, a work of philosophy and poetry about the pursuit of happiness. Boethius's work *De trinitate* as well as *De hebdomadibus* occasioned commentaries by Aquinas. For more information, see Ralph McInerny, *Boethius and Aquinas* (Washington, DC: The Catholic University of America Press, 1990).

Reply to Objection 2. Speculation is about universal and necessary things, which, in themselves, are not distant, since they are everywhere and always, though they are distant from us, in so far as we fail to know them. Hence foresight does not apply properly to speculative, but only to practical, matters.

Objection 3. Further, the chief act of practical wisdom is to command, while its secondary act is to judge and to take counsel. But none of these seems to be properly implied by foresight. Therefore foresight is not part of practical wisdom.

Reply to Objection 3. Right order to an end, which is included in the notion of foresight, contains rectitude of counsel, judgment, and command, without which no right order to the end is possible.

QUESTION 52

THE GIFT OF COUNSEL

ARTICLE 1 ~~ **Should counsel be considered among the gifts of the Holy Spirit?**

Yes, despite objections to the contrary, It is written (Is 11:2): "(The Spirit of the Lord) shall rest upon him . . . the spirit of counsel, and of courage."

I answer that, As stated above (I–II, q. 68, a. 1), the gifts of the Holy Spirit are dispositions whereby the soul is rendered amenable to the motion of the Holy Spirit. Now God moves everything according to the mode of the thing moved:[1] thus He moves the corporeal creature through time and place, and the spiritual creature through time, but not through place, as Augustine declares[2] (*Gen. ad lit.* viii, 20, 22). Again, it is proper to the rational creature to be moved through the research of reason to perform any particular action, and this

---

[1] In other words, grace perfects nature rather than contradicting it. God acts in creation and acts also in a supernatural way through grace. God's providence respects the nature of each created thing and in so doing respects God's own creative will. God therefore directs human beings in a way that respects the natural gifts that He has given, reason and will. By means of these natural gifts, perfected by graces and gifts of the Holy Spirit, human beings return to God.

[2] St. Augustine of Hippo (b. 354–d. 430) is one of the most influential thinkers of all time. His life story, a development from pagan intellectual to Catholic bishop and saint, is detailed in his *Confessions*. Augustine was a prolific author of philosophical dialogues, scripture commentaries, sermons, and other influential works.

research is called counsel. Hence the Holy Spirit is said to move the rational creature by way of counsel. Therefore counsel is reckoned among the gifts of the Holy Spirit.

Objection 1. It would seem that counsel should not be reckoned among the gifts of the Holy Spirit. The gifts of the Holy Spirit are given as a help to the virtues, according to Gregory (*Moral.* ii, 49). Now for the purpose of taking counsel, man is sufficiently perfected by the virtue of practical wisdom, or even of *euboulia* [deliberating well], as is evident from what has been said (q. 47, a. 1, ad 2; q. 51, aa 1, 2). Therefore counsel should not be reckoned among the gifts of the Holy Spirit.

Reply to Objection 1. Practical wisdom or *euboulia* [deliberating well], whether acquired or infused, directs man in the research of counsel according to principles that the reason can grasp; hence practical wisdom or *euboulia* [deliberating well] makes man take good counsel either for himself or for another. Since, however, human reason is unable to grasp the singular and contingent things which may occur, the result is that "the thoughts of mortal men are fearful, and our counsels uncertain" (Wis 9:14). Hence in the research of counsel, man requires to be directed by God, who comprehends all things: and this is done through the gift of counsel, whereby man is directed as though counseled by God,[3] just

---

3 John Henry Cardinal Newman's hymn, composed at sea on a stormy night, captures the yearning of a heart for the Holy Spirit's gift of counsel.

Lead kindly light! Amid the encircling gloom,
Lead Thou me on;
The night is dark, and I am far from home,
Lead Thou me on;
Keep Thou my feet; I do not ask to see
The distant scene; one step enough to me.

I was not ever thus, nor prayed that Thou
Should'st lead me on;
I loved to choose and see my path; but now
Lead Thou me on:
I loved the garish day, and spite of fears,
Pride ruled my will. Remember not past years.

So long Thy power has blessed me, sure it still
Will lead me on

as, in human affairs, those who are unable to take counsel for themselves seek counsel from those who are wiser.

Objection 2. Further, the difference between the seven gifts of the Holy Spirit and the gratuitous graces[4] seems to be that the latter are not given to all, but are divided among various people, whereas the gifts of the Holy Spirit are given to all who have the Holy Spirit. But counsel seems to be one of those things which are given by the Holy Spirit specially to certain persons, according to 1 Maccabees 2:65: "Behold . . . your brother Simon is a man of counsel." Therefore counsel should be numbered among the gratuitous graces rather than among the seven gifts of the Holy Spirit.

Reply to Objection 2. That a man be of such good counsel as to counsel others may be due to a gratuitous grace; but that a man be counseled by God as to what he ought to do in matters necessary for salvation is common to all holy persons.

Objection 3. Further, it is written (Rom 8:14): "Whosoever are led by the Spirit of God, they are the sons of God." But counseling is not consistent with being led by another. Since, then, the gifts of the Holy Spirit are most befitting the children of God, who "have received the spirit of adoption of sons," it would seem that counsel should not be numbered among the gifts of the Holy Spirit.

Reply to Objection 3. The children of God are moved by the Holy Spirit according to their mode, without prejudice to their free-will

---

O'er moor and fen, o'er crag and torrent, till
The night is gone;
And with the morn those angel faces smile
Which I have loved long since, and lost awhile.

[4] In *Summa theologiae* I–II, q. 111, a. 5, Thomas speaks of the distinction between these two kinds of graces: "[S]anctifying grace ordains a man immediately to a union with his last end, whereas gratuitous grace ordains a man to what is preparatory to the end; i.e., by prophecy and miracles and so forth, men are induced to unite themselves to their last end." The objection is that counsel would seem to be a gratuitous grace, a special intervention for a particular person akin to the power of prophecy or healing, rather than an aspect of sanctifying grace, including the gifts of the Holy Spirit, which is had by all persons of living faith.

which is the "faculty of will and reason" [Sent. iii, D, 24]. Accordingly the gift of counsel is befitting the children of God in so far as the reason is instructed by the Holy Spirit about what we have to do.[5]

---

[5] God's counsel, in the case of the infused virtue of prudence, or human counsel, in the case of acquired prudence, helps our intelligence, i.e., aids our understanding in doing what is right. In the case of infused prudence, as with the other infused virtues, grace does not undermine or destroy nature but perfects it.

QUESTION 53

IMPRUDENCE

ARTICLE 1 ⟿ **Is imprudence a sin?**

Yes, despite objections to the contrary, The spiritual treasure of grace is not taken away save by sin. But it is taken away by imprudence, according to Proverbs 21:20, "There is a treasure to be desired, and oil in the dwelling of the just, and the imprudent man shall spend it." Therefore imprudence is a sin.

I answer that, Imprudence may be taken in two ways: first, as a privation; secondly, as a contrary. Properly speaking it is not taken as a negation, so as merely to signify the absence of prudence, for this can be without any sin.[1] Taken as a privation, imprudence denotes lack of that practical wisdom which a man can and ought to have, and in this sense imprudence is a sin by reason of a man's negligence in striving to have prudence.

Imprudence is taken as a contrary[2] in so far as the movement or act of reason is in opposition to practical wisdom: for instance, whereas the

---

[1] For instance, a person without acquired prudence, such as a small child, does not sin by the mere fact of not having prudence. Someone who could not learn, such as a mentally handicapped person, would not sin in not having practical wisdom. A lack of practical wisdom is sinful if the agent could have and should have acquired prudence but did not. In this sense, imprudence is a moral evil, a lack of a perfection that a person ought to have.

[2] This article hinges on the differences between a negation, a privation, and a contrary. A negation is a lack of a characteristic that a being is not capable of having nor should possess; e.g., horses don't have wings. A privation is a lack of a quality a being is capable of possessing and ought to possess; e.g., a horse

right reason of prudence acts by taking counsel, the person lacking practical wisdom despises counsel, and the same applies to the other conditions which require consideration in the act of practical wisdom. In this way imprudence is a sin in respect of prudence considered under its proper aspect, since it is not possible for a man to act against practical wisdom except by infringing the rules on which the right reason of practical wisdom depends. Therefore, if this should happen through aversion from the Divine Law, it will be a mortal sin, as when a man acts precipitately through contempt and rejection of the Divine teaching, whereas if he act beside the Law and without contempt, and without detriment to things necessary for salvation, it will be a venial sin.

Objection 1. It would seem that imprudence is not a sin. For every sin is voluntary, according to Augustine [*De Vera Relig.* xiv], whereas imprudence is not voluntary, since no man wishes to be imprudent. Therefore imprudence is not a sin.

Reply to Objection 1. No man desires the deformity of imprudence, but the rash man wills the act of imprudence, because he wishes to act

---

without legs suffers a privation, not merely a negation. A contrary is when terms are in the same genus but are separated by the greatest possible difference, such as good/bad, black/white, and odd/even. So the pure negation of prudence, a simple lack of it, may not be sinful in the case of children. Since prudence requires experience, and children cannot have had time to acquire the needed experience, children do not have prudence. This *negation* may be contrasted to the *privation* of an adult lacking prudence, a characteristic that a normal functioning adult can and should have. This privation can itself be distinguished from a person having the opposite of prudence, imprudence. This person has just the opposite characteristics of the person with practical wisdom. One could imagine situations where there is a privation of a characteristic (the person is not strong, but can and ought to be strong), but there is no contrary present (though not strong, the person is also not weak, but rather average in strength). So a person may "lack prudence" in three ways, which set a person increasingly far from virtue. In pure negation, the habit is simply not there through no fault of the person in question. In a privation, the habit is lacking in a case where it can and should be present. And in a contrary, the person not only does not have the habit of practical wisdom but has the opposite characteristic, imprudence.

with lack of due consideration. Hence the Philosopher says (*Ethic.* vi, 5) that "he who sins willingly against prudence is less to be commended."[3]

Objection 2. Further, none but original sin comes to man with his birth. But imprudence comes to man with his birth; therefore the young are imprudent; and yet it is not original sin which is opposed to original justice. Therefore imprudence is not a sin.

Reply to Objection 2. This argument takes imprudence in the negative sense. It must be observed, however, that lack of prudence or of any other virtue is included in the lack of original justice which perfected the entire soul. Accordingly all such lack of virtue may be ascribed to original sin.

Objection 3. Further, every sin is taken away by repentance. But imprudence is not taken away by repentance. Therefore imprudence is not a sin.

Reply to Objection 3. Repentance restores infused practical wisdom, and thus the lack of this prudence ceases; but acquired prudence is not restored as to the habit, although the contrary act is taken away, wherein, properly speaking, the sin of imprudence consists.[4]

ARTICLE 5 ~~ **Is inconstancy [lack of persistence] a vice against practical wisdom?**

Yes, despite objections to the contrary, It belongs to practical wisdom to prefer the greater good to the lesser. Therefore to forsake the greater

---

[3] No one desires evil for its own sake because what is seen as good, and good alone, attracts the will. Everything is chosen under the notion or formality of the good *(sub ratione boni)*, but sometimes this good is merely illusory rather than truly good. However, in doing wrong a person desires to have the good to which evil is attached more than he wishes to avoid the evil attached by seeking some other good. It is not that a person sets out to be imprudent, but a person may voluntarily seek some apparent good and is willing (that is, voluntarily choosing) to accept as a price the imprudence involved in the action.

[4] Confession may restore the infused virtues if they are lost (faith, hope, love, as well as infused prudence, infused justice, infused courage, and infused temperance), but only the repeated choices of the person lead to attaining the acquired virtues or vices.

good belongs to imprudence. Now this is inconstancy. Therefore lack of persistence belongs to imprudence.

I answer that, Lack of persistence denotes withdrawal from a definite good purpose. Now the origin of this withdrawal is in the appetite, for a man does not withdraw from a previous good purpose except on account of something being inordinately pleasing to him; nor is this withdrawal completed except through a defect of reason, which is deceived in rejecting what before it had rightly accepted. And since it can resist the impulse of the passions, if it fails to do this, it is due to its own weakness in not standing to the good purpose it has conceived; hence inconstancy, as to its completion, is due to a defect in the reason. Now just as all rectitude of the practical reason belongs in some degree to practical wisdom, so all lack of that rectitude belongs to imprudence. Consequently inconstancy, as to its completion, belongs to imprudence. And just as undue haste is due to a defect in the act of counsel, and thoughtlessness to a defect in the act of judgment, so lack of persistence arises from a defect in the act of command.[5] For a man is stated to be inconstant because his reason fails in commanding what has been counseled and judged.

Objection 1. It would seem that inconstancy is not a vice contained under imprudence. For inconstancy consists seemingly in a lack of perseverance in matters of difficulty. But perseverance in difficult matters belongs to courage. Therefore inconstancy is opposed to courage rather than to practical wisdom.

---

[5] In this sentence, one can see how each vice is a failure of a virtue. Sin, like any form of evil, must ride parasitic upon some good because evil is a lack of a due good. In each of the "three chief acts" of practical wisdom, an agent may fail. Where there is a lack of due counsel, there is undue haste. In such a situation, the agent may fail to take note of possible means to the end. Where there is a lack of proper judgment, there is thoughtlessness. Here a means is chosen that is not well fitted to achieving the end. Finally, where there is a defect in the act of command, there is inconstancy. In this case, sufficient care is taken in considering the various possible means (counsel), a sound judgment is made about which means to use, but the chosen means is not made use of. Practical wisdom is truly practical in that if someone in practice fails to carry out what prudence requires, the agent cannot be said to be practically wise.

Reply to Objection 1. The good of practical wisdom is shared by all the moral virtues,[6] and accordingly perseverance in good belongs to all moral virtues, chiefly, however, to courage, which suffers a greater impulse to the contrary.

Objection 2. Further, it is written (Jas 3:16): "Where jealousy and contention are, there are inconstancy and every evil work." But jealousy pertains to envy. Therefore lack of persistence pertains not to imprudence but to envy.

Reply to Objection 2. Envy and anger, which are the source of contention, cause lack of persistence on the part of the appetite, to which power the origin of lack of persistence is due, as stated above.

---

[6] All moral virtues involve prudence, for it takes practical wisdom to find the mean in which the virtues of courage, temperance, and justice consist.

QUESTION 55

COUNTERFEIT
PRACTICAL WISDOM

ARTICLE 1 ⏤ **Is prudence of the flesh a sin?**

Yes, despite objections to the contrary, No man is an enemy to God save for wickedness, according to Wisdom 14:9: "To God the wicked and his wickedness are hateful alike." Now it is written (Rom 8:7): "The prudence [Vulg.: 'wisdom'] of the flesh is an enemy to God." Therefore prudence of the flesh is a sin.

I answer that, As stated above (q. 47, a. 13), prudence regards things which are directed to the end of life as a whole. Hence prudence of the flesh signifies properly the practical wisdom of a man who looks upon carnal goods as the last end of his life.[1] Now it is evident that this is a sin, because it involves a disorder in man with respect to his last end, which does not consist in the goods of the

---

[1] By carnal goods, Thomas means not only sexual pleasure, but also other goods of the body, such as food, drink, clothes, and health. All these things are good, but none of these things are the greatest good. Human beings having all the carnal goods in the world would still not be happy because we need more than this to make us truly happy. In particular, we have a drive to know the pure truth and to obtain an unfailing, untarnished good. Thus, the person who acts as if one or a combination of fleshly goods were the greatest good deprives himself (and the community) of full sharing in authentic human happiness.

body, as stated above (I–II, q. 2, a. 5).[2] Therefore, prudence of the flesh is a sin.

Objection 1. It would seem that prudence of the flesh is not a sin. For prudence is more excellent than the other moral virtues, since it governs them all. But no justice or temperance is sinful. Neither, therefore, is any prudence a sin.

Reply to Objection 1. Justice and temperance include in their very nature that which ranks them among the virtues, viz. equality and the curbing of concupiscence; hence they are never taken in a bad sense. On the other hand, prudence is so called from foreseeing [*providendo*], as stated above (q. 47, a. 1; q. 49, a. 6), which can extend to evil things also. Therefore, although practical wisdom is taken simply in a good sense, yet, if something be added, it may be taken in a bad sense: and it is thus that the prudence of the flesh is directed to the love of the flesh.

Objection 2. Further, it is not a sin to act prudently for an end which it is lawful to love. But it is lawful to love the flesh, "for no man ever hated his own flesh" (Eph 5:29). Therefore prudence of the flesh is not a sin.

Reply to Objection 2. The flesh is on account of the soul, as matter is on account of the form, and the instrument on account of the principal agent. Hence the flesh is loved lawfully, if it be directed to the good of the soul as its end. If, however, a man place his last end in a good of the flesh, his love will be inordinate and unlawful, and it is thus that the prudence of the flesh is directed to the love of the flesh.

---

2 In *Summa contra Gentiles* III, ch. 32, Thomas argues that perfect human happiness cannot consist in goods of the body such as strength, speed, or longevity. Such things are unstable, for accident or disease can take any one or all of these good things away, but happiness is something lasting and stable. Furthermore, these perfections are shared with animals or even surpassed by animals: "in bodily goods the human being is surpassed by many animals; for instance, by the elephant in longevity, by the lion in strength, by the stag in fleetness" (*ST* I–II, q. 2, a. 5). But human happiness should be something distinctly *human*, and therefore not shared with lower animals. Although health, strength, and physical vitality are goods for human beings, it is also true that these things are not the ultimate and perfect good for human beings. One can be, in other words, very healthy and yet very unhappy.

Article 2 ~~ Is prudence of the flesh a mortal sin?

No, despite objections to the contrary, That which diminishes a sin has not of itself the nature of a mortal sin. Now the thoughtful quest of things pertaining to the care of the flesh, which seems to pertain to carnal prudence, diminishes sin [cf. Prov 6:30]. Therefore prudence of the flesh has not of itself the nature of a mortal sin.

I answer that, As stated above (q. 47, a. 2, ad 1; a. 13), a man is said to be prudent in two ways: first, simply, i.e., in relation to the end of life as a whole; secondly, relatively, i.e., in relation to some particular end; thus a man is said to be prudent in business or something else of the kind. Accordingly if prudence of the flesh be taken as corresponding to prudence in its absolute signification, so that a man place the last end of his whole life in the care of the flesh, it is a mortal sin, because he turns away from God by so doing, since he cannot have several last ends, as stated above (I–II, q. 1, a. 5).[3]

If, on the other hand, prudence of the flesh be taken as corresponding to particular prudence, it is a venial sin. For it happens sometimes that a man has an inordinate affection for some pleasure of the flesh, without turning away from God by a mortal sin, in which case he does not place the end of his whole life in carnal pleasure. To apply oneself to obtain this pleasure is a venial sin and pertains to prudence of the flesh. But if a man actually refers the care of the flesh to a good end, as when one is careful about one's food in order to sustain

---

[3] Thomas himself asks in *ST* I–II, q. 1, a. 5: Why can't there be more than one final end? The reason lies in part in the nature of choice and the nature of the final end. One's final end is that overriding and consummate goal of life—whatever is desired the most and not to be sacrificed for some other goal. Reality sometimes demands choice among competing goods: the student must either study now for the exam or go out and socialize with friends; but he cannot do both at once. The ultimate end may be understood in two ways. Formally, it is that which is desired above all other things as complete and fulfilling. All human beings desire perfect happiness. However, where is a person to find perfect happiness? The shared "formality" agreed upon by all gives way to a wild diversity "materially" speaking. The final end for one person may be wealth; for another, bodily pleasure; for a third, power; or for another, loving and knowing God. Each agrees formally in seeking perfect happiness; each disagrees materially about where that happiness is to be found.

one's body, this is no longer prudence of the flesh, because then one uses the care of the flesh as a means to an end.

Objection 1. It would seem that prudence of the flesh is a mortal sin. For it is a mortal sin to rebel against the Divine law, since this implies contempt of God. Now "the prudence of the flesh . . . is not subject to the law of God" (Rom 8:7). Therefore prudence of the flesh is a mortal sin.

Reply to Objection 1. The Apostle is speaking of that carnal prudence whereby a man places the end of his whole life in the goods of the flesh, and this is a mortal sin.

Objection 2. Further, every sin against the Holy Spirit is a mortal sin. Now prudence of the flesh seems to be a sin against the Holy Spirit, for "it cannot be subject to the law of God" (Rom 8:7), and so it seems to be an unpardonable sin, which is proper to the sin against the Holy Spirit. Therefore prudence of the flesh is a mortal sin.

Reply to Objection 2. Prudence of the flesh does not imply a sin against the Holy Spirit. For when it is stated that "it cannot be subject to the law of God," this does not mean that he who has prudence of the flesh cannot be converted and submit to the law of God, but that carnal prudence itself cannot be subject to God's law, even as neither can injustice be just, nor heat cold, although that which is hot may become cold.

Objection 3. Further, the greatest evil is opposed to the greatest good, as stated in *Ethic.* viii, 10. Now prudence of the flesh is opposed to that prudence which is the chief of the moral virtues. Therefore prudence of the flesh is chief among mortal sins, so that it is itself a mortal sin.

Reply to Objection 3. Every sin is opposed to practical wisdom, just as practical wisdom is shared by every virtue. But it does not follow that every sin opposed to practical wisdom is most grave, but only when it is opposed to prudence in some very grave matter.

ARTICLE 3 ～ Is craftiness a special sin?

Yes, despite objections to the contrary, The Apostle says (2 Cor 4:2): "We renounce the hidden things of dishonesty, not walking in craftiness, nor adulterating the word of God."[4] Therefore craftiness is a sin.

I answer that, Practical wisdom is "right reason applied to action," just as science is "right reason applied to knowledge." In speculative matters one may sin against rectitude of knowledge in two ways: in one way, when the reason is led to a false conclusion that appears to be true; in another way, when the reason proceeds from false premises, which appear to be true, either to a true or to a false conclusion. Even so a sin may be against practical wisdom, through having some resemblance thereto, in two ways: first, when the purpose of the reason is directed to an end which is good not in truth but in appearance, and this pertains to prudence of the flesh; secondly, when, in order to obtain a certain end, whether good or evil, a man uses means that are not true but fictitious and counterfeit, and this belongs to the sin of craftiness.[5] This is consequently a sin opposed to practical wisdom, and distinct from prudence of the flesh.

---

4 Here Thomas quotes briefly from St. Paul's Second Letter to the Corinthians. Although Thomas is most well known for his *Summa theologiae*, and among philosophers for his commentaries on Aristotle, the Angelic Doctor also spent a large portion of his time commenting on Scripture. Indeed, his official duties as a professor at the University of Paris demanded not that he write *Summas* of theology or interpret Aristotle, but rather that he lecture on Sacred Scripture. Thomas commented on the Gospels of Matthew and John, on the Letters of St. Paul and in the Old Testament on Isaiah, Jeremiah, Lamentations, and Job. At the request of Pope Urban IV, Thomas compiled the *Catena aurea*, which he completed in 1264. The *Catena* is a compilation of quotations from the Church Fathers, such as Jerome, Augustine, and John Chrysostom, arranged to follow the Gospels line by line. This work manifests Thomas's deep knowledge of the Patristic tradition and has been widely distributed. In the nineteenth century, John Henry Cardinal Newman translated and added a preface to this work. Many, but not all, of Thomas's commentaries on Scripture are available in English translation.

5 Craftiness (Latin: *astutia*) is sometimes translated as "cunning," which brings out the negative connotation of the word. The cunning person is very intelligent, but the intelligence of the cunning person is in service of wrongdoing, not the good.

Objection 1. It would seem that craftiness is not a special sin. For the words of Holy Scripture do not induce anyone to sin; and yet they induce us to be crafty, according to Proverbs 1:4: "To give craftiness to little ones." Therefore craftiness is not a sin.

Reply to Objection 1. As Augustine observes (*Contra Julian.* iv, 3) just as practical wisdom is sometimes improperly taken in a bad sense, so is craftiness sometimes taken in a good sense, and this on account of their mutual resemblance. Properly speaking, however, craftiness is taken in a bad sense, as the Philosopher states in *Ethic.* vi, 12.

Objection 2. Further, it is written (Prov 13:16): "The crafty man does all things with counsel." Therefore, he does so either for a good or for an evil end. If for a good end, there is no sin seemingly, and if for an evil end, it would seem to pertain to carnal or worldly prudence. Therefore craftiness is not a special sin distinct from prudence of the flesh.

Reply to Objection 2. Craftiness can take counsel both for a good end and for an evil end; nor should a good end be pursued by means that are false and counterfeit but by such as are true. Hence craftiness is a sin if it be directed to a good end.

ARTICLE 6 ~~ **Is anxious care about temporal things contrary to prudence?**

Yes, despite objections to the contrary, Our Lord said (Mt 6:31): "Be not anxious . . . saying, What shall we eat, or what shall we drink, or wherewith shall we be clothed?" And yet such things are very necessary.[6]

---

6 Thomas realizes that people need food, drink, and clothing in order to survive. Such things are important and are not matters of indifference to the Christian believer. Indeed, the importance of external goods (such as food, clothing, and shelter) is presupposed by one of the Ten Commandments, "You shall not steal." After all, if external goods were of absolutely no accord, why would taking someone's external goods be in any way wrong? Further, the importance of such goods is illustrated in the corporal works of mercy, in which we are commanded by Jesus, on pain of damnation, to feed, clothe, and shelter those in need. "[As] you did it to one of the least of these my brethren, you did it to me" (Mt 25:40). Nevertheless, although food, clothing, and shelter

I answer that, To have anxious care denotes an earnest endeavor to obtain something. Now it is evident that the endeavor is more earnest when there is fear of failure, so that there is less solicitude when success is assured. Accordingly to have anxious care about temporal things may be unlawful in three ways: First on the part of the object of our concern, that is, if we seek temporal things as an end. Hence Augustine says (*De Operibus Monach.* xxvi): "When Our Lord said: 'Be not fearful,'. . . . He intended to forbid them either to make such things their end, or for the sake of these things to do whatever they were commanded to do in preaching the Gospel."[7] Secondly, anxious care for temporal things may be unlawful, through too much earnestness in endeavoring to obtain temporal things, the result being that a man is drawn away from spiritual things which ought to be the chief object of his search; therefore it is written (Mt 13:22) that "the care of this world . . . chokes up the word." Thirdly, anxious care is sinful through over much fear, when, to wit, a man fears to lack necessary things if he does what he ought to do. Now our Lord gives three motives for laying aside this fear: first, on account of the yet greater favors bestowed by God on man, independently of his solicitude, viz. his body and soul (Mt 6:26); secondly, on account of the care with which God watches over animals and plants without the assistance of man, according to the requirements of their nature; thirdly, because of Divine providence, through ignorance of which the gentiles are anxious in seeking temporal goods before all others. Consequently He concludes that we should be anxious most of all about spiritual goods, hoping that temporal goods also may be granted us according to our needs, if we do what we ought to do.

Objection 1. It would seem lawful to be anxious about temporal matters because a superior should be anxious for his subjects, according to

---

are important, they are not the *most important* thing. And since they are not the most important, it is unreasonable and contrary to proper love of God to have undue anxiety about them.

[7] As Augustine teaches in *De doctrina christiana (On Christian Doctrine)*, God alone should be enjoyed as an end, while things are to be made use of for that end. In other words, to set one's heart as ultimately relying upon and seeking anything else than God is to set oneself up for failure in terms of ultimate human fulfillment.

Romans 12:8: "He that rules, with solicitude." Now according to the Divine ordering, man is placed over temporal things, according to Psalm 8:8: "You have subjected all things under his feet," etc. Therefore man should be anxious about temporal things.

Reply to Objection 1. Temporal goods are subjected to man that he may use them according to his needs, not that he may place his end in them and be over anxious about them.

Objection 2. Further, everyone is anxious about the end for which he works. Now it is lawful for a man to work for the temporal things whereby he sustains life. Therefore the Apostle says (2 Thess 3:10): "If any man will not work, neither let him eat." Therefore it is lawful to be anxious about temporal things.

Reply to Objection 2. The anxious care of a man who gains his bread by bodily labor is not superfluous but proportionate; hence Jerome says on Matthew 6:31, "Be not anxious," that "labor is necessary, but solicitude must be banished," namely superfluous solicitude which unsettles the mind.[8]

Objection 3. Further, anxious care about works of mercy is praiseworthy, according to 2 Timothy 1:17: "When he was come to Rome, he carefully sought me." Now anxious care about temporal things is sometimes connected with works of mercy: for instance, when a man is anxious to watch over the interests of orphans and poor persons. Therefore, anxious care about temporal things is not unlawful.

Reply to Objection 3. In the works of mercy, anxious care about temporal things is directed to charity as its end. Therefore it is not unlawful, unless it be superfluous.

---

8 Thomas is not advocating a carelessness about temporal matters, but rather that these matters be given due or proportionate care. Many people are tempted to care about such things as if they were the "be all and end all," the very meaning of human life. But what is most important is not what a person owns or what a person does, but rather who the person is, a friend of God in fact or in potentiality.

QUESTION 56

THE PRECEPTS
CONCERNING
PRACTICAL WISDOM

ARTICLE 1 ∾ Should the Ten Commandments have included a precept of practical wisdom?

No, despite objections to the contrary, It is clear to anyone who goes through the precepts of the decalogue.

I answer that, As stated above (I–II, q. 100, a. 3; a. 5, ad 1) when we were treating of precepts, the commandments of the decalogue, being given to the whole people, are a matter of common knowledge to all, as coming under the purview of natural reason.[1] Now foremost among the things dictated by natural reason are the ends of human life, which are to the practical order what naturally known principles are to the speculative order, as shown above (q. 47, a. 6).[2] Now practical

---

[1] The Ten Commandments, although revealed by God, are principles of natural law that are accessible to human reason. God reveals what could be known naturally as an aid to human beings, who often suppress moral knowledge via rationalizations to facilitate wrongdoing.

[2] The passage to which Thomas refers twice in this article, II–II, question 47, article 5, reads as follows: "Now, just as, in the speculative reason, there are certain things naturally known, about which is 'understanding,' and certain things of which we obtain knowledge through them, viz. conclusions, about which is 'science,' so in the practical reason, certain things pre-exist, as naturally known principles, and such are the ends of the moral virtues, since the end is in practical matters what principles are in speculative matters, as stated above (q. 23, a. 7, ad 2; I–II, q. 13, a. 3), while certain things are in the practical reason by way of conclusions, and such are the means which we gather

wisdom is not about the end, but about the means, as stated above (q. 47, a. 6). Hence it was not fitting that the precepts of the decalogue should include a precept relating directly to practical wisdom.[3] And yet all the precepts of the decalogue are related to practical wisdom, in so far as it directs all virtuous acts.

Objection 1. It would seem that the precepts of the decalogue should have included a precept of practical wisdom. For the chief precepts should include a precept of the chief virtue. Now the chief precepts are those of the decalogue. Since, then, practical wisdom is the chief of the moral virtues, it seems that the precepts of the decalogue should have included a precept of practical wisdom.[4]

Reply to Objection 1. Although practical wisdom is simply foremost among all the moral virtues, yet justice, more than any other virtue, regards its object under the aspect of something due, which is a necessary condition for a precept, as stated above (q. 44, a. 1; I–II, q. 99, aa 1, 5). Hence it behooved the chief precepts of the Law, which are those of the decalogue, to refer to justice rather than to practical wisdom.

---

from the ends themselves. About these is prudence, which applies universal principles to the particular conclusions of practical matters. Consequently it does not belong to prudence to appoint the end to moral virtues, but only to regulate the means." The end is in practical matters, that is, the ultimate goal is in practice, what principles are in speculative matters, that is, the presuppositions of reasoning. In practice, we begin with the end or goal in mind before consideration can be given to the suitable means to achieve that goal. In reasoning, we presuppose certain fundamental truths, when considering any particular matter.

3 In other words, the precepts of the Ten Commandments needed to be of such clarity that the detailed and circumstantial nature of precepts pertaining to prudence were not suitable for inclusion. As Thomas puts it in I–II, q. 100, a. 5, ad 1: "[T]he precepts of the Decalogue need to be such as the people can understand at once. Now a precept implies the notion of duty. But it is easy for a man, especially for a believer, to understand that, of necessity, he owes certain duties to God and to his neighbor."

4 The objection suggests that the importance of prudence should be reflected in the Ten Commandments. The most important law of the Old Testament should reflect the most important virtue. Instead, the Ten Commandments focus on matters of justice, such as not depriving someone of life, property, reputation, or due honor.

Objection 2. Further, the teaching of the Gospel contains the Law especially with regard to the precepts of the decalogue. Now the teaching of the Gospel contains a precept of practical wisdom (Mt 10:16): "Be . . . prudent as serpents." Therefore the precepts of the decalogue should have included a precept of practical wisdom.

Reply to Objection 2. The teaching of the Gospel is the doctrine of perfection. Therefore it needed to instruct man perfectly in all matters relating to right conduct, whether ends or means: therefore it behooved the Gospel teaching to contain precepts also of practical wisdom.

Objection 3. Further, the other lessons of the Old Testament are directed to the precepts of the decalogue: therefore it is written (Mal 4:4): "Remember the law of Moses My servant, which I commanded him in Horeb." Now the other lessons of the Old Testament include precepts of practical wisdom, for instance (Prov 3:5): "Lean not upon your own practical wisdom"; and further on (Prov 4:25): "Let your eyelids go before your steps." Therefore the Law also should have contained a precept of practical wisdom, especially among the precepts of the decalogue.

Reply to Objection 3. Just as the rest of the teaching of the Old Testament is directed to the precepts of the decalogue as its end, so it behooved man to be instructed by the subsequent lessons of the Old Testament about the act of practical wisdom which is directed to the means.[5]

---

[5] In this reply, Thomas gives a sense of the importance of salvation history. God relates to His people in a way that is appropriate for them at that time. There is, then, a certain unfolding of providential care throughout history that reaches its climax in the Incarnation, Passion, Death, and Resurrection of Christ. Before Christ, God prepares His people to receive the Savior. After Christ, God's people relate to God through Christ. Matthew Levering's *Christ's Fulfillment of Torah and Temple: Salvation According to Thomas Aquinas* (Notre Dame, IN: University of Notre Dame Press, 2002) provides a rich synthesis of Thomas's teaching, echoing Augustine, that the Old Covenant is revealed in the New, and the New Covenant is concealed in the Old. Over time, God leads His people to a deeper understanding of who He is and who they should become.

JUSTICE

JUSTICE

ACCORDING TO St. Thomas, justice is a virtue that enables us to render to each person that which is his or her right, what is due to each person, what each person ought to receive. The proper object of justice is right (*ius*), understood as the proper order of interrelationships established by divine or human reason. Justice is expressed in actions aimed at what is right in our relations with other persons. Unlike other virtues, justice is always "other"-regarding.

Historically justice has been understood in a number of ways. Justice has been taken to be equivalent to doing what is right in any action and as such synonymous with virtue as a whole. Justice has been understood also as a general virtue of the lawgiver and its proper object the common good of the political community. Justice has also been understood as one of the particular virtues. St. Thomas manages to coordinate these different perspectives on justice as a general virtue, as one particular cardinal virtue, and as an integral part of the Christian life. In typical fashion, Thomas takes both what is "new" (namely, for the thirteenth-century, Aristotle's *Ethics*) and what is "old" (the Augustinian theological tradition) and integrates them into one vision. With justice, given the various ways in which the term has been understood, Thomas's task is especially difficult.

St. Thomas views justice both as a general and as a specific virtue. He sees justice as a general virtue in two senses: the first as being equated with moral goodness as a general condition for doing what is morally good in any situation; and the second as the architectonic virtue, which directs the exercise of the other virtues to its own object, the common good, which transcends the good of the individual, toward which the other particular virtues are directed. Justice in this latter sense of general virtue is what St. Thomas calls legal, as it pertains to the law, which governs in accordance with the common good. The moral value of legal justice lies in the observance of valid laws of the community out of respect for the common good.

Justice as a particular virtue is "particular justice." By means of this virtue, we are disposed to act rightly in all matters having to do with other persons, neither withholding from another what is due, nor injuring another. Since particular justice concerns our relationships with other individual persons, by virtue of this justice our actions are directed toward the common good. And since our relationships with others are mediated through exterior actions, the proper sphere of particular justice is in external actions. These actions must conform to objective criteria of fairness and equality. Justice as a particular virtue is a good habit of the will enabling us characteristically to desire whatever we judge by practical wisdom (in conformity with the law) to be right (fair and equal) in our interpersonal relationships. By virtue of justice we are also motivated to seek the common good over our own private good since our private good is actually part of the common good.

Justice, then, is a virtue whose exercise is essentially directed toward what is right (fair and equal) in our relationships with others: with the community as a whole in the case of legal justice, or with other individuals in the case of particular justice.

Acts of Justice

In his analysis of the particular virtues, St. Thomas begins by asking what is the object of the virtue and what are the characteristic actions by which the virtue aims at that object. He ends by considering the precepts of the divine law (found in sacred scripture) that correspond to that virtue.

St. Thomas sets out what he calls the "parts of justice" in question 61 of the *Secunda Secundae*. These he identifies as "distributive" and "commutative." In the course of his analysis of distributive and commutative justice, he explains how each of these forms of justice attains the object (or mean) of justice. Distributive justice focuses on the questions that arise for us when we are charged with distributing shareable goods to others in the community. The norm of distributive justice in specific situations is set by reference to whatever is the organizing principle of the community in question (q. 61, a. 1). This norm varies with respect to the kinds of goods distributed: honors are distributed with reference to personal worth, public offices are to be distributed with reference to individual qualifications, and so forth (q. 63, a. 1). Distributive justice renders what is due to each person as determined by the criterion of proportionality between individual worthiness and the kinds of goods to be distributed. For example, in the military, rewards such as greater pay or leave time should be given to those who demonstrate the greatest achievement in terms of military service. In terms of distributive justice, the general should make sure that the brave Achilles receives a greater reward than the boy bringing water for the reserve horses. Commutative justice, on the other hand, preserves an equality between persons by rendering what is due to each with respect to the quantity of the things exchanged between persons in situations in which the suffering or loss of one is balanced by the suffering or loss of another (q. 61, a. 4). If you agree to weed the garden for me for $50, then I ought to pay you $50 if you weed the garden.

St. Thomas goes on to develop further the meaning of commutative justice through his analysis of restitution (the primary act of commutative justice) (q. 62) and of the sins opposed to commutative justice. From questions 64 to 76 he takes up an analysis of sins against commutative justice that involve involuntary transactions resulting in bodily harm, damage to one's connections or goods, injustice in legal proceedings, or loss of social standing due to slander or other forms of speech outside a strictly judicial environment. Sins against the neighbor involving sexual acts, such as adultery, are taken up in his analysis of sins against temperance, since these are sins of lust as well as sins against justice (q. 65, a 4, ad 3). Next, he turns to those offenses that occur in the course of voluntary transactions. Here he treats of various forms of economic injustice, including fraud and usury (qq. 77–78). In these cases, the neighbor is not given what is due, and so an injustice takes place. Murder, slander, theft, assault, and so on do not give what is due, but rather take what is due away from the one to whom it is due. My property is *my* property, so if you steal it from me you have violated justice, what is due to me (my property) was not left in my care but rather stolen from me. A similar analysis could be done in terms of the other kinds of acts that violate justice. In murder, someone takes away my life. In slander, someone takes away my good reputation. In each case, I am stripped of what was due to me, what I had a right to retain and keep.

At question 79, St. Thomas looks at what he calls the integral parts of justice, which he gives as "to avoid evil and to do good" (q. 79, a. 1). In this context he explains that good and evil should be understood specifically with reference to the good of our neighbor and the common good, in such a way that we do good by promoting the common good of the community and respecting the just claims of other persons, and we avoid evil by avoiding harm to the community or to other individual persons. St. Thomas calls these the integral parts of justice, since each is required for a perfect, or complete, act of justice.

In questions 80 to 120 St. Thomas devotes himself to the virtues "annexed" to justice and the sins opposed to these virtues. By virtues "annexed" to justice he means those virtues that resemble justice in some way: either with regard to obligations to those to whom full recompense can never be made, such as God or our parents, or as qualities that are morally desirable but not strictly obligatory, for example, liberality or friendliness (q. 81, a. 6).

Preeminent among the moral virtues annexed to justice is that of religion. St. Thomas understands religion as the moral virtue by which we offer due honor to God in acts of worship (q. 81, aa 1, 5, 7). The inclination to show honor to God through acts of worship is part of our nature as rational creatures, and in this sense religion is a part of the natural law, even though exactly how we perform these acts of worship is established by human or divine law (q. 85, a. 1). Because we are embodied rational creatures our thinking requires the senses and so we need to express our acts of worshiping God by means of exterior signs. These signs provide the sphere of operation proper to the virtue of religion (q. 85, a. 7). Although religion is preeminent among the moral virtues, it is distinct from and subordinate to the theological virtues (q. 81, aa 5–6). Religion, then, is not a matter simply for "religious" or "spiritual" people. Rather, all people, in virtue of being created by God and sustained by God, owe God worship out of justice. Just as it would be the height of ingratitude to treat your mother with disdain or indifference given all she has done for you, so too, to fail to render God his due is to be a moral failure.

After discussing the acts of religion and the sins opposed to it (qq. 82–100), St. Thomas looks at other moral virtues annexed to justice as well as their correlative sins or vices (qq. 101–22). These virtues include piety toward our parents, gratitude toward our benefactors, obedience to our superiors, as well as friendliness, affability, and liberality toward others. St. Thomas ends his analysis of justice with an examination of "piety" as the gift of the Holy Spirit that he associates with justice. Piety is the gift of the Spirit that disposes us to pay due reverence to God as our loving Father (q. 101, a. 1).

QUESTION 57

WHAT IS RIGHT

ARTICLE 1 ‹‹ Is right the object of justice?

Yes, despite objections to the contrary, Isidore says (*Etym.* v, 2) that "*jus* [right] is so called because it is just." Now the "just" is the object of justice,[1] for the Philosopher declares (*Ethic.* v, 1) that "all are agreed in giving the name of justice to the habit that makes men capable of doing just actions."[2]

I answer that, It is proper to justice, as compared with the other virtues, to direct man in his relations with others, because it denotes a kind of equality, as its very name implies; indeed we are wont to say that things are adjusted when they are made equal, for equality is in reference of one thing to some other. On the other hand, the other virtues perfect man in those matters only which befit him in relation

---

[1] In the words of John Finnis, "The word *ius* (which can be spelled *jus* and is the root of 'just', 'justice', 'judiciary', 'injury', etc.) has a variety of quite distinct though related meanings. When Aquinas says that *ius* is the object of justice, he means: what justice is about, and what doing justice secures, is the right of some other person or persons—what is due to them, what they are entitled to, what is rightfully theirs." John Finnis, *Aquinas: Moral Political and Legal Theory* (Oxford: Oxford University Press, 1998), 133.

[2] Here we see an example of Thomas's consistent outlook that faith and reason are harmonious. Isidore of Seville, the Catholic saint and Doctor of the Church, stands alongside the Greek philosopher Aristotle in holding that right is the object of justice. Thomas emphasizes throughout his work the harmony between faith and reason, revelation and rationality.

to himself.[3] Accordingly, that which is right in the works of the other virtues, and to which the intention of the virtue tends as to its proper object, depends on its relation to the agent only, whereas the right in a work of justice, besides its relation to the agent, is set up by its relation to others. For a man's work is said to be just when it is related to some other by way of some kind of equality, for instance the payment of the wage due for a service rendered.[4] And so a thing is said to be just, as having the rectitude of justice, when it is the term of an act of justice, without one taking into account the way in which it is done by the agent, whereas in the other virtues nothing is declared to be right unless it is done in a certain way by the agent.[5] For this reason justice has its own special proper object over and above the other virtues, and this object is called the just, which is the same as "right." Hence it is evident that right is the object of justice.

Objection 1. It would seem that right is not the object of justice. For the jurist Celsus[6] says [*Digest.* i, 1; *De Just. et Jure* 1] that "right is the art

---

[3] For example, temperance perfects people in relation to their own bodily pleasures (not the pleasures of others), and courage perfects people in relation to their own fears (not the fears of others).

[4] In a just exchange of labor for pay, the employer would pay what is just or due to the employee and the employee would likewise perform a just act by providing goods or services equal to the amount of pay earned. It is possible for either party to be unjust in that the employer could pay less than is equal to the work or service provided or the worker could provide goods or services not equal to the wage provided.

[5] In other words, an act can be said to accord with justice regardless of the disposition of the agent. If I owe you $25 and then I pay you $25, the act that I have performed is just even if I hate you or do the act reluctantly. On the other hand, an act of temperance, for example, demands not merely that I do that which objectively accords with temperance (e.g., neither too much nor too little bodily pleasure) but also that I do the temperate act in a certain way, namely with enjoyment rather than pain. For if I do an act that in other ways is temperate, but it gives me great pain to do so, and I only act temperately because under pressure from others, then I have not performed a truly temperate act. The virtue of justice, like the other virtues requires that one acts with joy or ease.

[6] Publius Iuventius Celsus was a prominent legal mind of ancient Rome in the beginning of the second century, who served a number of terms as a top elected magistrate in the ancient Roman Republic. The jurist Celsus is not to

of goodness and equality." Now art is not the object of justice, but is by itself an intellectual virtue. Therefore right is not the object of justice.

Reply to Objection 1. It is usual for words to be distorted from their original signification so as to mean something else: thus the word "medicine" was first employed to signify a remedy used for curing a sick person, and then it was drawn to signify the art by which this is done.[7] In like manner the word *"jus"* [right] was first of all used to denote the just thing itself, but afterwards it was transferred to designate the art whereby what is just is known, and further to denote the place where justice is administered—thus a man is said to appear *"in jure"*[8]—and yet further, we say even that a man, who has the office of exercising justice, administers the *"jus"* even if his sentence be unjust.

Objection 2. Further, "Law," according to Isidore (*Etym.* v, 3), "is a kind of right." Now law is the object not of justice but of prudence; therefore the Philosopher [*Ethic.* vi, 8] reckons "legislative" as one of the parts of prudence. Therefore right is not the object of justice.

Reply to Objection 2. Even as there preexists in the mind of the craftsman an expression of the things to be made externally by his craft, which expression is called the rule of his craft, so too there preexists in the mind an expression of the particular just work which the reason determines, and which is a kind of rule of prudence. If this rule be expressed in writing it is called a "law," which according to Isidore

---

be confused with the late second-century Celsus whose anti-Christian works were cited by Origen.

7 One word such as "health" can mean the quality of health itself (a well-functioning organism), a sign of health (healthy complexion), or a cause of health (healthy food). These meanings are not exactly the same (univocal), but neither are they totally unrelated as are equivocal words, which mean totally different things, such as "bat," which could be either equipment for the game of baseball or a winged, flying animal. Analogical meaning is neither univocal nor totally equivocal, but a mean between univocal predication and equivocal predication, in which meanings are related to one another as in the various senses of the word "health" described above or *"jus"* as spoken of in the reply to objection one. For more on this subject, see Ralph McInerny, *Aquinas and Analogy* (Washington, DC: The Catholic University of America Press, 1996).

8 The Dominican editors note that in English we speak of a court of law, a barrister at law, etc.

(*Etym.* v, 1) is "a written decree," and so law is not the same as right, but an expression of right.

Objection 3. Further, justice, before all, subjects man to God: for Augustine says (*De Moribus Eccl.* xv) that "justice is love serving God alone, and consequently governing aright all things subject to man." Now right [*jus*] does not pertain to Divine things, but only to human affairs, for Isidore says (*Etym.* v, 2) that "'*fas*' is the Divine law, and '*jus*,' the human law." Therefore right is not the object of justice.

Reply to Objection 3. Since justice implies equality, and since we cannot offer God an equal return, it follows that we cannot make Him a perfectly just repayment.[9] For this reason the Divine law is not properly called "*jus*" but "*fas*" because, to wit, God is satisfied if we accomplish what we can. Nevertheless justice tends to make man repay God as much as he can, by subjecting his mind to Him entirely.

ARTICLE 2 ⸻ **Is right fittingly divided into natural right and positive right?**

Yes, despite objections to the contrary, The Philosopher says (*Ethic.* v, 7) that "political justice is partly natural and partly legal," i.e., established by law.

---

[9] Before Thomas, St. Anselm of Canterbury (1033–1109), in his work *Cur Deus Homo* or *Why God Became Man*, made this point that human beings can never perfectly repay God. A contemporary example can illustrate the argument. Let's say that Bill Gates lent a person 10 billion dollars, and that person lost all the money on poor investments. Even if that person worked 24 hours a day and gave all the money earned to Bill Gates, it would be virtually impossible to pay back what is owed to the Microsoft mogul. Similarly, we owe everything to God—our health, our talents, our very lives. In justice, since God has given us so much, we owe God everything. In sinning, we do not give God what is due to God. Thus, we incur a debt to God that we can never repay ourselves. Even if we were to be perfectly sinless for the rest of our lives, doing this would be giving God what was due to Him in the first place, not making up for what was due to God on account of sin. Only God would not already be indebted to God and only a human being should make up for the debts of humankind. In the words of St. Athanasius, God had to become a human (the Incarnation) so that humans could become members of God's family (through the adoption of grace).

I answer that, As stated above (a. 1) the "right," or the "just," is a work that is adjusted to another person according to some kind of equality. Now a thing can be adjusted to a man in two ways: first, by its very nature, as when a man gives so much that he may receive equal value in return, and this is called "natural right." In another way, a thing is adjusted or commensurated to another person, by agreement, or by common consent, when, to wit, a man deems himself satisfied, if he receive so much. This can be done in two ways: first, by private agreement, as that which is confirmed by an agreement between private individuals; secondly, by public agreement, as when the whole community agrees that something should be deemed as though it were adjusted and commensurated to another person, or when this is decreed by the prince who is placed over the people, and acts in its stead, and this is called "positive right."[10]

Objection 1. It would seem that right is not fittingly divided into natural right and positive right. For that which is natural is unchangeable, and is the same for all. Now nothing of the kind is to be found in human affairs, since all the rules of human right fail in certain cases, nor do they obtain force everywhere. Therefore there is no such thing as natural right.

---

[10] Natural right is not a mere matter of convention but rather of what is due to a being in virtue of its nature. Positive right, on the other hand, is a matter of convention and agreement, that is, what is posited by legal stipulation. One has a natural right to life, liberty, and property, but a positive right, for example, to travel in certain places, to enter into specified financial agreements, or to operate particular kinds of machinery. What places are private property and what places are not, what kind of financial agreements are binding and under what circumstances, and who can drive a semi-truck are matters that are determined by individuals together or by the community at large. On the other hand, individuals or communities do not bestow a right to life or a right to liberty on human beings, but rather human beings have a natural right, on account of the kind of beings that they are, to life and liberty. Throughout the history of philosophy and legal theory, some have claimed that there are only positive rights and that morality is simply a matter of convention. Cephalus in Plato's *Republic* represents this point of view. Socrates, in the *Republic* and elsewhere, as well as Aquinas, takes up the opposite viewpoint. Some rights are merely conventional, but others are natural.

Reply to Objection 1. That which is natural to one whose nature is unchangeable must be such always and everywhere. But human nature is changeable;[11] therefore that which is natural to man may sometimes fail. Thus the restitution of a deposit to the depositor is in accordance with natural equality, and if human nature were always right, this would always have to be observed; but since it happens sometimes that man's will is unrighteous, there are cases in which a deposit should not be restored, lest a man of unrighteous will make evil use of the thing deposited, as when a madman or an enemy of the commonweal demands the return of his weapons.[12]

Objection 2. Further, a thing is called "positive" when it proceeds from the human will. But a thing is not just simply because it proceeds from the human will, else a man's will could not be unjust. Since then the "just" and the "right" are the same, it seems that there is no positive right.

Reply to Objection 2. The human will can, by common agreement, make a thing to be just, provided it be not, of itself, contrary to natural justice, and it is in such matters that positive right has its place.[13]

---

11 Human nature for Aquinas is not changeable (cf. I–II, q. 94, a. 6), but that which pertains to human affairs can change. It may be useful and obligatory to return a sword, but if in the particular situation the person is intent on using the sword to harm others then the sword should not be returned. If human affairs were utterly stable and predictable, then coming to correct judgments in the moral life would be much easier.

12 Note that Thomas does not agree with the objection that "all the rules of human right fail in certain cases," although the example in the reply is of a rule that *does* fail to apply in all cases, namely, "return stolen objects." For Thomas, most moral rules are what might be called *prima facie* guides, good for the most part but not in all circumstances. However, as will be made more clear later in Thomas's discussion of murder and lying, there are some things that a just person will *never* willingly do. Indeed, in the response to the second objection, Thomas makes clear that natural right gives rise to acts that should never be done, acts whose moral nature does not change regardless of what is posited as legal in a given society.

13 It is a matter of positive right to drive on one side of the street rather than the other. Nothing in natural law dictates that driving should be on the left (or right) side of the street. However, once the positive law has been promulgated that everyone should drive on the left side of the street, it becomes unjust to

Hence the Philosopher says (*Ethic.* v, 7) that "in the case of the legal just, it does not matter in the first instance whether it takes one form or another, it only matters when once it is laid down." If, however, a thing is, of itself, contrary to natural right, the human will cannot make it just, for instance by decreeing that it is moral to steal or to commit adultery. Hence it is written (Is 10:1): "Woe to them that make wicked laws."

Objection 3. Further, Divine right is not natural right, since it transcends human nature.[14] In like manner, neither is it positive right, since it is based not on human, but on Divine, authority. Therefore right is unfittingly divided into natural and positive.

Reply to Objection 3. The Divine right is that which is promulgated by God. Such things are partly those that are naturally just, yet their justice is hidden to man, and partly those that are made just by God's decree. Hence also Divine right may be divided in respect of these two things, even as human right is. For the Divine law commands certain things because they are good,[15] and forbids others, because they are evil,[16] while others are good because they are prescribed,[17] and others evil because they are forbidden.[18]

---

violate this legal stipulation. To violate what is legally just is to do wrong as long as what is legally just accords with what is naturally just, even though what is legally just arises from the will of one human being (monarchy) or many human beings (democracy).

[14] In other words, divine right does not arise from human nature but rather from the divine nature.

[15] For instance, honoring mother and father.

[16] For instance, murder and idolatry.

[17] For example, worshiping God in a certain manner.

[18] Examples of such things would be disobeying a superior in a matter that would not otherwise be wrong. For example, a bishop may order a priest of his diocese not to leave the diocese without his permission, but the priest does so anyway. There is nothing in itself objectionable about a priest leaving his diocese, but that action becomes wrong because forbidden by a legitimate authority making a legitimate request.

QUESTION 58

~~~~~~~~~~~~~~~~

JUSTICE

ARTICLE 1 ⁓ **Is justice fittingly defined as being the perpetual and constant will to render to each one his right?**

Yes, despite objections I answer that, The aforesaid definition of justice is fitting if understood aright. For since every virtue is a habit that is the principle of a good act, a virtue must be defined by means of the good act bearing on the matter proper to that virtue. Now the proper matter of justice consists of those things that belong to our relations with other men, as shall be shown further on (a. 2). Hence the act of justice in relation to its proper matter and object is indicated in the words, "Rendering to each one his right," since, as Isidore says (*Etym.* x), "a man is said to be just because he respects the rights [*jus*] of others."

Now in order that an act bearing upon any matter whatever be virtuous, it must be voluntary, stable, and firm, because the Philosopher says (*Ethic.* ii, 4) that in order for an act to be virtuous it needs first of all to be done "knowingly," secondly to be done "by choice" and "for a due end," thirdly to be done "immovably", that is, from a virtuous character. Now the first of these is included in the second, since "what is done through ignorance is involuntary" (*Ethic.* iii, 1). Hence the definition of justice mentions first the "will," in order to show that the act of justice must be voluntary; and mention is made afterwards of its "constancy" and "perpetuity" in order to indicate the firmness of the act.

Accordingly, this is a complete definition of justice, save that the act is mentioned instead of the habit, which takes its species from that act, because habit implies relation to act. And if anyone would reduce it to the proper form of a definition, he might say that "justice is a habit whereby a man renders to each one his due by a constant and perpetual will": and this is about the same definition as that given by the Philosopher (*Ethic.* v, 5), who says that "justice is a habit whereby a man is said to be capable of doing just actions in accordance with his choice."[1]

Objection 3. Further, no will is perpetual save God's. If, therefore, justice is a perpetual will, in God alone will there be justice.

Reply to Objection 3. The will may be called perpetual in two ways: first, on the part of the will's act, which endures for ever, and thus God's will alone is perpetual; secondly, on the part of the subject, because, to wit, a man wills to do a certain thing always. This is a necessary condition of justice. For it does not satisfy the conditions of justice that one wish to observe justice in some particular matter for the time being, because one could scarcely find a man willing to act unjustly in every case; and it is requisite that one should have the will to observe justice at all times and in all cases.

Objection 4. Further, whatever is perpetual is constant, since it is unchangeable. Therefore it is needless in defining justice to say that it is both "perpetual" and "constant."

Reply to Objection 4. Since "perpetual" does not imply perpetuity of the act of the will, it is not superfluous to add "constant": for while the "perpetual will" denotes the purpose of observing justice always, "constant" signifies a firm perseverance in this purpose.

Objection 5. Further, it belongs to the sovereign to give each one his right. Therefore, if justice gives each one his right, it follows that it is in none but the sovereign, which is absurd.

---

[1] In this article, Thomas seeks the definition of the virtue of justice, not the definition of "justice" abstractly considered. The virtue of justice consists in the habit whereby a person renders to each one his due by a constant and perpetual will. What precisely is "due," what a person has legitimate claim to, is a related, but different, question than how to define the virtue of justice.

Reply to Objection 5. A judge renders to each one what belongs to him, by way of command and direction, because a judge is the "personification of justice," and "the sovereign is its guardian" (*Ethic.* v, 4). On the other hand, the subjects render to each one what belongs to him, by way of execution.

Objection 6. Further, Augustine says (*De Moribus Eccl.* xv) that "justice is love serving God alone." Therefore it does not render to each one his right.

Reply to Objection 6. Just as love of God includes love of our neighbor, as stated above (q. 25, a. 1), so too the service of God includes rendering to each one his due.[2]

ARTICLE 3 ⸺ Is justice a virtue?[3]

Yes, despite objections to the contrary, Gregory says (*Moral.* ii, 49) that "the entire structure of good works is built on four virtues," viz. temperance, prudence, fortitude and justice.

I answer that, A human virtue is one "which renders a human act and man himself good" [*Ethic.* ii, 6], and this can be applied to justice. For a man's act is made good through attaining the rule of reason, which is the rule whereby human acts are regulated. Hence, since justice regulates human operations, it is evident that it renders man's operations good, and, as Tully declares (*De Officiis* i, 7), good men are

---

[2] In the *Summa contra Gentiles*, Thomas argues that the love of God includes love of neighbor because those who love someone also love those who are related and loved by that person. For example, if I truly love my wife, I will also love those that she is related to and loves. God loves all human beings and is related to them as their Creator and Final End. So all those who truly love God should also love other people. As the First Letter of John says, "If anyone says, 'I love God,' yet hates his brother, he is a liar. For anyone who does not love his brother, whom he has seen, cannot love God, whom he has not seen" (1 Jn 4:20).

[3] This article is an excellent example of Thomas's synthesis of various sources. Despite certain differences, great "authorities" of history—respected authors whose views are taken seriously—are woven into a coherent unity. New Testament and Old Testament sources, a Greek philosopher and a Roman orator, a pope and monk, all contribute to a deeper understanding of justice as a virtue. Thomas seeks truth wherever and from whomever it can be found.

so called chiefly from their justice; therefore, as he says again (*De Officiis* i, 7), "the luster of virtue appears above all in justice."

Objection 1. It would seem that justice is not a virtue. For it is written (Lk 17:10): "When you shall have done all these things that are commanded you, say: We are unprofitable servants; we have done that which we ought to do." Now it is not unprofitable to do a virtuous deed: for Ambrose says (*De Officiis* ii, 6): "We look to a profit that is estimated not by pecuniary gain but by the acquisition of godliness." Therefore to do what one ought to do is not a virtuous deed. And yet it is an act of justice. Therefore justice is not a virtue.

Reply to Objection 1. When a man does what he ought, he brings no gain to the person to whom he does what he ought, but only abstains from doing him a harm. He does, however, profit himself, in so far as he does what he ought, spontaneously and readily, and this is to act virtuously.[4] Hence it is written (Wis 8:7) that Divine wisdom "teaches temperance, and prudence, and justice, and fortitude, which are such things as men (i.e., virtuous men) can have nothing more profitable in life."

Objection 2. Further, that which is done of necessity, is not meritorious. But to render to a man what belongs to him, as justice requires, is of necessity. Therefore it is not meritorious. Yet it is by virtuous actions that we gain merit. Therefore justice is not a virtue.

Reply to Objection 2. Necessity is twofold. One arises from *constraint*, and this removes merit, since it runs counter to the will. The other arises from the obligation of a *command*, or from the necessity of obtaining an end, when, to wit, a man is unable to achieve the end of virtue without doing some particular thing. The latter necessity does not remove merit, when a man does voluntarily that which is necessary

---

[4] To act virtuously is not simply to do that which morality demands, but to do it in a particular way, spontaneously and readily. With a virtuous act one executes what morality demands but does so freely, willingly, joyfully, and easily. To do what is right unwillingly, under compulsion, or only under duress is not to act virtuously, although neither is it to act viciously. Such acts pave the way to virtue, though they fail to achieve the fullness of virtue.

in this way. It does, however, exclude the credit of supererogation, according to 1 Corinthians 9:16, "If I preach the Gospel, it is no glory to me, for a necessity lies upon me."[5]

Objection 3. Further, every moral virtue is about matters of action. Now those things which are wrought externally are not things concerning behavior but concerning handicraft, according to the Philosopher (*Metaph.* ix). Therefore, since it belongs to justice to produce externally a deed that is just in itself, it seems that justice is not a moral virtue.

Reply to Objection 3. Justice is concerned about external things, not by making them, which pertains to art, but by using them in our dealings with other men.[6]

---

[5] To say that a person "must" do something has various meanings, including physical necessity and moral necessity. If a person must do something because of *physical necessity*, this does not pertain to morality, which is about human actions, acts that come from a person's reason and will. If someone stronger than I grabs my hand and makes me hit another person, then I must hit this other person. But this *physical necessity* removes my action from moral evaluation. Although it is my hand that hits, I *as a moral agent*, do not hit anyone, but rather the strongman is the moral agent. In this sense of *physical necessity*, if I must do something good or bad, then I am not responsible for the good or bad done in a moral sense. On the other hand, a moral necessity, such as I must refrain from harming innocent people, does not impose a physical necessity that interferes with my reason and will. I can perform human actions, subject to moral analysis, if under a moral necessity but not if under a physical necessity. A moral necessity is one in which duty must be discharged in order to attain to virtue. Finally, Thomas notes that some matters are not of moral necessity (a duty for all) but rather are matters of supererogation, matters of going above and beyond the call of duty. To give some money to those in need is a moral necessity, but to give all one's money is a matter of supererogation. Another way to put the same distinction is between matters of precept (moral necessities) on the one hand and matters of counsel (supererogation) on the other.

[6] Implicit in Thomas's answer is the distinction between morality (*actio*) [act] and fabrication/production (*factio*). Morality pertains to human action considered as coming from a person's reason and will. In the case of fabrication, art, or *factio* pertains to the creation of effects in the world. Justice does concern external things, but considered as expressions of the heart and mind of a human agent. In the case of fabrication, on the other hand, one simply judges what was made, done, or changed in the world without taking into account the agent. Ethics properly understood cannot be simply a matter of judging "what was done" in the world.

ARTICLE 8 ～～ **Does particular justice have a special matter?**

Yes, despite objections to the contrary, The Philosopher reckons (*Ethic.* v, 2) particular justice to be specially about those things which belong to social life.

I answer that, Whatever can be rectified by reason is the matter of moral virtue, for this is defined in reference to right reason, according to the Philosopher (*Ethic.* ii, 6). Now the reason can rectify not only the internal passions of the soul, but also external actions, and also those external things of which man can make use.[7] And yet it is in respect of external actions and external things by means of which men can communicate with one another, that the relation of one man to another is to be considered, whereas it is in respect of internal passions that we consider man's rectitude in himself. Consequently, since justice is directed to others, it is not about the entire matter of moral virtue, but only about external actions and things, under a certain special aspect of the object, in so far as one man is related to another through them.

Objection 2. Further, Augustine says (QQ. lxxxiii, qu. 61) that "the soul has four virtues whereby, in this life, it lives spiritually, viz. temperance, prudence, fortitude and justice;" and he says that "the fourth is justice, which pervades all the virtues." Therefore particular justice, which is one of the four cardinal virtues, has no special matter.

Reply to Objection 2. As stated above (I–II, q. 61, aa 3, 4), the cardinal virtues may be taken in two ways: first, as special virtues, each having a determinate matter; secondly, as certain general modes of virtue. In this latter sense Augustine speaks in the passage quoted: for he says

---

7 To "rectify," to make "right" or just, in a certain sense is not a specific virtue, but another way of speaking about being virtuous in general. The virtuous person has a just or rightly ordered soul in that the virtuous person is rightly disposed in all aspects of life, with respect to fear, bodily pleasure, and other people. Socrates emphasized this sense of justice in his *Republic*. On the other hand, to be just is also a specific virtue, pertaining not to overall moral well-being but to interactions with other people. In asking, "Does particular justice have a special matter?", Thomas is seeking to understand this latter sense of justice.

that "prudence is knowledge of what we should seek and avoid, temperance is the curb on the lust for fleeting pleasures, fortitude is strength of mind in bearing with passing trials, justice is the love of God and our neighbor which pervades the other virtues, that is to say, is the common principle of the entire order between one man and another."[8]

Objection 3. Further, justice directs man sufficiently in matters relating to others. Now a man can be directed to others in all matters relating to this life. Therefore the matter of justice is general and not special.

Reply to Objection 3. A man's internal passions, which are a part of moral matter, are not in themselves directed to another man, which belongs to the specific nature of justice; yet their effects, i.e., external actions, are capable of being directed to another man. Consequently, it does not follow that the matter of justice is general.

ARTICLE 9 ⟶ **Is justice about the passions?**

No, despite objections to the contrary, The Philosopher says (*Ethic.* v, 1) that justice is about operations.

I answer that, The true answer to this question may be gathered from a twofold source. First, from the subject of justice, i.e., from the will, whose movements or acts are not passions, as stated above (I–II, q. 22, a. 3; I–II, q. 59, a. 4), for it is only the sensitive appetite whose movements are called passions. Hence justice is not about the passions, as are temperance and fortitude, which are in the irascible and concupiscible parts. Secondly, on the part of the matter, because justice is about man's relations with another, and we are not directed immediately to another by the internal passions. Therefore justice is not about the passions.

Objection 1. It would seem that justice is about the passions. For the Philosopher says (*Ethic.* ii, 3) that "moral virtue is about pleasure and pain." Now pleasure, or delight, and pain are passions, as stated above

---

[8] General modes of virtues pervade the entire moral life and are involved in each good action. Particular, or special, virtues have a specific subject matter that makes, say, fighting in battle uniquely involved with courage and not, say, temperance.

[I–II, q. 23, a. 4; q. 31, a. 1; q. 35, a. 1] when we were treating of the passions. Therefore justice, being a moral virtue, is about the passions.

Reply to Objection 1. Not every moral virtue is about pleasure and pain as its proper matter, since fortitude is about fear and daring; but every moral virtue is directed to pleasure and pain, as to ends to be acquired, for, as the Philosopher says (*Ethic.* vii, 11), "pleasure and pain are the principal end in respect of which we say that this is an evil, and that a good;" and in this way, too, they belong to justice, since "a man is not just unless he rejoice in just actions" (*Ethic.* i, 8).[9]

Objection 2. Further, justice is the means of rectifying a man's operations in relation to another man. Now such like operations cannot be rectified unless the passions be rectified, because it is owing to disorder of the passions that there is disorder in the aforesaid operations: thus sexual lust leads to adultery, and overmuch love of money leads to theft. Therefore justice must be about the passions.

Reply to Objection 2. External operations are, as it were, between external things, which are their matter, and internal passions, which are their origin. Now it happens sometimes that there is a defect in one of these, without there being a defect in the other. Thus a man may steal another's property, not through the desire to have the thing, but through the will to hurt the man; or vice versa, a man may covet another's property without wishing to steal it. Accordingly the directing of operations in so far as they tend towards external things belongs to justice, but in so far as they arise from the passions, it belongs to the other moral virtues which are about the passions. Hence justice hinders theft of another's property, in so far as stealing is contrary to the equality that should be maintained in

---

[9] For Thomas, as for Aristotle, a person must enjoy performing acts of virtue to be considered truly virtuous. If one does what is just, but does not enjoy it, then one is merely "continent," that is, self-controlled. On the other hand, if one does what is wrong and does not enjoy it but regrets it, then one is "incontinent." The vicious person does what is wrong and enjoys doing what is wrong. This differs from a Kantian perspective on ethics, in which the best action is one performed from duty and only on account of duty regardless of one's desires or inclinations. In the Catholic tradition, a person is only proclaimed a saint with heroic virtue if that person also exhibited joy and pleasure in being virtuous for the love of God. Saints are not sad.

external things, while liberality hinders it as resulting from an immoderate desire for wealth. Since, however, external operations take their species not from the internal passions, but from external things as being their objects,[10] it follows that external operations are essentially the matter of justice rather than of the other moral virtues.

ARTICLE 11 ⤳ Is the act of justice to render to each one his own?

Yes, despite objections to the contrary, Ambrose says (*De Offic.* i, 24): "It is justice that renders to each one what is his, and claims not another's property; it disregards its own profit in order to preserve the common equity."

I answer that, As stated above (aa 8, 10), the matter of justice is an external operation in so far as either it or the thing we use by it is made proportionate to some other person to whom we are related by justice. Now each man's own is that which is due to him according to equality of proportion. Therefore the proper act of justice is nothing else than to render to each one his own.

Objection 1. It would seem that the act of justice is not to render to each one his own. For Augustine (*De Trin.* xiv, 9) ascribes to justice the act of succoring the needy. Now in caring for the needy we give them what is not theirs but ours. Therefore the act of justice does not consist in rendering to each one his own.

Reply to Objection 1. Since justice is a cardinal virtue, other secondary virtues, such as mercy, liberality, and the like, are connected with it, as we shall state further on (q. 80, a. 1). Therefore to succor the needy, which belongs to mercy or pity, and to be liberally beneficent, which pertains to liberality, are by a kind of reduction ascribed to justice as to their principal virtue.

---

[10] Moral activity can have both an internal and external aspect. Stealing as an external operation is wrong, but a given act of stealing may also be disordered in terms of the passion from which it arose. So one might steal out of hatred or out of greed or out of lust, and these actions, though alike as stealing and contrary to justice, differ in terms of the motivating passion giving rise to them. For Thomas, *both* the "internal" and "external" aspects of the moral act are important.

Objection 3. Further, it belongs to justice not only to distribute things duly, but also to repress injurious actions, such as murder, adultery and so forth. But the rendering to each one of what is his seems to belong solely to the distribution of things. Therefore the act of justice is not sufficiently described by saying that it consists in rendering to each one his own.

Reply to Objection 3. As the Philosopher states (*Ethic.* v, 4), in matters of justice, the name of "profit" is extended to whatever is excessive, and whatever is deficient is called "loss." The reason for this is that justice is first of all and more commonly exercised in voluntary interchanges of things, such as buying and selling, wherein those expressions are properly employed; and yet they are transferred to all other matters of justice. The same applies to the rendering to each one of what is his own.[11]

ARTICLE 12 ~~ **Is justice the foremost among all moral virtues?**

Yes, despite objections to the contrary, Tully says (*De Offic.* i, 7): "Justice is the most resplendent of the virtues, and gives its name to a good man."

I answer that, If we speak of legal justice,[12] it is evident that it stands foremost among all the moral virtues, for as much as the common good transcends the individual good of one person.[13] In this sense the Philosopher declares (*Ethic.* v, 1) that "the most excellent of the virtues would seem to be justice, and more glorious than either

---

11 Murder, for example, violates justice because a person's life is his own and to take a person's life is to cause him to lose that which is properly his. Similarly, in the marriage vow of fidelity, a husband gives himself *qua* sexual partner to his wife alone, and his wife gives herself *qua* sexual partner to her husband alone. Adultery violates justice by giving what should be reserved to one person alone to another.

12 Legal justice is giving to each what is due according to the positive law.

13 Note that justice is foremost among all the moral virtues, the virtues acquired by human actions. However, the theological virtues of faith, hope, and love excel all the acquired virtues because they have God as their object and because these virtues enable us to attain a good that far exceeds any good that can be had by human effort, namely eternal salvation. The foremost virtue among theological virtues is charity because among all theological virtues charity binds us most closely to God and makes us worthy of eternal life.

the evening or the morning star." But, even if we speak of particular justice, it excels the other moral virtues for two reasons. The first reason may be taken from the subject, because justice is in the more excellent part of the soul, viz. the rational appetite or will, whereas the other moral virtues are in the sensitive appetite, to which pertain the passions that are the matter of the other moral virtues. The second reason is taken from the object, because the other virtues are commendable in respect of the sole good of the virtuous person himself, whereas justice is praiseworthy in respect of the virtuous person being well disposed towards another, so that justice is somewhat the good of another person, as stated in *Ethic.* v, 1. Hence the Philosopher says (*Rhet.* i, 9): "The greatest virtues must be those which are most profitable to other persons, because virtue is a faculty of doing good to others. For this reason the greatest honors are accorded the brave and the just, since bravery is useful to others in warfare, and justice is useful to others both in warfare and in time of peace."

Objection 1. It would seem that justice does not stand foremost among all the moral virtues, because it belongs to justice to render to each one what is his, whereas it belongs to liberality to give of one's own, and this is more virtuous. Therefore liberality is a greater virtue than justice.

Reply to Objection 1. Although the liberal man gives of his own,[14] yet he does so in so far as he takes into consideration the good of his own virtue, while the just man gives to another what is his, through consideration of the common good. Moreover, justice is observed towards all, whereas liberality cannot extend to all. Again, liberality, which gives of a man's own, is based on justice, whereby one renders to each man what is his.

Objection 2. Further, nothing is adorned by a less excellent thing than itself. Now magnanimity is the ornament both of justice and of all the virtues, according to *Ethic.* iv, 3. Therefore magnanimity is more excellent than justice.

---

[14] The "liberal" man in the sense used here by Thomas refers to the *liber,* the "free" person who willingly disposes of his possessions for the good of others.

Reply to Objection 2. When magnanimity is added to justice it increases the latter's goodness; and yet without justice it would not even be a virtue.

Objection 3. Further, virtue is about that which is "difficult" and "good," as stated in *Ethic.* ii, 3. But fortitude is about more difficult things than justice is, since it is about dangers of death, according to *Ethic.* iii, 6. Therefore fortitude is more excellent than justice.

Reply to Objection 3. Although fortitude is about the most difficult things, it is not about the best, for it is only useful in warfare, whereas justice is useful both in war and in peace, as stated above.

INJUSTICE

ARTICLE 2 ~~ **Is a person unjust through doing an unjust thing?**

No, despite objections to the contrary, The Philosopher says (*Ethic.* v, 6) that "a man may do an unjust thing without being unjust."[1]

I answer that, Even as the object of justice is something equal in external things, so too the object of injustice is something unequal, through more or less being assigned to some person than is due to him. To this object the habit of injustice is compared by means of its proper act which is called an injustice. Accordingly, it may happen in two ways that a man who does an unjust thing is not unjust: first, on account of a lack of correspondence between the operation and its proper object. For the operation takes its species and name from its direct and not from its indirect object: and in things directed to an end the direct is that which is intended, and the indirect is what is beside the intention. Hence if a man do that which is unjust, without intending to do an unjust thing, for instance if he do it through ignorance,

---

[1] The distinctions Thomas makes in this article are very important for moral theology, indeed moral reasoning of any kind, philosophical or theological. He distinguishes between act and agent, between what is done and who is doing it, between the act itself and culpability for the act. Someone can do something materially unjust but not be an unjust person as, for example, when a good person mistakenly takes someone else's property honestly believing it to be his own. This distinction can save us from rushing to judgment when observing someone's behavior. With the act/agent distinction, we can affirm that the act itself is wrong while withholding judgment about whether the person performing the act is a bad person.

being unaware that it is unjust, properly speaking he does an unjust
thing, not directly, but only indirectly, and, as it were, doing materially
that which is unjust: hence such an operation is not called an injustice.[2] Secondly, this may happen on account of a lack of proportion
between the operation and the habit. For an injustice may sometimes
arise from a passion, for instance, anger or desire, and sometimes from
choice, for instance when the injustice itself is the direct object of one's
complacency. In the latter case, properly speaking, it arises from a
habit, because whenever a man has a habit, whatever befits that habit
is, of itself, pleasant to him. Accordingly, to do what is unjust intentionally and by choice is proper to the unjust man, in which sense the
unjust man is one who has the habit of injustice; but a man may do
what is unjust, unintentionally or through passion, without having the
habit of injustice.

Objection 1. It would seem that a man is called unjust through doing
an unjust thing. For habits are specified by their objects, as stated
above (I–II, q. 54, a. 2). Now the proper object of justice is the just,
and the proper object of injustice is the unjust. Therefore a man should
be called just through doing a just thing, and unjust through doing an
unjust thing.

Reply to Objection 1. A habit is specified by its object in its direct
and formal acceptation, not in its material and indirect acceptation.[3]

---

2 For example, a person may pick up someone else's coat mistakenly believing
it to be his own. Such a person does materially that which is unjust, but does
not formally steal. Both Aristotle and Christian morality agree on the priority of the "interior" in the moral life. It is possible for someone to do the
wrong thing objectively speaking and yet, if this be done unknowingly, such
an act is not accounted a moral failure on the part of the agent. Nevertheless,
such an act may have seriously adverse effects for all those involved, so agents
must always take due care to ensure that they are properly informed.

3 Thomas uses a similar analysis when considering acts with two effects. The
effects of an act that are "direct" or "formally intended" are more morally significant than effects that are "indirect" or "merely material." For example,
when a person goes jogging many different effects are brought about, including wearing down running shoes, making a shirt damp with perspiration, getting exercise, moving from point A to point B, and staying in shape. Some of
these effects are intentionally brought about, such as staying in shape, getting

Objection 2. Further, the Philosopher declares (*Ethic.* v, 9) that they hold a false opinion who maintain that it is in a man's power to do suddenly an unjust thing, and that a just man is no less capable of doing what is unjust than an unjust man. But this opinion would not be false unless it were proper to the unjust man to do what is unjust. Therefore a man is to be deemed unjust from the fact that he does an unjust thing.

Reply to Objection 2. It is not easy for any man to do an unjust thing from choice, as though it were pleasing for its own sake and not for the sake of something else: this is proper to one who has the habit, as the Philosopher declares (*Ethic.* v, 9).

ARTICLE 4 ∾ **Does anyone who does an unjust act sin mortally?**

Yes, despite objections to the contrary, Whatever is contrary to the law of God is a mortal sin. Now whoever does an injustice does that which is contrary to the law of God, since it amounts either to theft, or to adultery, or to murder, or to something of the kind, as will be shown further on (q. 64 and following). Therefore whoever does an injustice sins mortally.[4]

I answer that, As stated above (I–II, q. 12, a. 5), when we were treating of the distinction of sins, a mortal sin is one that is contrary to charity, which gives life to the soul. Now every injury inflicted on another person is of itself contrary to charity, which moves us to will the good of another. And so since injustice always consists in an injury inflicted on another person, it is evident that to do an injustice is a mortal sin according to its genus.

Objection 1. It would seem that not everyone who does an injustice sins mortally. For venial sin is opposed to mortal sin. Now it is sometimes a

---

exercise, and moving from point A to point B. However, wearing down running shoes or making a shirt damp with perspiration are, presumably, not the goal of the activity. These "side-effects" may indeed be important in moral evaluation but they do not define the act as such, but are "accidental" to the intentional act of the agent.

[4] Thomas qualifies this elsewhere (II–II, q. 66, a. 6, reply to 3) in so far as he holds that not *every* theft is a mortal sin, e.g., stealing something trivial, such as an apple.

venial sin to do an injury: for the Philosopher says (*Ethic.* v, 8) in reference to those who act unjustly: "Whatever they do not merely in ignorance but through ignorance is a venial matter." Therefore not everyone that does an injustice sins mortally.

Reply to Objection 1. This saying of the Philosopher is to be understood as referring to ignorance of fact, which he calls "ignorance of particular circumstances" [*Ethic.* iii, 1], and which deserves pardon, and not to ignorance of the law which does not excuse; and he who does an injustice through ignorance does no injustice except accidentally, as stated above (q. 59, art. 2).

Objection 2. Further, he who does an injustice in a small matter departs but slightly from the mean. Now this seems to be insignificant and should be accounted among the least of evils, as the Philosopher declares (*Ethic.* ii, 9). Therefore not everyone that does an injustice sins mortally.

Reply to Objection 2. He who does an injustice in small matters falls short of the perfection of an unjust deed,[5] in so far as what he does may be deemed not altogether contrary to the will of the person who suffers from the act: for instance, if a man takes an apple or some such thing from another man, in which case it is probable that the latter is not hurt or displeased.[6]

---

5 "Perfection" in this context means "thoroughly done" and is compatible with the act being morally wrong. The "perfect" thief does his work of stealing thoroughly but is not on that account a morally good person, but rather good only in a certain realm of activity, namely as one who steals.

6 Put another way, a mortal sin, a separation from God that objectively merits eternal punishment, requires free consent and understanding as well as a seriously grave offense. Stealing an apple, while wrong, is not seriously wrong. So an act can be unjust, evil to perform, without it necessarily being a serious evil. The gravity of the offense depends upon a number of factors, one of which is the harm done against the person. Trivial harms are not matter for mortal sins, but rather venial. Serious harms, such as murdering a person, or stealing significant property or money, are seriously grave offenses.

QUESTION 60

JUDGMENT

ARTICLE 2 ~~ **Is it moral to judge people?**

Yes, despite objections to the contrary, It is written (Dt 16:18): "You shall appoint judges and magistrates in all your gates . . . that they may judge the people with just judgment."

I answer that, Judgment is moral in so far as it is an act of justice. Now it follows from what has been stated above (a. 1, ad 1, ad 3) that three conditions are requisite for a judgment to be an act of justice: first, that it proceed from the inclination of justice; secondly, that it come from one who is in authority; thirdly, that it be pronounced according to the right ruling of prudence. If any one of these be lacking, the judgment will be faulty and immoral: first, when it is contrary to the rectitude of justice, and then it is called "perverted" or "unjust"; secondly, when a man judges about matters wherein he has no authority, and this is called judgment "by usurpation"; thirdly, when the reason lacks certainty, as when a man, without any solid motive, forms a judgment on some doubtful or hidden matter, and then it is called judgment by "suspicion" or "rash" judgment.

Objection 1. It would seem immoral to judge. For nothing is punished except what is immoral. Now those who judge are threatened with punishment, which those who judge not will escape, according to Matthew 7:1, "Judge not, and you shall not be judged." Therefore it is immoral to judge.

Reply to Objection 1. In these words our Lord forbids rash judgment which is about the inward intention, or other uncertain things, as Augustine states (*De Serm. Dom. in Monte* ii, 18). Or else He forbids judgment about Divine things, which we ought not to judge, but simply believe, since they are above us, as Hilary declares in his commentary on Matthew 5. Or again according to Chrysostom [*Hom. xvii in Matth.* in the *Opus Imperfectum* falsely ascribed to St. John Chrysostom], He forbids the judgment which proceeds not from benevolence but from bitterness of heart.[1]

Objection 2. Further, it is written (Rom 14:4): "Who are you that judges another man's servant. To his own lord he stands or falls." Now God is the Lord of all. Therefore, to no man is it moral to judge.

Reply to Objection 2. A judge is appointed as God's servant; therefore it is written (Dt 1:16): "Judge that which is just," and further on (Dt 1:17), "because it is the judgment of God."

Objection 3. Further, no man is sinless, according to 1 John 1:8, "If we say that we have no sin, we deceive ourselves." Now it is immoral for a sinner to judge, according to Romans 2:1, "You are inexcusable, O man, whosoever you are, that judges; for wherein you judge another, you condemn yourself, for you do the same things which you judge." Therefore to no man is it ethical to judge.

---

[1] This passage indicates the fullness of meaning present in Scripture for Thomas. Three different interpretations are given, but no resolution as to which is the "right" reading. Indeed, his point may be that there is no *single* "correct" reading. Although misinterpretations of Scripture are certainly possible, Scripture always remains mysterious and pregnant with meaning in a way no other text is. St. Thomas says as much explicitly: "[T]he authority of Sacred Scripture is not derogated when it is differently explained, the faith being saved, because the Holy Spirit made it fruitful with a greater truth than any man can discover" (*Commentary on the Sentences of Peter Lombard*, book 2, Dist. XII, q.1, art. 2; in *Aquinas: Selected Writings*, trans. and ed. Ralph McInerny [London: Penguin Books, 1998], 92). For this reason, deeper insight into Scripture is always possible. For more, see Christopher Kaczor, "Thomas Aquinas on the Development of Doctrine," *Theological Studies* 62 (June 2001): 283–302.

Reply to Objection 3. Those who stand guilty of grievous sins should not judge those who are guilty of the same or lesser sins, as Chrysostom [*Hom.* xxiv] says. In the words of Matthew 7:1, "Judge not." Above all does this hold when such sins are public, because there would be an occasion of scandal arising in the hearts of others. If, however, they are not public but hidden, and there be an urgent necessity for the judge to pronounce judgment, because it is his duty, he can reprove or judge with humility and fear. Hence Augustine says (*De Serm. Dom. in Monte* ii, 19): "If we find that we are guilty of the same sin as another man, we should groan together with him, and invite him to strive against it together with us." And yet it is not through acting thus that a man condemns himself so as to deserve to be condemned once again, but when, in condemning another, he shows himself to be equally deserving of condemnation on account of another or a like sin.

ARTICLE 4 ∞ Should doubts be interpreted for the best?

Yes, despite objections to the contrary, A gloss[2] on Romans 14:3, "He that eats not, let him not judge him that eats," says: "Doubts should be interpreted in the best sense."

I answer that, As stated above (a. 3, ad 2), from the very fact that a man thinks ill of another without sufficient cause, he injures and despises him. Now no man ought to despise or in any way injure another man without urgent cause; and, consequently, unless we have evident indications of a person's wickedness, we ought to deem him good, by interpreting for the best whatever is doubtful about him.[3]

---

2 Medieval texts often came accompanied by a "gloss," or interpretation, in the margins of the main text. Often, a gloss sought to clarify obscure, technical, or transliterated foreign words or phrases.

3 This point is important for moral development. An eagerness to find fault in others, an inclination toward negative interpretations of acts and motives, poisons many human relationships. Often, looking for the "bad news" in others arises from a desire to make oneself feel superior and is a form of pride. Of course, a certain realism about human behavior is not excluded by what Thomas is saying. People sometimes do have bad motives and behavior, and we must not pretend as if this were not so. However, charity leads a person to seek what is good in others, to reject a "hermeneutic of suspicion" in favor of benign interpretations of others.

Objection 1. It would seem that doubts should not be interpreted for the best, because we should judge from what happens for the most part. But it happens for the most part that evil is done, since "the number of fools is infinite" (Eccles 1:15), "for the imagination and thought of man's heart are prone to evil from his youth" (Gen 8:21). Therefore doubts should be interpreted for the worst rather than for the best.

Reply to Objection 1. He who interprets doubtful matters for the best may happen to be deceived more often than not; yet it is better to err frequently through thinking well of a wicked man, than to err less frequently through having an evil opinion of a good man, because in the latter case an injury is inflicted, but not in the former.

Objection 2. Further, Augustine says (*De Doctr. Christ.* i, 27) that "he leads a godly and just life who is sound in his estimate of things, and turns neither to this side nor to that." Now he who interprets a doubtful point for the best turns to one side. Therefore this should not be done.

Reply to Objection 2. It is one thing to judge of things and another to judge of men.[4] For when we judge of things, there is no question of the good or evil of the thing about which we are judging, since it will take no harm no matter what kind of judgment we form about it; but there is question of the good of the person who judges, if he judge truly, and of his evil, if he judge falsely, because "the true is the good of the intellect, and the false is its evil," as stated in *Ethic.* vi, 2. There-

---

[4] The reason we should judge persons differently than things arises in part from the imperative of charity. We have charity toward persons, such as other human beings and God, but we do not have charity toward things. Hence, our judgment of persons and things differs. Things, for instance, have a value based on the laws of supply and demand. In our market economy, the value of a thing is determined by whether it is wanted by others. The more it is wanted, the higher the demand, and the more valuable it is. Persons, on the other hand, have innate dignity and worth, even if they are not "valued" by others who "want" them. It is thus a grave moral mistake, contrary to both charity and justice, to treat people as if they were things. Of course, practical wisdom does mitigate against a Pollyannaish failure to acknowledge reality. The store clerk, for example, should be suspicious and "on guard" if gang members walk into his store late at night.

fore everyone should strive to make his judgment accord with things as they are. On the other hand, when we judge of men, the good and evil in our judgment is considered chiefly on the part of the person about whom judgment is being formed; for he is deemed worthy of honor from the very fact that he is judged to be good, and deserving of contempt if he is judged to be evil. For this reason we ought, in this kind of judgment, to aim at judging a man good, unless there is evident proof of the contrary. And though we may judge falsely, our judgment in thinking well of another pertains to our good feeling and not to the evil of the intellect, even as neither does it pertain to the intellect's perfection to know the truth of contingent singulars in themselves.

Objection 3. Further, man should love his neighbor as himself. Now with regard to himself, a man should interpret doubtful matters for the worst, according to Job 9:28, "I feared all my works." Therefore it seems that doubtful matters affecting one's neighbor should be interpreted for the worst.

Reply to Objection 3. One may interpret something for the worst or for the best in two ways: first, by a kind of supposition; and thus, when we have to apply a remedy to some evil, whether our own or another's, in order for the remedy to be applied with greater certainty of a cure, it is expedient to take the worst for granted, since if a remedy be efficacious against a worse evil, much more is it efficacious against a lesser evil.[5] Secondly, we may interpret something for the best or for the worst, by deciding or determining, and in this case when judging of things we should try to interpret each thing according as it is, and when judging of persons, to interpret things for the best as stated above.

---

[5] "By supposition" here seems to mean that one can act *as if* the worse were true so as to help cure a person of a malady (physical or moral) without coming to a conclusive judgment that in fact the less favorable interpretation of a person's action is true. "Trust, but verify" seems to embody this sort of thinking in which you do not call the person's trustworthiness into account, but still act on the supposition that deception is possible so as to help and aid the other.

QUESTION **61**

THE PARTS OF JUSTICE

ARTICLE 1 ⌁ **Is justice suitably divided into commutative justice and distributive justice?**

Yes, despite objections to the contrary, The Philosopher assigns two parts to justice and says (*Ethic.* v, 2) that "one directs distributions, the other, commutations."

I answer that, As stated above (q. 58, aa 7, 8), particular justice is directed to the private individual, who is compared to the community as a part to the whole. Now a twofold order may be considered in relation to a part. On the one hand, there is the order of one part to another, to which corresponds the order of one private individual to another. This order is directed by commutative justice, which is concerned about the mutual dealings between two persons. On the other hand, there is the order of the whole towards the parts, to which corresponds the order of that which belongs to the community in relation to each single person. This order is directed by distributive justice, which distributes common goods proportionately. Hence there are two species of justice, distributive and commutative.[1]

---

[1] This distinction is essential to understanding the nature of justice. What may be unjust within one "sphere of justice" may not be unjust within another "sphere of justice." For instance, one private individual may not kidnap another or take his money, for this action violates the due order between individuals as governed by commutative justice. However, the governmental authority may punish wrongdoers by imprisonment or by taking money from others (in taxes or fines), both as forms of distributive justice. These two kinds

Objection 1. It would seem that the two species of justice are unsuitably assigned, viz. distributive and commutative. That which is hurtful to the many cannot be a species of justice, since justice is directed to the common good. Now it is hurtful to the common good of the many, if the goods of the community are distributed among many, both because the goods of the community would be exhausted, and because the morals of men would be corrupted. For Tully says (*De Offic.* ii, 15): "He who receives becomes worse, and the more ready to expect that he will receive again." Therefore distribution does not belong to any species of justice.

Reply to Objection 1. Just as a private individual is praised for moderation in his bounty, and blamed for excess therein, so too ought moderation to be observed in the distribution of common goods, wherein distributive justice directs.[2]

Objection 2. Further, the act of justice is to render to each one what is his own, as stated above (q. 58, a. 2). But when things are distributed, a man does not receive what was his, but becomes possessed of something which belonged to the community. Therefore this does not pertain to justice.

Reply to Objection 2. Even as part and whole are somewhat the same, so too that which pertains to the whole, pertains somewhat to

---

     of justice (commutative and distributive) help morally distinguish acts that may not differ in external appearance, such as theft as opposed to fines/taxes, assault as opposed to arresting, kidnapping as opposed to imprisoning.

2 Thus although a governmental authority may do actions that a private individual may not do, nevertheless justice limits the legitimate action of the government. Because the state has care for the common good, and the state's authority is given precisely in order to secure the common good, any exercise of authority that contradicted this good would be illegitimate. In a similar way, what a parent may do to govern and raise his own child far exceeds that which a stranger may legitimately do for that same child. But parental authority is hardly absolute. Indeed, this authority is only legitimately exercised for the well-being of the child in question. Acts of parental authority that undermine the well-being of the parent's child are contrary to the very point of parental authority, namely to secure the child's well-being. Similarly, the authority of the state arises from and is limited by the common good for which the state has care. In both cases, authority is not an exercise in raw power, but a service undertaken and limited by the good of those served.

the part also: so that when the goods of the community are distributed among a number of individuals, each one receives that which, in a way, is his own.

Objection 3. Further, justice is not only in the sovereign, but also in the subject, as stated above (q. 58, a. 6). But it belongs exclusively to the sovereign to distribute. Therefore distribution does not always belong to justice.

Reply to Objection 3. The act of distributing the goods of the community belongs to none but those who exercise authority over those goods; and yet distributive justice is also in the subjects to whom those goods are distributed in so far as they are contented by a just distribution. Moreover distribution of common goods is sometimes made not to the state but to the members of a family, and such distribution can be made by authority of a private individual.

Objection 4. Further, "distributive justice regards common goods" (*Ethic.* v, 4). Now matters regarding the community pertain to legal justice. Therefore distributive justice is a part, not of particular, but of legal justice.

Reply to Objection 4. Movement takes its species from the term "whereunto." Hence it belongs to legal justice to direct to the common good those matters which concern private individuals, whereas, on the contrary, it belongs to particular justice to direct the common good to particular individuals by way of distribution.

Objection 5. Further, unity or multitude do not change the species of a virtue. Now commutative justice consists in rendering something to one person, while distributive justice consists in giving something to many. Therefore they are not different species of justice.

Reply to Objection 5. Distributive and commutative justice differ not only in respect of unity and multitude, but also in respect of different kinds of due: because common property is due to an individual in one way, and his personal property in another way.

RESTITUTION

ARTICLE 5 ⟿ **Must restitution always be made to the person from whom a thing has been taken?**

Yes, despite objections to the contrary, It is written (Rom 13:7): "Render . . . to all men their dues; tribute to whom tribute is due, custom to whom custom."

I answer that, Restitution re-establishes the equality of commutative justice, which equality consists in the equalizing of thing to thing, as stated above (q. 62, a. 2; q. 58, a. 10). Now this equalizing of things is impossible, unless he that has less than his due receive what is lacking to him: and for this to be done, restitution must be made to the person from whom a thing has been taken.[1]

Objection 1. It would seem that restitution need not always be made to the person from whom a thing has been taken. For it is not ethical to injure anyone. Now it would sometimes be injurious to the man himself, or to others, were one to restore to him what has been taken from

---

[1] This question concerns returning, for example, items that were stolen. If a thief takes $10,000 from an old widow, he must not only repent of the wrongdoing but also restore what was taken. He may not make use of the money himself, and he must also *return* all the money to the person from whom he took it. As Thomas notes, certain factors may complicate matters. It could turn out that the money is now gone and cannot be repaid. Or it may happen that the widow has since died. Thomas's point here is that in principle, even if in a practical way one cannot or ought not return what was taken, the goal is restitution of that which was lost or damaged.

him: if, for instance, one were to return a madman his sword. Therefore restitution need not always be made to the person from whom a thing has been taken.

Reply to Objection 1. When the thing to be restored appears to be grievously injurious to the person to whom it is to be restored, or to some other, it should not be restored to him there and then, because restitution is directed to the good of the person to whom it is made,[2] since all possessions come under the head of the useful. Yet he who retains another's property must not appropriate it, but must either reserve it, that he may restore it at a fitting time, or hand it over to another to keep it more securely.

Objection 2. Further, if a man has given a thing immorally, he does not deserve to recover it. Now sometimes a man gives immorally that which another accepts immorally, as in the case of the giver and receiver who are guilty of simony.[3] Therefore it is not always necessary to make restitution to the person from whom one has taken something.

Reply to Objection 2. A person may give a thing immorally in two ways: first, through the giving itself being illicit and against the law, as is the case when a man gives a thing simoniacally. Such a man deserves to lose what he gave. Therefore restitution should not be made to him; and, since the receiver acted against the law in receiving, he must not retain the price, but must use it for some pious object. Secondly, a man gives immorally through giving for an immoral purpose, albeit the giving itself is not immoral, as when a woman receives payment for fornication: therefore she may keep what she has received. If, however, she has extorted overmuch by fraud or deceit, she would be bound to restitution.

---

[2] Justice is not blind to the good of others but is an instantiation of that good. To do justice in returning something one must take into account the proper time, place, and manner of the return. Justice has to do with securing or defending the good of others, so this good of others orders the way in which justice is done. Obviously, justice requires, therefore, the exercise of prudence or practical wisdom, the virtue that concerns itself with the concrete particularity of the moral life.

[3] Simony is the buying and selling of spiritual things, such as Sacraments or ecclesiastical offices, such as the office of bishop (cf. Acts 8:14–24).

Objection 3. Further, no man is bound to do what is impossible.[4] Now it is sometimes impossible to make restitution to the person from whom a thing has been taken, either because he is dead, or because he is too far away, or because he is unknown to us. Therefore restitution need not always be made to the person from whom a thing has been taken.

Reply to Objection 3. If the person to whom restitution is due is unknown altogether, restitution must be made as far as possible, for instance by giving an alms for his spiritual welfare (whether he be dead or living), but not without previously making a careful inquiry about his person. If the person to whom restitution is due be dead, restitution should be made to his heir, who is looked upon as one with him. If he be very far away, what is due to him should be sent to him, especially if it be of great value and can easily be sent, else it should be deposited in a safe place to be kept for him, and the owner should be advised of the fact.

Objection 4. Further, we owe more compensation to one from whom we have received a greater favor. Now we have received greater favors from others (our parents for instance) than from a lender or depositor. Therefore sometimes we ought to care for some other person rather than make restitution to one from whom we have taken something.

---

[4] Although this is an objection, Thomas does accept this principle. Morality does not demand the impossible. Even though temptations might abound, temptations are not "necessitations" of wrongdoing. There do arise situations, however, called by Thomas *perplexus secundum quid,* in which a person cannot help but do wrong. If a married man with children fathers other children outside his marriage, he can find himself unable to father properly both sets of children. He cannot simultaneously be married to both women, so he will either neglect his wife and their children together or neglect the children fathered outside marriage. He does wrong if he stays with his wife (because he neglects his other children), but he also does wrong if he neglects the children fathered within the marriage. By doing wrong previously, in this example adultery, the man finds himself without any unproblematic resolution. However, aside from cases of previous wrongdoing, Aquinas does not recognize any so-called "tragic" situations in the sense of cases in which a person must do wrong whatever he or she may choose.

Reply to Objection 4. A man is bound, out of his own property, to care for his parents, or those from whom he has received greater benefits; but he ought not to compensate a benefactor out of what belongs to others; and he would be doing this if he were to compensate one with what is due to another. Exception must be made in cases of extreme need, for then he could and should even take what belongs to another in order to succor a parent.[5]

---

[5] Later in II–II, q. 66, a. 7, Thomas argues that in case of absolute need, where no other means is possible, it is morally permissible to take what is legally the property of another so as to secure the survival of those in need.

QUESTION **64**

~~~~~~~~~~~~~~~~~~~~~~~~~

MURDER

ARTICLE 1 ~~Is it immoral to kill any living thing?

No, despite objections to the contrary, Augustine says (*De Civ. Dei* i, 20): "When we hear it said, 'You shall not kill,' we do not take it as referring to trees, for they have no sense, nor to irrational animals, because they have no fellowship with us. Hence it follows that the words, 'You shall not kill' refer to the killing of a man."[1]

I answer that, There is no sin in using a thing for the purpose for which it is. Now the order of things is such that the imperfect are for the perfect, even as in the process of generation nature proceeds from imperfection to perfection. Hence it is that just as in the generation of a man there is first a living thing, then an animal, and lastly a man,[2]

---

[1] Even more precisely, murder as forbidden by the fifth commandment is the "intentional killing of an innocent person." So if the death is not from an intentional act, but rather merely foreseen, the killing is not murder (though it may still be wrong, for we often have a duty to prevent the deaths of others). Why is there an important difference between intending someone's death and merely foreseeing but not preventing it? The acting person is more fully formed by what he intends than by what he foresees. We necessarily set our hearts on what we intend (health) but may not set our hearts on what is merely foreseen as connected with what we intend (to wear out our running shoes). The dentist who foresees that a necessary dental procedure will cause great pain may be justified in doing the procedure anyway; on the other hand, the dentist who sets out to cause pain as the goal acts wrongly.

[2] St. Thomas's account of human generation reflects an outdated understanding of the facts of embryology. He "thought that the male's seed did not become one with the female's material contribution, which he believed was in such a

so too things, like the plants, which merely have life, are all alike for animals, and all animals are for man. Therefore it is not immoral if man use plants for the good of animals, and animals for the good of man,[3] as the Philosopher states (*Polit.* i, 3).[4]

Now the most necessary use would seem to consist in the fact that animals use plants, and men use animals, for food, and this cannot be done unless these be deprived of life: therefore, it is ethical both to take life from plants for the use of animals, and from animals for the use of men. In fact this is in keeping with the commandment of God Himself: for it is written (Gen 1:29, 30): "Behold I have given you every herb . . . and all trees . . . to be your meat, and to all beasts of the earth"; and again (Gen 9:3): "Everything that moves and lives shall be meat to you."[5]

---

crude state that effort was needed to bring the maternal contribution to even a minimal state of life; that is false, for we know now that the sperm and the egg prior to fertilization are highly and equally organized, though 'half-organized,' as it were, such that the union of the two at fertilization results in a single body that is materially one, and formally or organizationally one, and is indeed organizationally more sophisticated than either the sperm or the egg had been on its own, prior to fertilization—after fertilization occurs, of course, it is improper in the discipline of biology to speak further of 'the sperm' or 'the egg,' since those two erstwhile realities no longer exist, but have become 'parts' of another whole. Thomas thought that the embryo was the passive recipient of the semen's agency, since the semen worked-over and shaped, and 'built' the structures in the passive embryo, first developing in it the structures necessary for nutrition, then eventually sensation, and so on; that [too] is false." Mark Johnson, "The Moral Status of Embryonic Human Life" in *What is Man, O Lord? The Human Person in a Biotech Age: Eighteenth Workshop for Bishops*, ed. Edward J. Furton and Louise A. Mitchell (Boston: The National Catholic Bioethics Center, 2002), 196.

[3] Note that destruction of living things is permissible for the good of human beings. Wanton destruction of plant life or animal life is not endorsed, and Thomas's view is fully compatible with a care for the environment as well as animal life.

[4] Note that Aquinas suggests that it is licit to *use* plants and animals, not abuse plants and animals. Use implies a legitimate stewardship of resources, not a reckless carelessness with natural things given as gifts by God.

[5] Long before there were people advocating "animal rights," medieval authors considered the objection that killing animals was wrong. But many modern advocates of "animal rights" do not so much raise animals to the status of human beings as reduce human beings to the status of mere animals. Despite

Objection 1. It would seem immoral to kill any living thing. For the Apostle says (Rom 13:2): "They that resist the ordinance of God purchase to themselves damnation [Vulg.: 'He that resists the power, resists the ordinance of God: and they that resist, purchase themselves damnation']." Now Divine providence has ordained that all living things should be preserved, according to Psalm 146:8, 9, "Who makes grass to grow on the mountains . . . Who gives to beasts their food." Therefore it seems immoral to take the life of any living thing.

Reply to Objection 1. According to the Divine ordinance, the life of animals and plants is preserved not for themselves but for man. Hence, as Augustine says (*De Civ. Dei* i, 20), "by a most just ordinance of the Creator, both their life and their death are subject to our use."

Objection 3. Further, in the Divine law a special punishment is not appointed save for a sin. Now a special punishment had to be inflicted, according to the Divine law, on one who killed another man's ox or sheep (Ex 22:1). Therefore the slaying of animals is a sin.

Reply to Objection 3. He that kills another's ox, sins, not through killing the ox, but through injuring another man in his property. Therefore this is not a species of the sin of murder but of the sin of theft or robbery.

ARTICLE 2 ⤖ **Is capital punishment moral?**

Yes, despite objections to the contrary, It is written (Ex 22:18): "Wizards you shall not suffer to live;" and (Ps 100:8): "In the morning I put to death all the wicked of the land."

I answer that, As stated above (a. 1), it is ethically permissible to kill animals, in so far as they are naturally directed to man's use, as the imperfect is directed to the perfect. Now every part is directed to the

---

this kind of reductionism, it is wrong to abuse needlessly or inflict cruelty on animals—not because animals are the moral equals to humans but rather because humans should not indulge in cruelty to any creature lest this inclination be turned also on human beings. Needless infliction of pain, like needless destruction of beautiful objects, is wrong in itself though neither animals nor works of art have "rights."

whole, as imperfect to perfect, Therefore every part is naturally for the sake of the whole. For this reason we observe that if the health of the whole body demands the excision of a member, through its being decayed or infectious to the other members, it will be both praiseworthy and advantageous to have it cut away. Now every individual person is compared to the whole community as part to whole. Therefore, if a man be dangerous and infectious to the community, on account of some sin, it is praiseworthy and advantageous that he be killed in order to safeguard the common good, since "a little leaven corrupts the whole lump" (1 Cor 5:6).[6]

Objection 1. It would seem immoral to kill men who have sinned. For our Lord in the parable (Mt 13) forbade the uprooting of the cockle, which denotes wicked men, according to a gloss. Now whatever is forbidden by God is a sin. Therefore it is a sin to kill a sinner.

Reply to Objection 1. Our Lord commanded them to forbear from uprooting the cockle in order to spare the wheat, i.e., the good. This occurs when the wicked cannot be slain without the good being killed with them, either because the wicked lie hidden among the good, or because they have many followers, so that they cannot be killed without danger to the good, as Augustine says (*Contra Parmen.* iii, 2). Therefore our Lord teaches that we should rather allow the wicked to live, and

---

6 Note that Thomas's approval of the death penalty is conditional. He argues that "if" a criminal is dangerous and infectious to the community, the death penalty is justified—but not required. In our contemporary circumstances, Pope John Paul II writes in *Evangelium Vitae* that "the state ought not go to the extreme of executing the offender except in cases of absolute necessity: in other words, when it would not be possible otherwise to defend society. Today however, as a result of steady improvements in the organization of the penal system, such cases are very rare, if not practically non-existent" (*EV* 56). Just as one ought not to amputate a limb that can be treated through less severe means, so too the state should not put criminals to death if bloodless means will protect innocent life. For useful accounts of contemporary Catholic teaching, see Avery Cardinal Dulles, "Catholicism and Capital Punishment," *First Things* (April 2001): 30–35, and Christopher Kaczor, "Capital Punishment and the Catholic Tradition: Contradiction, Change in Circumstance, or Development of Doctrine," *Nova et Vetera* 2:1 (English Edition), Fall 2004: 279–304.

that vengeance is to be delayed until the last judgment, rather than that the good be put to death together with the wicked. When, however, the good incur no danger, but rather are protected and saved by the slaying of the wicked, then the latter may be morally put to death.[7]

Objection 2. Further, human justice is conformed to Divine justice. Now according to Divine justice sinners are kept back for repentance, according to Ezekiel 33:11, "I desire not the death of the wicked, but that the wicked turn from his way and live." Therefore it seems altogether unjust to kill sinners.

Reply to Objection 2. According to the order of His wisdom, God sometimes slays sinners forthwith in order to deliver the good, whereas sometimes He allows them time to repent, according as He knows what is expedient for His elect. This also does human justice imitate according to its powers; for it puts to death those who are dangerous to others, while it allows time for repentance to those who sin without grievously harming others.[8]

Objection 3. Further, it is not moral, for any good end whatever, to do that which is evil in itself,[9] according to Augustine (*Contra Mendac.* vii)

---

7 The danger to the good could be physical or spiritual. To the degree that the criminal justice system cannot distinguish the guilty from the innocent, the good are in physical danger. To the degree that the death penalty is viewed as an act of vengeance rather than retributive justice, the good are in spiritual danger of becoming more engrossed in the "culture of death" that views human life as dispensable.

8 Helpful to consider here is what Thomas wrote earlier in II–II, q. 43, a. 7 Reply to Objection 1: "In the infliction of punishment it is not the punishment itself that is the end in view, but its medicinal properties in checking sin; therefore punishment partakes of the nature of justice, in so far as it checks sin. But if it is evident that the infliction of punishment will result in more numerous and more grievous sins being committed, the infliction of punishment will no longer be a part of justice. It is in this sense that Augustine is speaking, when, to wit, the excommunication of a few threatens to bring about the danger of a schism, for in that case it would be contrary to the truth of justice to pronounce excommunication." Justice, then, is not blind to but rather seeks what promotes the common good.

9 A good act is a good act even if something evil ends up arising from it; likewise an evil act is an evil act even if something good arises from it. The act of marital intercourse is good, even if the child that originates from that act

and the Philosopher (*Ethic.* ii, 6). Now to kill a man is evil in itself, since we are bound to have charity towards all men, and "we wish our friends to live and to exist," according to *Ethic.* ix, 4. Therefore it is nowise moral to kill a man who has sinned.

Reply to Objection 3. By sinning man departs from the order of reason, and consequently falls away from the dignity of his manhood, in so far as he is naturally free, and exists for himself, and he falls into the slavish state of the beasts, by being disposed of according as he is useful to others. This is expressed in Psalm 48:21: "Man, when he was in honor, did not understand; he has been compared to senseless beasts, and made like to them," and Proverbs 11:29: "The fool shall serve the wise." Hence, although it be evil in itself to kill a man so long as he preserve his dignity, yet it may be good to kill a man who has sinned, even as it is to kill a beast. For a bad man is worse than a beast, and is more harmful, as the Philosopher states (*Polit.* i, 1 and *Ethic.* vii, 6).[10]

ARTICLE 5 ~~ Is suicide moral?

No, despite objections to the contrary, Augustine says (*De Civ. Dei* i, 20): "Hence it follows that the words 'You shall not kill' refer to the killing of a man—not another man; therefore, not even yourself. For he who kills himself, kills nothing else than a man."

I answer that, It is altogether immoral to kill oneself, for three reasons. First, because everything naturally loves itself, the result being that everything naturally keeps itself in being, and resists corruptions so far as it can. Therefore suicide is contrary to the inclination of nature,

---

leads an evil life as an adult. The act of adultery is evil, even if a child, who is good and made in God's image, originates from the union. The fact that evil sometimes leads to good or good sometimes leads to evil does not change evil into good or good into evil.

[10] Yet John Paul II has stated: "Not even a murderer loses his personal dignity, and God himself pledges to guarantee this" and that "great care must be taken to respect every life, even that of criminals and unjust aggressors" (*EV* 9, 57), and Thomas himself states that even those in hell do not completely lose the goodness of their nature (*ST* I–II, q. 85, a. 2, ad 3). Indeed, punishment presupposes the dignity of the one punished because any just punishment presupposes personal responsibility, and hence the dignity of an acting person.

and to charity whereby every man should love himself. Hence suicide
is always a mortal sin, as being contrary to the natural law and to charity.[11] Secondly, because every part, as such, belongs to the whole.
Now every man is part of the community, and so, as such, he belongs
to the community. Hence by killing himself he injures the community, as the Philosopher declares (*Ethic.* v, 11).[12] Thirdly, because life
is God's gift to man, and is subject to His power, Who kills and makes
to live. Hence whoever takes his own life sins against God, even as he
who kills another's slave sins against that slave's master, and as he who
usurps to himself judgment of a matter not entrusted to him. For it
belongs to God alone to pronounce sentence of death and life, according to Deuteronomy 32:39, "I will kill and I will make to live."

---

[11] Some philosophers have spoken of "wrongful life" meaning that some lives are
not worth living or that some people are better off dead. This is a grave concep-
tual confusion. Undoubtedly, the good of life can lead to painful circumstances
but this does not make life wrongful or evil any more than the suffering that can
come from vision (such as looking at the sun) or intelligence (such as knowing
you are disliked) would make these intrinsically good aspects of sight or the
mind "evils." Good is good and evil is evil, even when good comes from evil or
evil comes from good. I might become a better person because I was tortured,
but that does not make torturing me in itself good. A person might become evil
because too much liberty was given him by his parents in the wrong circumstances, but that does not make liberty evil. Life is a good, so loving yourself
involves caring for your life and never intentionally taking your own life.

[12] It might be objected by an advocate of physician-assisted suicide (PAS) that a
sick person killing himself does not hurt the community but rather helps it by
conserving financial resources. However, although medical costs for the gravely
disabled are indeed high, studies have indicated that in fact PAS "is not likely to
save substantial amounts of money in absolute or relative terms, either for particular institutions or for the nation as a whole." Ezekiel J. Emanuel and Mar-
garet Battin, "What are the Potential Cost Savings from Legalizing Physician
Assisted Suicide," *The New England Journal of Medicine* 339:3 (July 16, 1998):
171. Furthermore, physician-assisted suicide endangers the common good. The
"right to die" becomes for many people the "duty to die." Even those who have
not consented to euthanasia are endangered by it. The 1991 Dutch government study of euthanasia, the Remmelink Report, indicated that more people
were killed without their consent than killed with their consent in Holland following euthanasia's decriminalization. Chapter ten of Robert Spitzer's *Healing
the Culture* (San Francisco: Ignatius Press, 2000) frankly describes the severe
cultural problems that arise from legalizing euthanasia.

Objection 1. It would seem ethically permissible for a man to kill himself. For murder is a sin in so far as it is contrary to justice. But no man can do an injustice to himself, as is proved in *Ethic.* v, 11. Therefore no man sins by killing himself.

Reply to Objection 1. Murder is a sin, not only because it is contrary to justice, but also because it is opposed to charity, which a man should have towards himself: in this respect suicide is a sin in relation to oneself. In relation to the community and to God, it is sinful, by reason also of its opposition to justice.

Objection 2. Further, it is ethically permissible, for one who exercises public authority, to kill evil-doers. Now he who exercises public authority is sometimes an evil-doer. Therefore he may ethically kill himself.

Reply to Objection 2. One who exercises public authority may ethically put to death an evil-doer, since he can pass judgment on him. But no man is judge of himself. Therefore it is not ethical for one who exercises public authority to put himself to death for any sin whatever, although he may ethically commit himself to the judgment of others.[13]

Objection 3. Further, it is ethical for a man to suffer spontaneously a lesser danger that he may avoid a greater: thus it is ethical for a man to cut off a decayed limb even from himself, that he may save his whole body. Now sometimes a man, by killing himself, avoids a greater evil, for example an unhappy life, or the shame of sin. Therefore a man may kill himself.

Reply to Objection 3. Man is made master of himself through his free-will: therefore he can ethically dispose of himself as to those matters which pertain to this life, which is ruled by man's free-will. But the

---

[13] It is often difficult to come to an objective, true assessment of oneself. The common ancient Greek dictum "Know Thyself" would be unnecessary if self-knowledge were self-evident. For this reason, people should not judge themselves in the sense of being judge, jury, and executioner in their own capital case. Some people are prone to exaggerate their guilt; others are prone to minimize it. For the same reason, progress in the spiritual life is best undertaken in consultation with a spiritual director, rather than as an isolated individual going it alone.

passage from this life to another and happier one is subject not to man's free-will but to the power of God. Hence it is not ethical for man to take his own life that he may pass to a happier life, nor that he may escape any unhappiness whatsoever of the present life, because the ultimate and most fearsome evil of this life is death, as the Philosopher states (*Ethic.* iii, 6). Therefore to bring death upon oneself in order to escape the other afflictions of this life is to adopt a greater evil in order to avoid a lesser. In like manner, it is immoral to take one's own life on account of one's having committed a sin, both because by so doing one does oneself a very great injury, by depriving oneself of the time needful for repentance, and because it is not ethical to slay an evildoer except by the sentence of the public authority. Again it is immoral for a woman to kill herself lest she be violated, because she ought not to commit on herself the very great sin of suicide, to avoid the lesser sin of another. For she commits no sin in being violated by force,[14] provided she does not consent, since "without consent of the mind there is no stain on the body," as the Blessed Lucy declared. Now it is evident that fornication and adultery are less grievous sins than taking a man's, especially one's own, life: since the latter is most grievous, because one injures oneself, to whom one owes the greatest love.[15] Moreover, it is most dangerous since no time is left wherein to expiate it by repentance. Again, it is not ethical for anyone to take his own life for fear he should consent to sin, because "evil must not be done that good may come" (Rom 3:8) or that evil may be avoided, especially if the evil be

---

[14] Sin, to be sin, must be voluntary. No one sins through the action of another person alone. Force can take a person's life, liberty, or property, but not even the strongest force can undermine a person's virtue.

[15] Earlier in the *Summa*, in his treatment of the theological virtue of love (II–II, q. 26), Thomas speaks of the order of love (*ordo charitatis*). The virtue of love, like the other virtues, is guided by practical intelligence, which recognizes that those in closest proximity to us should be loved most. God is the most worthy of love, followed by those most closely connected to us. In contrast to the "telescopic philanthropy" decried by Charles Dickens in *Bleak House,* charity begins at home. It is relatively easy and costs me little to express good will for people half-way across the globe but much more challenging to practice goodwill with whoever is sitting across from me at the breakfast table.

of small account and an uncertain event, for it is uncertain whether one will at some future time consent to a sin, since God is able to deliver man from sin under any temptation whatever.[16]

Objection 4. Further, Samson killed himself, as related in Judges 16, and yet he is numbered among the saints (Heb 11). Therefore it is ethical for a man to kill himself.

Reply to Objection 4. As Augustine says (*De Civ. Dei* i, 21), "not even Samson is to be excused that he crushed himself together with his enemies under the ruins of the house, except the Holy Spirit, Who had wrought many wonders through him, had secretly commanded him to do this." He assigns the same reason in the case of certain holy women, who at the time of persecution took their own lives, and who are commemorated by the Church.[17]

Objection 5. Further, it is related (2 Mac 14:42) that a certain Razias killed himself, "choosing to die nobly rather than to fall into the hands of the wicked, and to suffer abuses unbecoming his noble birth." Now nothing that is done nobly and bravely is immoral. Therefore suicide is not immoral.

---

[16] Pope John Paul II notes that "temptations can be overcome, sins can be avoided, because together with the commandments the Lord gives us the possibility of keeping them: 'His eyes are on those who fear him, and he knows every deed of man. He has not commanded any one to be ungodly, and he has not given any one permission to sin' (Sir 15:19–20). Keeping God's law in particular situations can be difficult, extremely difficult, but it is never impossible. This is the constant teaching of the Church's tradition, and was expressed by the Council of Trent: 'But no one, however much justified, ought to consider himself exempt from the observance of the command-ments, nor should he employ that rash statement, forbidden by the Fathers under anathema, that the commandments of God are impossible of obser-vance by one who is justified. For God does not command the impossible, but in commanding he admonishes you to do what you can and to pray for what you cannot, and he gives his aid to enable you. His commandments are not burdensome (cf. 1 Jn 5:3); his yoke is easy and his burden light (cf. Mt 11:30)'" (*The Splendor of Truth*, Aug. 6, 1993, 102).

[17] The case of Samson might not even be considered suicide strictly speaking, for suicide involves the intention to end one's life. Samson's act might be described as intending to kill unjust oppressors and merely foreseeing that his life will be lost as a result, as a soldier might do in a just war.

Reply to Objection 5. It belongs to fortitude that a man does not shrink from being slain by another, for the sake of the good of virtue, and that he may avoid sin. But that a man take his own life in order to avoid penal evils has indeed an appearance of fortitude (for which reason some, among whom was Razias, have killed themselves thinking to act from fortitude), yet it is not true fortitude, but rather a weakness of soul unable to bear penal evils, as the Philosopher (*Ethic.* iii, 7) and Augustine (*De Civ. Dei* 22, 23) declare.[18]

ARTICLE 6 — Is it moral to kill the innocent?

No, despite objections to the contrary, It is written (Ex 23:7): "The innocent and just person you shall not put to death."

I answer that, An individual man may be considered in two ways: first, in himself; secondly, in relation to something else. If we consider a man in himself, it is immoral to kill any man, since in every man though he be sinful, we ought to love the nature which God has made,[19] and which is destroyed by slaying him. Nevertheless, as stated above (a. 2), the slaying of a sinner becomes moral in relation to the common good, which is corrupted by sin. On the other hand, the life of righteous men preserves and forwards the common good, since they are the chief part of the community. Therefore it is in no way moral to slay the innocent.[20]

---

[18] Thomas here underscores the importance of intention as opposed to foresight. The person committing suicide intends, tries, and chooses to take his own life. The person who is a martyr foresees, allows, or permits his life to be lost rather than give up some greater good, like fidelity to the Gospel. This distinction between intention and foresight is tremendously important in ethics generally and in assessing individual cases of conduct. A person who intends to inflict severe pain is a torturer. A person who merely foresees that severe pain may be inflicted but isn't trying to inflict pain is not; he may be just a dentist.

[19] Even the worst sinner is not entirely evil, for evil is always a lack of due perfection parasitic upon goodness of some kind. The sinner has an evil will, a will that lacks its due perfection, but still has a nature as a human being that is good. In loving even sinners, the Christian imitates God himself: "God demonstrates his own love for us in this: While we were still sinners, Christ died for us" (Rom 5:8).

[20] This teaching was underscored with particular urgency by Pope John Paul II in *The Gospel of Life*: "[T]he absolute inviolability of innocent human life is a moral truth clearly taught by Sacred Scripture, constantly upheld in the Church's Tradition and consistently proposed by her Magisterium. This consistent teaching is

Objection 1. It would seem that in some cases it is moral to kill the innocent. The fear of God is never manifested by sin, since on the contrary "the fear of the Lord driveth out sin" (Sir 1:27). Now Abraham was commended in that he feared the Lord, since he was willing to slay his innocent son. Therefore one may, without sin, kill an innocent person.

Reply to Objection 1. God is Lord of death and life, for by His decree both the sinful and the righteous die. Hence he who at God's command kills an innocent man does not sin, as neither does God Whose behest he executes: indeed his obedience to God's commands is a proof that he fears Him.

---

the evident result of that 'supernatural sense of the faith' which, inspired and sustained by the Holy Spirit, safeguards the People of God from error when 'it shows universal agreement in matters of faith and morals'. Faced with the progressive weakening in individual consciences and in society of the sense of the absolute and grave moral illicitness of the direct taking of all innocent human life, especially at its beginning and at its end, the Church's Magisterium has spoken out with increasing frequency in defense of the sacredness and inviolability of human life. The Papal Magisterium, particularly insistent in this regard, has always been seconded by that of the Bishops, with numerous and comprehensive doctrinal and pastoral documents issued either by Episcopal Conferences or by individual Bishops. The Second Vatican Council also addressed the matter forcefully, in a brief but incisive passage. Therefore, by the authority which Christ conferred upon Peter and his Successors, and in communion with the Bishops of the Catholic Church, I confirm that the direct and voluntary killing of an innocent human being is always gravely immoral. This doctrine, based upon that unwritten law which man, in the light of reason, finds in his own heart (cf. Rom 2:14–15), is reaffirmed by Sacred Scripture, transmitted by the Tradition of the Church and taught by the ordinary and universal Magisterium. The deliberate decision to deprive an innocent human being of his life is always morally evil and can never be licit either as an end in itself or as a means to a good end. It is in fact a grave act of disobedience to the moral law, and indeed to God himself, the author and guarantor of that law; it contradicts the fundamental virtues of justice and charity. Nothing and no one can in any way permit the killing of an innocent human being, whether a fetus or an embryo, an infant or an adult, an old person, or one suffering from an incurable disease, or a person who is dying. Furthermore, no one is permitted to ask for this act of killing, either for himself or herself or for another person entrusted to his or her care, nor can he or she consent to it, either explicitly or implicitly. Nor can any authority legitimately recommend or permit such an action." (*The Gospel of Life*, 57; notes omitted.)

Objection 2. Further, among those sins that are committed against one's neighbor, the more grievous seem to be those whereby a more grievous injury is inflicted on the person sinned against. Now to be killed is a greater injury to a sinful than to an innocent person, because the latter, by death, passes forthwith from the unhappiness of this life to the glory of heaven. Since, then, it is moral in certain cases to kill a sinful man, much more is it moral to slay an innocent or a righteous person.

Reply to Objection 2. In weighing the gravity of a sin we must consider the essential rather than the accidental. Therefore he who kills a just man sins more grievously than he who slays a sinful man: first, because he injures one whom he should love more, and so acts more in opposition to charity; secondly, because he inflicts an injury on a man who is less deserving of one, and so acts more in opposition to justice; thirdly, because he deprives the community of a greater good; fourthly, because he despises God more, according to Luke 10:16, "He that despises you despises Me." On the other hand, it is accidental to the slaying that the just man whose life is taken be received by God into glory.

ARTICLE 7 ⸺ **Is it moral to kill a person in self-defense?**[21]

Yes, despite objections to the contrary, It is written (Ex 22:2) "If a thief be found breaking into a house or undermining it, and be wounded so as to die, he that slew him shall not be guilty of blood." Now it is much more moral to defend one's life than one's house. Therefore neither is a man guilty of murder if he kill another in defense of his own life.

I answer that, Nothing hinders one act from having two effects, only one of which is intended, while the other is beside the intention. Now moral acts take their species according to what is intended, and not

---

[21] This is perhaps the most commented upon article in the entire *Secunda Secundae.* Aquinas here introduces what has come to be known as "the principle of double-effect," or "double-effect reasoning," in philosophical and theological discussions. The Jesuit Jean-Pierre Gury gave double-effect reasoning its standard formula in the nineteenth century: (1) the act itself must not be evil, (2) evil may not be used as a means, (3) the evil may not be intended, and (4) there must be a serious reason for allowing the evil effect. For more on the history of double-effect and related matters, see Christopher Kaczor, "Double-Effect Reasoning: From Jean Pierre Gury to Peter Knauer," *Theological Studies* 59(June 1999): 297–316.

according to what is beside the intention, since this is accidental as explained above (q. 43, a. 3; I–II, q. 72, a. 1).[22] Accordingly, the act of self-defense may have two effects, one is the saving of one's life, the other is the slaying of the aggressor. Therefore this act, since one's intention is to save one's own life, is not immoral, seeing that it is natural to everything to keep itself in "being," as far as possible. And yet, though proceeding from a good intention, an act may be rendered immoral if it be out of proportion to the end. Therefore if a man, in self-defense, uses more than necessary violence, it will be immoral, whereas if he repel force with moderation his defense will be moral, because according to the jurists [*Cap. Significasti, De Homicid. volunt. vel casual.*], "it is lawful to repel force by force, provided one does not exceed the limits of a blameless defense."[23] Nor is it necessary for salvation that a man omit the act of moderate self-defense in order to avoid killing the other man, since one is bound to take more care of one's own life than of another's.[24]

---

[22] Actions with two effects take place quite often in medicine where a given treatment will help the patient recover health but may also have bad side-effects. Such treatments may be licit to give since the intention of the doctor is to restore health and not induce the bad side-effects. The action is defined, therefore, by what that agent wants, chooses, tries, or intends to do rather than by side-effects that are not part of the desired act.

[23] Thomas indicates here that licit self-defense must use the least amount of force possible. If non-lethal force will stop the aggressor, one may not use lethal force.

[24] In his treatment of charity in *Secunda Secundae*, q. 26, a. 5, "Should a man love his neighbor more than his own body?," Thomas considers and replies to an objection relevant to this article.

"**Objection 3**. Further, a man imperils that which he loves less for the sake of what he loves more. Now every man is not bound to imperil his own body for his neighbor's safety: this belongs to the perfect, according to John 15:13: 'Greater love than this no man has, that a man lay down his life for his friends.' Therefore a man is not bound, out of charity, to love his neighbor more than his own body.

Reply to Objection 3. Every man is immediately concerned with the care of his own body, but not with his neighbor's welfare, except perhaps in cases of urgency: therefore, charity does not necessarily require a man to imperil his own body for his neighbor's welfare, except in a case where he is under obligation to do so, and if a man of his own accord offer himself for that purpose, this belongs to the perfection of charity."

But as it is immoral to take a man's life,[25] except for the public authority acting for the common good, as stated above (a. 3), it is not moral for a man to intend killing a man in self-defense,[26] except for such as have public authority, who while intending to kill a man in self-defense, refer this to the public good, as in the case of a soldier fighting against the foe, and in the minister of the judge struggling with robbers, although even these sin if they be moved by private animosity.

Thomas, in other words, is appealing to a principle he uses throughout the *Summa* in determining what should be loved more, namely the principle of proximity, in arguing that a man should love his own body more than the neighbor. However, if someone were to refer the sacrifice of his own body to some higher good (for instance, a father allowing a wild animal to kill him in order to save his children out of love of God), then this would not only be permissible but an act of highest perfection, for there is no greater love than to lay down one's life for a friend.

[25] Earlier in the *Summa*, II–II, q. 41, article 1, Thomas explains in a different way his teaching on self-defense: "Hence strife is a kind of private war, because it takes place between private persons, being declared not by public authority, but rather by an inordinate will. Therefore strife is always sinful. In fact it is a mortal sin in the man who attacks another unjustly, for it is not without mortal sin that one inflicts harm on another even if the deed be done by the hands. But in him who defends himself, it may be without sin, or it may sometimes involve a venial sin, or sometimes a mortal sin; and this depends on his intention and on his manner of defending himself. For if his sole intention be to withstand the injury done to him, and he defend himself with due moderation, it is no sin, and one cannot say properly that there is strife on his part. But if, on the other hand, his self-defense be inspired by vengeance and hatred, it is always a sin. It is a venial sin, if a slight movement of hatred or vengeance obtrudes itself, or if he does not much exceed moderation in defending himself; but it is a mortal sin if he makes for his assailant with the fixed intention of killing him, or inflicting grievous harm on him."

[26] As with the article generally, there is some dispute about the meaning of this phrase and how it would apply to given cases. Some say that this excludes any action that is certainly lethal to the aggressor (e.g., cutting off the head of the aggressor with a sword in a case where this was the only possible method of defense); others say that so long as the action is only for the sake of defense and does not exceed what is strictly needed for defense, one may even use force that is, as a matter of practical certainty, lethal. On this view, for instance, a defender could licitly cut off the head of an attacker. Are all foreseen effects that are necessarily connected with the intended effects also thereby intended? For one answer, see Christopher Kaczor, *Proportionalism and the Natural Law Tradition* (Washington, DC: The Catholic University of America Press, 2002), Chapter Three.

Objection 1. It would seem that nobody may morally kill a man in self-defense. For Augustine says to Publicola (Ep. xlvii): "I do not agree with the opinion that one may kill a man lest one be killed by him, unless one be a soldier, exercise a public office, so that one does it not for one-self but for others, having the power to do so, provided it be in keeping with one's person." Now he who kills a man in self-defense kills him lest he be killed by him. Therefore this would seem to be immoral.

Reply to Objection 1. The words quoted from Augustine refer to the case when one man intends to kill another to save himself from death. The passage quoted in the Second Objection is to be understood in the same sense. Hence he says pointedly, "for the sake of these things," whereby he indicates the intention. This suffices for the Reply to the Second Objection.

Objection 2. Further, he says (*De Lib. Arb.* i, 5): "How are they free from sin in sight of Divine providence, who are guilty of taking a man's life for the sake of these contemptible things?" Now among contemptible things he reckons "those which men may forfeit unwillingly," as appears from the context (*De Lib. Arb.* i, 5): and the chief of these is the life of the body. Therefore it is immoral for any man to take another's life for the sake of the life of his own body.

Objection 4. Further, murder is a more grievous sin than fornication or adultery. Now nobody may morally commit simple fornication or adultery or any other mortal sin in order to save his own life, since the spiritual life is to be preferred to the life of the body. Therefore no man may morally take another's life in self-defense in order to save his own life.

Reply to Objection 4. The act of fornication or adultery is not necessarily directed to the preservation of one's own life, as is the act whence sometimes results the taking of a man's life.[27]

Objection 5. Further, if the tree be evil, so is the fruit, according to Matthew 7:17. Now self-defense itself seems to be immoral, according

---

27 The act of adultery is itself wrong, whereas the act of self-defense is not in itself wrong, nor is self-defense defined by what sometimes follows from the act of self-defense, namely the loss of the attacker's life.

to Romans 12:19: "Not defending yourselves, my dearly beloved." Therefore its result, which is the slaying of a man, is also immoral.

Reply to Objection 5. The defense forbidden in this passage is that which comes from revengeful spite. Hence a gloss says: "Not defending yourselves—that is, not striking your enemy back."

ARTICLE 8 — Is one guilty of murder through killing someone by chance?

No, despite objections to the contrary, Augustine says to Publicola (*Ep.* xlvii): "When we do a thing for a good and lawful purpose, if thereby we unintentionally cause harm to anyone, it should by no means be imputed to us."[28] Now it sometimes happens by chance that a person is killed as a result of something done for a good purpose. Therefore the person who did it is not accounted guilty.

I answer that, According to the Philosopher (*Phys.* ii, 6), "chance is a cause that acts beside one's intention." Hence chance happenings, strictly speaking, are neither intended nor voluntary. And since every sin is voluntary, according to Augustine (*De Vera Relig.* xiv), it follows that chance happenings, as such, are not sins.

Nevertheless, it happens that what is not actually and directly voluntary and intended is voluntary and intended accidentally, according as that which removes an obstacle is called an accidental cause. Therefore he who does not remove something whence homicide results, whereas he ought to remove it, is in a sense guilty of voluntary homicide. This happens in two ways: first, when a man causes another's death through occupying himself with immoral things which he ought to avoid;[29] secondly, when he does not take sufficient care.[30] Hence,

---

[28] Note that this differs from those who kill, though unintentionally, as a result of excessive drinking or drug abuse. In such cases, a "good and lawful purpose" is missing and so the death, though not murder, is still wrongful.

[29] Motorists should avoid driving drunk. Therefore, if a drunk driver kills another on the road by accident, he nevertheless sins since he was engaged in wrongful behavior (drinking and driving) in causing the death.

[30] Again, imagine a motorist who knowingly does not take sufficient care during rainy or snowy road conditions. If an accident happens, the motorist is guilty of wrongdoing because he failed in his duty to take into account the

according to jurists, if a man pursues a lawful occupation and takes due care, the result being that a person loses his life, he is not guilty of that person's death, whereas if he be occupied with something immoral, or even with something lawful, but without due care, he does not escape being guilty of murder, if his action results in someone's death.[31]

Objection 1. It would seem that one is guilty of murder through killing someone by chance. For we read (Gen 4:23, 24) that Lamech slew a man in mistake for a wild beast,[32] and that he was accounted guilty of murder. Therefore one incurs the guilt of murder through killing a man by chance.

Reply to Objection 1. Lamech did not take sufficient care to avoid taking a man's life: and so he was not excused from being guilty of homicide.

Objection 2. Further, it is written (Ex 21:22): "If . . . one strike a woman with child, and she miscarry indeed . . . if her death ensue thereupon, he shall render life for life." Yet this may happen without any intention of causing her death. Therefore one is guilty of murder through killing someone by chance.

Reply to Objection 2. He that strikes a woman with child does something immoral: therefore, if there results the death either of the woman or of the animated fetus, he will not be excused from homicide, especially seeing that death is the natural result of such a blow.[33]

---

condition of the road. If he had driven more carefully, as he should have, no one would have died.

31 In other words, it is immoral to endanger others, to put their lives in substantial risk of being lost, without a serious reason.

32 The Dominican translators note: "The text of the Bible does not say so, but this was the Jewish traditional commentary on Gn 4:23."

33 Although Thomas held that both contraception and abortion were morally wrong, he held the belief of what later became known as "delayed ensoulment" or "delayed hominization," a theory according to which the human fetus was not fully a human being until many weeks following conception. For more on the faulty understanding of biology on which Thomas's view was based, see the note in the body of question 64, article 1 above.

QUESTION 65

INJURIES COMMITTED AGAINST A PERSON

ARTICLE 3 ~~ **Is it moral to imprison a man?**

Yes, despite objections to the contrary, We read in Leviticus 24 that a man was imprisoned for the sin of blasphemy.

I answer that, In bodily goods three things may be considered in due order: first, the substantial integrity of the body, and this is injured by death or maiming; secondly, pleasure or rest of the senses, and to this striking or anything causing a sense of pain is opposed. Thirdly, the movement or use of the members, and this is hindered by binding or imprisoning or any kind of detention.[1]

Therefore it is immoral to imprison or in any way detain a man, unless it be done according to the order of justice,[2] either in punishment, or as a measure of precaution against some evil.

---

[1] Virtually everyone agrees that it is legitimate to imprison criminals, but there is a lively dispute in the contemporary world about capital punishment and the infliction of bodily pain on others as punishment (e.g., caning). Thomas treats each of these three forms of punishment as instances of depriving the criminal of some good of which the criminal is no longer worthy.

[2] Of course, it may be in principle permissible to imprison a criminal and yet still illicit to imprison the person in certain circumstances. Someone who once voluntarily assaulted another person should be imprisoned, but it would not be just to imprison the person for life, in an overly crowded cell, with no chance to exercise. Just punishment does not exceed what is due for the crime.

Objection 1. It would seem immoral to imprison a man. An act which deals with undue matter is evil in its genus, as stated above (I–II, q. 18, a. 2). Now man, having a free-will, is undue matter for imprisonment, which is inconsistent with free-will. Therefore it is immoral to imprison a man.

Reply to Objection 1. A man who abuses the power entrusted to him deserves to lose it, and therefore, when a man by sinning abuses the free use of his members, he becomes a fitting matter for imprisonment.

Objection 2. Further, human justice should be ruled by Divine justice. Now according to Sirach 15:14, "God left man in the hand of his own counsel." Therefore it seems that a man ought not to be coerced by chains or prisons.

Reply to Objection 2. According to the order of His wisdom, God sometimes restrains a sinner from accomplishing a sin, according to Job 5:12: "Who brings to nought the designs of the malignant, so that their hand cannot accomplish what they had begun, while sometimes He allows them to do what they will." In like manner, according to human justice, men are imprisoned, not for every sin but for certain ones.

Objection 3. Further, no man should be forcibly prevented except from doing an evil deed; and any man can morally prevent another from doing this. If, therefore, it were moral to imprison a man, in order to restrain him from evil deeds, it would be moral for anyone to put a man in prison; and this is clearly false. Therefore the same conclusion follows.

Reply to Objection 3. It is moral for anyone to restrain a man for a time from doing some immoral deed there and then: as when a man prevents another from throwing himself over a precipice, or from striking another. But to him alone who has the right of disposing in general of the actions and of the life of another does it belong primarily to imprison or fetter, because by so doing he hinders him from doing not only evil but also good deeds.

VICES CONTRARY TO COMMUTATIVE JUSTICE IN DEEDS

QUESTION 66

THEFT AND JUSTICE

ARTICLE 2 ⁓ **Is private property moral?**

Yes, despite objections to the contrary, Augustine says (*De Haeres.*, haer. 40): "The 'Apostolici' are those who with extreme arrogance have given themselves that name, because they do not admit into their communion persons who are married or possess anything of their own, such as both monks and clerics who in considerable number are to be found in the Catholic Church." Now the reason why these people are heretics is because severing themselves from the Church, they think that those who enjoy the use of the above things, which they themselves lack, have no hope of salvation. Therefore it is erroneous to maintain that it is immoral for a man to possess property.

I answer that, Two things are competent to man in respect of exterior things. One is the power to procure and dispense them, and in this regard it is moral for man to possess property. Moreover, this is necessary to human life for three reasons. First, because every man is more careful to procure what is for himself alone than that which is common to many or to all: since each one would shirk the labor and leave to another that which concerns the community, as happens where there is a great number of servants. Secondly, because human affairs are conducted in more orderly fashion if each man is charged with taking care of some particular thing himself, whereas there would be confusion if everyone had to look after any one thing indeterminately. Thirdly, because a more peaceful state is ensured to man if each one is contented

with his own. Hence it is to be observed that quarrels arise more frequently where there is no division of the things possessed.[1]

The second thing that is competent to man with regard to external
things is their use. In this respect, man ought to possess external things,
not as his own, but as common, so that, to wit, he is ready to communicate them to others in their need.[2] Hence the Apostle says (1 Tim
6:17, 18): "Charge the rich of this world . . . to give easily, to communicate to others," etc.

Objection 1. It would seem immoral for a man to possess a thing as his
own. For whatever is contrary to the natural law is immoral. Now
according to the natural law all things are common property: and the
possession of property is contrary to this community of goods. Therefore
it is immoral for any man to appropriate any external thing to himself.

Reply to Objection 1. Community of goods is ascribed to the natural law, not that the natural law dictates that all things should be possessed in common and that nothing should be possessed as one's own,
but because the division of possessions is not according to the natural
law, but rather arose from human agreement which belongs to positive law,[3] as stated above (q. 57, aa 2, 3). Hence the ownership of possessions is not contrary to the natural law, but an addition thereto
devised by human reason.

---

[1] Catholic social teaching from Leo XIII's *Rerum Novarum* (1891) through John
Paul II's *Centessimus Annus* (1991) has defended the right to private property
against the claim that the state should own all things. In addition to the reasons
given here by Thomas, it is also important to note that private property helps
secure human freedom. Without owning possessions, a person's ability to act
freely is greatly hindered. Indeed, without possessions of any kind, a person can
be reduced to a kind of slavery, where labor is not rewarded or where speaking
against the exercise of state authority is action taken at enormous potential risk.
Of course, private property can also become a kind of idol, where the goal and
meaning of human life is assessed simply in terms of dollars and cents.

[2] Love of neighbor pertains not simply to not harming one's neighbor but also
to aiding one's neighbor. All our talents and abilities, as well as the use of
material goods, are properly ordered to helping our neighbor.

[3] In other words, although private property considered as an institution
accords with the natural law, any given distribution of private property is not
a matter of natural law but positive law and determination. In general, a person has a right to private property, but a person does not have (by natural

Objection 2. Further, Basil,[4] in expounding the words of the rich man quoted above (a. 1, obj. 2), says: "The rich who deem as their own property the common goods they have seized upon are like to those who by going beforehand to the play prevent others from coming, and appropriate to themselves what is intended for common use." Now it would be immoral to prevent others from obtaining possession of common goods. Therefore, it is immoral to appropriate to oneself what belongs to the community.

Reply to Objection 2. A man would not act immorally if by going beforehand to the play he prepared the way for others, but he acts immorally if by so doing he hinders others from going. In like manner, a rich man does not act immorally if he anticipates someone in taking possession of something which at first was common property, and gives others a share, but he sins if he excludes others indiscriminately from using it. Hence Basil says (*Hom. in Luc.* xii, 18): "Why are you rich while another is poor, unless it be that you may have the merit of a good stewardship, and he the reward of patience?"

Objection 3. Further, Ambrose[5] says [*Serm.* lxiv, *de temp.*], and his words are quoted in the Decretals[6] [Dist. xlvii, can. *Sicut hi.*]: "Let no man call his own that which is common property": and by "common"

---

law) a right to *this* piece of land, *that* car, or any *particular* house. Natural law grants a right to private property, but positive law may dictate that what was once the private property of one should become the property of another. If a freeway is being built, what was formerly your house may be given over to public use (eminent domain).

[4] St. Basil the Great (b. ca. A.D. 329, d. A.D. 379) is a distinguished doctor of the Church who fought brilliantly against the heresies of his day, including denials of the Trinity.

[5] St. Ambrose of Milan (b. ca. A.D. 340, d. A.D. 397) was bishop of Milan, author of many influential works, a defender of the full divinity of Christ against the Arian heresy, and as is made clear in Book V of the *Confessions*, a source of consolation to St. Monica and instrumental in the conversion of St. Augustine of Hippo.

[6] A decretal is a papal decision communicated regarding an individual inquiry, normally pertaining to a matter of discipline or question in canon law. Collections of these decisions were collected and commented upon in the Middle Ages.

he means external things, as is clear from the context. Therefore, it seems immoral for a man to appropriate an external thing to himself.

Reply to Objection 3. When Ambrose says: "Let no man call his own that which is common," he is speaking of ownership as regards use. Therefore he adds: "He who spends too much is a robber."

ARTICLE 5 ~~ **Is theft always a sin?**

Yes, despite objections to the contrary, It is written (Ex 20:15): "You shall not steal."

I answer that, If anyone considers what is meant by theft, he will find that it is sinful on two counts: first, because of its opposition to justice, which gives to each one what is his, so that for this reason theft is contrary to justice, through being a taking of what belongs to another; secondly, because of the guile or fraud committed by the thief, by laying hands on another's property secretly and cunningly. Therefore it is evident that every theft is a sin.

Objection 1. It would seem that theft is not always a sin. For no sin is commanded by God, since it is written (Sir 15:21): "He has commanded no man to do wickedly." Yet we find that God commanded theft, for it is written (Ex 12:35, 36): "And the children of Israel did as the Lord had commanded Moses [Vulg.: 'as Moses had commanded'] . . . and they stripped the Egyptians." Therefore theft is not always a sin.

Reply to Objection 1. It is no theft for a man to take another's property either secretly or openly by order of a judge who has commanded him to do so, because it becomes his due by the very fact that it is adjudicated to him by the sentence of the court. Hence still less was it a theft for the Israelites to take away the spoils of the Egyptians at the command of the Lord, Who ordered this to be done on account of the ill-treatment accorded to them by the Egyptians without any cause: therefore it is written significantly (Wis 10:19): "The just took the spoils of the wicked."[7]

---

[7] Along with the "adultery" of Hosea and the command to kill Isaac, the despoiling of the Egyptians [in which God commands the Israelites to take goods from the Egyptians] is a classic case in which God *seemingly* com

Objection 2. Further, if a man finds a thing that is not his and takes it, he seems to commit a theft, for he takes another's property. Yet this seems moral according to natural equity, as the jurists hold. [See *loc. cit.* in *Reply*.] Therefore it seems that theft is not always a sin.

Reply to Objection 2. With regard to a treasure-trove a distinction must be made. For some there are that were never in anyone's possession, for instance precious stones and jewels, found on the seashore, and such the finder is allowed to keep [Dig. I, viii, *De divis. rerum:* Inst. II, i, *De rerum divis.*]. The same applies to treasure hidden underground long since and belonging to no man, except that according to civil law the finder is bound to give half to the owner of the land, if the treasure trove be in the land of another person [Inst. II, i, 39: Cod. X, xv, *De Thesauris*]. Hence in the parable of the Gospel (Mt 13:44) it is said of the finder of the treasure hidden in a field that he bought the field, as though he purposed thus to acquire the right of possessing the whole treasure. On the other hand, the treasure-trove may be nearly in someone's possession: and then if anyone take it with the intention, not of keeping it, but of returning it to the owner who does not look upon such things as unclaimed, he is not guilty of theft. In like manner, if the thing found appears to be unclaimed, and if the finder believes it to be so, although he keep it, he does not commit a theft [Inst. II, i, 47]. In any other case the sin of theft is committed [Dig. XLI, i, *De acquirend, rerum dominio*, 9: Inst. II, i, 48]: therefore Augustine says in a homily (Serm. clxxviii. *De Verb. Apost.*): "If you have found a thing and not returned it, you have stolen it" (Dig. xiv, 5, can. *Si quid invenisti*).

ARTICLE 6 ~~ **Is theft a mortal sin?**

Yes, despite objections to the contrary, No man is condemned by the Divine judgment save for a mortal sin. Yet a man is condemned for theft, according to Zechariah 5:3, "This is the curse that goes forth

---

mands someone to do something wrong. In fact, as Thomas notes above, in q. 104, a. 4, God does not command what is evil.

over the face of the earth; for every thief shall be judged as is there written." Therefore theft is a mortal sin.[8]

I answer that, As stated above, (II–II, q. 59, a. 4; q. 72, a. 5), a mortal sin is one that is contrary to charity as the spiritual life of the soul. Now charity consists principally in the love of God, and secondarily in the love of our neighbor, which is shown in our wishing and doing him well. But theft is a means of doing harm to our neighbor in his belongings; and if men were to rob one another habitually, human society would be undone. Therefore theft, as being opposed to charity, is a mortal sin.

Objection 1. It would seem that theft is not a mortal sin. For it is written (Prov 6:30): "The fault is not so great when a man has stolen." But every mortal sin is a great fault. Therefore theft is not a mortal sin.

Reply to Objection 1. The statement that theft is not a great fault is in view of two cases: first, when a person is led to thieve through necessity. This necessity diminishes or entirely removes sin, as we shall show further on (II–II, q. 66 a. 7). Hence the text continues: "For he steals to fill his hungry soul." Secondly, theft is stated not to be a great fault in comparison with the guilt of adultery, which is punished with death. Hence the text goes on to say of the thief that "if he be taken, he shall restore sevenfold . . . but he that is an adulterer . . . shall destroy his own soul."

Objection 2. Further, mortal sin deserves to be punished with death. But in the Law theft is punished not by death but by indemnity, according to Exodus 12:1, "If any man steal an ox or a sheep . . . he shall restore five oxen for one ox, and four sheep for one sheep." Therefore theft is not a mortal sin.

---

[8] Mortal sin must have serious matter, cf. II–II q. 66, a. 6, ad 3. Theft is wrong because it is opposed to human well-being. In cases of theft where what is stolen is of such little importance that it does not adversely affect the victim's well-being, the theft will not be a mortal sin but rather a venial sin. In some cases, where there is no other way to secure human flourishing, reallocation of property should take place voluntarily, and if it does not, then what would in other cases be "theft" in fact is not wrong at all, as Thomas argues in the next article.

Reply to Objection 2. The punishments of this life are medicinal rather than retributive. For retribution is reserved to the Divine judgment, which is pronounced against sinners "according to the truth" (Rom 2:2). Therefore, according to the judgment of the present life the death punishment is inflicted, not for every mortal sin, but only for such as inflict an irreparable harm, or again for such as contain some horrible deformity. Hence, according to the present judgment the pain of death is not inflicted for theft which does not inflict an irreparable harm, except when it is aggravated by some grave circumstance, as in the case of sacrilege which is the theft of a sacred thing, of peculation, which is theft of common property, as Augustine states (*Tract.* 1, *super Joan.*), and of kidnapping, which is stealing a man, for which the pain of death is inflicted (Ex 21:16).

Objection 3. Further, theft can be committed in small even as in great things. But it seems unreasonable for a man to be punished with eternal death for the theft of a small thing, such as a needle or a quill. Therefore theft is not a mortal sin.

Reply to Objection 3. Reason accounts as nothing that which is little, so that a man does not consider himself injured in very little matters, and the person who takes such things can presume that this is not against the will of the owner. And if a person take such like very little things, he may be proportionately excused from mortal sin. Yet if his intention is to rob and injure his neighbor, there may be a mortal sin even in these very little things, even as there may be through consent in a mere thought.

ARTICLE 7 ～ **Is it moral to steal through stress of need?**[9]

Yes, despite objections to the contrary, In cases of need all things are common property,[10] so that there would seem to be no sin in taking another's property, for need has made it common.

I answer that, Things that are of human right cannot derogate from natural right or Divine right. Now according to the natural order established by Divine Providence, inferior things are ordained for the purpose of succoring man's needs by their means. Therefore, the division and appropriation of things which are based on human law do not preclude the fact that man's needs have to be remedied by means of these very things. Hence whatever certain people have in superabundance is due, by natural law, to the purpose of succoring the poor. For this reason Ambrose [*Loc. cit.,* 2, obj. 3] says, and his words are embodied in the Decretals (Dist. xlvii, can. *Sicut* ii): "It is the hungry man's bread that you withhold, the naked man's cloak that you store away, the money that you bury in the earth is the price of the poor man's ransom and freedom."

Since, however, there are many who are in need, while it is impossible for all to be succored by means of the same thing, each one is entrusted with the stewardship of his own things, so that out of them he may come to the aid of those who are in need. Nevertheless, if the need be so manifest and urgent that it is evident that the present need must be remedied by whatever means be at hand (for instance when a

---

[9] This question was posed in dramatic fashion in *Les Miserables.* Does Jean Valjean, who stole bread to feed his starving family, deserve to be punished? St. Thomas's answer is no. In cases where basic necessities for human survival are lacking, and there is no other way to secure these necessities, taking them from those who have in abundance is not wrongful, for those basic necessities are rightfully theirs as human beings.

[10] Note that Thomas speaks of cases of "need" not cases of "want." At issue here are situations of famine or disaster, where people's lives are at risk for want of basic necessities such as food, shelter, or clothing. Material items that others may desire, but that are not basic necessities, such as DVDs, CDs, or TVs, may not be taken even if desire for these things is great. In addition, such reallocation must be a last resort. One may not take basic necessities if these necessities could be provided through one's own work or through the voluntary assistance of others, be it governmental agencies or private charities.

person is in some imminent danger, and there is no other possible remedy), then it is moral for a man to succor his own need by means of another's property, by taking it either openly or secretly, nor is this properly speaking theft or robbery.

Objection 1. It would seem immoral to steal through stress of need. For penance is not imposed except on one who has sinned. Now it is stated (Extra, *De furtis,* Cap. *Si quis*): "If anyone, through stress of hunger or nakedness, steal food, clothing or beast, he shall do penance for three weeks." Therefore it is not moral to steal through stress of need.

Reply to Objection 1. This decretal considers cases where there is no urgent need.[11]

Objection 2. Further, the Philosopher says (*Ethic.* ii, 6) that "there are some actions whose very name implies wickedness," and among these he reckons theft. Now that which is wicked in itself may not be done for a good end. Therefore a man cannot morally steal in order to remedy a need.

Reply to Objection 2. It is not theft, properly speaking, to take secretly and use another's property in a case of extreme need: because that which he takes for the support of his life becomes his own property by reason of that need.[12]

Objection 3. Further, a man should love his neighbor as himself. Now, according to Augustine (*Contra Mendac.* vii), it is immoral to steal in order to succor one's neighbor by giving him alms. Therefore neither is it moral to steal in order to remedy one's own needs.

---

[11] It is only permissible to take basic necessities from others when there is no other recourse for securing what is needed. In the contemporary Western world, with both private charities as well as governmental agencies providing basic necessities, it is difficult to imagine situations where taking property in the possession of others would be permissible.

[12] It is always wrong to steal, but stealing involves taking that to which one has no right. What Thomas is proposing in this article is that the poor have a right to basic necessities needed to live when no other means are available to secure them. What legally belongs to the rich, morally speaking belongs to the poor in such situations.

Reply to Objection 3. In a case of a like need a man may also take secretly another's property in order to succor his neighbor in need.

QUESTION 70

INJUSTICE WITH REGARD
TO THE PERSON
OF THE WITNESS

ARTICLE 4 ‑‑ **Is it always a mortal sin to give false evidence?**

Yes, despite objections to the contrary, It is written (Prov 19:5): "A false witness shall not be unpunished."

I answer that, False evidence has a threefold deformity.[1] The first is owing to perjury, since witnesses are admitted only on oath and on this count it is always a mortal sin.[2] Secondly, owing to the violation of justice, and on this account it is a mortal sin generically, even as any kind of injustice. Hence the prohibition of false evidence by the precept of the decalogue is expressed in this form when it is said (Ex 20:16), "You shall not bear false witness against your neighbor." For one does nothing against a man by preventing him from doing someone an injury, but only by taking away what is his due.[3] Thirdly, owing to the false-

---

[1] One act can be wrong on multiple counts. An example would be incest with a child. This is wrong because it is a form of extramarital sex, wrong because someone older is taking advantage of someone underage, and wrong because it is a grave violation of the proper relationship between parent and child.

[2] When one takes an oath, one binds oneself to doing (or not doing) that which is promised. What would otherwise be permissible, for instance to marry or to have personal property, becomes impermissible if one has taken an oath not to do so. For more on the importance of oaths, as well as the links between oaths, covenant relationships, and the seven sacraments of the Church, see Scott Hahn, *The Promise and Power of the Sacraments* (New York: Doubleday, 2004).

[3] The administration of criminal justice and the defense and vindication of the innocent (including both those who are falsely accused of a crime as well as

hood itself, by reason of which every lie is a sin: on this account, the giving of false evidence is not always a mortal sin.

Objection 1. It would seem that it is not always a mortal sin to give false evidence. For a person may happen to give false evidence, through ignorance of fact. Now such ignorance excuses from mortal sin. Therefore the giving of false evidence is not always a mortal sin.

Reply to Objection 1. In giving evidence a man ought not to affirm as certain, as though he knew it, that about which he is not certain and he should confess his doubt in doubtful terms, and that which he is certain about, in terms of certainty. Owing, however, to the frailty of the human memory, a man sometimes thinks he is certain about something that is not true; and then if after thinking over the matter with due care he deems himself certain about that false thing, he does not sin mortally if he asserts it, because the evidence which he gives is not directly and intentionally, but accidentally, contrary to what he intends.

Objection 2. Further, a lie that benefits someone and hurts no man is officious, and this is not a mortal sin. Now sometimes a lie of this kind occurs in false evidence, as when a person gives false evidence in order to save a man from death, or from an unjust sentence which threatens him through other false witnesses or a perverse judge. Therefore in such cases it is not a mortal sin to give false evidence.

Reply to Objection 2. An unjust judgment is not a judgment. Therefore the false evidence given in an unjust judgment, in order to prevent injustice, is not a mortal sin by virtue of the judgment, but only by reason of the oath violated.

Objection 3. Further, a witness is required to take an oath in order that he may fear to commit a mortal sin of perjury. But this would not be necessary if it were already a mortal sin to give false evidence. Therefore the giving of false evidence is not always mortal sin.

---

innocent people who have been victimized by someone guilty of a crime) depend upon truthful testimony in court. Hence, to bear false witness against one's neighbor is morally impermissible and seriously wrong.

Reply to Objection 3. Men abhor chiefly those sins that are against God, as being most grievous, and among them is perjury, whereas they do not abhor so much sins against their neighbor. Consequently, for the greater certitude of evidence, the witness is required to take an oath.[4]

---

[4] As Thomas explains elsewhere (II–II, q. 98, a. 3), perjury is the crime of taking a false oath, and this can pertain to the promise to tell the truth or to other kinds of promises in which God is invoked to aid in the task, "so help me God," and called to reward or punish the one taking the oath. For this reason, those taking an oath often put one hand on a Bible and the other towards heaven, symbolically saying, "May the curses in this book be given to me if I lie, and the rewards in this book be given to me if I speak truly." For more on oaths and self-curses as this relates to the sacramental life, see Scott Hahn, *Swear to God: The Promise and Power of the Sacraments* (New York: Doubleday, 2004).

QUESTION 71

INJUSTICE IN JUDGMENT ON THE PART OF COUNSEL

ARTICLE 3 ~ **Does a lawyer sin by defending an unjust cause?**

Yes, despite objections to the contrary, It is said (2 Paralip. 19:2): "You help the ungodly . . . and therefore you did deserve . . . the wrath of the Lord." Now a lawyer, by defending an unjust cause, helps the ungodly. Therefore he sins and deserves the wrath of the Lord.

I answer that, It is immoral to cooperate in an evil deed, by counseling, helping, or in any way consenting, because to counsel or assist an action is, in a way, to do it,[1] and the Apostle says (Rom 1:32) that "they

---

[1] This important point is often spoken of in terms of formal and material cooperation. Formal cooperation is intending to help someone carry out an evil act, such as counseling them in how to do the evil, encouraging them in doing the evil, approving the evil, or otherwise aiding them precisely in their wrongdoing. In formal cooperation the agent makes the evil intention of the person he is helping his own. For example, imagine a man planning a bank robbery who enlists the aid of his sister in helping him get away from the scene of the crime. If his sister agrees to help him pull off the armed heist, she formally cooperates and sins. In material cooperation, on the other hand, help or aid is also given to someone doing evil, but the help or aid is not given with the intention of helping or aiding in wrongdoing. Material cooperation is justifiable for a proportionately serious reason. For example, imagine the storeowner of a hunting shop who sold the gun that was used in the heist, or a cab driver who picks up the robber after the heist (not realizing he is a robber) enabling him to escape police. In the case of both the storeowner and the taxi driver, material cooperation was given but not formal cooperation. Both provide the means without

. . . are worthy of death, not only they that do" a sin, "but they also that consent to them that do" it. Hence it was stated above (q. 62, a. 7), that all such are bound to restitution. Now it is evident that a lawyer provides both assistance and counsel to the party for whom he pleads. Therefore, if knowingly he defends an unjust cause, without doubt he sins grievously, and is bound to restitution of the loss unjustly incurred by the other party by reason of the assistance he has provided. If, however, he defends an unjust cause unknowingly, thinking it just, he is to be excused according to the measure in which ignorance is excusable.

Objection 1. It would seem that a lawyer does not sin by defending an unjust cause. For just as a physician proves his skill by healing a desperate disease, so does a lawyer prove his skill if he can defend an unjust cause. Now a physician is praised if he heals a desperate malady. Therefore a lawyer also commits no sin, but ought to be praised, if he defends an unjust cause.

Reply to Objection 1. The physician injures no man by undertaking to heal a desperate malady, whereas the advocate who accepts service in an unjust cause unjustly injures the party against whom he pleads unjustly. Hence the comparison fails. For though he may seem to deserve praise for showing skill in his art, nevertheless he sins by reason of injustice in his will, since he abuses his art for an evil end.

Objection 2. Further, it is always moral to desist from committing a sin. Yet a lawyer is punished if he throws up his brief (Decret. II, qu. iii, can. *Si quem poenit.*). Therefore a lawyer does not sin by defending an unjust cause, when once he has undertaken its defense.

Reply to Objection 2. If a lawyer believes from the outset that the cause is just, and discovers afterwards while the case is proceeding that it

---

which the theft could not be successfully accomplished, but neither shares in the wrongdoing of the thief. However, in some cases, not even material cooperation may be permissible, as when the evil done by material cooperation is great and the good secured is insignificant. For more on this distinction, see Joseph Boyle, "Collaboration and Integrity: How to Think Clearly about Moral Problems of Cooperation," in *Issues for a Catholic Bioethic*, ed. Luke Gormally (London: Linacre Center, 1999), 187–99.

is unjust, he ought not to throw up his brief in such a way as to help the other side, or so as to reveal the secrets of his client to the other party. But he can and must give up the case, or induce his client to give way, or make some compromise without prejudice to the opposing party.

Objection 3. Further, it would seem to be a greater sin for a lawyer to use unjust means in defense of a just cause (e.g. by producing false witnesses, or alleging false laws) than to defend an unjust cause, since the former is a sin against the form, the latter against the matter of justice. Yet it is seemingly moral for a lawyer to make use of such underhanded means, even as it is moral for a soldier to lay ambushes in a battle. Therefore it would seem that a lawyer does not sin by defending an unjust cause.

Reply to Objection 3. As stated above (q. 40, a. 3), it is moral for a soldier, or a general, to lay ambushes in a just war, by prudently concealing what he has a mind to do, but not by means of fraudulent falsehoods, since we should keep faith even with a foe, as Tully says (*De offic.* iii, 29). Hence it is moral for a lawyer, in defending his case, prudently to conceal whatever might hinder its happy issue, but it is immoral for him to employ any kind of falsehood.[2]

---

[2] This distinction also applies to the conduct of those who are not lawyers. Thomas argues that lying is always wrong (II–II, q. 110, a. 3), but it is not always wrong to withhold information. These two actions are not the same, for in virtually every communication many things are withheld from the other in virtue of the realities of speech (e.g., if we are to talk about politics, we cannot also at the same time talk about how to shoot a basketball). Of course, in some circumstances withholding information, though not lying, strictly speaking, nevertheless is wrong, for instance when the other person has a right to know the truth withheld.

QUESTION *73*

BACKBITING

ARTICLE 2 ~~ **Is it a mortal sin to speak ill of absent persons in order to undermine their reputation?**

Yes, despite objections to the contrary, It is written (Rom 1:30): "Backbiters, hateful to God," which epithet, according to a gloss, is inserted, "lest it be deemed a slight sin because it consists in words."

I answer that, As stated above (q. 72, a. 2), sins of word should be judged chiefly from the intention of the speaker. Now backbiting by its very nature aims at blackening a man's good name. Therefore, properly speaking, to backbite is to speak ill of an absent person in order to blacken his good name. Now it is a very grave matter to blacken a man's good name, because of all temporal things a man's good name seems the most precious, since for lack of it he is hindered from doing many things well. For this reason it is written (Sir 41:15): "Take care of a good name, for this shall continue with you, more than a thousand treasures precious and great." Therefore backbiting, properly speaking, is a mortal sin. Nevertheless it happens sometimes that a man utters words whereby someone's good name is tarnished, and yet he does not intend this, but something else. This is not backbiting strictly and formally speaking, but only materially and accidentally as it were. And if such defamatory words be uttered for the sake of some necessary good, and with attention to the due circumstances, it is not a sin and cannot be called backbiting.[1] But if they be uttered out of lightness of heart or for some unnecessary motive, it is not a mortal sin, unless perchance the spoken word be of such a grave nature as to cause a notable injury to a man's good name, especially in matters pertaining to his moral character, because from the very nature of the words this would be a mortal sin. And one is bound to restore a man his good name, no less than any other thing one has taken from him, in the manner stated above (q. 62, a. 2) when we were treating of restitution.[2]

Objection 1. It would seem that backbiting is not a mortal sin. For no act of virtue is a mortal sin. Now, to reveal an unknown sin, which pertains to backbiting, as stated above (a. 1, ad 3), is an act of the

---

[1] For example, revealing that another is committing child abuse is something that may undermine the abuser's reputation, yet is obligatory in order to secure the well-being of the child.

[2] Fr. Richard John Neuhaus illustrates nicely the near impossibility of making restitution for harming someone's good name: "The story is told of St. Philip Neri (1515–95) that he gave a most unusual penance to a novice who was guilty of spreading malicious gossip. He told him to take a feather pillow to the top of a church tower on a blustery day and there release all the feathers to the wind. Then he was to come down from the tower, collect all the feathers dispersed over the far countryside, and put them back into the pillow. Of course the poor novice couldn't do it, and that was precisely Philip's point about the great evil of tale bearing. Slander and calumny have a way of spreading to the four winds and, once released, can never be completely recalled. Even when accusations are firmly nailed as false, the reputations of those falsely accused bear a lingering taint. "Oh yes," it is vaguely said, "wasn't he once accused of. . . ."

The words of the Bard that you learned in grade school are entirely to the point:

Who steals my purse steals trash; 'tis something,
  nothing;
'Twas mine, 'tis his, and has been slave to
  thousands;
But he that filches from me my good name
Robs me of that which not enriches him,
And makes me poor indeed.

Richard John Neuhaus, "Naked Public Square," *First Things* (March 2002), www.firstthings.com/ftissues/ft0203/public.html#feathers.

virtue of charity, whereby a man denounces his brother's sin in order that he may amend; or else it is an act of justice, whereby a man accuses his brother. Therefore backbiting is not a mortal sin.

Reply to Objection 1. As stated above, it is not backbiting to reveal a man's hidden sin in order that he may mend, whether one denounce it, or accuse him for the good of public justice.

Objection 2. Further, a gloss on Proverbs 24:21, "Have nothing to do with detractors," says: "The whole human race is in peril from this vice." But no mortal sin is to be found in the whole of mankind, since many refrain from mortal sin, whereas they are venial sins that are found in all. Therefore backbiting is a venial sin.

Reply to Objection 2. This gloss does not assert that backbiting is to be found throughout the whole of mankind, but "almost," both because "the number of fools is infinite" [Eccles 1:15], and few are they that walk in the way of salvation [Cf. Mt 7:14], and because there are few or none at all who do not at times speak from lightness of heart, so as to injure someone's good name at least slightly, for it is written (Jas 3:2): "If any man offend not in word, the same is a perfect man."

Objection 3. Further, Augustine in a homily *On the Fire of Purgatory* [*Serm.* civ in the appendix to St. Augustine's work] reckons it a slight sin "to speak ill without hesitation or forethought." But this pertains to backbiting. Therefore backbiting is a venial sin.

Reply to Objection 3. Augustine is referring to the case when a man utters a slight evil about someone, not intending to injure him, but through lightness of heart or a slip of the tongue.

VICES CONTRARY TO COMMUTATIVE JUSTICE IN ECONOMIC MATTERS

QUESTION 78

USURY

ARTICLE 1 ⟿ **Is it a sin to take usury for money lent?**[1]

Yes, despite objections to the contrary, It is written (Ex 22:25): "If you lend money to any of your people who are poor, that dwells with you, you shall not be hard upon them as an extortioner, nor oppress them with usuries."

I answer that, To take usury for money lent is unjust in itself, because this is to sell what does not exist, and this evidently leads to inequality, which is contrary to justice. In order to make this evident, we must observe that there are certain things the use of which consists in their consumption: thus we consume wine when we use it for drink, and we consume wheat when we use it for food. Therefore in such like things the use of the thing must not be reckoned apart from the thing itself, and whoever is granted the use of the thing is granted the thing itself, and for this reason, to lend things of this kind is to transfer the ownership. Accordingly, if a man wanted to sell wine separately from the use of the wine, he would be selling the same thing twice, or he would be selling what does not exist; therefore he would evidently commit a sin of injustice. In like manner, he commits an injustice who lends wine or wheat, and asks for double payment, viz. one, the

---

[1] This article is important in part because it illustrates a development of doctrine in Catholic teaching since Aquinas. Other examples of such development include issues of religious liberty and slavery.

return of the thing in equal measure, the other, the price of the use, which is called usury.[2]

On the other hand, there are things the use of which does not consist in their consumption: thus to use a house is to dwell in it, not to destroy it. Therefore in such things both may be granted: for instance, one man may hand over to another the ownership of his house while reserving to himself the use of it for a time, or vice versa, he may grant the use of the house, while retaining the ownership. For this reason a man may lawfully make a charge for the use of his house, and, besides this, reclaim the house from the person to whom he has granted its use, as happens in renting and letting a house.

Now money, according to the Philosopher (*Ethic.* v, 5; *Polit.* i, 3), was invented chiefly for the purpose of exchange: and consequently the proper and principal use of money is its consumption or alienation whereby it is sunk in exchange. Hence it is by its very nature immoral to take payment for the use of money lent, which payment is known as

---

[2] Thomas draws a distinction between the use of a thing and the thing in itself. Some items one can use without the item being destroyed in its very use; for instance a house can be rented out and returned in good condition. On the other hand, the use of other things, like, say, the eating of an apple, destroys the very thing used. Thus, you could not rent the eating of an apple, but only sell it, and in selling it the transaction would be complete. Since money, on this model, is a thing consumed in its use, to charge a person interest on a loan is to demand payment for selling the money (principal) and another payment for renting the money (interest). As Finnis notes in his book *Aquinas*: "To make any further charge in respect of the loan of money is unjust, and the name for this sort of charge—this sort of wrong—is usury. . . . For (as we saw) in making a loan of this sort I willy-nilly transfer ownership (and thus the risks of loss) along with use. The two cannot be separated; to transfer the one is to transfer the other, and to use a thing of this sort is to 'consume' it, i.e., to lose both possession and ownership of it, either by transfer to someone else (in the case of money as such) or by destruction of the thing 'lent' (as in the case of bread or wine)." John Finnis, *Aquinas* (Cambridge: Cambridge University Press, 1996), 205–6. Justice in exchange can be understood as an equality between what is given on both sides of the exchange. So if someone lends amount X, then in justice the borrower must repay amount X, no more and no less. To demand more is to be unjust.

usury, and just as a man is bound to restore other ill-gotten goods, so is he bound to restore the money which he has taken in usury.[3]

Objection 1. It would seem that it is not a sin to take usury for money lent. For no man sins through following the example of Christ. But Our Lord said of Himself (Lk 19:23): "At My coming I might have exacted it," i.e., the money lent, "with usury." Therefore it is not a sin to take usury for lending money.

Reply to Objection 1. In this passage usury must be taken figuratively for the increase of spiritual goods which God exacts from us, for

---

[3] Aquinas's conclusions about lending at interest were adequate given the financial assumptions and market conditions of his time, but must be adjusted to account for contemporary circumstances. In a similar way, in medieval times, to remove the heart of someone would be the same as to kill him; but today to remove someone's heart may be part of a heart transplant operation. For us today, to cut off someone's head is nothing other than an act of killing; but it is at least possible that someday such separation would not be always fatal. Murder is always wrong, but which kinds of acts are actually the same as killing an innocent person varies with circumstances. Similarly usury is always wrong, but what counts as usury depends upon circumstances, and contemporary developments indicate that not all lending at interest counts as usury.

Although there has been development in determining what constitutes usury, there has been no contradiction or radical rejection of previous teachings on the subject in the Catholic tradition. As John T. Noonan, Jr. points out: "[A]s far as dogma in the technical Catholic sense is concerned, there is only one dogma at stake. Dogma is not to be loosely used as synonymous with every papal rule or theological verdict. Dogma is a defined, revealed doctrine taught by the Church at all times and places. Nothing here meets the test of dogma except this assertion, that usury, the act of taking profit on a loan without a just title, is sinful. Even this dogma is not specifically, formally defined by any pope or council. It is, however, taught by the tradition of the Church, as witnessed by papal bulls and briefs, conciliar acts, and theological opinion. This dogmatic teaching remains unchanged. What is a just title, what is technically to be treated as a loan, are matters of debate, positive law, and changing evolution. The development of these points is great. But the pure and narrow dogma is the same today as in 1200." John Noonan, *The Scholastic Analysis of Usury* (Cambridge: Harvard University Press, 1957), 399–400. Put another way, the Church maintains that usury is wrong, but does not hold and never did hold that all charging whatsoever of amounts beyond the principal is wrong.

He wishes us ever to advance in the goods which we receive from Him: and this is for our own profit, not for His.

Objection 2. Further, according to Psalm 18:8, "The law of the Lord is unspotted," because, to wit, it forbids sin. Now usury of a kind is allowed in the Divine law, according to Deuteronomy 23:19, 20: "You shall not fenerate [lend on interest] to your brother money, nor corn, nor any other thing, but to the stranger;" nay more, it is even promised as a reward for the observance of the Law, according to Deuteronomy 28:12: "You shall fenerate to many nations, and shalt not borrow of any one." Therefore it is not a sin to take usury.

Reply to Objection 2. The Jews were forbidden to take usury from their brethren, i.e., from other Jews. By this we are given to understand that to take usury from any man is evil simply, because we ought to treat every man as our neighbor and brother, especially in the state of the Gospel, whereto all are called. Hence it is said without any distinction in Psalm 14:5: "He that has not put out his money to usury," and (Ezek 18:8): "Who has not taken usury [Vulg.: 'If a man . . . has not lent upon money, nor taken any increase . . . he is just']." They were permitted, however, to take usury from foreigners, not as though it were moral, but in order to avoid a greater evil, lest, to wit, through greed to which they were prone according to Isaiah 56:11, they should take usury from the Jews who were worshippers of God.

Where we find it promised to them as a reward, "You shall fenerate to many nations," etc., fenerating is to be taken in a broad sense for lending, as in Sirach 29:10, where we read: "Many have refused to fenerate, not out of wickedness," i.e., they would not lend. Accordingly the Jews are promised in reward an abundance of wealth, so that they would be able to lend to others.

Objection 3. Further, in human affairs justice is determined by civil laws. Now civil law allows usury to be taken. Therefore it seems to be moral.

Reply to Objection 3. Human laws leave certain things unpunished, on account of the condition of those who are imperfect, and who would be deprived of many advantages, if all sins were strictly forbidden and punishments appointed for them. Therefore human law has permitted usury, not that it looks upon usury as harmonizing with justice, but lest the advantage of many should be hindered. Hence it is that in civil law [Inst. II, iv, *de Usufructu*] it is stated that "those things according to natural reason and civil law which are consumed by being used do not admit of usufruct,"[4] and that "the senate did not (nor could it) appoint a usufruct to such things, but established a quasi-usufruct," namely by permitting usury. Moreover, the Philosopher, led by natural reason, says (*Polit.* i, 3) that "to make money by usury is exceedingly unnatural."

---

[4] Usufruct is the legal right to make use of or benefit from what belongs to another.

QUESTION *79*

THE QUASI-INTEGRAL
PARTS OF JUSTICE

ARTICLE 3 ~ **Is omission a special sin?**

Yes, despite objections to the contrary, It is written (Jas 4:17): "To him . . . who knows to do good and does it not, to him it is sin."

I answer that, Omission signifies the non-fulfillment of a good, not indeed of any good, but of a good that is due. Now good under the aspect of due belongs properly to justice: to legal justice, if the thing due depends on Divine or human law; to special justice, if the thing due is something in relation to one's neighbor. Therefore, in the same way as justice is a special virtue, as stated above (q. 58, aa 6, 7), omission is a special sin distinct from the sins which are opposed to the other virtues; and just as doing good, which is the opposite of omitting it, is a special part of justice, distinct from avoiding evil, to which transgression is opposed, so too is omission distinct from transgression.[1]

Objection 1. It would seem that omission is not a special sin. For every sin is either original or actual. Now omission is not original sin, for it is not contracted through origin, nor is it actual sin, for it may be altogether without act, as stated above (I–II, q. 71, a. 5) when we were treating of sins in general. Therefore omission is not a special sin.

---

[1] Hence, in the penitential rite of the Mass a believer prays: "I confess to Almighty God and to you my brothers and sisters that I have sinned through my own fault, in my thoughts and in my words, in what I have done and in *what I have failed to do.*"

Reply to Objection 1. Omission is not original but actual sin, not as though it had some act essential to it, but for as much as the negation of an act is reduced to the genus of act, and in this sense non-action is a kind of action, as stated above (I–II, q. 71, a. 6, ad 1).

Objection 3. Further, it is possible to fix the time when any special sin begins. But this is not possible in the case of omission, since one is not altered by not doing a thing, no matter when the omission occurs, and yet the omission is not always sinful. Therefore omission is not a special sin.

Reply to Objection 3. Just as the sin of transgression is opposed to negative precepts which regard the avoidance of evil, so the sin of omission is opposed to affirmative precepts, which regard the doing of good. Now affirmative precepts bind not for always, but for a fixed time, and at that time the sin of omission begins. But it may happen that then one is unable to do what one ought, and if this inability is without any fault on his part, he does not omit his duty, as stated above (ad 2; I–II, q. 71, a. 5). On the other hand, if this inability is due to some previous fault of his (for instance, if a man gets drunk at night, and cannot get up for matins,[2] as he ought to), some say that the sin of omission begins when he engages in an action that is illicit and incompatible with the act to which he is bound. But this does not seem to be true, for supposing one were to rouse him by violence and that he went to matins, he would not omit to go, so that, evidently, the previous drunkenness was not an omission, but the cause of an omission.

Consequently, we must say that the omission begins to be imputed to him as a sin when the time comes for the action; and yet this is on account of a preceding cause by reason of which the subsequent omission becomes voluntary.

Objection 4. Further, every special sin is opposed to a special virtue. But it is not possible to assign any special virtue to which omission is opposed, both because the good of any virtue can be omitted, and because justice to which it would seem more particularly opposed,

---

[2] The first of seven periods of prayer each day, matins was traditionally observed by monks and nuns at midnight, 2:00 a.m, or sunrise.

always requires an act, even in declining from evil, as stated above (a. 1, ad 2), while omission may be altogether without act. Therefore omission is not a special sin.

Reply to Objection 4. Omission is directly opposed to justice, as stated above, because it is a non-fulfillment of a good of virtue, but only under the aspect of due, which pertains to justice. Now more is required for an act to be virtuous and meritorious than for it to be sinful and demeritorious, because "good results from an entire cause, whereas evil arises from each single defect" [Dionysius, *De Div. Nom.* iv].[3] Therefore the merit of justice requires an act, whereas an omission does not.

ARTICLE 4 ﹏ **Is a sin of omission worse than a sin of commission?**

No, despite objections to the contrary, It is easier to refrain from evil deeds than to accomplish good deeds. Therefore it is a graver sin not to refrain from an evil deed, i.e., "to transgress," than not to accomplish a good deed, which is "to omit."

I answer that, The gravity of a sin depends on its remoteness from virtue. Now contrariety is the greatest remoteness, according to the *Metaphysics.* Therefore a thing is further removed from its contrary than from its simple negation; thus black is further removed from white than not-white is, since every black is not-white, but not conversely.[4] Now it is evident that transgression is contrary to an act of virtue, while omission denotes the negation thereof: for instance it is a sin of omission, if

---

[3] Throughout the Middle Ages, Dionysius was believed to be an author of ancient authority, a member of court who was converted to Christianity by St. Paul (Acts 17: 34). In fact, the author of the often-cited work *On the Divine Names* wrote no earlier than the second half of the fifth century, as is clear from the evident influence of later neo-Platonic philosophers on his thought. During the Renaissance, doubts began to be expressed about the apostolic origins of Dionysius but not all were convinced until the end of the nineteenth century, at which point the author of *On the Divine Names,* the *Celestial Hierarchies,* and other works became known as *Pseudo-*Dionysius.

[4] Non-white is a negation of white; but black is a contrary of white. Thomas's point here is that black is as far removed from white as possible, whereas non-white may be, for example, grey and thus not as far removed from being white as black is. In this context, not to perform an act of virtue (a negation) is not as bad, other things being equal, as to perform an act of vice (a contrary).

one fail to give one's parents due reverence, while it is a sin of transgression to revile them or injure them in any way. Hence it is evident that, simply and absolutely speaking, transgression is a graver sin than omission, although a particular omission may be graver than a particular transgression.

Objection 2. Further, the greater evil is opposed to the greater good, as the Philosopher declares (*Ethic.* viii, 10). Now to do good is a more excellent part of justice than to decline from evil, to which transgression is opposed, as stated above (a. 1, ad 3). Therefore omission is a graver sin than transgression.

Reply to Objection 2. The opposite of "doing good" is both "not doing good," which is an omission, and "doing evil," which is a transgression: but the first is opposed by contradiction, the second by contrariety, which implies greater remoteness. Therefore transgression is the more grievous sin.

Objection 3. Further, sins of transgression may be either venial or mortal. But sins of omission seem to be always mortal, since they are opposed to an affirmative precept. Therefore omission would seem to be a graver sin than transgression.

Reply to Objection 3. Just as omission is opposed to affirmative precepts, so is transgression opposed to negative precepts: therefore both, strictly speaking, have the character of mortal sin. Transgression and omission, however, may be taken broadly for any infringement of an affirmative or negative precept, disposing to the opposite of such precept: and so taking both in a broad sense they may be venial sins.

JUSTICE TOWARD GOD: THE VIRTUE OF RELIGION

QUESTION 81

~~~~~~~~~~~

RELIGION

ARTICLE 1 ~~ **Does religion direct man to God alone?**

Yes, despite objections to the contrary, I answer that, As Isidore says (*Etym.* x), "according to Cicero, a man is said to be religious from 'religio,' because he often ponders over, and, as it were, reads again [*relegit*] the things which pertain to the worship of God," so that religion would seem to take its name from reading over those things which belong to Divine worship because we ought frequently to ponder over such things in our hearts, according to Proverbs 3:6, "In all thy ways think on Him". According to Augustine (*De Civ. Dei* x. 3) it may also take its name from the fact that "we ought to seek God again, whom we lost by our neglect." Or again, religion may be derived from "religare" (to bind together), wherefore Augustine says (*De Vera Relig.* 55): "May religion bind us to the one Almighty God." However, whether religion takes its name from frequent reading, or from a repeated choice of what has been lost through negligence, or from a bond, it denotes properly a relation to God. For it is He to Whom we ought to be bound as to our unfailing principle, to Whom also our choice should be resolutely directed as to our last end, and Whom we lose when we neglect Him by sin, and should recover by believing in Him and confessing our faith.

ARTICLE 2 ~~ **Is religion a virtue?**

Yes, despite objections to the contrary, I answer that, As stated above, (q. 58, a. 3; I–II, q. 55, aa 3, 4) "a virtue is that which makes its possessor good, and his act good likewise," wherefore we must needs say that every good act belongs to a virtue. Now it is evident that to render anyone his due has the aspect of good, since by rendering a person his due, one becomes suitably proportioned to him, through being ordered to him in a becoming manner. But order comes under the aspect of good, just as mode and species, according to Augustine (*De Nat. Boni* iii). Since, then, it belongs to religion to pay due honor to someone, namely, to God, it is evident that religion is a virtue.

ARTICLE 3 ❦ Is religion one virtue?

Yes, despite objections to the contrary, I answer that, As stated above (I–II, q. 54, a. 2, ad 1), habits are differentiated according to a different aspect of the object. Now it belongs to religion to show reverence to one God under one aspect, namely, as the first principle of creation and government of things. Therefore He Himself says (Mal 1:6) "If . . . I be a father, where is My honor?" For it belongs to a father to beget and to govern. Therefore, it is evident that religion is one virtue.

ARTICLE 4 ❦ Is religion a special virtue, distinct from the others?

Yes, despite objections to the contrary, I answer that, Since virtue is directed to the good, wherever there is a special aspect of good there must be a special virtue. Now the good to which religion is directed is to give due honor to God. Again, honor is due to someone under the aspect of excellence; and to God a singular excellence is competent since He infinitely surpasses all things and exceeds them in every way. Therefore, to Him is special honor due: even as in human affairs we see that different honor is due different personal excellences, one kind to a father, another to the king, and so on. Hence it is evident that religion is a special virtue.

ARTICLE 5 ❦ Is religion a theological virtue?

No, despite objections to the contrary, It is reckoned a part of justice, which is a moral virtue.

I answer that, As stated above (a. 4), religion pays due worship to God.[1] Hence two things are to be considered in religion: first, that which

---

[1] As Thomas notes in q. 81, a. 1, religion "denotes properly a relation to God. For it is He to Whom we ought to be bound as to our unfailing principle, to

it offers to God, viz. worship, and this is by way of matter and object in religion; secondly, that to which something is offered, viz. God, to Whom worship is paid. And yet the acts whereby God is worshiped do not reach out to God Himself, as when we believe God we reach out to Him by believing, for which reason it was stated (q. 1, aa 1, 2, 4) that God is the object of faith, not only because we believe that there is a God (*credimus Deum*), but because we believe God (*credimus Deo*).[2]

Now due worship is paid to God, in so far as certain acts whereby God is worshiped, such as the offering of sacrifices and so forth, are done out of reverence for God. Hence it is evident that God is related to religion not as matter or object, but as end: and consequently religion is not a theological virtue whose object is the last end, but a moral virtue which is properly about things referred to the end.[3]

Objection 1. It would seem that religion is a theological virtue. Augustine says (*Enchiridion* iii) that "God is worshiped by faith, hope and charity," which are theological virtues. Now it belongs to religion to pay worship to God. Therefore religion is a theological virtue.

Reply to Objection 1. The power or virtue whose action deals with an end moves by its command the power or virtue whose action deals with matters directed to that end. Now the theological virtues, faith, hope, and charity, have an act in reference to God as their proper object: therefore, by their command, they cause the act of religion, which performs certain deeds directed to God: and so Augustine says that God is worshiped by faith, hope, and charity.

Whom also our choice should be resolutely directed as to our last end, and Whom we lose when we neglect Him by sin, and should recover by believing in Him and confessing our faith."

[2] We may believe that there is a God (*credimus Deum*), but fail to place our trust in God (*credimus Deo*). But we believe God (*credere Deo*) in so far as we hold fast to God as reliable, trustworthy, and unfailing. A deist believes that there is a God (*credimus Deum*), but believes that this God is totally separated and unconcerned with earthly affairs and so does not trust in God (*credere Deo*) that God will provide, love, nurture, and forgive human beings. This important distinction, originally from St. Augustine of Hippo, is explored earlier in the *Summa* by Thomas in II–II, q. 2, a. 2.

[3] Religion therefore is not God, but rather a "binding" of human beings to God.

Objection 3. Further, every virtue is either theological, or intellectual, or moral, as is clear from what has been said (I–II, qq. 57, 58, 62). Now it is evident that religion is not an intellectual virtue, because its perfection does not depend on the consideration of truth; nor is it a moral virtue, which consists properly in observing the mean between too much and too little. For one cannot worship God too much, according to Sirach 43:33, "Blessing the Lord, exalt Him as much as you can; for He is above all praise." Therefore it remains that it is a theological virtue.

Reply to Objection 3. Religion is neither a theological nor an intellectual, but a moral virtue, since it is a part of justice, and observes a mean, not in the passions, but in actions directed to God, by establishing a kind of equality in them. And when I say "equality," I do not mean absolute equality, because it is not possible to pay God as much as we owe Him, but equality in consideration of man's ability and God's acceptance.

And it is possible to have too much in matters pertaining to the Divine worship, not as regards the circumstance of quantity, but as regards other circumstances, as when Divine worship is paid to whom it is not due, or when it is not due, or unduly in respect of some other circumstance.[4]

ARTICLE 6 ⸱⸱ Should religion be preferred to the other moral virtues?

Yes, despite objections to the contrary, The precepts pertaining to religion are given precedence (Ex 20) as being of greatest importance. Now the order of precepts is proportionate to the order of virtues,[5] since the

---

[4] So although God is the best and most worthy of our time and attention, there are circumstances when we should focus our immediate attention on other things, even though even at these times God can remain our final end and the ultimate reason we do whatever we do. Nevertheless, acts of this virtue excel acts of other virtues, other things being equal, as Thomas makes clear in the next article.

[5] The precepts of which Thomas speaks, namely the Ten Commandments, are ordered from most important (no gods before me) to least important (not coveting the neighbor's goods).

precepts of the Law prescribe acts of virtue. Therefore religion is the chief of the moral virtues.[6]

I answer that, Whatever is directed to an end takes its goodness from being ordered to that end, so that the nearer it is to the end the better it is. Now moral virtues, as stated above (a. 5; q. 4, a. 7), are about matters that are ordered to God as their end. And religion approaches nearer to God than the other moral virtues, in so far as its actions are directly and immediately ordered to the honor of God. Hence religion excels among the moral virtues.

Objection 1. It would seem that religion should not be preferred to the other moral virtues. The perfection of a moral virtue consists in its observing the mean, as stated in *Ethic.* ii, 6. But religion fails to observe the mean of justice, since it does not render an absolute equal to God. Therefore religion is not more excellent than the other moral virtues.

Reply to Objection 1. Virtue is praised because of the will, not because of the ability: and therefore, if a man fall short of equality, which is the mean of justice, through lack of ability, his virtue deserves no less praise, provided there be no failing on the part of his will.

Objection 2. Further, what is offered by one man to another is the more praiseworthy, according as the person it is offered to is in greater need. Therefore it is written (Is 57:7): "Deal your bread to the hungry." But God needs nothing that we can offer Him, according to Psalm 15:2, "I have said: You are my God, for You have no need of my goods." Therefore religion would seem less praiseworthy than the other virtues whereby man's needs are relieved.

---

6 In his reply to the first objection in article 1, St. Thomas states that religion has two kinds of acts: first, those that are its proper and immediate acts, by which we are directed to God alone, for instance, sacrifice, adoration, and the like. But second, religion has other acts that are means to the honor of God as their end, acts such as charitable works toward the neighbor, like visiting the fatherless, and taking care of widows, and proper care of oneself in keeping oneself uncontaminated by the world. Truly "religious" people are virtuous in their practice of religion in both these kinds of acts. The law of love given by Christ is to love God with all our heart, soul, mind, and strength, and to love our neighbor as we love ourselves for God's sake.

Reply to Objection 2. In offering a thing to a man on account of its usefulness to him, the more needy the man the more praiseworthy the offering, because it is more useful, whereas we offer a thing to God not on account of its usefulness to Him, but for the sake of His glory, and on account of its usefulness to us.[7]

Objection 3. Further, the greater the obligation to do a thing, the less praise does it deserve, according to 1 Corinthians 9:16, "If I preach the Gospel, it is no glory to me: a necessity lies upon me." Now the more a thing is due, the greater the obligation of paying it. Since, then, what is paid to God by man is in the highest degree due to Him, it would seem that religion is less praiseworthy than the other human virtues.

Reply to Objection 3. Where there is an obligation to do a thing it loses the luster of supererogation, but not the merit of virtue, provided it be done voluntarily. Hence the argument proves nothing.

---

[7] Our worship of God helps and aids us. Since God is perfect in Himself, God has no need for our worship. Yet our very being and our worship are among God's gifts to us. In worshiping God we perfect ourselves by doing what we were created to do. Just as a pen is good through its functioning as an instrument of writing, and a car is good through functioning as a mode of transportation, our specific function is the proper use of reason and will. The most exalted way to use our reason and will is in connection with the most noble object we could know or love, namely God. Prayer and worship are raising our minds and hearts (intellect and will) to God, and so fulfilling of our purpose. As Thomas says in the next article, "We pay God honor and reverence, not for His sake (because He is of Himself full of glory, to which no creature can add anything), but for our own sake, because by the very fact that we revere and honor God, our mind is subjected to Him, wherein its perfection consists, since a thing is perfected by being subjected to its superior."

PRAYER

ARTICLE 2 — **Does it make sense to pray?**

Yes, despite objections to the contrary, It is written (Lk 18:1): "We ought always to pray, and not to faint."

I answer that, Among the ancients there was a threefold error concerning prayer. Some held that human affairs are not ruled by Divine providence, whence it would follow that it is useless to pray and to worship God at all: of these it is written (Mal 3:14): "You have said: He labors in vain that serves God." Another opinion held that all things, even in human affairs, happen of necessity, whether by reason of the unchangeableness of Divine providence, or through the compelling influence of the stars, or on account of the connection of causes: and this opinion also excluded the utility of prayer. There was a third opinion of those who held that human affairs are indeed ruled by Divine providence, and that they do not happen of necessity; yet they deemed the disposition of Divine providence to be changeable, and that it is changed by prayers and other things pertaining to the worship of God. All these opinions were disproved in the first part (q. 19, aa 7, 8; q. 22, aa 2, 4; q. 115, a. 6; q. 116).[1] Therefore it behooves us so to

---

[1] In the very beginning of the *Summa*, in the famous "five ways" to prove that God exists, Thomas argues that God is unmoved mover, uncaused cause, and pure actuality. Since God is pure actuality, there is no potentiality whatsoever in God. So prayers do not and cannot "change" God's mind, "moving" God from potentially fulfilling a prayer to actually fulfilling the prayer, since from

account for the utility of prayer as neither to impose necessity on human affairs subject to Divine providence, nor to imply changeableness on the part of the Divine disposition.

In order to throw light on this question, we must consider that Divine providence disposes not only what effects shall take place, but also from what causes and in what order these effects shall proceed. Now among other causes human acts are the causes of certain effects. Therefore it must be that men do certain actions not that thereby they may change the Divine disposition, but that by those actions they may achieve certain effects according to the order of the Divine disposition; and the same is to be said of natural causes. And so is it with regard to prayer.[2] For we pray not that we may change the Divine disposition, but that we may obtain by request that which God has disposed to be fulfilled by our prayers, in other words, "that by asking, men may deserve to receive what Almighty God from eternity has disposed to give," as Gregory says (*Dial.* i, 8).[3]

Objection 1. It would seem that it is unbecoming to pray. Prayer seems to be necessary in order that we may make our needs known to

---

all eternity God enjoys perfectly every perfection. If God had potentiality, then He would not be the "fullness of being."

[2] God causes some things directly, for example miracles. However, God often works through secondary causes or intermediaries. In the natural order, God works through secondary causes, such as the care given by parents in securing the well-being of children. Similarly, God can work through the secondary cause of prayer, a human act, in securing human well-being. He deems that some things be accomplished through physical activity (making a bed), other things through mental activity (finding the solution to a physics problem), and still other things through prayers (of petition).

[3] Children sometimes have difficulties learning to ask for things in a mannerly way. Parents, therefore, often resolve to give their children something on the condition that they ask nicely: "Say please." In saying please, the child does not change the parent's mind, for she remains before and after resolved to give the child something if he says please. Likewise, God does not change His mind when we ask Him for something in prayer. Rather, from all eternity, He has resolved to act in history provided that we petition him in prayer. Just as the mother works to better the child through making him use good manners in making requests, so too God intends our perfection through prompting us to commune with Him in prayers of petition.

the person to whom we pray. But according to Matthew 6:32, "Your Father knoweth that you have need of all these things." Therefore it is not becoming to pray to God.

Reply to Objection 1. We need to pray to God, not in order to make known to Him our needs or desires but that we ourselves may be reminded of the necessity of having recourse to God's help in these matters.

Objection 2. Further, by prayer we bend the mind of the person to whom we pray, so that he may do what is asked of him. But God's mind is unchangeable and inflexible, according to 1 Kings 15:29, "But the Triumpher in Israel will not spare, and will not be moved to repentance." Therefore it is not fitting that we should pray to God.

Reply to Objection 2. As stated above, our motive in praying is not that we may change the Divine disposition, but that, by our prayers, we may obtain what God has appointed.

Objection 3. Further, it is more liberal to give to one who asks not, than to one who asks because, according to Seneca (*De Beneficiis* ii, 1), "nothing is bought more dearly than what is bought with prayers." But God is supremely liberal. Therefore it would seem unbecoming to pray to God.

Reply to Objection 3. God bestows many things on us out of His liberality, even without our asking for them; but that He wishes to bestow certain things on us at our asking, is for the sake of our good, namely, that we may acquire confidence in having recourse to God, and that we may recognize in Him the Author of our goods. Hence Chrysostom says [Implicitly (*Hom. ii, de Orat.: Hom. xxx in Genes.*); Cf. *Caten. Aur.* on Luke 18]: "Think what happiness is granted you, what honor bestowed on you, when you converse with God in prayer, when you talk with Christ, when you ask what you will, whatever you desire."

ARTICLE 3 ⁓ **Is prayer an act of religion?**

Yes, despite objections to the contrary, I answer that, As stated above (q. 81, aa 2, 4), it belongs to religion to show honor to God, therefore all those things through which reverence is shown to God belong to religion. Now human beings show reverence to God by means of prayer, in so far as they subject themselves to Him, and by praying confess that they need Him as the Author of their goods. Hence it is evident that prayer is properly an act of religion.

ARTICLE 4 ～ Should we pray to God alone?

No, despite objections to the contrary, It is written (Job 5:1), "Call . . . if there be any that will answer you, and turn to some of the saints."

I answer that, Prayer is offered to a person in two ways: first, as to be fulfilled by him; secondly, as to be obtained through him. In the first way we offer prayer to God alone, since all our prayers ought to be directed to the acquisition of grace and glory, which God alone gives, according to Psalm 83:12, "The Lord will give grace and glory." But in the second way we pray to the saints, whether angels or men, not that God may through them know our petitions, but that our prayers may be effective through their prayers and merits. Hence it is written (Rev 8:4) that "the smoke of the incense," namely "the prayers of the saints ascended up before God." This is also clear from the very style employed by the Church in praying, since we beseech the Blessed Trinity "to have mercy on us," while we ask any of the saints "to pray for us."[4]

Objection 1. It would seem that we ought to pray to God alone. Prayer is an act of religion, as stated above (a. 3). But God alone is to be worshiped by religion. Therefore we should pray to God alone.

---

[4] Although some Protestant Christians object to the intercession of saints, the principle follows from what is clearly taught in Scripture. Those who have died in Christ are not dead but rather alive, praying to God. Jesus said: "And as for the dead being raised, have you not read in the book of Moses, in the passage about the bush, how God said to him, 'I am the God of Abraham, and the God of Isaac, and the God of Jacob'? He is not God of the dead, but of the living . . ." (Mk 12:26–27). These saints in heaven are aware of what we say and what we do: "Therefore, since we are surrounded by so great a cloud of witnesses, let us also lay aside every weight, and sin which clings so closely . . ." (Heb 12:1). Since the saints in heaven hear us and see us, we can ask them to pray for us, just as Scripture urges that we ask living holy people to pray for us (Jas 5:16).

Reply to Objection 1. To Him alone do we offer religious worship when praying, from Whom we seek to obtain what we pray for, because by so doing we confess that He is the Author of our goods, but not to those whom we call upon as our advocates in God's presence.

Objection 2. Further, it is useless to pray to one who is ignorant of the prayer. But it belongs to God alone to know one's prayer, both because frequently prayer is uttered by an interior act which God alone knows, rather than by words, according to the saying of the Apostle (1 Cor 14:15), "I will pray with the spirit, I will pray also with the understanding," and again because, as Augustine says (*De Cura pro Mort.* xiii) the "dead, even the saints, know not what the living, even their own children, are doing." Therefore we ought to pray to God alone.

Reply to Objection 2. The dead, if we consider their natural condition, do not know what takes place in this world, especially the interior movements of the heart. Nevertheless, according to Gregory (*Moral.* xii, 21),[5] whatever it is fitting for the blessed to know about what happens to us, even as regards the interior movements of the heart, is made known to them in the Word: and it is most becoming to their exalted position that they should know the petitions we make to them by word or thought; and consequently the petitions which we raise to them are known to them through Divine manifestation.

Objection 3. Further, if we pray to any of the saints, this is only because they are united to God. Now some yet living in this world, or even some who are in Purgatory, are closely united to God by grace, and yet we do not pray to them. Therefore neither should we pray to the saints who are in Paradise.

Reply to Objection 3. Those who are in this world or in Purgatory do not yet enjoy the vision of the Word, so as to be able to know what

---

[5] Pope Gregory the Great (d. 604) is one of only a handful of popes to be accorded the title "the Great" along with Leo the Great (d. 461), Nicholas the Great (d. 867), and John Paul the Great (d. 2005). The epithet is not formally given by any official process but rather simply by acclamation and the use of the faithful.

we think or say. Therefore we do not seek their assistance by praying to them, but ask it of the living by speaking to them.

ARTICLE 6 ⁓ Should we ask God for temporal things when we pray?[6]

Yes, despite objections to the contrary, It is written (Prov 30:8): "Give me only the necessaries of life."

I answer that, As Augustine says (*ad Probam, de orando Deum,* Ep. cxxx, 12): "It is moral to pray for what it is moral to desire." Now it is moral to desire temporal things, not indeed principally, by placing our end therein, but as helps whereby we are assisted in tending towards beatitude, in so far, to wit, as they are the means of supporting the life of the body, and are of service to us as instruments in performing acts of virtue,[7] as also the Philosopher states (*Ethic.* i, 8). Augustine too says the same to Proba (*ad Probam, de orando Deum,* Ep. cxxx, 6, 7) when he states that "it is not unbecoming for anyone to desire enough for a livelihood, and no more; for this sufficiency is desired, not for its own sake, but for the welfare of the body, or that we should desire to be clothed in a way befitting one's station, so as not to be out of keeping with those among whom we have to live. Accordingly we ought to pray that we may keep these things if we have them, and if we have them not, that we may gain possession of them."

Objection 1. It would seem that man ought not to ask God for temporal things when he prays. We seek what we ask for in prayer. But we should not seek for temporal things, for it is written (Mt 6:33): "Seek

---

6 For example, should we pray to have a good job? Should we pray that the bus isn't too late? That we find our lost book? Or on the other hand, should our prayer concern only spiritual things, such as praying for an increase in faith or charity?

7 Temporal goods such as health, financial well-being, and worldly success are goods, but not the greatest good. That they are goods is shown not just by the fact that we may pray for them, but also by the prohibition against damaging them in other people. If wealth were evil, stealing would be a service, not a crime. However, though all these things are good, one can seek what is good in an unreasonable way. To seek money as if money were that in which one could find perfect happiness is to be unreasonable (and to thwart one's own happiness).

. . . first the kingdom of God, and His justice: and all these things shall be added unto you," that is to say, temporal things, which, says He, we are not to seek, but they will be added to what we seek. Therefore, temporal things are not to be asked of God in prayer.

Reply to Objection 1. We should seek temporal things not in the first but in the second place. Hence Augustine says (*De Serm. Dom. in Monte* ii, 16): "When He says that this" (i.e., the kingdom of God) "is to be sought first, He implies that the other" (i.e., temporal goods) "is to be sought afterwards, not in time but in importance, this as being our good, the other as our need."[8]

Objection 2. Further, no one asks save for that which he is solicitous about. Now we ought not to have solicitude for temporal things, according to the saying of Matthew 6:25, "Be not solicitous for your life, what you shall eat." Therefore we ought not to ask for temporal things when we pray.

Reply to Objection 2. Not all solicitude about temporal things is forbidden, but that which is superfluous and inordinate, as stated above (II–II, q. 56, art. 6).

Objection 3. Further, by prayer our mind should be raised up to God. But by asking for temporal things, it descends to things beneath it, against the saying of the Apostle (2 Cor 4:18), "While we look not at the things which are seen, but at the things which are not seen. For the things which are seen are temporal, but the things which are not seen are eternal." Therefore man ought not to ask God for temporal things when he prays.

Reply to Objection 3. When our mind is intent on temporal things in order that it may rest in them, it remains immersed therein; but when it is intent on them in relation to the acquisition of beatitude, it is not lowered by them, but raises them to a higher level.

---

[8] In other words, to put friendship with God first does not mean that it is *chronologically* first but first in terms of *importance*. It may be the case that on any given day one must first seek material goods before nurturing friendship with God. However, even in this case, any legitimate task, even the most mundane, can be done for the greater glory of God.

Objection 4. Further, man ought not to ask of God other than good and useful things. But sometimes temporal things, when we have them, are harmful, not only in a spiritual sense, but also in a material sense. Therefore we should not ask God for them in our prayers.

Reply to Objection 4. From the very fact that we ask for temporal things not as the principal object of our petition, but as subordinate to something else, we ask God for them in the sense that they may be granted to us in so far as they are expedient for salvation.

ARTICLE 8 ∾ **Should we pray for our enemies?**

Yes, despite objections to the contrary, It is written (Mt 5:44): "Pray for them that persecute and calumniate you."

I answer that, To pray for another is an act of charity, as stated above (a. 7). Therefore we are bound to pray for our enemies in the same manner as we are bound to love them. Now it was explained above in the treatise on charity (q. 25, aa 8, 9), how we are bound to love our enemies, namely, that we must love in them their nature, not their sin,[9] and that to love our enemies in general is a matter of precept, while to love them in the individual is not a matter of precept, except in the preparedness of the mind, so that a man must be prepared to love his enemy even in the individual and to help him in a case of necessity, or if his enemy should beg his forgiveness. But to love one's enemies absolutely in the individual, and to assist them, is an act of perfection.[10]

In like manner, it is a matter of obligation that we should not exclude our enemies from the general prayers which we offer up for

---

[9] To love the sinner and to hate the sin is not a contradiction in terms. Sin is nothing other than a separation from God, a blow (fatal or injurious) to our relationship with God that undermines our true happiness. If we love people, we will hate that which harms them, undermines them, and destroys their happiness. The doctor who loves his patient hates her cancer. So it is precisely from love of neighbor that a hatred for sin arises. This hatred is not opposed to love of neighbor, or despite love of neighbor, but precisely on account of love of neighbor.

[10] An example of such an act was done by President Abraham Lincoln, who was once encouraged by an aid to take revenge on a political enemy and destroy him. Lincoln chose instead to reach out to the other person stating, "I destroy my enemies when I make them my friends."

others; but it is a matter of perfection, and not of obligation, to pray for them individually, except in certain special cases.

Objection 1. It would seem that we ought not to pray for our enemies. According to Romans 15:4, "whatever was written, was written for our learning." Now Holy Writ contains many imprecations against enemies; thus it is written (Ps 6:10): "Let all my enemies be ashamed and be . . . troubled; let them be ashamed and be troubled very speedily [Vulg.: 'Let them be turned back and be ashamed']." Therefore we too should pray against rather than for our enemies.

Reply to Objection 1. The imprecations contained in Holy Writ may be understood in four ways. First, according to the custom of the prophets "to foretell the future under the veil of an imprecation," as Augustine states [*De Serm. Dom. in Monte* i, 21]. Secondly, in the sense that certain temporal evils are sometimes inflicted by God on the wicked for their correction. Thirdly, because they are understood to be pronounced, not against the men themselves, but against the kingdom of sin, with the purpose, to wit, of destroying sin by the correction of men. Fourthly, by way of conformity of our will to the Divine justice with regard to the damnation of those who are obstinate in sin.

Objection 2. Further, to be revenged on one's enemies is harmful to them. But holy men seek vengeance of their enemies according to Apocalypse 6:10, "How long . . . do You not . . . revenge our blood on them that dwell on earth?" Therefore, they rejoice in being revenged on their enemies, according to Psalm 57:11, "The just shall rejoice when he shall see the revenge." Therefore we should not pray for our enemies, but against them.

Reply to Objection 2. As Augustine states in the same book (*De Serm. Dom. in Monte* i, 22), "the martyrs' vengeance is the overthrow of the kingdom of sin, because they suffered so much while it reigned"; or as he says again (QQ. *Vet. et Nov. Test.* lxviii), "their prayer for vengeance is expressed not in words but in their minds, even as the blood of Abel cried from the earth." They rejoice in vengeance not for its own sake, but for the sake of Divine justice.

Objection 3. Further, man's deed should not be contrary to his prayer. Now sometimes it is permissible for men to attack their enemies, else all wars would be immoral, which is opposed to what we have said above (q. 40, a. 1). Therefore we should not pray for our enemies.

Reply to Objection 3. It is moral to attack one's enemies, that they may be restrained from sin: and this is for their own good and for the good of others. Consequently it is even moral in praying to ask that temporal evils be inflicted on our enemies in order that they may mend their ways. Thus prayer and deed will not be contrary to one another.

SACRIFICES

ARTICLE 1 ∾ **Is offering a sacrifice to God part of the law of nature?**

Yes, despite objections to the contrary, At all times and among all nations there has always been the offering of sacrifices. Now that which is observed by all is seemingly natural. Therefore the offering of sacrifices is of the natural law.

I answer that, Natural reason tells man that he is subject to a higher being, on account of the defects which he perceives in himself, and in which he needs help and direction from someone above him: and whatever this superior being may be, it is known to all under the name of God. Now just as in natural things the lower are naturally subject to the higher, so too it is a dictate of natural reason in accordance with man's natural inclination that he should tender submission and honor, according to his mode, to that which is above man. Now the mode befitting to man is that he should employ sensible signs in order to signify anything, because he derives his knowledge from sensibles. Hence it is a dictate of natural reason that man should use certain sensibles, by offering them to God in sign of the subjection and honor due to Him, like those who make certain offerings to their lord in recognition of his authority. Now this is what we mean by a sacrifice, and consequently the offering of sacrifice is of the natural law.[1]

---

[1] Offering sacrifice to God, an act of the virtue of religion that is a part of justice, is not simply a matter of revealed duty. Human beings, by nature, can and

Objection 1. It would seem that offering a sacrifice to God is not of the natural law. Things that are of the natural law are common among all men. Yet this is not the case with sacrifices: for we read of some, e.g. Melchisedech (Gen 14:18), offering bread and wine in sacrifice, and of certain animals being offered by some, and others by others. Therefore the offering of sacrifices is not of the natural law.

Reply to Objection 1. As stated above (I–II, q. 95, a. 2), certain things belong generically to the natural law, while their determination belongs to the positive law; thus the natural law requires that evildoers should be punished; but that this or that punishment should be inflicted on them is a matter determined by God or by man. In like manner, the offering of sacrifice belongs generically to the natural law, and consequently all are agreed on this point, but the determination of sacrifices is established by God or by man, and this is the reason for their difference.

Objection 2. Further, things that are of the natural law were observed by all just men. Yet we do not read that Isaac offered sacrifice, nor that Adam did so, of whom nevertheless it is written (Wis 10:2) that wisdom "brought him out of his sin." Therefore the offering of sacrifice is not of the natural law.

Reply to Objection 2. Adam, Isaac, and other just men offered sacrifice to God in a manner befitting the times in which they lived,[2] according to Gregory, who says (*Moral.* iv, 3) that in olden times original sin was remitted through the offering of sacrifices. Nor does Scrip-

---

should offer worship to God in justice. In justice, since human beings receive all good things that they enjoy either directly or indirectly from God, all human persons owe everything to God. The sacrifice that is given to God symbolizes and reinforces the total gift of self that each human being owes in justice to God.

2 Although it pertains to justice and the natural law to offer sacrifice to God, the precise form that this sacrifice takes does not need to be the same in all times and places. Similarly, all children owe honor to their parents, but the way in which this is expressed differs in time and place. In contemporary culture, not to show special respect to one's mother on the second Sunday in May (Mother's Day) by a call, card, or gift would be neglectful. Other cultures, however, have different days or ways in which to show honor to mothers.

ture mention all the sacrifices of the just, but only those that have something special connected with them. Perhaps the reason why we read of no sacrifice being offered by Adam may be that, as the origin of sin is ascribed to him, the origin of sanctification ought not to be represented as typified in him. Isaac was a type of Christ, being himself offered in sacrifice; and so there was no need that he should be represented as offering a sacrifice.

Objection 3. Further, Augustine says (*De Civ. Dei* x, 5, 19) that sacrifices are offered in signification of something. Now words, which are chief among signs, as he again says (*De Doctr. Christ.* ii, 3), signify, not by nature but by convention, according to the Philosopher (*Peri Herm.* i, 2). Therefore sacrifices are not of the natural law.

Reply to Objection 3. It is natural to man to express his ideas by signs, but the determination of those signs depends on man's pleasure.[3]

---

[3] Again, that all people are to worship God does not mean that they must worship Him in the exact same time or manner. A wide diversity is possible by way of fulfilling this duty.

QUESTION 92

SUPERSTITION

ARTICLE 1 ～ **Is superstition a vice contrary to religion?**

Yes, despite objections to the contrary, Augustine says (*De Decem Chord. Serm.* ix): "You strike the first chord in the worship of one God, and the beast of superstition has fallen." Now the worship of one God belongs to religion. Therefore superstition is contrary to religion.[1]

I answer that, As stated above (q. 81, a. 5), religion is a moral virtue. Now every moral virtue observes a mean, as stated above (I–II, q. 64, a. 1). Therefore a twofold vice is opposed to a moral virtue: one by way of excess, the other by way of deficiency. Again, the mean of virtue may be exceeded, not only with regard to the circumstance called "how much," but also with regard to other circumstances: so that, in certain virtues, such as magnanimity and magnificence, vice exceeds the mean of virtue, not through tending to something greater

---

[1] Common examples of superstition include putting faith in horoscopes, tarot cards, ouija boards, astrology, and occult dealings. Actions such as these are contrary in justice to what is due to God and contrary to the first commandment of having no false gods. "If anyone take observation of the stars in order to foreknow casual or fortuitous future events, or to know with certitude future human actions, his conduct is based on a false and vain opinion; and so the operation of the demon introduces itself therein. Therefore it will be a superstitious and immoral divination. On the other hand, if one were to apply the observation of the stars in order to foreknow those future things that are caused by heavenly bodies, for instance, drought or rain and so forth, it will be neither an immoral nor a superstitious divination." *ST* II–II, q. 95, a. 5.

than the virtue, but possibly to something less, and yet it goes beyond the mean of virtue, through doing something to whom it ought not, or when it ought not, and in like manner as regards other circumstances, as the Philosopher shows (*Ethic.* iv, 1, 2, 3).

Accordingly, superstition is a vice contrary to religion by excess, not that it offers more to the divine worship than true religion, but because it offers divine worship either to whom it ought not, or in a manner it ought not.

Objection 1. It would seem that superstition is not a vice contrary to religion. One contrary is not included in the definition of the other. But religion is included in the definition of superstition: for the latter is defined as being "immoderate observance of religion," according to a gloss on Colossians 2:23, "Which things have indeed a show of wisdom in superstition." Therefore superstition is not a vice contrary to religion.

Reply to Objection 1. Just as we speak metaphorically of good among evil things—thus we speak of a good thief—so too sometimes the names of the virtues are employed by transposition in an evil sense. Thus prudence is sometimes used instead of cunning, according to Luke 16:8, "The children of this world are more prudent in their generation than the children of light." It is in this way that superstition is described as religion.

Objection 2. Further, Isidore says (*Etym.* x): "Cicero [*De Natura Deorum* ii, 28] states that the superstitious were so called because they spent the day in praying and offering sacrifices that their children might survive [*superstites*] them." But this may be done even in accordance with true religious worship. Therefore superstition is not a vice opposed to religion.

Reply to Objection 2. The etymology of a word differs from its meaning. For its etymology depends on what it is taken from for the purpose of signification, whereas its meaning depends on the thing to which it is applied for the purpose of signifying it. Now these things differ sometimes: for "lapis" [a stone] takes its name from hurting the foot [*laedere pedem*], but this is not its meaning, else iron, since it hurts the foot, would be a stone. In like manner, it does not follow that "superstition" means that from which the word is derived.

Objection 3. Further, superstition seems to denote an excess. But religion admits of no excess, since, as stated above (q. 81, a. 5, ad 3), there is no possibility of rendering to God, by religion, the equal of what we owe Him. Therefore superstition is not a vice contrary to religion.

Reply to Objection 3. Religion does not admit of excess, in respect of absolute quantity, but it does admit of excess in respect of proportionate quantity, in so far, to wit, as something may be done in divine worship that ought not to be done.[2]

---

[2] Thus we can never love God too much, have too much hope in Him, or too much faith in Him. Nevertheless, we might worship God superstitiously by, for instance, sacrificing animals in worship. Thomas expands: "[I]f that which is done be, in itself, not conducive to God's glory, nor raise man's mind to God, nor curb inordinate concupiscence, or again if it be not in accordance with the commandments of God and of the Church, or if it be contrary to the general custom—which, according to Augustine [*Ad Casulan.* Ep. xxxvi], 'has the force of law'—all this must be reckoned excessive and superstitious, because consisting, as it does, of mere externals, it has no connection with the internal worship of God. Hence Augustine (*De Vera Relig.* iii) quotes the words of Luke 17:21, 'The kingdom of God is within you,' against the 'superstitious,' those, to wit, who pay more attention to externals" (*ST* II–II, q. 93, a. 2).

Q u e s t i o n **101**

PIETY

ARTICLE 1 ⁓ **Does piety extend to particular human individuals?**

Yes, despite objections to the contrary, Tully says (*De Invent. Rhet.* ii) that "it is by piety that we do our duty towards our kindred and well-wishers of our country and render them faithful service."

I answer that, Man becomes a debtor to other men in various ways, according to their various excellence and the various benefits received from them. On both counts God holds first place, for He is supremely excellent, and is for us the first principle of being and government. In the second place, the principles of our being and government are our parents and our country, which have given us birth and nourishment. Consequently man is debtor chiefly to his parents and his country, after God. Therefore just as it belongs to religion to give honor [*cultum*] to God, so does it belong to piety, in the second place, to give honor to one's parents and one's country.

The honor due to our parents includes the honor given to all our kindred, since our kinsfolk are those who descend from the same parents, according to the Philosopher (*Ethic.* viii, 12). The honor given to our country includes homage to all our fellow-citizens and to all the friends of our country. Therefore piety extends chiefly to these.[1]

---

[1] Of course, the honor due to God (*latria*) differs radically not just in degree but also in kind from the honor due Mary or the saints (*dulia*) or to parents or country. Aquinas himself gives the reason: "For God has absolute and paramount lordship over the creature wholly and singly, which is entirely subject to

His power, whereas man partakes of a certain likeness to the divine lordship, forasmuch as he exercises a particular power over some man or creature. Therefore, *dulia*, which pays due service to a human lord, is a distinct virtue from *latria*, which pays due service to the lordship of God" (*ST* II–II, q. 103, a. 3). Nevertheless, to honor one's father and mother is not only a commandment revealed by God but also a duty known through natural law. The following articles of question 101 (aa 2–4), though not included here, treat of interesting difficulties that may come about in the apparent tensions that can arise between properly honoring parents and giving God what is due to God alone. For Thomas, the circumstances of the situation are very important in determining the correct course of action. Even though God is always given a primacy of place, sometimes the best way to serve God may not be, for example, to enter into religious life if one's parents are in grave need of care and there is no other way that they can receive the due care.

QUESTION 104

~~~~~~~~~~~~~~~~~~~~~~~~~~~~~~

OBEDIENCE

ARTICLE 4 ⤳ **Should God be obeyed in all things?**

Yes, despite objections to the contrary, It is written (Ex 24:7): "All things that the Lord has spoken we will do, and we will be obedient."[1]

I answer that, As stated above (II–II q. 104, a. 1), he who obeys is moved by the command of the person he obeys, just as natural things are moved by their motive causes. Now just as God is the first mover of all things that are moved naturally, so too is He the first mover of all wills, as shown above (I–II, q. 9, a. 6). Therefore, just as all natural things are subject to the divine motion by a natural necessity, so too all wills, by a kind of necessity of justice, are bound to obey the divine command.[2]

---

[1] How are we to know what God wills for us? The broad parameters of God's will are made clear by the public teaching of God's Church. The voice of conscience is, as John Henry Cardinal Newman said, "the aboriginal vicar of Christ" (John Henry Newman, *The Rule of Our Warfare: John Henry Newman adn the True Christian Life* [New Jersey: Scepter Publishing, 2003], 60). For the Catholic Christian, this subjective and private vicar (conscience) is properly formed and illuminated through the teaching of the Church community, especially the bishops and the objective and public vicar of Christ, the pope. Secondly, reception of the sacraments and personal prayer can help illumine the will of God in a person's life. Each person's path will be different, and so each person is called to find and follow a personal vocation, a call from God to holiness uniquely suited and adapted to the individual.

[2] Every human person is created to know, love, and serve God, and this takes place through obedience to God. Without submitting one's mind to truth we cannot properly know God, without preferring God to earthly things we cannot properly love God, and without submitting one's will to God we cannot

Objection 1. It seems that God need not be obeyed in all things. For it is written (Mt 9:30, 31) that our Lord, after healing the two blind men, commanded them, saying: "See that no man know this. But they going out spread His fame abroad in all that country." Yet they are not blamed for so doing. Therefore it seems that we are not bound to obey God in all things.

Reply to Objection 1. Our Lord in telling the blind men to conceal the miracle had no intention of binding them with the force of a divine precept, but, as Gregory says (*Moral.* xix), "gave an example to His servants who follow Him that they might wish to hide their virtue and yet that it should be proclaimed against their will, in order that others might profit by their example."

Objection 2. Further, no one is bound to do anything contrary to virtue. Now we find that God commanded certain things contrary to virtue: thus He commanded Abraham to slay his innocent son (Gen 22); and the Jews to steal the property of the Egyptians (Ex 11), which things are contrary to justice; and Hosea to take to himself a woman who was an adulteress (Hos 3), and this is contrary to chastity. Therefore God is not to be obeyed in all things.[3]

Reply to Objection 2. Even as God does nothing contrary to nature (since "the nature of a thing is what God does therein," according to a gloss on Romans 11), and yet does certain things contrary to the usual

---

properly serve God. And of course, without knowing, loving, and serving God, human beings cannot be happy. As Augustine states in his *Confessions* to God: "Our hearts are restless until they rest in You." So our obedience to God is nothing more than finding our own happiness, a happiness which cannot be had without our being just persons. Giving God what is God's due involves obeying him.

3 Plato's *Euthyphro* takes up the question whether the gods command what is right by nature or whether whatever the gods command is right. A "divine command" theory of ethics holds the latter view, that morality is simply a matter of following divine commands whatever those divine commands may be. In this objection, it is noted that the commands of God can seem contrary to the call of virtue. For a nice explanation of St. Thomas's solution to this seeming dilemma, see Brian Davies, *An Introduction to the Philosophy of Religion* (Oxford: Oxford University Press, 2004), 276.

(*solitum*) course of nature, so too God can command nothing contrary to virtue since virtue and rectitude of human will consist chiefly in conformity with God's will and obedience to His command, although it be contrary to the wonted mode of virtue. Accordingly, then, the command given to Abraham to slay his innocent son was not contrary to justice, since God is the author of life and death. Nor again was it contrary to justice that He commanded the Jews to take things belonging to the Egyptians, because all things are His, and He gives them to whom He will. Nor was it contrary to chastity that Hosea was commanded to take an adulteress, because God Himself is the ordainer of human generation, and the right manner of intercourse with woman is that which He appoints. Hence it is evident that the persons aforesaid did not sin, either by obeying God or by willing to obey Him.[4]

---

[4] In this famous passage, Thomas treats three cases (and there are other similar ones) in which God seems to command that someone does something that is intrinsically evil or always wrong to perform. Murder, theft, and adultery are all acts that are wrong in themselves, and here God seems to order that these acts be done. It may be easiest to understand such cases by considering theft first. Theft "is contrary to justice, through being a taking of what belongs to another" (II–II, q. 66, a. 5). Theft is always wrong, but "what belongs to another" is something that can and does change. If I give you money for your radio, and you agree to sell me your radio for that amount of money, in taking the radio from you I do not rob you since what did belong to you now belongs to me. So if the owner of property gives away or sells the property, then the property no longer belongs to the owner. Now God is the "owner" of all things, since all things were directly or indirectly created by God and only remain in existence because of God. So, if God gives the gold of the Egyptians to the Israelites, they do nothing wrong whatsoever in taking it. In a similar way, adultery is sexual intercourse between "a married person and one unmarried, or between a married person and the spouse of another" (See *Catechism of the Catholic Church*, 2380). But like possession of property, marriage is a state created by God and also governed by God, and so this state can be created between a man and a woman as happened in the case of Hosea. Finally, just as God is Lord over property and marriage, so too God is the Lord of life. Every human life is created by God who infuses each human soul (I–II, q. 118, a. 2), and on account of original sin (I–II, q. 85), God in no way does or allows something unjust in separating soul from body and ending that earthly life. That Abraham did not actually kill Isaac but is stopped by the message of an angel is significant, particularly in the time in which human sacrifice was

ARTICLE 5 ~~ Are subjects bound to obey their superiors in all things?

No, despite objections to the contrary, It is written (Acts 5:29): "We ought to obey God rather than men." Now sometimes the things commanded by a superior are against God. Therefore superiors are not to be obeyed in all things.

I answer that, As stated above (aa 1, 4), he who obeys is moved at the bidding of the person who commands him, by a certain necessity of justice, even as a natural thing is moved through the power of its mover by a natural necessity. . . . There are two reasons for which a subject may not be bound to obey his superior in all things: first, on account of the command of a higher power. For as a gloss says on Romans 13:2, "They that resist [Vulg.: 'He that resists'] the power, resist the ordinance of God" [cf. St. Augustine, *De Verb. Dom.* viii]. "If a commissioner issue an order, are you to comply, if it is contrary to the bidding of the proconsul? Again, if the proconsul command one thing, and the emperor another, will you hesitate to disregard the former and serve the latter? Therefore, if the emperor commands one thing and God another, you must disregard the former and obey God."[5] Secondly, a subject is not bound to obey his superior if the latter command him to do something wherein he is not subject to him. For Seneca says (*De Beneficiis* iii): "It is wrong to suppose that slavery falls upon the whole man: for the better part of him is excepted." His body is subjected and assigned to his master, but his soul is his own.

---

common. In any case, many contemporary Scripture scholars suggest that in these passages God is not really commanding such acts to be done, and so the problem that Thomas treats would not really arise.

[5] The obedience that one owes to one's parents or religious authorities is subordinate to the obedience due to God. Therefore, if a government, parent, or religious authority were to command that someone do something that God has forbidden, then not only may someone disobey, one must disobey. No government, parent, or religious authority may ever justly ask obedience of a person in a particular matter if this would mean disobedience to God. A soldier should obey his commanding officer, unless that officer commands him, for example, to kill intentionally innocent children; children should obey parents, unless parents tell them to do that which is evil, such as stealing.

Consequently in matters touching the internal movement of the will, man is not bound to obey his fellow-man, but God alone.

Nevertheless man is bound to obey his fellow-man in things that have to be done externally by means of the body, and yet, since by nature all men are equal, he is not bound to obey another man in matters touching the nature of the body, for instance in those relating to the support of his body or the begetting of his children. Therefore servants are not bound to obey their masters, nor children their parents, in the question of contracting marriage or of remaining in the state of virginity or the like. But in matters concerning the disposal of actions and human affairs, a subject is bound to obey his superior within the sphere of his authority: for instance a soldier must obey his general in matters relating to war, a servant his master in matters touching the execution of the duties of his service, a son his father in matters relating to the conduct of his life and the care of the household, and so forth.[6]

Objection 1. It seems that subjects are bound to obey their superiors in all things. For the Apostle says (Col 3:20): "Children, obey your parents in all things;" and farther on (Col 3:22): "Servants, obey in all things your masters according to the flesh." Therefore, in like manner other subjects are bound to obey their superiors in all things.

Reply to Objection 1. When the Apostle says "in all things," he refers to matters within the sphere of a father's or master's authority.

Objection 2. Further, superiors stand between God and their subjects, according to Deuteronomy 5:5, "I was the mediator and stood between the Lord and you at that time, to show you His words." Now there is no going from extreme to extreme, except through that which stands between. Therefore the commands of a superior must be esteemed the commands of God. Therefore the Apostle says (Gal 4:14): "You . . . received me as an angel of God, even as Christ Jesus;"

---

6 Obedience to human authority is always limited by the sphere of governance proper to the human authority. Thus, no person ever owes complete obedience to another human being, although a person may owe strict obedience to another within a certain sphere of governance (e.g., the soldier to the officer with respect to military affairs).

and (1 Thess 2:13): "When you had received of us the word of the hearing of God, you received it, not as the word of men, but, as it is indeed, the word of God." Therefore, as man is bound to obey God in all things, so is he bound to obey his superiors.

Reply to Objection 2. Man is subject to God simply as regards all things, both internal and external. Therefore he is bound to obey Him in all things. On the other hand, inferiors are not subject to their superiors in all things, but only in certain things and in a particular way, in respect of which the superior stands between God and his subjects, whereas in respect of other matters the subject is immediately under God, by Whom he is taught either by the natural or by the written law.

Objection 3. Further, just as religious in making their profession take vows of chastity and poverty, so do they also vow obedience. Now a religious is bound to observe chastity and poverty in all things. Therefore he is also bound to obey in all things.

Reply to Objection 3. Religious profess obedience as to the regular mode of life, in respect of which they are subject to their superiors: therefore they are bound to obey in those matters only which may belong to the regular mode of life, and this obedience suffices for salvation. If they be willing to obey even in other matters, this will belong to the superabundance of perfection, provided, however, such things be not contrary to God or to the rule they profess, for obedience in this case would be immoral.

Accordingly we may distinguish a threefold obedience: one, sufficient for salvation, and consisting in obeying when one is bound to obey; secondly, perfect obedience, which obeys in all things moral; thirdly, indiscreet obedience, which obeys even in matters immoral.

QUESTION 105

DISOBEDIENCE

ARTICLE 2 — **Is disobedience the most serious of sins?**

No, despite objections to the contrary, Contempt of the commander is a more grievous sin than contempt of his command. Now some sins are against the very person of the commander, such as blasphemy and murder. Therefore disobedience is not the most grievous of sins.[1]

I answer that, Not every disobedience is equally a sin: for one disobedience may be greater than another, in two ways. First, on the part of the superior commanding, since, although a man should take every care to obey each superior, yet it is a greater duty to obey a higher than a lower authority, in sign of which the command of a lower authority is set aside if it be contrary to the command of a higher authority. Consequently the higher the person who commands, the more grievous is it to disobey him: so that it is more grievous to disobey God than man.[2] Secondly, on the part of the things commanded. For the person commanding does not equally desire the fulfillment of all his commands: since

---

1 To claim that something is wrong, even seriously wrong, is not to claim that it is equally wrong. Stealing is always wrong, but it is worse to steal a great deal of money than a little bit of money and worse to steal from someone poor than from someone rich. Similarly, disobedience is wrong, but it is not as bad as murder or blasphemy. Even the Ten Commandments are not equally important, for it is much more important to avoid worshiping false gods than to avoid coveting a neighbor's goods.

2 For example, other things being equal, it is worse for the private in the army to disobey the commander-in-chief than the general, worse to disobey the general than the captain, worse to disobey the captain than a sergeant.

every such person desires above all the end, and that which is nearest to the end. Therefore disobedience is the more grievous, according as the unfulfilled commandment is more in the intention of the person commanding.[3] As to the commandments of God, it is evident that the greater the good commanded, the more grievous the disobedience of that commandment, because since God's will is essentially directed to the good, the greater the good the more does God wish it to be fulfilled.[4] Consequently he that disobeys the commandment of the love of God sins more grievously than one who disobeys the commandment of the love of our neighbor. On the other hand, man's will is not always directed to the greater good: hence, when we are bound by a mere precept of man, a sin is more grievous, not through setting aside a greater good, but through setting aside that which is more in the intention of the person commanding.

---

[3] Obedience, like all the virtues, is governed by intelligence perfected by the virtue of practical wisdom. Obedience is more important and necessary the more it is linked with achieving the end. Hence, disobedience in a trivial matter, relatively unrelated to the end, differs markedly from disobedience in an important matter, intimately related to achieving the goal of the one directing.

[4] The Ten Commandments are ordered in terms of importance. "You shall have no god before me" forbids idolatry and enjoins worship of the one true God. The next two commandments in a sense follow this first one. "You shall not take the name of the Lord your God in vain" (give proper respect to that which pertains to God) and "keep holy the Sabbath day" (make special time to honor God properly). After commandments pertaining to God (the so-called First Tablet) come commandments pertaining to neighbor (the Second Tablet). "Honor your father and mother" immediately comes next because parents share in God's governing and proportionate honor is due to them as we saw in q. 101, a. 1 on piety. "You shall not murder." This is the most important of the "negative" commandments, since life is needed for any of our activities in terms of honoring God or parents. "You shall not commit adultery" because, in part, the possible generation of human life requires appropriate conditions. "You shall not steal" because without personal sustenance our life would end. "You shall not bear false witness" since individual human lives are only sustained by the human community, which cannot survive without truth-telling, particularly in crucial situations such as court. "You shall not covet your neighbor's spouse and goods" because stealing and adultery both begin with the desire to steal or commit adultery. St. Bonaventure wrote an interesting commentary on the commandments in his book *Collations on the Ten Commandments*, trans. Paul Spaeth (New York: The Franciscan Institute, St. Bonaventure University, 1995).

Accordingly, the various degrees of disobedience must correspond with the various degrees of precepts: because the disobedience in which there is contempt of God's precept, from the very nature of disobedience, is more grievous than a sin committed against a man, apart from the latter being a disobedience to God. And I say this because whoever sins against his neighbor acts also against God's commandment. And if the divine precept be contemned in a yet graver matter, the sin is still more serious. The disobedience that contains contempt of a man's precept is less grievous than the sin which contemns the man who made the precept, because reverence for the person commanding should give rise to reverence for his command. In like manner a sin that directly involves contempt of God, such as blasphemy, or the like, is more grievous (even if we mentally separate the disobedience from the sin) than would be a sin involving contempt of God's commandment alone.

THANKFULNESS

ARTICLE 1 ⟿ **Is thankfulness a special virtue, distinct from other virtues?**

Yes, despite objections to the contrary, Tully reckons thankfulness a special part of justice (*De Invent. Rhet.* ii).

I answer that, As stated above (I–II, q. 60, a. 3), the nature of the debt to be paid must needs vary according to various causes giving rise to the debt, yet so that the greater always includes the lesser. Now the cause of debt is found primarily and chiefly in God, in that He is the first principle of all our goods; secondarily it is found in our father, because he is the proximate principle of our begetting and upbringing; thirdly it is found in the person that excels in dignity, from whom general favors proceed; fourthly it is found in a benefactor, from whom we have received particular and private favors, on account of which we are under particular obligation to him.

Accordingly, since what we owe God, or our father, or a person excelling in dignity, is not the same as what we owe a benefactor from whom we have received some particular favor, it follows that after religion, whereby we pay God due worship, and piety, whereby we honor our parents, and observance, whereby we honor persons excelling in dignity, there is thankfulness or gratitude, whereby we give thanks to our benefactors.[1] And it is distinct from the foregoing virtues, just as

---

[1] The virtue of thankfulness is a matter of justice, not just good manners. In justice, we owe God everything for God ultimately is the source of all the

each of these is distinct from the one that precedes, as falling short thereof.

Objection 1. It seems that thankfulness is not a special virtue, distinct from other virtues. For we have received the greatest benefits from God, and from our parents. Now the honor which we pay to God in return belongs to the virtue of religion, and the honor with which we repay our parents belongs to the virtue of piety. Therefore thankfulness, or gratitude, is not distinct from the other virtues.

Reply to Objection 1. Just as religion is superexcelling piety, so is it excelling thankfulness or gratitude. Therefore giving thanks to God was reckoned above (q. 83, a. 17) among things pertaining to religion.

Objection 2. Further, proportionate repayment belongs to commutative justice, according to the Philosopher (*Ethic.* v, 4). Now the purpose of giving thanks is repayment (*Ethic.* 5, 4). Therefore thanksgiving, which belongs to gratitude, is an act of justice. Therefore gratitude is not a special virtue, distinct from other virtues.

Reply to Objection 2. Proportionate repayment belongs to commutative justice, when it answers to the legal due: for instance when it is contracted that so much be paid for so much. But the repayment that belongs to the virtue of thankfulness or gratitude answers to the moral debt, and is paid spontaneously.[2] Hence thanksgiving is less thankful when compelled, as Seneca observes (*De Beneficiis* iii).

---

goods we enjoy. It follows from this "owing" of God that God should be given worship—a unique and fitting worship, in particular the Eucharist (thanksgiving in Greek) for all that God has done for us. But other human beings also have benefited us, in particular our own parents to whom is due not the worship fitting for God alone but rather honor and "piety." "Thanksgiving" in the sense used here by Thomas is giving what is due to those who have in other ways benefited us, for example, clergy, teachers, coaches, neighbors, and others who have served us in various ways.

[2] The thanksgiving due to those who have benefited us (benefactors) is not a matter of strict legal repayment. In many cases, such repayment in a literal sense would be impossible. However, a benefit should be returned to such persons in so far as the time and opportunity arises.

Objection 3. Further, acknowledgment of favor received is requisite for the preservation of friendship, according to the Philosopher (*Ethic.* viii, 13; ix, 1). Now friendship is associated with all the virtues, since they are the reason for which man is loved. Therefore thankfulness, or gratitude, to which it belongs to repay favors received, is not a special virtue.

Reply to Objection 3. Since true friendship is based on virtue, whatever there is contrary to virtue in a friend is an obstacle to friendship, and whatever in him is virtuous is an incentive to friendship. In this way friendship is preserved by repayment of favors, although repayment of favors belongs specially to the virtue of gratitude.

INGRATITUDE

ARTICLE 1 ~ **Is ingratitude always a sin?**

Yes, despite objections to the contrary, Ingratitude is reckoned among other sins (2 Tim 3:2), where it is written: "Disobedient to parents, ungrateful, wicked," and so on.

I answer that, As stated above (q. 106, a. 4, ad 1, a. 6), a debt of gratitude is a moral debt required by virtue. Now a thing is a sin from the fact of its being contrary to virtue. Therefore it is evident that every ingratitude is a sin.[1]

Objection 1. It seems that ingratitude is not always a sin. For Seneca says (*De Beneficiis* iii) that "he who does not repay a favor is ungrateful." But sometimes it is impossible to repay a favor without sinning, for instance if one man has helped another to commit a sin. Therefore, since it is not a sin to refrain from sinning, it seems that ingratitude is not always a sin.

Reply to Objection 1. Gratitude regards a favor received, and he that helps another to commit a sin does him not a favor but an injury: and so no thanks are due to him, except perhaps on account of his good will, supposing him to have been deceived, and to have thought to help

---

[1] This form of wrongdoing, usually a sin of omission, is apparently quite common. Few people recognize, let alone properly thank or attempt to repay, many others who have done them tremendous services. Benefactors, teachers, relatives, friends, and country, have given literally innumerable gifts to us all, but are often not given proper thanks.

him in doing good, whereas he helped him to sin. In such a case the repayment due to him is not that he should be helped to commit a sin, because this would be repaying not good but evil, and this is contrary to gratitude.

Objection 2. Further, every sin is in the power of the person who commits it: because, according to Augustine (*De Lib. Arb.* iii; Retract. i), "no man sins in what he cannot avoid." Now sometimes it is not in the power of the sinner to avoid ingratitude, for instance when he has not the means of repaying. Again, forgetfulness is not in our power, and yet Seneca declares (*De Beneficiis* iii) that "to forget a kindness is the height of ingratitude." Therefore ingratitude is not always a sin.

Reply to Objection 2. No man is excused from ingratitude through inability to repay, for the very reason that the mere will suffices for the repayment of the debt of gratitude, as stated above (q. 106, a. 6, ad 1).

Forgetfulness of a favor received amounts to ingratitude, not indeed the forgetfulness that arises from a natural defect, which is not subject to the will, but that which arises from negligence.[2] For, as Seneca observes (*De Beneficiis* iii), "when forgetfulness of favors lays hold of a man, he has apparently given little thought to their repayment."

ARTICLE 2 ← Is ingratitude a special sin?

Yes, despite objections to the contrary, Ingratitude is opposed to gratitude or thankfulness, which is a special virtue. Therefore it is a special sin.

I answer that, Every vice is denominated from a deficiency of virtue, because deficiency is more opposed to virtue: thus illiberality is more opposed to liberality than prodigality is. Now a vice may be opposed to the virtue of gratitude by way of excess, for instance if one were to show gratitude for things for which gratitude is not due, or sooner than it is due, as stated above (q. 106, a. 4). But still more

---

[2] There is no sin where there is no voluntary act. If someone is struck with force on the head and thereby forgets what others have done for him, that person does not sin. However, to neglect proper care in recalling what others have done would be wrong.

opposed to gratitude is the vice denoting deficiency of gratitude, because the virtue of gratitude, as stated above (q. 106, a. 6), inclines to return something more. Therefore ingratitude is properly denominated from being a deficiency of gratitude. Now every deficiency or privation takes its species from the opposite habit: for blindness and deafness differ according to the difference of sight and hearing. Therefore, just as gratitude or thankfulness is one special virtue, so also is ingratitude one special sin.

It has, however, various degrees corresponding in their order to the things required for gratitude. The first of these is to recognize the favor received, the second to express one's appreciation and thanks, and the third to repay the favor at a suitable place and time according to one's means. And since what is last in the order of generation is first in the order of destruction, it follows that the first degree of ingratitude is when a man fails to repay a favor, the second when he declines to notice or indicate that he has received a favor,[3] while the third and supreme degree is when a man fails to recognize the reception of a favor, whether by forgetting it[4] or in any other way. Moreover, since opposite affirmation includes negation, it follows that it belongs to the first degree of ingratitude to return evil for good, to the second to find fault with a favor received, and to the third to esteem kindness as though it were unkindness.

Objection 1. It seems that ingratitude is not a special sin. For whoever sins acts against God his sovereign benefactor. But this pertains to ingratitude. Therefore ingratitude is not a special sin.

---

3 Thus, simply writing a thank you note or telling someone sincerely and from the heart "thank you" is, for Thomas, an important moral act. Thomas's ethics, as we see from this example, is thoroughly practical and "every day." Ethics is not just something that arises in "moral dilemmas," e.g., where there are six people and only two life jackets available. Moral success can take place in everyday decisions, such as writing thank you notes.

4 As Thomas clarified in the previous article, if forgetfulness is entirely unwillful, (e.g., you get in a car accident and have amnesia), then there is no wrongdoing involved. However, forgetting something can be wrong when that something can and should be remembered. Such forgetting shows that a given thing is not important, since what one finds extremely important is not easily forgotten.

Reply to Objection 1. In every sin there is material ingratitude to God, inasmuch as a man does something that may pertain to ingratitude. But formal ingratitude is when a favor is actually viewed with contempt, and this is a special sin.

Objection 2. Further, no special sin is contained under different kinds of sin. But one can be ungrateful by committing different kinds of sin, for instance by calumny, theft, or something similar committed against a benefactor. Therefore ingratitude is not a special sin.

Reply to Objection 2. Nothing hinders the formal aspect of some special sin from being found materially in several kinds of sin, and in this way the aspect of ingratitude is to be found in many kinds of sin.[5]

ARTICLE 4 ∼ Should favors be withheld from the ungrateful?

No, despite objections to the contrary, It is written (Lk 6:35) that "God . . . is kind to the unthankful, and to the evil." Now we should prove ourselves His children by imitating Him (Lk 6:36). Therefore we should not withhold favors from the ungrateful.

    I answer that, There are two points to be considered with regard to an ungrateful person. The first is what he deserves to suffer, and thus it is certain that he deserves to be deprived of our favor. The second is, what ought his benefactor to do? For in the first place he should not easily judge him to be ungrateful, since, as Seneca remarks (*De Beneficiis* iii), "a man is often grateful although he repays not," because perhaps he has not the means or the opportunity of repaying. Secondly, he should be inclined to turn his ungratefulness into gratitude, and if he does not achieve this by being kind to him once, he may by being so a second time. If, however, the more he repeats his favors, the more ungrateful and evil the other becomes, he should cease from bestowing his favors upon him.[6]

---

[5] A single act, then, may embody more than one way to do wrong. To punch your benefactor in response to his gift is wrong in so far as it is generally wrong to assault others, wrong on account of the special respect due to benefactors, and wrong as a form of ingratitude for a gift.

[6] Granting favors, like all acts that are good in kind, must be done with practical wisdom. Prudence determines whether this is the right time, place, and person

Objection 1. It seems that favors should be withheld from the ungrateful. For it is written (Wis 16:29): "The hope of the unthankful shall melt away as the winter's ice." But this hope would not melt away unless favors were withheld from him. Therefore favors should be withheld from the ungrateful.

Reply to Objection 1. The passage quoted speaks of what the ungrateful man deserves to suffer.

Objection 2. Further, no one should afford another an occasion of committing sin. But the ungrateful in receiving a favor is given an occasion of ingratitude. Therefore favors should not be bestowed on the ungrateful.

Reply to Objection 2. He that bestows a favor on an ungrateful person affords him an occasion not of sin but of gratitude and love. And if the recipient makes the favor an occasion of ingratitude, this is not to be imputed to the person doing the favor.

Objection 3. Further, "By what things a man sins, by the same also he is tormented" (Wis 11:17). Now he that is ungrateful when he receives a favor sins against the favor. Therefore he should be deprived of the favor.

Reply to Objection 3. He that bestows a favor must not at once act the part of a punisher of ingratitude, but rather that of a kindly physician, by healing the ingratitude with repeated favors.

---

to grant a favor, taking into account the specific circumstances and likely outcomes. If granting a favor makes a person even worse off, as this example supposes, then it is no kindness to grant the favor and indeed it is charitable not to grant the favor. Although some things should never be done because they are incompatible with proper love of God and neighbor (for example, idolatry and bearing false witness), what ought to be done in any given circumstance cannot be determined apart from use of practical wisdom in the concrete circumstances of life.

QUESTION **108**

VENGEANCE

ARTICLE 1 ~ Is vengeance permissible?

Yes, despite objections to the contrary, We should look to God for nothing save what is good and moral. But we are to look to God for vengeance on His enemies: for it is written (Lk 18:7): "Will not God revenge His elect who cry to Him day and night?" as if to say: "He will indeed." Therefore vengeance is not essentially evil and immoral.

I answer that, Vengeance consists in the infliction of a penal evil on one who has sinned. Accordingly, in the matter of vengeance, we must consider the mind of the avenger. For if his intention is directed chiefly to the evil of the person on whom he takes vengeance and rests there, then his vengeance is altogether immoral: because to take pleasure in another's evil belongs to hatred, which is contrary to the charity whereby we are bound to love all men. Nor is it an excuse that he intends the evil of one who has unjustly inflicted evil on him, as neither is a man excused for hating one that hates him: for a man may not sin against another just because the latter has already sinned against him, since this is to be overcome by evil, which was forbidden by the Apostle, who says (Rom 12:21): "Be not overcome by evil, but overcome evil by good."

If, however, the avenger's intention be directed chiefly to some good, to be obtained by means of the punishment of the person who has sinned (for instance that the sinner may amend, or at least that he may be restrained and others be not disturbed, that justice may be upheld, and God honored), then vengeance may be moral, provided other due circumstances be observed.[1]

Objection 1. It seems that vengeance is not moral. For whoever usurps what is God's sins. But vengeance belongs to God, for it is written (Dt 32:35, Rom 12:19): "Vengeance is mine, and I will repay." Therefore all vengeance is immoral.

Reply to Objection 1. He who takes vengeance on the wicked in keeping with his rank and position does not usurp what belongs to God but makes use of the power granted him by God. For it is written (Rom 13:4) of the earthly prince that "he is God's minister, an avenger to execute wrath upon him that doeth evil." If, however, a man takes vengeance outside the order of divine appointment, he usurps what is God's and therefore sins.[2]

---

[1] Punishment is a non-moral evil for the one undergoing it, but not necessarily a moral evil for the one who carries out the punishment. For Thomas, many things that physically may look the same are not morally the same. Robberies and fines both take a person's property; imprisonment and kidnapping both take a person's liberty; capital punishment and murder both take a person's life. But these acts, though physically similar, are morally quite different. As noted here, however, for a punishment to be truly just, "due circumstances" must be observed. So even if fining is not robbing, and imprisoning is not kidnapping, and judicial executing is not murdering, fining, imprisoning, and judicial executing may still be wrong—indeed may usually be wrong, in certain circumstances. However, these judicial acts are not intrinsically wrong in the way that robbing, kidnapping, and murdering are.

[2] Parents, for example, have due authority over their children arising from their duty to raise their children properly. This duty to care for and love children gives rise to their right as parents to educate their children, and a proper education includes not merely growth in knowledge but also growth in character. Discipline or punishment is one tool in aiding growth in character and thus may be used to train children. Parents have the right to punish their own children, not the children of other people, unless these others grant them permission. Likewise, those in public authority have responsibility for the common good and so may punish so as to rectify a disorder produced by the criminal and thereby to preserve the common good. If, on the other hand, a private person were to punish another citizen in a way reserved for the public authority, such a person would exceed the due order and would not serve justice but rather exhibits vigilantism.

Objection 2. Further, he that takes vengeance on a man does not bear with him. But we ought to bear with the wicked, for a gloss on Canticle 2:2, "As the lily among the thorns," says: "He is not a good man that cannot bear with a wicked one." Therefore we should not take vengeance on the wicked.

Reply to Objection 2. The good bear with the wicked by enduring patiently, and in due manner, the wrongs they themselves receive from them, but they do not bear with them so as to endure the wrongs they inflict on God and their neighbor. For Chrysostom [cf. *Opus Imperfectum, Hom. v in Matth.*, falsely ascribed to St. Chrysostom] says: "It is praiseworthy to be patient under our own wrongs, but to overlook God's wrongs is most wicked."[3]

Objection 3. Further, vengeance is taken by inflicting punishment, which is the cause of servile fear. But the New Law is not a law of fear, but of love, as Augustine states (*Contra Adamant.* xvii). Therefore, at least in the New Testament, all vengeance is immoral.

Reply to Objection 3. The law of the Gospel is the law of love, and therefore those who do good out of love, and who alone properly belong to the Gospel, ought not to be terrorized by means of punishment, but only those who are not moved by love to do good, and who, though they belong to the Church outwardly, do not belong to it in merit.

Objection 4. Further, a man is said to avenge himself when he takes revenge for wrongs inflicted on himself. But, seemingly, it is immoral even for a judge to punish those who have wronged him; for Chrysostom [cf. *Opus Imperfectum, Hom. v in Matth.*, falsely ascribed to St. Chrysostom] says: "Let us learn after Christ's example to bear our own wrongs with magnanimity, yet not to suffer God's wrongs, not even by listening to them." Therefore vengeance seems to be immoral.

---

3 Love of neighbor prompts many people to endure wrongs done against them personally. But the same love of neighbor may lead the same people not to endure wrongs done against those persons for whom they have responsibility.

Reply to Objection 4. Sometimes a wrong done to a person reflects on God and the Church: and then it is the duty of that person to avenge the wrong. For example, Elijah made fire descend on those who were come to seize him (2 Kings 1); likewise Elisha cursed the boys that mocked him (2 Kings 2); and Pope Sylverius excommunicated those who sent him into exile (XXIII, Q. iv, Cap. *Guilisarius*). But in so far as the wrong inflicted on a man affects his person, he should bear it patiently if this be expedient. For these precepts of patience are to be understood as referring to preparedness of the mind, as Augustine states (*De Serm. Dom. in Monte* i).

Objection 5. Further, the sin of a multitude is more harmful than the sin of only one: for it is written (Sir 26:5–7): "Of three things my heart has been afraid . . . the accusation of a city, and the gathering together of the people, and a false calumny." But vengeance should not be taken on the sin of a multitude, for a gloss on Matthew 13:29, 30, "Lest perhaps . . . you root up the wheat . . . suffer both to grow," says that "a multitude should not be excommunicated, nor should the sovereign." Neither, therefore, is any other vengeance moral.

Reply to Objection 5. When the whole multitude sins, vengeance must be taken on them, either in respect of the whole multitude—thus the Egyptians were drowned in the Red Sea while they were pursuing the children of Israel (Ex 14), and the people of Sodom were entirely destroyed (Gen 19)—or as regards part of the multitude, as may be seen in the punishment of those who worshipped the calf.

Sometimes, however, if there is hope of many making amends, the severity of vengeance should be brought to bear on a few of the principals, whose punishment fills the rest with fear; thus the Lord (Num 25) commanded the princes of the people to be hanged for the sin of the multitude.

On the other hand, if it is not the whole but only a part of the multitude that has sinned, then if the guilty can be separated from the innocent, vengeance should be wrought on them, provided, however, that this can be done without scandal to others, else the multitude should be spared and severity foregone. The same applies to the sovereign, whom the multitude follow. For his sin should be borne with, if it cannot be punished without scandal to the multitude, unless indeed his sin were such that it would do more harm to the multitude, either spiritually or temporally, than would the scandal that was feared to arise from his punishment.[4]

---

[4] For St. Thomas, punishment is not a matter of strict geometrical correspondence. Famously, Immanuel Kant held that murder *must* be punished with the death penalty: "If, however, he has committed a murder, he must die. In this case, there is no substitute that will satisfy the requirements of legal justice. There is no sameness of kind between death and remaining alive even under the most miserable conditions, and consequently there is also no equality between the crime and the retribution unless the criminal is judicially condemned and put to death." *The Metaphysical Elements of Justice* (New York: The Bobbs-Merrill Company, Inc., 1965), 104. Thomas, here and elsewhere, argues that justice is a virtue that is informed by practical wisdom. The ultimate goal of punishment is to restore, preserve, and forward the common good, so if some punishment undermines the common good, even if the crime committed fully merits the punishment in terms of strict retribution, the punishment should not be carried out.

Lying

Article 3 ⬩ Is every lie a sin?

Yes, despite objections to the contrary, It is written (Sir 7:14): "Be not willing to make any manner of lie."[1]

I answer that, An action that is naturally evil in respect of its genus can by no means be good and moral, since in order for an action to be good it must be right in every respect: because good results from a complete cause, while evil results from any single defect, as Dionysius asserts (*De Div. Nom.* iv). Now a lie is evil in respect of its genus, since it is an action bearing on undue matter. For as words are naturally signs of intellectual acts, it is unnatural and undue for anyone to signify by words something that is not in his mind.[2] Hence the Philosopher says (*Ethic.* iv, 7) that "lying is in itself evil and to be shunned, while truthfulness is

---

1 For a contemporary philosopher's treatment of lying, see Alasdair MacIntyre, "Truthfulness, Lies, and Moral Philosophers: What Can We Learn from Kant and Mill," in *The Tanner Lectures on Human Values 16*, ed. Grethe B. Peterson, (Salt Lake City: University of Utah Press, 1995), 307–61.

2 It is important to note that an obligation not to lie does not imply an obligation always to say what you believe is true. In many circumstances, one should simply remain silent or say something else true, but refrain from saying something untrue. If the unvarnished truth will hurt another person, and there is not a good reason for allowing someone to be hurt, then it is probably best not to speak this truth, and this concealment is *not* lying. In matters of speech as in all the moral life, the exercise of practical wisdom is necessary to know when to speak, when to remain silent, and to know what and how to speak when communication is appropriate.

good and worthy of praise." Therefore every lie is a sin, as also Augustine declares (*Contra Mendac.* i).[3]

Objection 1. It seems that not every lie is a sin. For it is evident that the evangelists did not sin in the writing of the Gospel. Yet they seem to have told something false since their accounts of the words of Christ and of others often differ from one another. Therefore seemingly one of them must have given an untrue account. Therefore not every lie is a sin.

Reply to Objection 1. It is immoral to hold that any false assertion is contained either in the Gospel or in any canonical Scripture, or that the writers thereof have told untruths, because faith would be deprived of its certitude that is based on the authority of Holy Writ. That the words of certain people are variously reported in the Gospel and other sacred writings does not constitute a lie. Hence Augustine says (*De Consens. Evang.* ii): "He that has the wit to understand that in order to know the truth it is necessary to get at the sense will conclude that he must not be the least troubled, no matter by what words that sense is expressed." Hence it is evident, as he adds (*De Consens. Evang.* ii), that "we must not judge that someone is lying, if several persons fail to describe in the same way and in the same words a thing which they remember to have seen or heard."

---

[3] Augustine is not alone in holding this view that lying is always wrong. Immanuel Kant as well as many later scholastic thinkers held the same view. For them, as for Aquinas, every lie is a sin. An important question is, of course, what is meant by "lie"? Augustine defined lying as communicating (what one believes to be) a falsehood in order to deceive. Aquinas narrowed the definition of a lie to communicating *contra mentem* or communicating something as true that one actually believes to be false. Later scholastics defined lying as communicating an untruth to one who has a right to the truth. Proportionalists defined lying as communicating an untruth without a proportionate reason. For more on the history of the moral teaching on lying, as well as a critique of the proportionalist view, see Christopher Kaczor, *Proportionalism and the Natural Law Tradition* (Washington, DC: The Catholic University of America Press, 2002), 190–95. Of course, to say something that in fact is untrue is not a lie *if* one sincerely believes that what one says is true. Lying and perjury are not always about saying something that is in fact false. I lie or perjure myself if I communicate what I believe to be false as if it were true, even if it turns out that my beliefs were mistaken (cf. *ST* II–II, q. 98, a. 1, ad 3).

Objection 2. Further, no one is rewarded by God for sin. But the midwives of Egypt were rewarded by God for a lie, for it is stated that "God built them houses" (Ex 1:21). Therefore a lie is not a sin.

Reply to Objection 2. The midwives were rewarded, not for their lie, but for their fear of God, and for their good-will, which latter led them to tell a lie. Hence it is expressly stated (Ex 2:21): "And because the midwives feared God, He built them houses." But the subsequent lie was not meritorious.

Objection 3. Further, the deeds of holy men are related in Sacred Scripture that they may be a model of human life. But we read of certain very holy men that they lied. Thus (Gen 12 and 20) we are told that Abraham said of his wife that she was his sister. Jacob also lied when he said that he was Esau, and yet he received a blessing (Gen 27:27–29). Again, Judith is commended (Jud 15:10, 11), although she lied to Holofernes. Therefore not every lie is a sin.

Reply to Objection 3. In Sacred Scripture, as Augustine observes (*Lib. De Mend.* v), the deeds of certain persons are related as examples of perfect virtue: and we must not believe that such persons were liars. If, however, any of their statements appear to be untruthful, we must understand such statements to have been figurative and prophetic. Hence Augustine says (*Lib. De Mend.* v): "We must believe that whatever is related of those who, in prophetical times, are mentioned as being worthy of credit, was done and said by them prophetically." As to Abraham, "when he said that Sara was his sister, he wished to hide the truth, not to tell a lie, for she is called his sister since she was the daughter of his father," Augustine says (QQ. *Super. Gen.* xxvi; *Contra Mendac.* x; *Contra Faust.* xxii). Therefore Abraham himself said (Gen 20:12): "She is truly my sister, the daughter of my father, and not the daughter of my mother," being related to him on his father's side. Jacob's assertion that he was Esau, Isaac's first-born, was spoken in a mystical sense, because, to wit, the latter's birthright was due to him by right: and he made use of this mode of speech being moved by the spirit of prophecy, in order to signify a mystery, namely, that the younger people, i.e., the Gentiles, should supplant the first-born, i.e., the Jews.

Some, however, are commended in the Scriptures, not on account of perfect virtue, but for a certain virtuous disposition,[4] seeing that it was owing to some praiseworthy sentiment that they were moved to do certain undue things. It is thus that Judith is praised, not for lying to Holofernes, but for her desire to save the people, to which end she exposed herself to danger. And yet one might also say that her words contain truth in some mystical sense.

Objection 4. Further, one ought to choose the lesser evil in order to avoid the greater: even so a physician cuts off a limb, lest the whole body perish. Yet less harm is done by raising a false opinion in a person's mind, than by someone slaying or being slain. Therefore a man may morally lie, to save another from committing murder, or another from being killed.

Reply to Objection 4. A lie is sinful not only because it injures one's neighbor, but also on account of its inordinateness, as stated above in this article. Now it is not permissible to make use of anything inordinate in order to ward off injury or defects from another: as neither is it moral to steal in order to give an alms, except perhaps in a case of necessity when all things are common. Therefore it is not moral to tell a lie in order to deliver another from any danger whatever. Nevertheless it is moral to hide the truth prudently, by keeping it back, as Augustine says (*Contra Mendac.* x).[5]

---

[4] Even though such persons had good intentions, not all of their deeds are worthy of imitation. Indeed, not all the examples given in Scripture show good behavior or even good intentions, but often show the consequences of bad behavior, such as the adultery of David (2 Sam:11) or the disobedience of Moses (Num:20). Indeed, aside from Christ, the major figures in Scripture from Adam onward all fail in one respect or another.

[5] An obvious objection raised to this view is this: What do you do in cases of extreme necessity, e.g., when the Nazis come and you are hiding Jews in the basement? Various answers have been proposed. Some moral philosophers have permitted what are called "mental reservations" in such cases. A mental reservation is a withholding of information in order to mislead (but not lie to) another. "Do you have Jews here?!" demands the SS officer. "No," you reply, "we don't have any Jews here." Of course, you are at the same time mentally reserving: "They're not right *here* in the entrance to the house; they are down in the basement." Others have noted that the Nazi regime was illegitimate and so an

Objection 5. Further, it is a lie not to fulfill what one has promised. Yet one is not bound to keep all one's promises: for Isidore says (*Synonym.* ii): "Break your faith when you have promised ill." Therefore not every lie is a sin.

Reply to Objection 5. A man does not lie, so long as he has a mind to do what he promises, because he does not speak contrary to what he has in mind, but if he does not keep his promise, he seems to act without faith in changing his mind. He may, however, be excused for two reasons: first, if he has promised something evidently immoral, because he sinned in making the promise, and did well to change his mind;[6] secondly, if circumstances have changed with regard to persons and the business at hand. For, as Seneca states (*De Beneficiis* iv), for a man to be bound to keep a promise, it is necessary for everything to remain unchanged: otherwise neither did he lie in promising—since

---

SS officer would have no right to the truth. If one defines a lie as communicating a falsehood to one who has a right to the truth, then telling the SS officer there are no Jews here would not count as a lie. Another strategy is to use words that can be taken in two ways. The story is told by Cardinal Newman of the enemies of St. Athanasius who, while seeking to kill him, passed by him in a boat on the other side of the river. They called out to him, "Have you seen Athanasius?" The saint replied, "He's not far off." With this, the enemies hurried down the river in hopes of finding him. [To mislead is not to lie.] Alexander Pruss proposes another answer. When the SS officer asks: "Do you have any Jews here?" the Nazi means by "Jews" nasty, dishonorable, and unlovable human beings. You believe that every human being is made in God's image, and so Jews are worthy of love, respect, and honor, as is everyone else. So, using his own meaning of the word "Jews," speaking his language so to speak, you respond, "No, we don't have any Jews here," since you don't have any nasty, dishonorable, unlovable human beings in your house, but rather human beings deserving of love, honor, and respect. See, Alexander Pruss, "Lying and Speaking Your Interlocutor's Language," *The Thomist* 63 (1999): 439–53. Note that such strategies to mislead others are not usually permissible. Although in extreme circumstances one can break a promise without moral fault, we usually have an obligation to keep our promises. So too when communicating we should speak the truth in a straightforward manner, unless justified by a serious reason.

6 If someone were to promise to do something evil, such as murder another, such a promise would not bind. Indeed, such a person would sin in making the promise and would do well in breaking it.

he promised what he had in his mind, due circumstances being taken for granted[7]—nor was he faithless in not keeping his promise, because circumstances are no longer the same. Hence the Apostle, though he did not go to Corinth, whither he had promised to go (2 Cor 1), did not lie, because obstacles had arisen which prevented him.

ARTICLE 4 ❦ **Is every lie a mortal sin?**

No, despite objections to the contrary, Augustine says on Psalm 5:7, "You will destroy," etc.: "There are two kinds of lie that are not grievously sinful yet are not devoid of sin, when we lie either in joking, or for the sake of our neighbor's good." But every mortal sin is grievous. Therefore jocose and officious lies are not mortal sins.

I answer that, A mortal sin is, properly speaking, one that is contrary to charity, whereby the soul lives in union with God, as stated above (q. 24, a. 12; q. 35, a. 3). Now a lie may be contrary to charity in three ways: first, in itself; secondly, in respect of the evil intended; thirdly, accidentally.

A lie may be in itself contrary to charity by reason of its false signification. For if this be about divine things, it is contrary to the charity of God, whose truth one hides or corrupts by such a lie, so that a lie of this kind is opposed not only to the virtue of charity, but also to the virtues of faith and religion: therefore it is a most grievous and a mortal sin. If, however, the false signification be about something the knowledge of which affects a man's good, for instance if it pertain to the perfection of science or to moral conduct, a lie of this description inflicts an injury on one's neighbor, since it causes him to have a false opinion. Therefore it is contrary to charity, as regards the love of our neighbor, and consequently is a mortal sin. On the other hand, if the false opinion engendered by the lie be about some matter the knowledge of which is of no consequence, then the lie in question does no harm to one's neighbor, for instance if a person be

---

[7] Nearly all promises are made with an implicit "other things being equal" proviso. If one promises to study with another person but on the way to studying has the opportunity to save someone's life, the prior promise to study is no longer binding.

deceived as to some contingent particulars that do not concern him. Therefore a lie of this kind, considered in itself, is not a mortal sin.[8]

As regards the end in view, a lie may be contrary to charity, through being told with the purpose of acting against God, and this is always a mortal sin, for it is opposed to religion; or in order to injure one's neighbor, in his person, his possessions, or his good name, and this also is a mortal sin, since it is a mortal sin to injure one's neighbor, and one sins mortally if one has merely the intention of committing a mortal sin. But if the end intended be not contrary to charity, neither will the lie, considered under this aspect, be a mortal sin, as in the case of a jocose lie, where some little pleasure is intended, or in an officious lie, where the good also of one's neighbor is intended. Accidentally a lie may be contrary to charity by reason of scandal or any other injury resulting therefrom: and thus again it will be a mortal sin, for instance if a man were not deterred through scandal from lying publicly.

Objection 1. It seems that every lie is a mortal sin. For it is written (Ps 6:7): "You will destroy all that speak a lie," and (Wis 1:11): "The mouth that belieth killeth the soul." Now mortal sin alone causes destruction and death of the soul. Therefore every lie is a mortal sin.

Reply to Objection 1. The passages quoted refer to the mischievous lie, as a gloss explains the words of Psalm 5:7, "You will destroy all that speak a lie."

Objection 2. Further, whatever is against a precept of the decalogue is a mortal sin. Now lying is against this precept of the decalogue: "You shall not bear false witness." Therefore every lie is a mortal sin.

Reply to Objection 2. Since all the precepts of the decalogue are directed to the love of God and our neighbor, as stated above (q. 44, a. 1, ad 3; I–II, q. 100, a. 5, ad 1), a lie is contrary to a precept of the

---

[8] Although all lies are wrong, not all lies are equally bad. It is worse to lie about things pertaining to God than to trivial matters of no great concern. Lies that undermine love of God and neighbor are mortal sins, while lies that cause no great harm and do not arise from an intention to hurt are venial sins. Often, it is a matter of judgment whether a particular lie is a mortal or a venial sin.

decalogue, in so far as it is contrary to the love of God and our neighbor. Hence it is expressly forbidden to bear false witness against our neighbor.[9]

Objection 3. Further, Augustine says (*De Doctr. Christ.* i, 36): "Every liar breaks his faith in lying, since forsooth he wishes the person to whom he lies to have faith in him, and yet he does not keep faith with him, when he lies to him: and whoever breaks his faith is guilty of iniquity." Now no one is said to break his faith or "to be guilty of iniquity," for a venial sin. Therefore no lie is a venial sin.

Reply to Objection 3. Even a venial sin can be called "iniquity" in a broad sense, in so far as it is beside the equity of justice; therefore it is written (1 Jn 3:4): "Every sin is iniquity [Vulg.: 'And sin is iniquity']." It is in this sense that Augustine is speaking.

---

[9] The commandment then forbids not simply bearing false witness but bearing false witness *against* our neighbor, lying so as to harm our neighbor.

QUESTION **118**

GREED[1]

ARTICLE 5 ⟶ **Is greed the greatest of sins?**

No, despite objections to the contrary, Adultery is a more grievous sin than theft, according to Proverbs 6:30. But theft pertains to greed. Therefore greed is not the most grievous of sins.

I answer that, Every sin, from the very fact that it is an evil, consists in the corruption or privation of some good, while, in so far as it is voluntary, it consists in the desire of some good.[2] Consequently the order of sins may be considered in two ways: first, on the part of the good that is despised or corrupted by sin, and then the greater the good the graver the sin. From this point of view a sin that is against God is most grievous; after this comes a sin that is committed against a man's person, and after this comes a sin against external things, which

---

[1] Greed denotes immoderate love of possessing external goods, especially money (*ST* II–II, q. 188, a. 1).

[2] Evil, whether moral evil or non-moral evil, always consists in a lack of due perfection. Hence, in the *Summa*, Thomas always first talks about a virtue (the due perfection of an agent, such as thankfulness) before talking about the corresponding vice (the lack of due perfection in an agent, such as ingratitude). Evil of body or of soul is parasitic on the good. At the same time, even an evil action is chosen under the formality of goodness (*sub ratione boni*). No agent chooses evil as evil for the sake of evil. Rather, even great evils such as terrorism are chosen as (misguided) means to a good (say, of establishing what is perceived to be a just social order).

are deputed to man's use, and this seems to belong to greed.[3] Secondly, the degrees of sin may be considered on the part of the good to which the human appetite is inordinately subjected; and then the lesser the good, the more deformed is the sin: for it is more shameful to be subject to a lower than to a higher good. Now the good of external things is the lowest of human goods: since it is less than the good of the body, and this is less than the good of the soul, which is less than the Divine good.[4] From this point of view the sin of greed, whereby the human appetite is subjected even to external things, has in a way a greater deformity. Since, however, corruption or privation of good is the formal element in sin, while conversion to a mutable good is the material element, the gravity of the sin is to be judged from the point of view of the good corrupted, rather than from that of the good to which the appetite is subjected. Hence we must assert that greed is not simply the most grievous of sins.

Objection 1. It seems that greed is the greatest of sins. For it is written (Sir 10:9): "Nothing is more wicked than a covetous man," and the text continues: "There is not a more wicked thing than to love money: for such a one puts even his own soul on sale." Tully also says (*De Offic.* i, under the heading, 'True magnanimity is based chiefly on two things'): "Nothing is so narrow or little minded as to love money." But this pertains to greed. Therefore greed is the most grievous of sins.

Reply to Objection 1. These authorities speak of greed on the part of the good to which the appetite is subjected. Hence (Sir 10:10) it is given as a reason that the covetous man "setteth his own soul to sale"; because, to wit, he exposes his soul—that is, his life—to danger for the sake of money. Hence the text continues: "Because while he lives

---

[3] The wrongfulness of a sin can be judged according to the goodness of the being corrupted or acted against. So the greater the good corrupted, the worse the wrongdoing. Similarly, the more valuable the object is, the worse it is to break that object—it is worse to break Michelangelo's *Pieta* than to break a plate at the cafeteria.

[4] The wrongfulness of a sin can also be accounted from the good to which someone turns: the lesser the good, the more deformed the sin. So, to break a fast for disgusting food is worse than to break a fast for delicious food, for to give in for a lesser good is worse than to give in to sin for a greater good.

he has cast away"—that is, despised—"his bowels," in order to make money. Tully also adds that it is the mark of a "narrow mind," namely, that one be willing to be subject to money.

Objection 2. Further, the more a sin is opposed to charity, the more grievous it is. Now greed is most opposed to charity: for Augustine says (QQ. 83, qu. 36) that "greed is the bane of charity." Therefore greed is the greatest of sins.

Reply to Objection 2. Augustine is taking greed generally, in reference to any temporal good, not in its special acceptation for greed, because greed for any temporal good is the bane of charity, inasmuch as a man turns away from the Divine good through cleaving to a temporal good.[5]

Objection 3. Further, the gravity of a sin is indicated by its being incurable: therefore the sin against the Holy Spirit is said to be most grievous, because it is unpardonable. But greed is an incurable sin; hence the Philosopher says (*Ethic.* iv, 1) that "old age and helplessness of any kind make men illiberal." Therefore greed is the most grievous of sins.

Reply to Objection 3. The sin against the Holy Spirit is incurable in one way, greed in another. For the sin against the Holy Spirit is incurable by reason of contempt: for instance, because a man rejects God's mercy, or His justice, or some one of those things whereby man's sins are healed. Therefore incurability of this kind points to the greater gravity of the sin. On the other hand, greed is incurable on the part of a human defect, a thing which human nature ever seeks to remedy, since the more deficient one is the more one seeks relief from external things, and consequently the more one gives way to greed. Hence incurability of this kind is an indication not of the sin's being more grievous, but of its being somewhat more dangerous.

---

5 Properly speaking, greed is an immoderate love of possessing things, especially money. In a general sense, however, one could speak of greed for power, or greed for fame, or greed for pleasure, and in this general sense Augustine indicates that greed is contrary to charity. For greed taken in this non-specific sense is what prompts a turn from the Uncreated Good to a mutable good.

Objection 4. Further, the Apostle says (Eph 5:5) that greed is "a serv-ing of idols." Now idolatry is reckoned among the most grievous sins. Therefore greed is also.

Reply to Objection 4. Greed is compared to idolatry on account of a certain likeness that it bears to it: because the greedy man, like the idol-ater, subjects himself to an external creature, though not in the same way. For the idolater subjects himself to an external creature by paying it Divine honor, whereas the covetous man subjects himself to an exter-nal creature by desiring it immoderately for use, not for worship. Hence it does not follow that greed is as grievous a sin as idolatry.[6]

---

6 Practically speaking, greed can be a form of idolatry when love of money replaces love of God, and the sole purpose of human life is seen in terms of accumulation of wealth and possessions: "He who dies with the most toys wins." Such materialism reduces human persons and human relationships to mere means to be used to accumulate wealth.

QUESTION **122**

THE PRECEPTS
OF JUSTICE

ARTICLE 1 ~~ **Are the precepts of the Ten Commandments precepts of justice?**

Yes, despite objections to the contrary, Seemingly justice is the sole virtue whereby we are directed to another. Now we are directed to another by all the precepts of the decalogue, as is evident if one consider each of them. Therefore all the precepts of the Ten Commandments pertain to justice.

I answer that, The precepts of the decalogue are the first principles of the Law, and the natural reason assents to them at once,[1] as to principles that are most evident.[2] Now it is altogether evident that the notion of duty, which is essential to a precept, appears in justice, which

---

[1] Why would God reveal in the Ten Commandments truths that could be known through natural reason? Thomas answers this question, with respect to God's existence, in chapter four of his *Summa contra Gentiles*. Although in principle people could come to know the basics of the moral law without revelation, God reveals these truths in order that there not be any confusion about them, nor room for rationalization. It is a mercy that God reveals these truths so as to help us to grow more easily in virtue and attain happiness.

[2] The Ten Commandments are revealed by God but are also precepts that accord with natural reason. The last chapter of C. S. Lewis's book *The Abolition of Man* (New York: Macmillan, 1947) illustrates the universality of the natural law across cultures. Using quotations from Greek, Roman, Chinese, Egyptian, Christian, Babylonian, Hindu, Jewish, Indian, and Norse cultures, Lewis shows that the fundamental truths expressed in loving God and neighbor are found throughout human history, even in cultures vastly diverse in many ways.

is of one towards another, because in those matters that relate to himself it would seem at a glance that man is master of himself, and that he may do as he likes, whereas in matters that refer to another it appears manifestly that a man is under obligation to render to another that which is his due. Hence the precepts of the decalogue pertain to justice. Therefore the first three precepts are about acts of religion, which is the chief part of justice; the fourth precept is about acts of piety, which is the second part of justice; and the six remaining are about justice commonly so called, which is observed among equals.

Objection 1. It seems that the precepts of the Decalogue are not precepts of justice. For the intention of a lawgiver is "to make the citizens virtuous in respect of every virtue," as stated in *Ethic.* ii, 1. Therefore, according to *Ethic.* v, 1, "the law prescribes about all acts of all virtues." Now the precepts of the Ten Commandments are the first principles of the whole Divine Law. Therefore the precepts of the decalogue do not pertain to justice alone.

Reply to Objection 1. The intention of the law is to make all men virtuous, but in a certain order, namely, by first of all giving them precepts about those things where the notion of duty is most manifest, as stated above.

Objection 3. Further, the Law contains chiefly precepts about acts of justice regarding the common good, for instance about public officers and the like. But there is no mention of these in the precepts of the decalogue. Therefore it seems that the precepts of the decalogue do not properly belong to justice.

Reply to Objection 3. Things that concern the common good must be administered in different ways according to the difference of men.[3] Hence they were to be given a place not among the precepts of the decalogue, but among the judicial precepts.

---

[3] Many matters of justice cannot be properly determined save in the highly specific and historical circumstances of individual societies, families, and relationships. However, certain fundamental principles, such as those found in the Ten Commandments, do apply universally.

Objection 4. Further, the precepts of the decalogue are divided into two tables, corresponding to the love of God and the love of our neighbor,[4] both of which regard the virtue of charity. Therefore the precepts of the Decalogue belong to charity rather than to justice.

Reply to Objection 4. The precepts of the decalogue pertain to charity as their end, according to 1 Timothy 1:5, "The end of the commandment is charity"; but they belong to justice inasmuch as they refer immediately to acts of justice.

ARTICLE 6 ～ Are the other six precepts of the Ten Commandments fittingly expressed?

Yes, despite objections to the contrary, Stands the authority of Scripture.

I answer that, Just as by the parts of justice a man pays that which is due to certain definite persons, to whom he is bound for some special reason, so too by justice properly so called he pays that which is due to all in general. Hence, after the three precepts pertaining to religion, whereby man pays what is due to God, and after the fourth precept pertaining to piety, whereby he pays what is due to his parents—which duty includes the paying of all that is due for any special reason—it was necessary in due sequence to give certain precepts pertaining to justice properly so called, which pays to all indifferently what is due to them.

Objection 1. It seems that the other six precepts of the decalogue are unfittingly expressed. For it is not sufficient for salvation that one refrain from injuring one's neighbor; but it is required that one pay one's debts, according to Romans 13:7, "Render . . . to all men their dues." Now the last six precepts merely forbid one to injure one's neighbor. Therefore these precepts are unfittingly expressed.

---

[4] The first few commandments (those contained in the first tablet) help direct us in terms of love of God ("no gods before Me, do not take the name of the Lord in vain, keep holy the Sabbath"). The second tablet helps guide us in terms of love of neighbor (honor your father and mother, you shall not kill, you shall not commit adultery, you shall not steal, you shall not bear false witness, you shall not covet your neighbor's spouse, you shall not covet your neighbor's goods).

Reply to Objection 1. Man is bound towards all persons in general to inflict injury on no one: hence the negative precepts, which forbid the doing of those injuries that can be inflicted on one's neighbor, had to be given a place, as general precepts, among the precepts of the decalogue. On the other hand, the duties we owe to our neighbor are paid in different ways to different people: hence it was not necessary to include affirmative precepts about those duties among the precepts of the decalogue.[5]

Objection 2. Further, these precepts forbid murder, adultery, stealing and bearing false witness. But many other injuries can be inflicted on one's neighbor, as appears from those which have been specified above (QQ. 72, *seq.*). Therefore it seems that the aforesaid precepts are unfittingly expressed.

Reply to Objection 2. All other injuries that are inflicted on our neighbor are reducible to those that are forbidden by these precepts, as taking precedence of others in point of generality and importance. For all injuries that are inflicted on the person of our neighbor are understood to be forbidden under the head of murder as being the principal of all. Those that are inflicted on a person connected with one's neighbor, especially by way of lust, are understood to be forbidden together with adultery; those that come under the head of damage done to property are understood to be forbidden together with theft; and those that are comprised under speech, such as detractions, insults, and so forth, are understood to be forbidden together with the bearing of false witness, which is more directly opposed to justice.

Objection 4. Further, murder is a more grievous sin than adultery or theft. But there is no precept forbidding the desire of murder. Therefore neither was it fitting to have precepts forbidding the desire of theft and of adultery.

---

[5] As in medicine, general directions are most easily given in the negative. One should not steal, but how and when and in what way one should repay one's debts is a matter of virtually infinite variation. Again, practical wisdom is needed to figure out what one should do to love one's neighbor, but the beginning of prudence is to realize what one should not do against one's neighbor.

Reply to Objection 4. Murder in itself is an object not of concupiscence but of horror, since it has not in itself the aspect of good. On the other hand, adultery has the aspect of a certain kind of good, i.e., of something pleasurable, and theft has an aspect of good, i.e., of something useful: and good of its very nature has the aspect of something concupiscible. Hence the concupiscence of theft and adultery had to be forbidden by special precepts, but not the concupiscence of murder.[6]

---

6 For more on this topic, see Jean Porter, "The Virtue of Justice," and Martin Rhonheimer, "Sins Against Justice," in *The Ethics of Aquinas*, ed. Stephen Pope (Washington, DC: Georgetown University Press, 2002).

COURAGE
(FORTITUDE)

COURAGE (FORTITUDE)

JUST AS there are different forms of justice, so too there are different senses of courage. St. Thomas distinguishes "general courage" from "special courage." General courage is a habit of the toughness or "guts", a resoluteness of mind, which enables us to overcome difficulties in attaining the good we intend to do. This kind of courage, however, is not necessarily a moral virtue. A thief might exhibit courage in this sense in fighting against the police. Special courage, on the other hand, is a moral virtue—specifically the cardinal virtue that enables us to be resolute in overcoming difficulties in doing what we know is truly the morally good thing to do.

This special, or cardinal, virtue of courage gives us a resoluteness of mind to endure any kind of danger or difficulty—even death itself—for the sake of doing what is morally good. A specifically Christian form of courage is a resoluteness of mind to endure any suffering—even death itself—for the sake of Christ (martyrdom).

According to St. Thomas, the cardinal virtue of courage requires the exercise of four related habits: magnanimity, magnificence, patience, and perseverance.

Magnanimity is the virtue that gives us the confidence we need to persevere in obtaining good things. Honor is among such good things. Magnanimity as a Christian virtue is the confidence we have in pursuing honor in view of the gifts we possess from God. By helping us to recognize our natural abilities and strengths as God-given, magnanimity enables us to work hard to perfect any talent (e.g., intelligence) we may have or to make use of any gift we may have received (e.g., wealth) for our own good and for the good of others to the praise and glory of God. If magnanimity gives us confidence in seeking honor out of a thankful recognition of our God-given gifts and talents, this virtue is not opposed to the Christian virtue of humility, which enables us to appreciate our creaturely lowliness before God in the recognition of our natural defects (q. 129, a. 3, ad 4).

St. Thomas lists four vices opposed to magnanimity. One such vice is pusillanimity (being a "shrinking violet"). Pusillanimity is the vice of shrinking back from making use of our God-given talents for our good and the good of others to God's glory. St. Thomas sees the scriptural example of such cowardice in the example of the third servant in Jesus' famous parable who, out of fear of his master, hid his talent in the ground rather than make use of it (q. 133, a. 1). If pusillanimity is the vice of shrinking from honor in not making use of the talents we have been given, the opposite vice is that of presumption. We are presumptuous when, for the sake of honor, we take on what is beyond our powers to achieve (q. 130, a. 1). Ambition, the third vice opposed to magnanimity, leads us to look for more honor than is rightfully due us (q. 131, a. 1). Finally, vainglory is the vice of seeking glory or honor for trivial pursuits, or from the wrong people, or for an end other than the honor of God or the salvation of our neighbor (q. 132, a. 1).

A second important habit related to courage, according to St. Thomas, is that of magnificence. Magnificence is a special virtue enabling us to accomplish or execute great things, specifically by contributing to expensive public projects, for God and the community. The vice opposed to magnificence is the pettiness of refusing to spend the appropriate amount on such projects.

Patience, a third important habit related to courage, has to do with "suffering well" in enduring grief or sorrows that lead us to turn away from virtue. Christian patience is the virtue of enduring such grief by considering our eventual heavenly beatitude. This kind of patience is an infused virtue caused by charity and acquired only by grace (q. 136, a.3).

Finally, perseverance is that habit related to courage that enables us to see things through to the end. One kind of perseverance enables us to be constant in completing a long and arduous morally good activity or project. The other kind enables us to be constant in well-doing throughout our lives and to the very end of our lives. This latter kind of perseverance is an infused virtue.

QUESTION **123**

COURAGE (FORTITUDE)

ARTICLE 1 ⌁ **Is courage a virtue?**

Yes, despite objections to the contrary, Augustine (*De Morib. Eccl.* xv, xxi, xxii) numbers courage among the virtues.[1]

I answer that, According to the Philosopher (*Ethic.* ii, 6),[2] "virtue is that which makes its possessor good, and renders his work good." Hence human virtue, of which we are speaking now, is that which makes a man good, and renders his work good. Now man's good is to

---

[1] Here Thomas cites St. Augustine of Hippo's book, *De moribus ecclesiae catholicae*, (*On the Morals of the Catholic Church*) in which Augustine proposes, using reason alone, to make clear the basics of morality. Augustine argues that each of the virtues cannot function properly unless ordered to the love of God and in so arguing offers a critique of pagan views of the virtues. Thomas himself makes a similar point in arguing that love of God (charity) can be the form of other virtues (*ST* II–II, q. 23, a. 8), directing them to supernatural ends fulfilling of the deepest desires of the human heart. Since the virtues, to be truly virtues, should help us attain the ultimate good for human beings, which is to enjoy God, and since charity orders us to this ultimate good, there can be no true virtue without charity (*ST* II–II, q. 23, a. 7). True virtues are therefore ordered, formed, and directed by charity to achieving perfect happiness with God.

[2] The importance of the "Philosopher," Aristotle, makes him not only one of Aquinas's most often quoted authorities but also led Thomas to undertake a series of commentaries on the works of Aristotle, including a Commentary on Aristotle's *Nicomachean Ethics*. Scholars have debated a great deal about the nature of these commentaries. For more, see Christopher Kaczor, "Is the *Sententia libri ethicorum* of Aquinas only an Interpretation of Aristotle?" in the *American Catholic Philosophical Quarterly* 78:3 (2004): 353–78.

be in accordance with reason, according to Dionysius (*Div. Nom.* iv, 22). Therefore it belongs to human virtue to make man good, to make his work accord with reason. This happens in three ways: first, by rectifying reason itself, and this is done by the intellectual virtues;[3] secondly, by establishing the rectitude of reason in human affairs, and this belongs to justice; thirdly, by removing the obstacles to the establishment of this rectitude in human affairs. Now the human will is hindered in two ways from following the rectitude of reason: first, through being drawn by some object of pleasure to something other than what the rectitude of reason requires, and this obstacle is removed by the virtue of temperance; secondly, through the will being disinclined to follow that which is in accordance with reason, on account of some difficulty that presents itself. In order to remove this obstacle, courage of the mind is requisite, whereby to resist the aforesaid difficulty, even as a man, by courage of body, overcomes and removes bodily obstacles.

Hence it is evident that courage is a virtue, in so far as it conforms man to reason.

Objection 1. It seems that courage is not a virtue. For the Apostle says (2 Cor 12:9): "Virtue is perfected in infirmity." But courage is contrary to infirmity. Therefore courage is not a virtue.

Reply to Objection 1. The virtue of the soul is perfected, not in the infirmity of the soul, but in the infirmity of the body, of which the Apostle was speaking. Now it belongs to courage of the mind to bear bravely with infirmities of the flesh, and this belongs to the virtue of patience or courage, as also to acknowledge one's own infirmity, and this belongs to the perfection that is called humility.

Objection 2. Further, if it is a virtue, it is either theological, intellectual, or moral. Now courage is not contained among the theological virtues, nor among the intellectual virtues, as may be gathered from

---

[3] These intellectual virtues include wisdom, understanding, and science (*scientia*). For more on the connection between intellectual virtues and the moral virtues (justice, prudence, temperance, courage), see Thomas Hibbs, *The Splendor of Virtue: Wisdom, Prudence, and the Human Good* (New York: Fordham University Press, 2001).

what we have said above (I–II, q. 57, a. 2; I–II, q. 62, a. 3). Neither, apparently, is it contained among the moral virtues, since according to the Philosopher (*Ethic.* iii, 7, 8): "Some seem to be brave through ignorance, or through experience, as soldiers," both of which cases seem to pertain to act rather than to moral virtue, "and some are called brave on account of certain passions": for instance, on account of fear of threats, or of dishonor, or again on account of sorrow, anger, or hope. But moral virtue does not act from passion but from choice, as stated above (I–II, q. 55, a. 4). Therefore courage is not a virtue.

Reply to Objection 2. Sometimes a person performs the exterior act of a virtue without having the virtue, and from some other cause than virtue.[4] Hence the Philosopher (*Ethic.* iii, 8) mentions five ways in which people are said to be brave by way of resemblance, through performing acts of courage without having the virtue. This may be done in three ways. First, because they tend to that which is difficult as though it were not difficult: and this again happens in three ways, for sometimes this is owing to ignorance, through not perceiving the greatness of the danger; sometimes it is owing to the fact that one is hopeful of overcoming dangers—when, for instance, one has often experienced escape from danger; and sometimes this is owing to a certain science and art, as in the case of soldiers who, through skill and practice in the use of arms, think little of the dangers of battle, as they reckon themselves capable of defending themselves against them; thus Vegetius says (*De Re Milit.* i),[5] "No man fears to do what he is confident of having learned to do well." Secondly, a man performs an act of courage without having the virtue, through the impulse of a passion, whether of sorrow that he wishes to cast off, or again of anger. Thirdly, [a man performs an act of courage] through choice, not indeed of a due end, but of some temporal advantage to be obtained, such as honor,

---

[4] For example, a person might do what justice demands, say, return a borrowed object, but not be a just person. Perhaps the object is returned because of fear of legal charges rather than returned because it is the just thing to do.

[5] Roman author Flavius Vegetius Renatus wrote this text around A.D. 390 to summarize the inherited wisdom of the day pertaining to military matters. Among the most famous of the bits of advice he gives is the adage: "Let him who desires peace prepare for war."

pleasure, or gain, or of some disadvantage to be avoided, such as blame, pain, or loss.[6]

Objection 3. Further, human virtue resides chiefly in the soul, since it is a "good quality of the mind," as stated above (*Ethic.* iii, 7, 8). But courage, seemingly, resides in the body, or at least results from the temperament of the body. Therefore it seems that courage is not a virtue.

Reply to Objection 3. The courage of the soul which is reckoned a virtue, as explained in the Reply to the First Objection, is so called from its likeness to courage of the body. Nor is it inconsistent with the notion of virtue that a man should have a natural inclination to virtue by reason of his natural temperament, as stated above (I–II, q. 63, a. 1).

ARTICLE 5 ∾ Is courage properly about dangers of death in battle?

Yes, despite objections to the contrary, The Philosopher says (*Ethic.* iii) that courage is chiefly about death in battle.

I answer that, As stated above (a. 4), courage strengthens a man's mind against the greatest danger, which is that of death. Now courage is a virtue; and it is essential to virtue ever to tend to good. Therefore it is in order to pursue some good that man does not fly from the danger of

---

[6] Here Thomas lists a number of ways in which someone might commit to a brave act, but not in fact be a brave person: (1) A person might not realize that he is in danger and does an act that, had he realized the danger, he would have never done. Believing (falsely) that my vest is bullet proof, I jump in front of a child about to be shot and take the bullet myself. (2) On account of great skill, a person may not fear situations that would cause many other people to be fearful and occasion bravery. If I were a tenth-degree black belt, I would not necessarily be brave if I were to fight against a single robber breaking into my house and threatening my life, though a person without training in self-defense would be brave in confronting him. (3) Sometimes people are impelled through great sorrow or anger to act bravely though they really don't have the virtue of courage. I am so angry that the robbers have come into my house that in a blind rage I attack them. (4) Finally, it is not bravery but something else when a person performs an otherwise brave act but is motivated by money or desire of something unrelated to virtue. For example, those that fight in battle, motivated solely by money or by fear of being punished if they flee, do not enjoy the virtue of courage, although they may perform acts similar to those who have the virtue.

death. But the dangers of death arising out of sickness, storms at sea, attacks from robbers, and the like do not seem to come on a man through his pursuing some good. On the other hand, the dangers of death which occur in battle come to man directly on account of some good, because, to wit, he is defending the common good by a just fight. Now a just fight is of two kinds. First, there is the general combat, for instance of those who fight in battle; secondly, there is the private combat, as when a judge or even private individual does not refrain from giving a just judgment through fear of the impending sword, or any other danger though it threaten death. Hence it belongs to courage to strengthen the mind against dangers of death, not only such as arise in a general battle, but also such as occur in singular combat, which may be called by the general name of battle. Accordingly it must be granted that courage is properly about dangers of death occurring in battle.

Moreover, a brave man behaves well in the face of danger of any other kind of death, especially since man may be in danger of any kind of death on account of virtue: thus may a man not fail to attend on a sick friend through fear of deadly infection, or not refuse to undertake a journey with some godly object in view through fear of shipwreck or robbers.[7]

Objection 1. It seems that courage is not properly about dangers of death in battle. For martyrs above all are commended for their courage.

---

[7] Courage, in its strictest sense, is a virtue concerned with danger of death in battle. It would seem, then, that one of the cardinal, or hinge, virtues plays no role whatsoever in ordinary human life. But this is mistaken according to Thomas. Courage is chiefly and most manifestly evident in the face of death, the paradigm case. Other situations, however, while not the paradigm cases of courage, nevertheless do manifest the virtue of courage or courage in a restricted sense (*ST* II–II, q. 123, a. 5). Although the greatest bodily evil is death, lesser evils also impinge on human life, such as loss of reputation, money, security, and pleasure. The pursuit of the good in the face of defamation, financial ruin, insecurity, and pain also manifests courage. In this way, courage is an everyday virtue of doing what is right despite the fears of various kinds of harm, most especially the harm of death, but also less paradigmatically the "little deaths" that inevitably face people when they seek to do God's will. As such, even those who never enter battle can develop the virtue of courage whenever they steel themselves against fears of any kind in the pursuit of doing good.

But martyrs are not commended in connection with battle. Therefore courage is not properly about dangers of death in battle.

Reply to Objection 1. Martyrs face the fight that is waged against their own person, and this for the sake of the sovereign good which is God. Therefore their courage is praised above all. Nor is it outside the genus of courage that regards warlike actions, for which reason they are said to have been valiant in battle. [*Office of Martyrs,* ex. Heb. 11:34.]

Objection 2. Further, Ambrose says (*De Offic.* i)[8] that "courage is applicable both to warlike and to civil matters"; and Tully (*De Offic.* i), under the heading, "That it pertains to courage to excel in battle rather than in civil life," says: "Although not a few think that the business of war is of greater importance than the affairs of civil life, this opinion must be qualified: and if we wish to judge the matter truly, there are many things in civil life that are more important and more glorious than those connected with war." Now greater courage is about greater things. Therefore courage is not properly concerned with death in battle.

Reply to Objection 2. Personal and civil business is differentiated from the business of war that regards general wars. However, personal and civil affairs admit of dangers of death arising out of certain conflicts which are private wars, and so with regard to these also there may be courage properly so called.

Objection 3. Further, war is directed to the preservation of a country's temporal peace: for Augustine says (*De Civ. Dei* xix) that "wars are waged in order to insure peace." Now it does not seem that one ought to expose oneself to the danger of death for the temporal peace of one's country, since this same peace is the occasion of much license in morals. Therefore it seems that the virtue of courage is not about the danger of death in battle.

Reply to Objection 3. The peace of the state is good in itself, nor does it become evil because certain persons make evil use of it. For there are

---

[8] St. Ambrose, bishop of Milan (c. A.D. 374–397).

many others who make good use of it; and many evils prevented by it, such as murders and sacrileges, are much greater than those which are occasioned by it, and which belong chiefly to the sins of the flesh.

ARTICLE 10 ➤ Does the brave person make use of anger in his action?

Yes, despite objections to the contrary, The Philosopher says (*Ethic.* iii, 8) that "anger helps the brave."

I answer that, As stated above (I–II, q. 24, a. 2), concerning anger and the other passions there was a difference of opinion between the Peripatetics and the Stoics.[9] For the Stoics excluded anger and all other passions of the soul from the mind of a wise or good man, whereas the Peripatetics,[10] of whom Aristotle was the chief, ascribed to virtuous men both anger and the other passions of the soul, albeit modified by reason. And possibly they differed not in reality but in their way of speaking. For the Peripatetics, as stated above (I–II, q. 24, a. 2), gave the name of passions to all the movements of the sensitive appetite,[11]

[9] The Stoic philosophical school included Seneca, Cicero, and Marcus Aurelius. They held that the ideal human person should be free of immoderate or uncontrolled emotion, including unrestrained anger. Stoic philosophy greatly enriched Christian reflection: for instance, the Stoics were the earliest advocates of "natural law" and offered their own philosophical interpretation of a divine *Logos* behind all reality. With respect to the emotions, Christians looked not to philosophical speculation for the model of the ideal human but to the Gospel accounts of Jesus, one who weeps (Jn 11:35) and becomes angry (Mk 3:1–5).

[10] The Peripatetics were Aristotelian philosophers.

[11] Appetite is for Thomas an internal inclination, the "inclination of a person desirous of a thing towards that thing" (*ST* I–II, q. 8, a. 1). Thomas distinguishes between an intellectual appetite and a sensitive appetite. The intellectual appetite desires the good as universally understood; the sensitive appetite desires the good as particular and limited to the senses (*ST* I, q. 59, a. 4). Angelic beings and human beings enjoy the intellectual appetite, for example, for knowledge of the truth; human beings and non-human animals enjoy the sensitive appetite, for example, for food. The sensitive appetite is itself divided into the concupiscible and the irascible appetites. The concupiscible seeks the good, "as something pleasant to the senses and suitable to nature (q. 82, a. 5)," such as food, drink, sexual pleasure, and relaxation. By the concupiscible appetite, a person is "inclined to seek what is suitable, according to the senses, and to fly from what is hurtful" (*ST* I, q. 81, a. 2). The irascible appetite manifests itself

however they may comport themselves. And since the sensitive appetite is moved by the command of reason, so that it may cooperate by rendering action more prompt, they held that virtuous persons should employ both anger and the other passions of the soul, modified according to the dictate of reason. On the other hand, the Stoics gave the name of passions to certain immoderate emotions of the sensitive appetite; therefore they called them sicknesses or diseases, and for this reason severed them altogether from virtue.

Accordingly the brave man employs moderate anger for his action, but not immoderate anger.[12]

Objection 1. It seems that the brave man does not use anger in his action. For no one should employ as an instrument of his action that which he cannot use at will. Now man cannot use anger at will, so as to take it up and lay it aside when he will. For, as the Philosopher says (*De Memoria* ii), when a bodily passion is in movement, it does not rest at once just as one wishes. Therefore a brave man should not employ anger for his action.

Reply to Objection 1. Anger that is moderated in accordance with reason is subject to the command of reason so that man uses it at his will, which would not be the case were it immoderate.

Objection 2. Further, if a man is competent to do a thing by himself, he should not seek the assistance of something weaker and more imperfect. Now the reason is competent to achieve by itself deeds of courage, wherein anger is impotent: therefore Seneca says (*De Ira* i): "Reason by itself suffices not only to make us prepared for action but

---

when human being or an animal "resists attacks that hinder what is suitable, and inflict harm" (*ST* I, q. 81, a. 2). The concipisicible appetite seeks the good as pleasing to the senses, and the irascible seeks the good "as something that wards off and repels what is hurtful," such as various dangers (*ST* I, q. 82, a. 5).

12 Anger is not "wrong" for Aquinas, and indeed Thomas holds that Christ himself exhibited anger (*ST* III, q. 15, a. 9; Jn 2:17). When someone seeks revenge to harm another not in accord with justice, then anger is blameworthy. On the other hand, in righting grievous wrongs, anger is not only legitimate but even praiseworthy. On whether it is lawful to be angry and whether anger is a sin, see *ST* II–II, q. 158, aa 1, 2 in this volume.

also to accomplish it. In fact, is there greater folly than for reason to seek help from anger, the steadfast from the unstaid, the trusty from the untrustworthy, the healthy from the sick?" Therefore a brave man should not make use of anger.

Reply to Objection 2. Reason employs anger for its action, not as seeking its assistance, but because it uses the sensitive appetite as an instrument, just as it uses the members of the body. Nor is it unbecoming for the instrument to be more imperfect than the principal agent, even as the hammer is more imperfect than the smith. Moreover, Seneca was a follower of the Stoics, and the above words were aimed by him directly at Aristotle.

Objection 3. Further, just as people are more earnest in doing deeds of courage on account of anger, so are they on account of sorrow or desire. Therefore the Philosopher says (*Ethic.* iii, 8) that wild beasts are incited to face danger through sorrow or pain, and adulterous persons dare many things for the sake of desire. Now courage employs neither sorrow nor desire for its action. Therefore, in like manner, it should not employ anger.

Reply to Objection 3. Whereas courage has two acts, namely endurance and aggression,[13] it employs anger, not for the act of endurance, because the reason by itself performs this act, but for the act of aggression, for which it employs anger rather than the other passions, since it belongs to anger to strike at the cause of sorrow, so that it directly cooperates with courage in attacking. On the other hand, sorrow by its very nature gives way to the thing that hurts; though accidentally it helps in aggression, either as being the cause of anger, as stated above (I–II, q. 47, a. 3), or as making a person expose himself to danger in order to escape from sorrow. In like manner desire, by its very nature, tends to a pleasurable good, to which it is directly contrary to withstand danger, yet accidentally sometimes it helps one to attack, in so far as one prefers to risk dangers rather than lack pleasure. Hence the Philosopher says (*Ethic.* iii, 5): "Of all the cases in which courage arises from a passion, the most natural is when a

---

[13] Thomas explores endurance in II–II, q.123, a.6.

man is brave through anger, making his choice and acting for a purpose," i.e., for a due end; "this is true courage."

ARTICLE 11 ⚬⚬ Is courage a cardinal virtue?

Yes, despite objections to the contrary, Gregory (*Moral.* xxii),[14]
Ambrose in his commentary on Luke 6:20, and Augustine (*De
Moribus Eccl.* xv) number courage among the four cardinal or princi-
pal virtues.

I answer that, As stated above (I–II, q. 61, aa 3, 4), those virtues
are said to be cardinal or principal which have a foremost claim to that
which belongs to the virtues in common. And among other conditions
of virtue in general is one that is stated to "act steadfastly", according to
Ethic. ii, 4. Now courage above all lays claim to praise for steadfastness,
because he that stands firm is so much the more praised, as he is more
strongly impelled to fall or recede. Now man is impelled to recede from
that which is in accordance with reason, both by the pleasing good and
the displeasing evil. But bodily pain impels him more strongly than
pleasure. For Augustine says (QQ. 83, qu. 36): "There is none that does
not shun pain more than he desires pleasure. For we perceive that even
the most untamed beasts are deterred from the greatest pleasures by the
fear of pain." And among the pains of the mind and dangers those are
mostly feared which lead to death, and it is against them that the brave
man stands firm. Therefore courage is a cardinal virtue.[15]

---

[14] St. Gregory the Great's work *Moralia in Job* reflects on the biblical story of
Job and why bad things should happen to good people. Gregory's reading of
the text includes literal, allegorical, and moral senses of Scripture. In the literal, he attempts to determine the meaning of the text, in the allegorical he
shows how Job prefigures Christ, and in the moral he draws the lessons that
we can learn from Job in order to live a better life, more fully alive in Christ.
Gregory's *Moralia in Job* became one of the most cited texts in the Middle
Ages and was available in many beautifully decorated manuscripts. Thomas
himself cites this work more than 350 times in the *Secunda secundae* alone.

[15] Without the cardinal virtue of courage, a person could never be totally committed to doing good and avoiding evil because any time death threatened, he
or she would be unable to endure the threat and would end up giving in to
wrongdoing rather than enduring evil. The courageous person enacts the
Socratic dictum that it is better to suffer evil than to do evil, even when the
evil that must be endured is the greatest physical evil—death itself.

Objection 2. Further, the object of virtue is good. But the direct object of courage is not good, but evil, for it is endurance of evil and toil, as Tully says (*De Inv. Rhet.* ii). Therefore courage is not a cardinal virtue.

Reply to Objection 2. Virtue is directed to the good of reason, which it ought to safeguard against the onslaught of evils. And courage is directed to evils of the body, as contraries which it withstands, and to the good of reason, as the end, which it intends to safeguard.

Objection 3. Further, the cardinal virtues are about those things upon which human life is chiefly occupied, just as a door turns upon a hinge *(cardine)*. But courage is about dangers of death that are of rare occurrence in human life. Therefore courage should not be reckoned a cardinal or principal virtue.

Reply to Objection 3. Though dangers of death are of rare occurrence, yet the occasions of those dangers occur frequently, since on account of justice, which he pursues, and also on account of other good deeds, man encounters mortal adversaries.[16]

ARTICLE 12 ~ **Is courage the greatest of virtues?**

No, despite objections to the contrary, Tully says (*De Offic.* i): "Justice is the most resplendent of the virtues and gives its name to a good man."

Further, the Philosopher says (*Rhet.* i, 19): "Those virtues are the greatest which are most profitable to others." Now liberality seems to be more useful than courage. Therefore it is a greater virtue.

I answer that, As Augustine says (*De Trin.* vi), "In things that are great, but not in bulk, to be great is to be good": therefore the better a virtue the greater it is. Now reason's good is man's good, according to Dionysius (*Div. Nom.* iv).[17] Prudence, since it is a perfection of reason, has the good essentially, while justice effects this good, since it belongs

---

16 As Clare Boothe Luce once joked, "No good deed goes unpunished." In the lives of the martyrs both the "red martyrs," who shed blood and the "white martyrs," who did not bleed but suffered for love of God and neighbor, attest to the fact that those who earnestly follow God often encounter fierce opposition.

17 Thomas wrote a short and unfinished commentary on this work of Pseudo-Dionysius, *On the Divine Names*. The commentary treats, among other things, the nature of love and goodness.

to justice to establish the order of reason in all human affairs, whereas the other virtues safeguard this good, inasmuch as they moderate the passions, lest they lead man away from reason's good. As to the order of the latter, courage holds the first place, because fear of dangers of death has the greatest power to make man recede from the good of reason; and after courage comes temperance, since also pleasures of touch excel all others in hindering the good of reason. Now to be a thing essentially ranks before effecting it, and the latter ranks before safeguarding it by removing obstacles thereto. Therefore, among the cardinal virtues, prudence ranks first, justice second, courage third, temperance fourth, and after these the other virtues.[18]

Objection 1. It seems that courage excels among all other virtues. For Ambrose says (*De Offic.* i): "Courage is higher, so to speak, than the rest."

Reply to Objection 1. Ambrose places courage before the other virtues in respect of a certain general utility, inasmuch as it is useful both in warfare and in matters relating to civil or home life. Hence he begins by saying (*De Offic.* i): "Now we come to treat of courage, which being higher, so to speak, than the others, is applicable both to warlike and to civil matters."[19]

Objection 2. Further, virtue is about that which is difficult and good. But courage is about most difficult things. Therefore it is the greatest of the virtues.

---

[18] In other words, the end has greater value than that which is for the sake of the end, and those things more closely related to the end have greater value than those things which are more distant from the end. The end of man is, understood in a certain way, to live according to reason which is prudence. Justice establishes exteriorly this order of reason flowing from prudence, and so justice is the second most important virtue. Two threats arise with regard to living according to reason, namely various evils. Death especially can be a powerful deterrent from doing what is right, giving rise to the need for courage. But the allure of bodily pleasure sought in a way that goes against reason can also lead a person astray, giving rise to the need for the virtue of temperance.

[19] Here also Thomas reminds us that although courage primarily concerns "battle" (either of a public kind, such as a soldier fighting a war, or of a private kind, such as a believer enduring persecution even unto death rather than renouncing faith), courage also pertains to life within the community and at home.

Reply to Objection 2. Virtue essentially regards the good rather than the difficult. Hence the greatness of a virtue is measured according to its goodness rather than its difficulty.[20]

Objection 3. Further, the person of a man is more excellent than his possessions. But courage is about a man's person, for it is this that a man exposes to the danger of death for the good of virtue, whereas justice and the other moral virtues are about other and external things. Therefore courage is the chief of the moral virtues.

Reply to Objection 3. A man does not expose his person to dangers of death except in order to safeguard justice: therefore the praise awarded to courage depends somewhat on justice. Hence Ambrose says (*De Offic.* i) that "courage without justice is an occasion of injustice, since the stronger a man is the more ready is he to oppress the weaker."

---

[20] St. Thomas does not measure the goodness of a person or virtue by the "difficulty" involved in being good. For Immanuel Kant, on the other hand, to act against all inclination from pure duty alone would be the mark of greatest moral goodness. For Thomas, the greatest moral goodness would be to do what is right and take pleasure in doing so. The saint is not therefore the dour person who acting on pure will alone does what is right; rather the saint takes joy in living the Christian life, despite whatever interior or exterior difficulties may be present.

QUESTION **124**

MARTYRDOM

ARTICLE 1 ⁓ **Is martyrdom an act of virtue?**

Yes, despite objections to the contrary, The reward of beatitude is not due save to acts of virtue. Now it is due to martyrdom, since it is written (Mt 5:10): "Blessed are they that suffer persecution for justice's sake, for theirs is the kingdom of heaven." Therefore martyrdom is an act of virtue.

I answer that, As stated above (q. 123, aa 1, 3),[1] it belongs to virtue to safeguard man in the good of reason. Now the good of reason consists in the truth as its proper object, and in justice as its proper effect, as shown earlier (q. 109, aa 1, 2; q. 123, a. 12). And martyrdom consists essentially in standing firmly in truth and justice against the assaults of persecution. Hence it is evident that martyrdom is an act of virtue.[2]

---

1 "[T]he will [can be] disinclined to follow that which is in accordance with reason, on account of some difficulty that presents itself. In order to remove this obstacle, courage of the mind is requisite, whereby to resist the aforesaid difficulty, even as a man, by courage of body, overcomes and removes bodily obstacles."

2 In II–II, q. 109, a. 1, Thomas writes of the end of virtue being the truth: "truth is not a virtue, but the object or end of a virtue." Since God is truth (I, q. 16, a. 5), to live in the truth is to be united to God. In *Veritatis Splendor*, Pope John Paul II highlights the importance of martyrdom and links martyrdom, as does Thomas, to freedom and truth. "Christ reveals, first and foremost, that the frank and open acceptance of truth is the condition for authentic freedom: 'You will know the truth, and the truth will set you free' (Jn 8:32).

Objection 1. It seems that martyrdom is not an act of virtue. For all acts of virtue are voluntary. But martyrdom is sometimes not voluntary, as in the case of the Innocents who were slain for Christ's sake, and of whom Hilary says (*Super Matth.* i) that "they attained the ripe age of eternity through the glory of martyrdom." Therefore martyrdom is not an act of virtue.

Reply to Objection 1. Some have said that in the case of the Innocents the use of their free will was miraculously accelerated, so that they suffered martyrdom even voluntarily. Since, however, Scripture contains no proof of this, it is better to say that these babes in being slain obtained by God's grace the glory of martyrdom, which others acquire by their own will. For the shedding of one's blood for Christ's sake takes the place of Baptism. Therefore, just as in the case of baptized children the merit of Christ is conducive to the acquisition of glory through the baptismal grace, so in those who were slain for Christ's sake the merit of Christ's martyrdom is conducive to the acquisition of the martyr's palm.[3] Hence Augustine says in a sermon on the Epiphany (*De Diversis*

This is truth which sets one free in the face of worldly power and which gives the strength to endure martyrdom. So it was with Jesus before Pilate: 'For this I was born, and for this I have come into the world, to bear witness to the truth' (Jn 18:37). The true worshippers of God must thus worship him 'in spirit and truth' (Jn 4:23): *in this worship they become free.* Worship of God and a relationship with truth are revealed in Jesus Christ as the deepest foundation of freedom. Furthermore, Jesus reveals by his whole life, and not only by his words, that freedom is acquired in love, that is, in the 'gift of self.' The one who says: 'Greater love has no man than this, that a man lay down his life for his friends' (Jn 15:13), freely goes out to meet his Passion (cf. Mt 26:46), and in obedience to the Father gives his life on the Cross for all men (cf. Phil 2:6–11). Contemplation of Jesus Crucified is thus the high-road which the Church must tread every day if she wishes to understand the full meaning of freedom: the gift of self in *service to God and one's brethren.* Communion with the Crucified and Risen Lord is the never-ending source from which the Church draws unceasingly in order to live in freedom, to give of herself and to serve." (*Veritatis Splendor* 87, notes omitted).

[3] There is therefore baptism by water, baptism by blood (e.g., those martyred who are still preparing for sacramental baptism with water), and baptism by desire. Baptism of some kind is necessary for salvation (III, q. 68, a. 2; *Catechism of the Catholic Church,* 1257–61). The ordinary means of baptism is by water, although baptism by blood or baptism by desire, of which Thomas

lxvi), as though he were addressing them: "A man that does not believe that children are benefited by the baptism of Christ will doubt of your being crowned in suffering for Christ. You were not old enough to believe in Christ's future sufferings, but you had a body wherein you could suffer for Christ Who was himself to suffer."

Objection 2. Further, nothing unlawful is an act of virtue. Now it is unlawful to kill oneself, as stated above (q. 64, a. 5), and yet martyrdom is achieved by so doing: for Augustine says (*De Civ. Dei* i) that "during persecution certain holy women, in order to escape from those who threatened their chastity, threw themselves into a river, and so ended their lives, and their martyrdom is honored in the Catholic Church with most solemn veneration." Therefore martyrdom is not an act of virtue.

Reply to Objection 2. Augustine says (*De Civ. Dei* i) that "possibly the Church was induced by certain credible witnesses of Divine authority thus to honor the memory of those holy women."[4]

---

speaks (III, q. 68, a. 11), are other possible means of incorporation into the Mystical Body of Christ.

[4] To commit suicide is wrong, but it is not suicide, according to Thomas, to kill oneself under obedience to a command from God. In Thomas's understanding of Scripture, God sometimes, however rarely, commands that a person act against what is normally required by morality. Three such examples include taking gold from the Egyptians, Hosea taking a prostitute as his wife, and Abraham being commanded to kill Isaac. In *ST* I–II, q. 94, a. 5, ad 2, Thomas explains that, because God is the Lord of all creation, to act on a Divine Command is not to act contrary to the dictates of morality, which is of course precisely to act in accord with Divine Wisdom and Love. If I own a car and allow Miles to make use of it, and then later tell Jennifer to take back the car from Miles, Jennifer has not "stolen" the car, even though it may appear that way to Miles (who was unaware that Jennifer took the car back on my instruction). Similarly, to take property at God's command is not to act wrongly, since ultimately all creation belongs to God. The institution of marriage also is part of God's creation, as is the gift of life. So to marry or take life at God's command is not immoral. Now, a large problem arises. What if someone claiming to be "God" appears to me tonight and tells me to kill scores of people? For the Catholic, such a possibility does not entail that I must follow through with the killing. Private revelations are judged as true or false depending in part on how they accord with public revelation as understood by the Church. If an alleged private revelation does not accord with what God has publicly revealed about

Objection 3. Further, it is praiseworthy to offer oneself to do an act of virtue. But it is not praiseworthy to court martyrdom; rather would it seem to be presumptuous and rash. Therefore martyrdom is not an act of virtue.

Reply to Objection 3. The precepts of the Law are about acts of virtue. Now it has been stated (I–II, q. 108, a. 1, ad 4) that some of the precepts of the Divine Law are to be understood in reference to the preparation of the mind, in the sense that man ought to be prepared to do such and such a thing, whenever expedient. In the same way certain things belong to an act of virtue as regards the preparation of the mind, so that in such and such a case a man should act according to reason. And this observation would seem very much to the point in the case of martyrdom, which consists in the right endurance of sufferings unjustly inflicted. Nor ought a man to give another an occasion of acting unjustly; yet if anyone act unjustly, one ought to endure it in moderation.[5]

ARTICLE 5 ‹‹ Is faith alone the cause of martyrdom?

No, despite objections to the contrary, It is written (Mt 5:10): "Blessed are they that suffer persecution for justice's sake," which pertains to martyrdom, according to a gloss, as well as Jerome's commentary on this passage. Now not only faith but also the other virtues pertain to justice. Therefore other virtues can be the cause of martyrdom.

    I answer that, As stated above (a. 4), martyrs are so called as being witnesses, because by suffering in body unto death they bear witness to the truth, not indeed to any truth, but to the truth which is in accordance with godliness, and was made known to us by Christ. Therefore

---

    how to behave, then the faithful Catholic can have confidence that the Holy Spirit is not communicating.

[5] St. Thomas More, for example, strenuously sought to avoid condemnation by the court of Henry VIII despite opposing Henry's views on divorce and papal supremacy. He remained silent in order to preserve his life until he could remain silent no longer. For more about More, see Gerard B. Wegemer, *Thomas More: A Portrait of Courage* (New York: Scepter Publishers, 1997).

Christ's martyrs are His witnesses. Now this truth is the truth of faith. Therefore the cause of all martyrdom is the truth of faith.[6]

But the truth of faith includes not only inward belief, but also outward profession, which is expressed not only by words, whereby one confesses the faith, but also by deeds, whereby a person shows that he has faith, according to James 2:18, "I will show you, by works, my faith." Hence it is written of certain people (Titus 1:16): "They profess that they know God but in their works they deny Him." Thus all virtuous deeds, inasmuch as they are referred to God, are professions of the faith whereby we come to know that God requires these works of us, and rewards us for them: and in this way they can be the cause of martyrdom. For this reason the Church celebrates the martyrdom of Blessed John the Baptist, who suffered death, not for refusing to deny the faith, but for condemning adultery.

Objection 1. It seems that faith alone is the cause of martyrdom. For it is written (1 Pet 4:15, 16): "Let none of you suffer as a murderer, or a thief, or a railer, or a coveter of other men's things. But if as a Christian, let him not be ashamed, but let him glorify God in this name." Now a man is said to be a Christian because he holds the faith of Christ. Therefore only faith in Christ gives the glory of martyrdom to those who suffer.

---

[6] In the twentieth century, there were more people who died for their faith, or in protection of other important virtues, than perhaps in any other century. Richard John Neuhaus notes: "During the Cold War, [David] Barrett's figure of 300,000 martyrs per year was widely used. His definition is important: 'A martyr is a Christian *believer* who *loses* his or her life *prematurely*, in a situation of *witness*, and as a result of human *hostility*' (emphasis in original). So, for example, while forty million Christians were killed in World War II, only three million can be called martyrs. In that number he includes the one million of the six million Jewish martyrs killed in the Holocaust who were Christian Jews. Since 1991, when organized Soviet assassinations of Christian leaders and other oppressions ceased, Barrett estimates that there are 150,000 Christian martyrs each year." Richard John Neuhaus, "The Public Square," *First Things* 70 (February 1997): 58–74. For more, see Robert Royal, *Catholic Martyrs of the Twentieth Century: A Comprehensive World History* (New York: Crossroad Publishing, 2006).

Reply to Objection 1. A Christian is one who is Christ's. Now a person is said to be Christ's, not only through having faith in Christ, but also because he is actuated to virtuous deeds by the Spirit of Christ, according to Romans 8:9, "If any man have not the Spirit of Christ, he is none of His," and again because in imitation of Christ he is dead to sins, according to Galatians 5:24, "They that are Christ's have crucified their flesh with the vices and concupiscence." Hence to suffer as a Christian is not only to suffer in confession of the faith, which is done by words, but also to suffer for doing any good work, or for avoiding any sin, for Christ's sake, because this all comes under the head of witnessing to the faith.[7]

Objection 2. Further, a martyr is a kind of witness. But witness is borne to the truth alone. Now one is not called a martyr for bearing witness to any truth, but only for witnessing to the Divine truth; otherwise a man would be a martyr if he were to die for confessing a truth of geometry or some other speculative science, which seems ridiculous. Therefore faith alone is the cause of martyrdom.

Reply to Objection 2. The truth of other sciences has no connection with the worship of the Godhead: hence it is not called truth according to godliness, and consequently the confession thereof cannot be said to be the direct cause of martyrdom. Yet, since every lie is a sin, as stated above (q. 110, aa 3, 4), avoidance of a lie, to whatever truth it

---

[7] Very few people in the western world will face the choice between execution and denying Christ, but abundant opportunities exist to suffer as a Christian. Being generous with works of charity will "cost" a great deal in terms of time, money, and effort. Bearing witness to the truth of marriage and the value of human life may cost a person ridicule in social life, professional disadvantage as a health care provider or educator, or non-confirmation as a judicial nominee. Avoiding sin for Christ's sake, undertaking penance, and extending kindness and forgiveness to others are all forms of "white martyrdom," where no red blood flows but one dies to oneself nonetheless. Lutheran Pastor Dietrich Bonhoeffer explores the necessity of personal sacrifice in the life of faith, in his book *The Cost of Discipleship* (Birmingham: Touchstone, 1995). In 1945, as a result of his personal witness for Christ and against the Nazis, as well as his aid to Jews, Bonhoeffer was sent to a concentration camp and killed by the Gestapo.

may be contrary, may be the cause of martyrdom inasmuch as a lie is a sin against the Divine Law.

Objection 3. Further, those virtuous deeds would seem to be of most account which are directed to the common good, since "the good of the nation is better than the good of the individual," according to the Philosopher (*Ethic.* i, 2). If, then, some other good were the cause of martyrdom, it would seem that before all those would be martyrs who die for the defense of their country. Yet this is not consistent with Church observance, for we do not celebrate the martyrdom of those who die in a just war. Therefore faith alone is the cause of martyrdom.

Reply to Objection 3. The good of one's country is paramount among human goods; yet the Divine good, which is the proper cause of martyrdom, is of more account than human good. Nevertheless, since a human good may become Divine, for instance when it is referred to God,[8] it follows that any human good in so far as it is referred to God, may be the cause of martyrdom.

---

[8] A human good may become divine when it is sought, loved, and promoted as good in reference to the divine. Marriage, for example, is a human good but is "divinized," so to speak, through the sacrament of marriage. We know that in loving one's spouse one also loves Christ. Every legitimate human activity may be sanctified through offering it to God, through bearing in mind that God's goodness is manifest throughout creation, and through working for God's glory.

QUESTION 125

FEAR

ARTICLE 1 ~ Is fear a sin?

Yes, despite objections to the contrary, Our Lord said (Mt 10:28): "Fear not them that kill the body," and it is written (Ezek 2:6): "Fear not, neither be afraid of their words."

I answer that, A human act is said to be a sin on account of its being inordinate, because the good of a human act consists in order, as stated above (q. 109, a. 2; q. 114, a. 1).[1] Now this due order requires that the appetite be subject to the ruling of reason. And reason dictates that certain things should be shunned and some sought after. Among things to be shunned, it dictates that some are to be shunned more than others, and among things to be sought after, that some are to be sought after more than others. Moreover, the more a good is to be

----

[1] Good consists in order because goodness is a due perfection, and that which is lacking in proper order does not have its due perfection (I, q. 5, a. 5). Consider, for example, the order of food consumption including chewing, swallowing, and digesting. It is part of good food consumption to follow this order, first chewing, then swallowing, and finally digesting. Without this order, there would be disorder and the body could not be nourished. This would constitute an evil for the body. Similarly, an aspect of the good of human action is its order. For example, in talking about the virtue of truthfulness (II–II, q. 109, a. 2), Thomas says: "[G]ood consists in order, it follows that a special aspect of good will be found where there is a special order. Now there is a special order whereby our externals, whether words or deeds, are duly ordered in relation to some thing, as sign to thing signified: and thereto man is perfected by the virtue of truth. Therefore it is evident that truth is a special virtue."

sought after, the more is the opposite evil to be shunned. The result is that reason dictates that certain goods are to be sought after more than certain evils are to be avoided.[2] Accordingly, when the appetite shuns what the reason dictates that we should endure rather than forfeit others that we should rather seek for, fear is inordinate and sinful.[3] On the other hand, when the appetite fears so as to shun what reason requires to be shunned, the appetite is neither inordinate nor sinful.[4]

Objection 1. It seems that fear is not a sin. For fear is a passion, as stated above (I–II, q. 23, a. 4; q. 42). Now we are neither praised nor blamed for passions, as stated in *Ethic.* ii. Since, then, every sin is blameworthy, it seems that fear is not a sin.

Reply to Objection 1. Fear in its generic acceptation denotes avoidance in general. Hence in this way it does not include the notion of good or

---

[2] For example, while pain is a physical evil to be avoided, the good of health is so important that the evil of getting a vaccination ought to be endured to secure health.

[3] Passions such as anger, fear, or desire are not considered in a general way good or evil. Once a passion is brought into human action, however, this act of reason and will, though motivated by passion, has a character of good or evil. In I–II, q. 24, a. 4, Thomas notes that "passions" can be considered simply as an instinctual, non-rational reaction or as a response that is informed by reason and will: "We ought, seemingly, to apply to passions what has been said in regard to acts (I–II, q. 18, aa 5, 6; q. 20, a. 1)—viz. that the species of a passion, as the species of an act, can be considered from two points of view. First, according to its natural genus; and thus moral good and evil have no connection with the species of an act or passion; secondly, according to its moral genus, inasmuch as it is voluntary and controlled by reason. In this way moral good and evil can belong to the species of a passion, in so far as the object to which a passion tends is, of itself, in harmony or in discord with reason: as is clear in the case of 'shame,' which is base fear; and of 'envy,' which is sorrow for another's good: for thus passions belong to the same species as the external act."

[4] Thomas accepts Augustine's definition of sin as "a word, deed, or desire contrary to the eternal law" (*Contra Faust.* xxii, 27; I–II, q. 71, a. 6). The eternal law is the divine wisdom ordering created reality (I–II, q. 93, a. 1). Thus a sin is not a sin simply because "God says so"; rather God's law is an expression of divine and perfect wisdom, love, and justice. Since God loves us, his law is a protection against our own tendency to self-disintegration in failing to love ourselves, others, and God properly.

evil, and the same applies to every other passion. Therefore the Philosopher says that passions call for neither praise nor blame, because, to wit, we neither praise nor blame those who are angry or afraid, but only those who behave thus in an ordinate or inordinate manner.[5]

Objection 2. Further, nothing that is commanded in the Divine Law is a sin, since the "law of the Lord is unspotted" (Ps 18:8). Yet fear is commanded in God's law, for it is written (Eph 6:5): "Servants, be obedient to them that are your lords according to the flesh, with fear and trembling." Therefore fear is not a sin.

Reply to Objection 2. The fear which the Apostle inculcates is in accordance with reason, namely that servants should fear lest they be lacking in the service they owe their masters.

Objection 3. Further, nothing that is naturally in man is a sin, for sin is contrary to nature according to Damascene (*De Fide Orth.* iii).[6] Now fear is natural to man. Therefore the Philosopher says (*Ethic.* iii, 7) that "a man would be insane or insensible to pain if nothing, not even earthquakes nor deluges, inspired him with fear." Therefore fear is not a sin.

Reply to Objection 3. Reason dictates that we should shun the evils that we cannot withstand, and the endurance of which profits us nothing. Hence there is no sin in fearing them.

ARTICLE 2 ~~ Is the sin of fear contrary to courage?

Yes, despite objections to the contrary, The Philosopher (*Ethic.* ii, 7; iii, 7) states that timidity is opposed to courage.

I answer that, As stated above (q. 19, a. 3; I–II, q. 43, a. 1), all fear arises from love, since no one fears save what is contrary to something

---

5 In other words, while an emotion like being afraid or angry is not good or evil in itself, in some cases, being afraid or angry may be blameworthy if unreasonable. As Thomas notes in the reply to the third objection, we should fear evils that can overcome us, evils the endurance of which does not profit us.

6 St. John Damascene (d. ca. 787) is one of the Greek Fathers of the Church and a person of accomplishment in both secular and religious matters. He compiled encyclopedic summaries of Christian theology that were of great use and value to generations of believers, in particular to Peter Lombard and Thomas Aquinas.

he loves. Now love is not confined to any particular kind of virtue or vice, but ordinate love is included in every virtue, since every virtuous man loves the good proper to his virtue, while inordinate love is included in every sin, because inordinate love gives rise to inordinate desire. Hence in like manner inordinate fear is included in every sin; thus the covetous man fears the loss of money, the intemperate man the loss of pleasure, and so on. But the greatest fear of all is that which has the danger of death for its object, as we find proved in *Ethic.* iii, 6. Therefore the inordinateness of this fear is opposed to courage which regards dangers of death. For this reason timidity is said to be in a certain sense opposed to courage.

Objection 1. It seems that the sin of fear is not contrary to courage because courage is about dangers of death, as stated above (q. 123, aa 4, 5). But the sin of fear is not always connected with dangers of death, for a gloss on Psalm 127:1, "Blessed are all they that fear the Lord," says that "it is human fear whereby we dread to suffer bodily dangers, or to lose worldly goods." Again, a gloss on Matthew 27:44, "He prayed the third time, saying the selfsame word," says that "evil fear is threefold, fear of death, fear of pain, and fear of contempt." Therefore the sin of fear is not contrary to courage.

Reply to Objection 1. The passages quoted refer to inordinate fear in its generic acceptation, which can be opposed to various virtues.

Objection 2. Further, the chief reason why a man is commended for courage is that he exposes himself to the danger of death. Now sometimes a man exposes himself to death through fear of slavery or shame. Thus Augustine relates (*De Civ. Dei* i) that Cato, in order not to be Caesar's slave, gave himself up to death. Therefore the sin of fear bears a certain likeness to courage instead of being opposed thereto.

Reply to Objection 2. Human acts are estimated chiefly with reference to the end, as stated above (I–II, q. 1, a. 3; q. 18, a. 6),[7] and it belongs to

---

[7] The end of human action has a primacy for Thomas that manifests itself by informing the means that are undertaken for that end. To choose something as an end rather than simply as a means is to indicate greater "depth" of commitment to that end. As Thomas says, "He who commits adultery in order to

a brave man to expose himself to danger of death for the sake of a good. But a man who exposes himself to danger of death in order to escape from slavery or hardships is overcome by fear, which is contrary to courage. Hence the Philosopher says (*Ethic.* iii, 7) that "to die in order to escape poverty, lust, or something disagreeable is an act not of courage but of cowardice: for to shun hardships is a mark of effeminacy."

Objection 3. Further, all despair arises from fear. But despair is opposed not to courage but to hope, as stated above (q. 20, a. 1; I–II, q. 40, a. 4). Neither, therefore, is the sin of fear opposed to courage.

Reply to Objection 3. As stated above (I–II, q. 45, a. 2), fear is the beginning of despair even as hope is the beginning of daring.[8] Therefore, just as courage, which employs daring in moderation, presupposes hope, so on the other hand despair proceeds from some kind of fear. It does not follow, however, that any kind of despair results from any kind of fear, but that only from fear of the same kind. Now the despair that is opposed to hope is referred to another kind, namely to

steal is more a thief than an adulterer" (I–II, q. 18, a. 6). As Janet Smith has noted, commenting on this passage: "One who steals to commit adultery is *more* of an adulterer (for this was the end of his act) than a thief (the object was to steal), but it is extremely important to note that he is both a thief and an adulterer, for he intended both to steal and to commit adultery." See Janet Smith, *Humanae Vitae: A Generation Later* (Washington, DC: The Catholic University of America Press, 1991), p. 217.

8 In I–II, q. 45, a. 2, Thomas addresses the relationship of despair and daring: "[E]very movement of the appetitive power is reducible to one either of pursuit or of avoidance. Again, pursuit or avoidance is of something either by reason of itself or by reason of something else. By reason of itself, good is the object of pursuit, and evil the object of avoidance; but by reason of something else, evil can be the object of pursuit, through some good attaching to it; and good can be the object of avoidance, through some evil attaching to it. Now that which is by reason of something else follows that which is by reason of itself. Consequently pursuit of evil follows pursuit of good; and avoidance of good follows avoidance of evil. Now these four things belong to four passions, since pursuit of good belongs to hope, avoidance of evil to fear, the pursuit of the fearful evil belongs to daring, and the avoidance of good to despair. It follows, therefore, that daring results from hope, since it is in the hope of overcoming the threatening object of fear that one attacks it boldly. But despair results from fear: since the reason why a man despairs is because he fears the difficulty attaching to the good he should hope for."

Divine things, whereas the fear that is opposed to courage regards dangers of death. Hence the argument does not prove.[9]

ARTICLE 4 ⚭ **Does fear excuse from sin?**

Yes, despite objections to the contrary, It is stated in the Decretals[10] (I, 1, *Cap. Constat.*): "A man who has been forcibly and unwillingly ordained by heretics has an ostensible excuse."

I answer that, As stated above (a. 3), fear is sinful in so far as it runs counter to the order of reason. Now reason judges certain evils to be shunned rather than others. Therefore it is no sin not to shun what is less to be shunned in order to avoid what reason judges to be more avoided: thus death of the body is more to be avoided than the loss of temporal goods. Hence a man would be excused from sin if through fear of death he were to promise or give something to a robber, and yet he would be guilty of sin were he to give to sinners rather than to the good to whom he should give in preference. On the other hand, if through fear a man were to avoid evils that according to reason are less to be avoided, and so incur evils that according to reason are more to be avoided, he could not be wholly excused from sin, because such like fear would be inordinate. Now the evils of the soul are more to be feared than the evils of the body, and evils of the body more than evils of external things. Therefore, if one were to incur evils of the soul, namely sins, in order to avoid evils of the body, such as blows or death, or evils of external things, such as loss of money, or if one were to endure evils of the body in order to avoid loss of money, one would

---

[9] It is not just any kind of fear that is opposed to courage, but fear of death. Fear of damnation is the kind of fear that can lead to despair, which is opposed to the theological virtue of hope. The objection is therefore using one kind of fear, fear of damnation, to draw a conclusion about another type of fear, fear of death. Fear of damnation is opposed to the virtue of hope; fear of death, on the other hand, is opposed to the virtue of courage.

[10] Decretals were judgments of popes on various matters collected together by an assortment of editors. The most famous collection at Thomas's time was gathered, put in order, and brought to better consistency by Gratian around 1140. *The Decretals of Gratian (Concordantia discordantium canonum)* was carefully studied, and many commentators added their own interpretations in the margins or even within the lines of the text.

not be wholly excused from sin.[11] Yet one's sin would be extenuated somewhat, for what is done through fear is less voluntary,[12] because when fear lays hold of a man he is under a certain necessity of doing a certain thing. Hence the Philosopher (*Ethic.* iii, 1) says that these things that are done through fear are not simply voluntary, but a mixture of voluntary and involuntary.

Objection 1. It seems that fear does not excuse from sin. For fear is a sin, as stated above (a. 1). But sin does not excuse from sin; rather does it aggravate it. Therefore fear does not excuse from sin.

Reply to Objection 1. Fear excuses, not in the point of its sinfulness, but in the point of its involuntariness.

Objection 2. Further, if any fear excuses from sin, most of all would this be true of the fear of death, to which, as the saying is, a courageous man is subject. Yet this fear, seemingly, is no excuse, because, since death comes, of necessity, to all, it does not seem to be an object of fear. Therefore fear does not excuse from sin.

Reply to Objection 2. Although death comes, of necessity, to all, yet the shortening of temporal life is an evil and consequently an object of fear.

---

11 Socrates's famous dictum that it is better to suffer evil than to do evil finds expression in Thomas's article. Human beings rightly fear evils that may befall them, such as loss of property, injury, death, and moral corruption. But just as all goods are not equal, so too all evils are not equal. It is unreasonable to suffer the loss of a greater good, for instance one's life, in order to protect a lesser good, such as one's wallet. The very worst evil that can befall a person is moral corruption, vice, and sin, and this is precisely because the greatest good a person can enjoy is friendship with God, charity, or sanctifying grace. So it is better to suffer evil (such as loss of property, injury, or even death) than to do evil (moral corruption). In the nineteenth century, John Henry Cardinal Newman wrote in his *Apologia pro vita sua*: "The Catholic Church holds it better for the sun and moon to drop from heaven, for the earth to fail, and for all the many millions on it to die of starvation in the extremest agony, as far as temporal affliction goes, than that one soul, I will not say, should be lost, but should commit one single venial sin, should tell one willful untruth, or should steal one poor farthing without excuse." (New York: Doubleday, 1956), p. 324.

12 Thus, the culpability of a person who acts under the influence of fear is less than someone who does the same thing without being influenced by fear.

Objection 3. Further, all fear is of evil, either temporal or spiritual. Now fear of spiritual evil cannot excuse sin, because instead of inducing one to sin, it withdraws one from sin, and fear of temporal evil does not excuse from sin, because according to the Philosopher (*Ethic.* iii, 6), "one should not fear poverty, nor sickness, nor anything that is not a result of one's own wickedness." Therefore it seems that in no sense does fear excuse from sin.

Reply to Objection 3. According to the opinion of Stoics, who held temporal goods not to be man's goods, it follows in consequence that temporal evils are not man's evils, and that therefore they are nowise to be feared. But according to Augustine (*De Lib. Arb.* ii) these temporal things are goods of the least account, and this was also the opinion of the Peripatetics. Hence their contraries are indeed to be feared, but not so much that one ought for their sake to renounce that which is good according to virtue.

QUESTION 126

FEARLESSNESS

ARTICLE 1 ⁓ Is fearlessness a sin?

Yes, despite objections to the contrary, It is said of the unjust judge (Lk 18:2) that "he feared not God nor regarded man."

I answer that, Since fear is born of love, we must seemingly judge alike of love and fear. Now it is here a question of that fear whereby one dreads temporal evils, and which results from the love of temporal goods. And every man has it instilled in him by nature to love his own life and whatever is directed thereto, and to do so in due measure, that is, to love these things not as placing his end therein, but as things to be used for the sake of his last end. Hence it is contrary to the natural inclination, and therefore a sin, to fall short of loving them in due measure. Nevertheless, one never lapses entirely from this love, since what is natural cannot be wholly lost: for which reason the Apostle says (Eph 5:29): "No man ever hated his own flesh." Therefore even those that slay themselves do so from love of their own flesh, which they desire to free from present stress. Hence it may happen that a man fears death and other temporal evils less than he ought, for the reason that he loves them less than he ought. But that he fear none of these things cannot result from an entire lack of love, but only from the fact that he thinks it impossible for him to be afflicted by the evils contrary to the goods he loves. This is sometimes the result of pride of soul presuming on self and despising others, according to the saying of Job 41:24, 25: "He [Vulg.: 'who'] was made to fear no one, he beholds every high thing"; and sometimes it happens through a defect in the reason; thus the Philosopher says (*Ethic.* iii, 7) that the Celts, through lack of intelligence, fear nothing.[13] It is therefore evident that fearlessness is a vice, whether it result from lack of love,[14] pride of soul, or dullness of understanding, yet the latter is excused from sin if it be invincible.[15]

Objection 1. It seems that fearlessness is not a sin. For that which is reckoned to the praise of a just man is not a sin. Now it is written in praise of the just man (Prov 28:1), "The just, bold as a lion, shall be without dread." Therefore it is not a sin to be without fear.

Reply to Objection 1. The just man is praised for being without fear that withdraws him from good, not that he is altogether fearless, for it is written (Sir 1:28): "He that is without fear cannot be justified."[16]

---

[13] Just as the emotion of fear can be irrational in some situations, so too lack of fear in some situations can be irrational. The exercise of practical wisdom enables us to discern rightly what to fear and what not to fear in any given situation.

[14] Fear arises from love. One only fears to lose one's health because one loves one's health. So fearlessness would indicate a lack of love, and love is a necessary component of full human flourishing, and a lack of love is a moral deficiency.

[15] Ignorance sometimes excuses from wrongdoing and sometimes does not. If a medical doctor does not know that two drugs, when taken simultaneously, bring about a lethal effect, and he prescribes both drugs to his patient, who subsequently dies from them, the physician has acted wrongly. A medical doctor can and should know how various drugs interact before prescribing them for patients. His ignorance is *culpable* ignorance and does not excuse. On the other hand, if an actor in a play shoots someone with a real gun and had no way to realize the prop gun was secretly replaced with a real pistol, the *inculpable* or *invincible* ignorance of the actor excuses him from wrongdoing. In other cases, a person wills to remain ignorant of something so as to continue "guilt free" in acting. Such willed ignorance does not excuse. Whether ignorance is culpable or inculpable, vincible or invincible, depends upon numerous factors such as age, experience, and the agent's role or occupation.

[16] Is a fear only bad if it actually causes the just person to turn away from the good, or is it also bad if it merely tempts him to turn away? Considered in themselves, the passions of fear, love, hope, despair, and daring are neither good nor evil (I–II, q. 24, a. 4). If in any given situation, however, a passion is in accord with reason, it is good, if not in accord with reason, bad.

Objection 2. Further, nothing is so fearful as death, according to the Philosopher (*Ethic.* iii, 6). Yet one ought not to fear even death, according to Matthew 10:28, "Fear not them that kill the body," etc., nor anything that can be inflicted by man, according to Isaiah 51:12, "Who are you, that you should be afraid of a mortal man?" Therefore it is not a sin to be fearless.

Reply to Objection 2. Death and whatever else can be inflicted by mortal man are not to be feared so that they make us forsake justice, but they are to be feared as hindering man in acts of virtue, either as regards himself, or as regards the progress he may cause in others. Hence it is written (Prov 14:16): "A wise man fears and declines from evil."

Objection 3. Further, fear is born of love, as stated above (q. 125, a. 2). Now it belongs to the perfection of virtue to love nothing earthly, since according to Augustine (*De Civ. Dei* xiv), "the love of God to the abasement of self makes us citizens of the heavenly city." Therefore it is seemingly not a sin to fear nothing earthly.

Reply to Objection 3. Temporal goods are to be despised as hindering us from loving and serving God, and on the same score they are not to be feared. Therefore it is written (Sir 34:16): "He that fears the Lord shall tremble at nothing." But temporal goods are not to be despised in so far as they are helping us instrumentally to attain those things that pertain to Divine fear and love.[17]

ARTICLE 2 — **Is fearlessness opposed to courage?**

Yes, despite objections to the contrary, The Philosopher (*Ethic.* iii) reckons fearlessness to be opposed to courage.

---

[17] Temporal goods are goods, not evils. For this reason, to deprive an innocent person of temporal goods, such as wealth, health, life, or reputation, is itself evil. Although temporal goods are good, however, they are not *the* Good, the Ultimate End of human life. Sin consists in turning away from Perfect Goodness so as to pursue that which is only good by participation. It is not the case, however, that temporal goods are opposed to the Divine Good, for often the pursuit of temporal goods in the correct manner is conducive to achieving the Ultimate End.

I answer that, As stated above (q. 123, a. 3), courage is concerned with fear and daring. Now every moral virtue observes the
rational mean in the matter about which it is concerned. Hence it
belongs to courage that man should moderate his fear according to
reason, namely that he should fear what he ought, and when he
ought, and so forth. Now this mode of reason may be corrupted
either by excess or by deficiency. Therefore, just as timidity is opposed
to courage by excess of fear, in so far as a man fears what he ought not,
and as he ought not, so too fearlessness is opposed thereto by deficiency of fear, in so far as a man fears not what he ought to fear.

Objection 1. It seems that fearlessness is not opposed to courage. For we
judge of habits by their acts. Now no act of courage is hindered by a man
being fearless, since if fear be removed, one is both brave to endure, and
daring to attack. Therefore fearlessness is not opposed to courage.

Reply to Objection 1. The act of courage is to endure death without
fear, and to be aggressive, not in any way whatsoever, but according to
reason: this the fearless man does not do.

Objection 2. Further, fearlessness is a vice, either through lack of due
love, or on account of pride, or by reason of folly. Now lack of due love
is opposed to charity, pride is contrary to humility, and folly to prudence
or wisdom. Therefore the vice of fearlessness is not opposed to courage.

Reply to Objection 2. Fearlessness by its specific nature corrupts the
mean of courage; therefore it is opposed to courage directly. But in
respect of its causes nothing hinders it from being opposed to other
virtues.[18]

Objection 3. Further, vices are opposed to virtue and extremes to the
mean. But one mean has only one extreme on the one side. Since, then,

---

[18] Thomas writes of the "unity of the virtues," in which anyone truly having
one virtue would also have the others. Here one can see how vices may also
be interlinked and causally related to one another. A lack of one virtue may
cause a deficiency in place of another. Yet being the cause of a deficiency is
not the same as being that deficiency. My lack of vision may lead to a car
accident that renders me unable to walk, but poor eyesight and being laid up
with injuries are not the same thing.

courage has fear opposed to it on the one side and daring on the other, it seems that fearlessness is not opposed thereto.

Reply to Objection 3. The vice of daring is opposed to courage by excess of daring, and fearlessness by deficiency of fear. Courage imposes the mean on each passion. Hence there is nothing unreasonable in its having different extremes in different respects.[19]

---

[19] The virtue of courage has two elements, fear and daring. Properly speaking, although both fear and daring have the same "matter," that is, they have to do with the danger of future hurt, fear and daring are contrary responses to the threat. Fear turns away from the danger, as it were, conceding the threat; daring takes on the danger so as to overcome it. As Thomas says in *ST* I–II, q. 45, a. 1: "Now that which is farthest removed from fear is daring, since fear turns away from the future hurt, on account of its victory over him that fears it, whereas daring turns on threatened danger because of its own victory over that same danger. Consequently it is evident that daring is contrary to fear." Both fear and daring may be in excess or deficiency, leading to not just two extremes (fearing too much/fearing too little), but four (in addition to extremes of fearing, also daring too much and daring too little).

QUESTION **129**

MAGNANIMITY

ARTICLE 3 ↠ **Is magnanimity a virtue?**

Yes, despite objections to the contrary, It is written in praise of certain men (2 Mac 15:18), "Nicanor hearing of the valor of Judas's[1] companions, and the greatness of courage [*animi magnitudinem*] with which they fought for their country, was afraid to try the matter by the sword." Now, only deeds of virtue are worthy of praise. Therefore magnanimity, which consists in greatness of courage, is a virtue.

I answer that, The essence of human virtue consists in safeguarding the good of reason in human affairs, for this is man's proper good. Now among external human things, honors take precedence of all others, as stated above (a. 1; I–II, q. 11, a. 2, obj. 3).[2] Therefore magnanimity, which observes the mode of reason in great honors, is a virtue.

---

[1] The Scripture passage is from the Old Testament and refers not to Judas Iscariot, who betrayed Christ for thirty pieces of silver, but rather to Judas Maccabeus, the great hero of Israel who fought against the forces of the Hellenic king Antiochus Epiphanes (see First and Second Maccabees, the last books of the Old Testament).

[2] In II–II, q. 129, a. 1, Thomas writes: "The things which come into man's use are external things, and among these, honor is the greatest simply, both because it is the most akin to virtue, since it is an attestation to a person's virtue, as stated above (II–II, q. 103, aa 1, 2), and because it is offered to God and to the best, and again because, in order to obtain honor even as to avoid shame, men set aside all other things."

Objection 1. It seems that magnanimity is not a virtue. For every moral virtue observes the mean. But magnanimity observes not the mean but the greater extreme, because the "magnanimous man deems himself worthy of the greatest things" (*Ethic.* iv, 3). Therefore magnanimity is not a virtue.

Reply to Objection 1. As the Philosopher again says (*Ethic.* iv, 3), "the magnanimous in point of quantity goes to extremes," in so far as he tends to what is greatest, "but in the matter of becomingness, he follows the mean," because he tends to the greatest things according to reason, for "he deems himself worthy in accordance with his worth" (*Ethic.* iv, 3), since his aims do not surpass his deserts.[3]

Objection 2. Further, he that has one virtue has them all, as stated above (I–II, q. 65, a. 1). But one may have a virtue without having magnanimity: since the Philosopher says (*Ethic.* iv, 3) that "whosoever is worthy of little things and deems himself worthy of them, is temperate, but he is not magnanimous." Therefore magnanimity is not a virtue.

Reply to Objection 2. The mutual connection of the virtues does not apply to their acts, as though every one were competent to practice the acts of all the virtues. Therefore the act of magnanimity is not becoming to every virtuous man, but only to great men. On the other hand, as regards the principles of virtue, namely prudence and grace, all virtues are connected together, since their habits reside together in the soul, either in act or by way of a proximate disposition thereto. Thus it is possible for one to whom the act of magnanimity is not competent to have the habit of magnanimity, whereby he is disposed to practice that act if it were competent to him according to his state.[4]

---

[3] The mean of virtue, Thomas reminds us here, does not consist in a mathematical mean but rather in a mean with respect to right reason. Although magnanimity prompts a person to strive for great things, this striving to be more than mediocre, average, or "in the middle," is fully in accord with understanding virtue as a mean when done in the right way, for the right reason, and in the right circumstances.

[4] Another example is the virtue of generosity with respect to money, a virtue that cannot be exercised by those in difficult financial situations, but which nevertheless may be possessed by the poor, who though without chances for

Objection 4. Further, no virtue is opposed to another virtue. But magnanimity is opposed to humility, since "the magnanimous deems himself worthy of great things, and despises others," according to *Ethic.* iv, 3. Therefore magnanimity is not a virtue.

Reply to Objection 4. There is in man something great which he possesses through the gift of God, and something defective which accrues to him through the weakness of nature. Accordingly, magnanimity makes a man deem himself worthy of great things in consideration of the gifts he holds from God: thus if his soul is endowed with great virtue, magnanimity makes him tend to perfect works of virtue; and the same is to be said of the use of any other good, such as science or external fortune. On the other hand, humility makes a man think little of himself in consideration of his own deficiency, and magnanimity makes him despise others in so far as they fall away from God's gifts, since he does not think so much of others as to do anything wrong for their sake. Yet humility makes us honor others and esteem them better than ourselves, in so far as we see some of God's gifts in them. Hence it is written of the just man (Ps 14:4): "In his sight a vile person is condemned," which indicates the contempt of magnanimity, "but he honors them that fear the Lord," which points to the reverential bearing of humility. It is therefore evident that magnanimity and humility are not contrary to one another, although they seem to tend in contrary directions, because they proceed according to different considerations.[5]

---

acts of financial generosity are fully disposed to perform such acts should the proper conditions arise (e.g., they get a great inheritance).

[5] This objection and reply is one of the most important in understanding the relationship between Christian ethics and Aristotelian ethics, for on the point of humility and magnanimity, the Gospels and Aristotle can appear irreconcilable. The potential contradiction is great. The Gospels champion humility; Aristotle considers magnanimity a virtue. Magnanimity and humility appear to be opposites, with the magnanimous person appearing proud to the humble and the humble person failing to recognize his greatness from the perspective of the magnanimous person. Here, Thomas tries to show that, properly understood, magnanimity and humility can co-exist in one person who is humble about what he can do on his own but magnanimous in light of the gifts God has given to him. The "haughty" aspect of the magnanimous person toward others is only with respect to the ways in which people fail to properly respect God. We are to love the sinner, but hate the sin. Sin is evil, and evil is

Objection 5. Further, the properties of every virtue are praiseworthy. But magnanimity has certain properties that call for blame. For, in the first place, the magnanimous is unmindful of favors; secondly, he is remiss and slow of action; thirdly, he employs irony [cf. q. 113] towards many; fourthly, he is unable to associate with others; fifthly, he holds to the barren things rather than to those that are fruitful. Therefore magnanimity is not a virtue.

Reply to Objection 5. These properties in so far as they belong to a magnanimous man call not for blame, but for very great praise. For in the first place, when it is said that the magnanimous is not mindful of those from whom he has received favors, this points to the fact that he takes no pleasure in accepting favors from others unless he repay them with yet greater favor; this belongs to the perfection of gratitude, in the act of which he wishes to excel, even as in the acts of other virtues. Again, in the second place, it is said that he is remiss and slow of action, not that he is lacking in doing what becomes him, but because he does not busy himself with all kinds of works, but only with great works, such as are becoming to him. He is also said, in the third place, to employ irony, not as opposed to truth, and so as either to say of himself vile things that are not true, or deny of himself great things that are true, but because he does not disclose all his greatness, especially to the large number of those who are beneath him, since, as also the Philosopher says (*Ethic.* iv, 3), "it belongs to a magnanimous man to be great towards persons of dignity and affluence, and unassuming towards the middle class." In the fourth place, it is said that he cannot associate with others: this means that he is not at home with others than his friends, because he altogether shuns flattery and hypocrisy, which belong to littleness of mind. But he associates with all, both great and little, according as he ought, as stated above (ad 1). It is also said, fifthly, that he prefers to have barren things, not indeed any, but good, i.e., virtuous; for in all things he prefers the virtuous to the useful, as being greater: since the useful is sought in order to supply a defect which is inconsistent with magnanimity.

---

    not to be loved. Despite sin, the goodness of the person as someone created in God's likeness and image always remains loveable.

QUESTION 130

PRESUMPTION

ARTICLE 1 -- **Is presumption a sin?**

Yes, despite objections to the contrary, It is written (Sir 37:3), "O wicked presumption, from where did you come?" and a gloss answers: "From a creature's evil will." Now all that comes of the root of an evil will is a sin. Therefore presumption is a sin.

I answer that, Since whatever is according to nature is ordered by the Divine Reason, which human reason ought to imitate, whatever is done in accordance with human reason in opposition to the order established in general throughout natural things is vicious and sinful. Now it is established throughout all natural things that every action is commensurate with the power of the agent; nor does any natural agent strive to do what exceeds its ability. Hence it is vicious and sinful, as being contrary to the natural order, that any one should assume to do what is above his power: and this is what is meant by presumption, as its very name shows. Therefore it is evident that presumption is a sin.[1]

---

[1] Presumption here is used in a different sense than it is in connection with the virtue of hope. In connection with hope, the sin of presumption is to assume that one will be saved on one's own power or to believe that one does not need God's grace in order to be saved (see II–II, q. 21, a. 2). The sense of presumption under consideration in this article treats what one might call a "grasping" for that which is well beyond a person's abilities in earthly affairs: for example, for an amateur to attempt dangerous stunts without the proper training. Presumption against the theological virtue of hope and presumption against the cardinal virtue of courage are both sins, but they are not the same sin. As Thomas notes in II–II, q. 130, a. 2, ad. 1. "It is not every presumption

Objection 1. It seems that presumption is not a sin. For the Apostle says: "Forgetting the things that are behind, I stretch forth [Vulg.: 'and stretching forth'] myself to those that are before." But it seems to savor of presumption that one should tend to what is above oneself. Therefore presumption is not a sin.

Reply to Objection 1. Nothing hinders that which is above the active power of a natural thing, and yet not above the passive power of that same thing: thus the air is possessed of a passive power by reason of which it can be so changed as to obtain the action and movement of fire, which surpass the active power of air.[2] Thus too it would be sinful and presumptuous for a man while in a state of imperfect virtue to attempt the immediate accomplishment of what belongs to perfect virtue. But it is not presumptuous or sinful for a man to endeavor to advance towards perfect virtue. In this way the Apostle stretched himself forth to the things that were before him, namely continually advancing forward.

Objection 2. Further, the Philosopher says (*Ethic.* i, 7), "we should not listen to those who would persuade us to relish human things because we are men, or mortal things because we are mortal, but we should relish those that make us immortal": and (*Metaph.* i) "that man should pursue divine things as far as possible." Now divine and immortal things are seemingly far above man. Since, then, presumption consists essentially in tending to what is above oneself, it seems that presumption is something praiseworthy, rather than a sin.

---

that is accounted a sin against the Holy Spirit, but that by which one contemns the Divine justice through inordinate confidence in the Divine mercy. The latter kind of presumption, by reason of its matter, inasmuch, to wit, as it implies contempt of something Divine, is opposed to charity, or rather to the gift of fear, whereby we revere God. Nevertheless, in so far as this contempt exceeds the proportion to one's own ability, it can be opposed to magnanimity."

[2] The active/passive power distinction marks the difference between changes in a thing brought about by an interior force as opposed to changes that a thing can undergo by reason of an outside force. I have an active power to walk; but I have a passive power to get a suntan. In the first case, I act in order to achieve some end: I walk to get to the store; in the second case, the sun acts upon me and I have the receptivity to be changed in a certain way.

Reply to Objection 2. Divine and immortal things surpass man according to the order of nature. Yet man is possessed of a natural power, namely the intellect, whereby he can be united to immortal and Divine things. In this respect the Philosopher says that "man ought to pursue immortal and divine things," not that he should do what it becomes God to do, but that he should be united to Him in intellect and will.

Objection 3. Further, the Apostle says (2 Cor 3:5): "Not that we are sufficient to think anything of ourselves, as of ourselves." If, then, presumption, by which one strives at that for which one is not sufficient, be a sin, it seems that man cannot lawfully even think of anything good, which is absurd. Therefore presumption is not a sin.

Reply to Objection 3. As the Philosopher says (*Ethic.* iii, 3), "what we can do by the help of others we can do by ourselves in a sense." Hence since we can think and do good by the help of God, this is not altogether above our ability. Hence it is not presumptuous for a man to attempt the accomplishment of a virtuous deed, but it would be presumptuous if one were to make the attempt without confidence in God's assistance.

QUESTION 131

AMBITION

ARTICLE 1 ~~ Is ambition a sin?

Yes, despite objections to the contrary, It is written (1 Cor 13:5) that "charity is not ambitious, seeks not her own." Now nothing is contrary to charity except sin. Therefore ambition is a sin.

I answer that, As stated above (q. 103, aa 1, 2), honor denotes reverence shown to a person in witness of his excellence. Now two things have to be considered with regard to man's honor. The first is that a man has not from himself the thing in which he excels, for this is, as it were, something Divine in him. Therefore on this count honor is due principally not to him but to God. The second point that calls for observation is that the thing in which man excels is given to him by God, that he may profit others thereby. Therefore a man ought so far to be pleased that others bear witness to his excellence as this enables him to profit others.

Now the desire of honor may be inordinate in three ways: first, when a man desires recognition of an excellence which he has not: this is to desire more than his share of honor; secondly, when a man desires honor for himself without referring it to God; thirdly, when a man's appetite rests in honor itself, without referring it to the profit of others. Since, then, ambition denotes inordinate desire of honor, it is evident that it is always a sin.[1]

---

1 "Ambition" here is used in a technical sense meaning an inordinate desire for honor, not as it might commonly be understood simply as a striving to do

Objection 1. It seems that ambition is not a sin. For ambition denotes the desire of honor. Now honor is in itself a good thing, and the greatest of external goods. Therefore those who care not for honor are reproved. Therefore ambition is not a sin; rather is it something deserving of praise, in so far as a good is laudably desired.

Reply to Objection 1. The desire for good should be regulated according to reason, and if it exceeds this rule it will be sinful. In this way it is sinful to desire honor in disaccord with the order of reason. Now those are reproved who care not for honor in accordance with reason's dictate that they should avoid what is contrary to honor.

Objection 2. Further, anyone may, without sin, desire what is due to him as a reward. Now honor is the reward of virtue, as the Philosopher states (*Ethic.* i, 12; iv, 3; viii, 14). Therefore ambition of honor is not a sin.

Reply to Objection 2. Honor is not the reward of virtue, as regards the virtuous man, in this sense that he should seek for it as his reward: since the reward he seeks is happiness, which is the end of virtue. But it is said to be the reward of virtue as regards others, who have nothing greater than honor whereby to reward the virtuous, which honor derives greatness from the very fact that it bears witness to virtue. Hence it is evident that it is not an adequate reward, as stated in *Ethic.* iv, 3.

Objection 3. Further, that which heartens a man to do good and disheartens him from doing evil is not a sin. Now honor heartens men to do good and to avoid evil; thus the Philosopher says (*Ethic.* iii, 8) that "with the bravest men, cowards are held in dishonor, and the brave in

---

great things. Ambition, as used by Thomas, is always a sin and differs from presumption, according to q. 131, a. 2, ad 2: "For if a man were to have an inordinate desire for a position of dignity, not for the sake of honor, but for the sake of a right use of a dignity exceeding his ability, he would not be ambitious but presumptuous." Both exceed the mean of just use of honor (magnanimity), but they exceed it in different ways. Ambition seeks honor inordinately, without reference to the divine and without using honor as a means for the good of others. On the other hand, "the presumptuous man attempts great deeds beyond his ability" and so exceeds the mean of magnanimity, but in a different way than the ambitious person (II–II, q. 131, a. 2, ad 1).

honor"; and Tully says (*De Tusc. Quaest.* i) that "honor fosters the arts." Therefore ambition is not a sin.

Reply to Objection 3. Just as some are heartened to do good and disheartened from doing evil by the desire of honor, if this be desired in due measure, so, if it be desired inordinately, it may become to man an occasion of doing many evil things, as when a man cares not by what means he obtains honor.[2] Therefore Sallust says (*Catilin.*) that "the good as well as the wicked covet honors for themselves, but the one," i.e., the good, "goes about it in the right way," whereas "the other," i.e., the wicked, "through lack of the good arts, makes use of deceit and falsehood." Yet they who, merely for the sake of honor, either do good or avoid evil, are not virtuous, according to the Philosopher (*Ethic.* iii, 8), where he says that they who do brave things for the sake of honor are not truly brave.

---

[2] In other words, that some consideration prompts one to do good or avoid evil is not a guarantee that this motivating factor is always good. One might do good and avoid evil in order to avoid embarrassment, and embarrassment is not in itself a serious evil. However, if one had an undue aversion to embarrassment, if "saving face" became the most important motivation in a person's life, then the inordinate avoiding of embarrassment would be sinful.

QUESTION 132

VAINGLORY

ARTICLE 5 ⟶ **Are the consequences of vainglory disobedience, boastfulness, hypocrisy, contention, obstinacy, discord, and love of novelties?**

Yes, despite objections to the contrary, Stands the authority of Gregory (*Moral.* xxxi), who there assigns the above consequences to vainglory.

I answer that, As stated above (q. 34, a. 5; q. 35, a. 4; I–II, q. 84, aa 3, 4), the vices that by their very nature are such as to be directed to the end of a certain capital vice are called its offspring.[1] Now the end of vainglory is the manifestation of one's own excellence, as stated above (aa 1, 4), and to this end a man may tend in two ways: in one way directly, either by words, and this is boasting, or by deeds, and then if they be true and call for astonishment, it is love of novelties which men are wont to wonder at most; but if they be false, it is hypocrisy. In another way, a man strives to make known his excellence by showing that he is not inferior to another, and this in four ways. First, as regards the intellect, and thus we have "obstinacy," by which a man is too much attached to his own opinion, being unwilling to believe one that is better. Secondly, as regards the will, and then we have "discord," whereby a man is unwilling

---

[1] Sometimes also called the "offspring" or "daughters of vainglory." Thomas speaks here about those vices that characteristically follow upon vainglory as offspring follow from parents. Small sins lead to bigger ones and additional ones. Happily, virtue operates the same way. Small acts of goodness lead to more, and eventually a stable disposition to seek what is truly good.

to give up his own will and agree with others. Thirdly, as regards "speech," and then we have "contention," whereby a man quarrels noisily with another. Fourthly as regards deeds, and this is "disobedience," whereby a man refuses to carry out the command of his superiors.

Objection 1. It seems that the offspring of vainglory are unsuitably reckoned to be "disobedience, boastfulness, hypocrisy, contention, obstinacy, discord, and presumption of novelties." For according to Gregory (*Moral.* xxiii), boastfulness is numbered among the species of pride. Now pride does not arise from vainglory; rather is it the other way about, as Gregory says (*Moral.* xxxi). Therefore boastfulness should not be reckoned among the offspring of vainglory.

Reply to Objection 1. As stated above (q. 112, a. 1, ad 2), boasting is reckoned a kind of pride as regards its interior cause, which is arrogance; but outward boasting, according to *Ethic.* iv, is directed sometimes to gain, but more often to glory and honor, and thus it is the result of vainglory.

Objection 2. Further, contention and discord seem to be the outcome chiefly of anger. But anger is a capital vice distinguished from vainglory. Therefore it seems that they are not the offspring of vainglory.

Reply to Objection 2. Anger is not the cause of discord and contention, except in conjunction with vainglory, in that a man thinks it a glorious thing for him not to yield to the will and words of others.

QUESTION 133

~~~~~~~~~~~~~~~~~~~~~~~~~~~~~~~

PUSILLANIMITY (FAINTHEARTEDNESS)

ARTICLE 1 ⟶ Is pusillanimity (faintheartedness) a sin?

Yes, despite objections to the contrary, Nothing in human conduct is to be avoided save sin. Now pusillanimity is to be avoided, for it is written (Col 3:21), "Fathers, provoke not your children to indignation, lest they be discouraged." Therefore pusillanimity is a sin.

I answer that, Whatever is contrary to a natural inclination is a sin, because it is contrary to a law of nature. Now everything has a natural inclination to accomplish an action that is commensurate with its power, as is evident in all natural things, whether animate or inanimate. Now just as presumption makes a man exceed what is proportionate to his power, by striving to do more than he can, so pusillanimity makes a man fall short of what is proportionate to his power, by refusing to tend to that which is commensurate thereto.[1] Therefore, as presumption is a

---

1 Rebecca Konyndyk DeYoung notes the causes of this vice: "First, pusillanimity results from measuring our value in comparison to others, and negatively so. The faint-hearted person is one who, when considering some action, looks around, sees others doing a much better job, is certain that she will look inferior in comparison or fare poorly by their standards or expectations, and therefore decides not to make the attempt. She shrinks back from acting because her measure of herself and her contributions depends on a 'horizontal' standard of comparison and a worldly measure of greatness. According to both, she finds herself wanting. Secondly, pusillanimity results from the wrong sort of self-reliance. In America, independence is *the* premier virtue.

sin, so is pusillanimity. Hence it is that the servant who buried in the earth the money he had received from his master, and did not trade with it through fainthearted fear, was punished by his master (Mt 25; Lk 19).[2]

Objection 1. It seems that pusillanimity is not a sin. For every sin makes a man evil, just as every virtue makes a man good. But a fainthearted man is not evil, as the Philosopher says (*Ethic.* iv, 3). Therefore pusillanimity is not a sin.

Reply to Objection 1. The Philosopher calls those evil who injure their neighbor; and accordingly the fainthearted is said not to be evil, because he injures no one, save accidentally, by omitting to do what

---

One is valuable and valued for 'autonomous' achievement, not for depending on others for help. For the pusillanimous person to ask for assistance—and therefore to admit that she needs it—would be to admit her inadequacy to others, something which she cannot bear to do; yet because she is certain that she could never act successfully on her own either, she shrinks back from the attempt altogether." DeYoung notes that Thomas's account of the virtue of courage corrects both difficulties: First, "[p]recisely because magnanimity depends on God's power and trusts his goodness, it protects us from smug presumption on the one hand and pusillanimous despair on the other. Both vices are caused by a view of the self and its accomplishments *without the aid of grace.* One takes the form of thinking our own power is sufficient for goodness and that we are independently worthy of honor; the other thinks that we are absolutely helpless and hopeless on our own and therefore there is no reason to even try to be good. So to the presumptuous person, God says, 'You *cannot* do this on your own'; and to those overwhelmed by a sense of their own inadequacy, God says, 'You don't *have* to do this on your own.' [Secondly the] standard of comparison on Aquinas's account is emphatically 'vertical': the measure of our worth does not ultimately depend on how we stack up against others. When we see ourselves in relation to God, we realize that both magnanimity and its complement, humility, are necessary for living in accord with a truthful view of ourselves." Rebecca Konyndyk DeYoung, "Aquinas's Virtues of Acknowledged Dependence: A New Measure of Greatness," *Faith and Philosophy* (April 2004): 214–27.

[2] Virtue consists in a mean. It is a kind of presumption for someone to exceed his or her gifts and abilities, for example a mediocre swimmer of middle age, attempting to become an Olympic swimmer. Pusillanimity, on the other hand, is a deficiency whereby one does not make use of talents and abilities that one

might be profitable to others. For Gregory says (*Pastoral.* i) that if "they who demur to do good to their neighbor in preaching be judged strictly, without doubt their guilt is proportionate to the good they might have done had they been less retiring."[3]

Objection 2. Further, the Philosopher says (*Ethic.* iv, 3) that "a faint-hearted man is especially one who is worthy of great goods, yet does not deem himself worthy of them." Now no one is worthy of great goods except the virtuous, since as the Philosopher again says (*Ethic.* iv, 3), "none but the virtuous are truly worthy of honor." Therefore the fainthearted are virtuous; and consequently pusillanimity is not a sin.

Reply to Objection 2. Nothing hinders a person who has a virtuous habit from sinning venially and without losing the habit, or mortally and with loss of the habit of gratuitous virtue. Hence it is possible for a man, by reason of the virtue which he has, to be worthy of doing certain great things that are worthy of great honor, and yet through not trying to make use of his virtue, he sins sometimes venially, sometimes mortally.[4]

Again, it may be replied that the fainthearted is worthy of great things in proportion to his ability for virtue, ability which he derives either from a good natural disposition, or from science, or from external fortune, and if he fails to use those things for virtue, he becomes guilty of pusillanimity.

---

has. It would be possible for one and the same person to be presumptuous in one respect, say in terms of athletic abilities, and pusillanimous in another respect, say in terms of academic abilities.

3 To omit an action may be sinful. The human community, and our smaller communities of school, family, or other voluntary groups, depend upon the effort of their members. Not only positively harming or injuring the good, but also failing to do the good that we could, constitutes a failing. Failing to develop one's talents, abilities, and aptitudes may unjustly deprive others of services, joys, and aids to which they are entitled.

4 The distinction between infused and acquired virtue is at work in this article. An infused virtue, a gift of God's grace, can be lost through a single mortal sin that deprives the soul of sanctifying grace and the infused virtues that accompany that grace. Acquired virtue, that habit of soul gained through repeated human acts, cannot be lost by a single act, although evil acts repeated over time do lead to a loss of virtue.

Objection 3. Further, "Pride is the beginning of all sin" (Sir 10:15). But pusillanimity does not proceed from pride, since the proud man sets himself above what he is, while the fainthearted man withdraws from the things he is worthy of. Therefore pusillanimity is not a sin.

Reply to Objection 3. Even pusillanimity may in some way be the result of pride: when, to wit, a man clings too much to his own opinion, whereby he thinks himself incompetent for those things for which he is competent. Hence it is written (Prov 26:16): "The sluggard is wiser in his own conceit than seven men that speak sentences." For nothing hinders him from depreciating himself in some things, and having a high opinion of himself in others. Therefore Gregory says (*Pastoral.* i) of Moses that "perchance he would have been proud, had he undertaken the leadership of a numerous people without misgiving; and again, he would have been proud, had he refused to obey the command of his Creator."

Objection 4. Further, the Philosopher says (*Ethic.* iv, 3) that "he who deems himself less worthy than he is, is said to be fainthearted." Now sometimes holy men deem themselves less worthy than they are: for instance, Moses and Jeremiah, who were worthy of the office God chose them for, which they both humbly declined (Ex 3:11; Jer 1:6). Therefore pusillanimity is not a sin.

---

5 Rebecca Konyndyk DeYoung notes in her article: "At the annunciation, Mary shows us that true greatness comes from looking to God for one's ultimate sense of worthiness, and the greatest achievements of virtue come from relying on God's power working in us. Paradoxically, Mary is greatest, most favored, and capable of both great virtue and great suffering for God's sake when she recognizes her absolute dependence on God, her status as a handmaid (Greek: *doula*—slave). She does not even refer to herself by her own name in the *Magnificat*—most of her song relates the great deeds of God. Yet at the same time she proclaims without hesitation that all generations to come will call her blessed—more honor and glory than any of the rest of us are likely to achieve. Throughout the account, Mary's source of self-appraisal is emphatically vertical: Elizabeth, *moved by the Holy Spirit,* confirms Mary's favor with the Lord and honors her for the greatness of her position, as was

Reply to Objection 4. Moses and Jeremiah were worthy of the office to which they were appointed by God, but their worthiness was of Divine grace;[5] yet they, considering the insufficiency of their own weakness, demurred, though not obstinately lest they should fall into pride.[6]

---

previously announced by the angelic messenger from God. By contrast, her reputation in her lifetime was likely of little account (she was from Nazareth in Galilee), if not shameful (because of her pregnancy out of wedlock). Mary sees herself rightly when she looks to the true source of her worthiness, her honor, and her ability to do great things. She is great on account of what the Lord has done for and through her. The mistakes of the pusillanimous person are threefold: to whom they are listening, against whom they are measuring themselves, on whom they are relying. In contrast, Mary could privilege Elizabeth's words of honor over the shame from her townsfolk because she knew where she stood before God. Greatness for her was fundamentally defined by God's favor and not by the expectations of others. Moreover, she accepted the great task to which she was called out of absolute trust in God's power and dependence on God's grace" ("Aquinas's Virtues of Acknowledged Dependence: A New Measure of Greatness," 222).

6 Pusillanimity may occur when someone is called to a great undertaking, for example, to be a father or mother to a large family, to organize a relief effort, or to offer needed services to a community group. As Thomas said in the reply to the previous objection, pride may be at work when people maintain their (belittling) viewpoint of themselves, thereby not shouldering the duties that they are capable of carrying. As Thomas notes in the next article, pusillanimity is also sometimes caused by fear of failure, which is unbearable to the proud. Humility consists in knowing the truth about oneself and living according to that truth, avoiding both presumption and pusillanimity.

QUESTION **136**

PATIENCE

ARTICLE 1 ↦ **Is patience a virtue?**

Yes, despite objections to the contrary, Augustine says (*De Patientia* i): "The virtue of the soul that is called patience is so great a gift of God, that we even preach the patience of Him who bestows it upon us."[1]

I answer that, As stated above (q. 123, a. 1), the moral virtues are directed to the good, inasmuch as they safeguard the good of reason against the impulse of the passions. Now among the passions sorrow is strong enough to hinder the good of reason, according to 2 Corinthians 7:10, "The sorrow of the world works death," and Sirach 30:25, "Sadness has killed many, and there is no profit in it." Hence the necessity for a virtue to safeguard the good of reason against sorrow,[2] lest reason give way to sorrow: and this patience does. Therefore Augustine says (*De Patientia* ii): "A man's patience it is whereby he bears evil with an equal mind," i.e., without being disturbed by sorrow, "lest he abandon

---

[1] The patience of Christ is paradigmatic. Knowing all things, he waited for others to learn. Capable of all things, he himself grew in wisdom and stature as a human. Aware of the future and end of all people, he nevertheless related to them in time as they were. In a most dramatic sense, the patience of the Lord was evident during his passion when he endured evils of all kinds but was never deterred from his goal.

[2] Sorrow is an interior displeasure of the soul arising from something repugnant to desire. It is an "inward pain" that may or may not accompany exterior displeasure of the body. Indeed, great bodily pleasure and sorrow may go together. For more on sorrow, see *ST* I–II, q. 35.

with an unequal mind the goods whereby he may advance to better things."[3] It is therefore evident that patience is a virtue.

Objection 1. It seems that patience is not a virtue. For the virtues are most perfect in heaven, as Augustine says (*De Trin.* xiv). Yet patience is not there, since no evils have to be borne there, according to Isaiah 49:10 and Revelation 7:16, "They shall not hunger nor thirst, neither shall the heat nor the sun strike them." Therefore patience is not a virtue.

Reply to Objection 1. The moral virtues do not remain in heaven as regards the same act that they have on the way, in relation, namely, to the goods of the present life, which will not remain in heaven; but they will remain in their relation to the end, which will be in heaven. Thus justice will not be in heaven in relation to buying and selling and other matters pertaining to the present life, but it will remain in the point of being subject to God. In like manner, the act of patience, in heaven, will not consist in bearing things, but in enjoying the goods to which we had aspired by suffering. Hence Augustine says (*De Civ. Dei* xiv) that "patience itself will not be in heaven, since there is no need for it except where evils have to be borne; yet that which we shall obtain by patience will be eternal."

Objection 2. Further, no virtue can be found in the wicked, since virtue is "that which makes its possessor good." Yet patience is sometimes found in wicked men, for instance in the covetous, who bear many evils patiently that they may amass money, according to Ecclesiastes 5:16, "All the days of his life he eats in darkness, and in many cares, and in misery and in sorrow." Therefore patience is not a virtue.

---

3 Augustine's understanding of patience as that virtue "whereby he bears evil with an equal mind lest he abandon with an unequal mind the goods whereby he may advance to better things" is important in a number of ways. Patience is not being unaware of an evil or pretending that evil is not really evil. Patience bears with evil so as not to abandon certain other goods. In certain circumstances, however, it is not patience but rather pusillanimity or cowardice that is evidenced when one continues to bear with evil. Sometimes an evil should be fought against rather than endured. At other times, however, patience with the evil is the better course. The importance of the virtue of prudence consists in having the discernment to make such decisions.

Reply to Objection 2. As Augustine says (*De Patientia* ii; v), "properly speaking those are patient who would rather bear evils without inflicting them than inflict them without bearing them. As for those who bear evils that they may inflict evil, their patience is neither marvelous nor praiseworthy, for it is no patience at all: we may marvel at their hardness of heart, but we must refuse to call them patient."[4]

ARTICLE 3 — **Is it possible to have patience without grace?**

No, despite objections to the contrary, It is written (Ps 61:6): "From Him," i.e., from God, "is my patience."

I answer that, As Augustine says (*De Patientia* iv), "the strength of desire helps a man to bear toil and pain: and no one willingly undertakes to bear what is painful, save for the sake of that which gives pleasure." The reason of this is because sorrow and pain are of themselves displeasing to the soul. Therefore it would never choose to suffer them for their own sake, but only for the sake of an end. Hence it follows that the good for the sake of which one is willing to endure evils is more desired and loved than the good the privation of which causes the sorrow that we bear patiently. Now the fact that a man prefers the good of grace to all natural goods, the loss of which may cause sorrow, is to be referred to charity, which loves God above all things.[5] Hence it is evident that patience, as a virtue, is caused by charity, according to 1 Corinthians 13:4, "Charity is patient."

---

4 Here, as in the *City of God*, Augustine emphasizes the internal aspect of morality. In the *City of God*, Augustine argues that the virtues of the Romans really masked the vice of glory, and in seeking glory, the other possible vices that they may have had were put in check. Just as a thief might develop a kind of faux courage, so too someone might develop an ersatz patience in service of an evil end. But for what appears to be virtue to count really as virtue, the end in mind must also be good. There is no virtue, but only imitations of virtue, that can be put in service of evil ends, for real virtue is ordered always to authentic happiness. On the important question of the "unity of the virtues," see I–II, q. 65, a. 1.

5 In other words, a person with the infused virtue of charity loves God more than any goods the pursuit of which would separate the agent from God (e.g., stealing money) even though lacking the good in question (in this case, money) may itself be a hardship.

But it is manifest that it is impossible to have charity save through grace, according to Romans 5:5, "The charity of God is poured forth in our hearts by the Holy Spirit Who is given to us." Therefore it is clearly impossible to have patience without the help of grace.[6]

Objection 1. It seems that it is possible to have patience without grace. For the more his reason inclines to a thing, the more is it possible for the rational creature to accomplish it. Now it is more reasonable to suffer evil for the sake of good than for the sake of evil. Yet some suffer evil for evil's sake, by their own virtue and without the help of grace; for Augustine says (*De Patientia* iii) that "men endure many toils and sorrows for the sake of the things they love sinfully." Much more, therefore, is it possible for man, without the help of grace, to bear evil for the sake of good, and this is to be truly patient.

Reply to Objection 1. The inclination of reason would prevail in human nature in the state of integrity. But in corrupt nature the inclination of concupiscence prevails, because it is dominant in man. Hence man is more prone to bear evils for the sake of goods in which the concupiscence delights here and now,[7] than to endure evils for the

---

6 Likewise, Thomas says it is impossible to have related virtues without the help of grace (II–II, q. 137, a. 4). Grace is especially important for perseverance. "To persist long in something good until it is accomplished belongs to a special virtue. Accordingly, just as temperance and courage are special virtues, for the reason that the one moderates pleasures of touch (which is of itself a difficult thing), while the other moderates fear and daring in connection with dangers of death (which also is something difficult in itself), so perseverance is a special virtue, since it consists in enduring delays in the above or other virtuous deeds, so far as necessity requires" (II–II, q. 137, a. 1). This virtue is especially important today as commitment to marriage or a religious vocation necessarily involves perseverance. Psychological studies indicate that every marital couple has irreconcilable differences of various kinds. Those in consecrated life or apostolic celibacy likewise face difficulties, doubts, trials, and challenges of various kinds. Perseverance helps people to remain committed to their vocation despite various (inevitable) difficulties in order to manifest fidelity to their promises and secure the goods that can only be attained through running the race of life to its completion.

7 The *Catechism of the Catholic Church* notes: "Etymologically, 'concupiscence' can refer to any intense form of human desire. Christian theology has given it a particular meaning: the movement of the sensitive appetite contrary to

sake of goods to come, which are desired in accordance with reason; and yet it is this that pertains to true patience.[8]

Objection 2. Further, some who are not in a state of grace have more abhorrence for sinful evils than for bodily evils: hence some heathens are related to have endured many hardships rather than betray their country or commit some other misdeed. Now this is to be truly patient. Therefore it seems that it is possible to have patience without the help of grace.

Reply to Objection 2. The good of a social virtue is commensurate with human nature; and consequently the human will can tend thereto without the help of sanctifying grace, yet not without the help of God's grace.[9] On the other hand, the good of grace is supernatural. Therefore man cannot tend thereto by a natural virtue. Hence the comparison fails.

Objection 3. Further, it is quite evident that some go through much trouble and pain in order to regain health of the body. Now the health of the soul is not less desirable than bodily health. Therefore, in like manner one may, without the help of grace, endure many evils for the health of the soul, and this is to be truly patient.

Reply to Objection 3. Even the endurance of those evils which a man bears for the sake of his body's health proceeds from the love a man

---

the operation of the human reason. The apostle St. Paul identifies it with the rebellion of the 'flesh' against the 'spirit.' Concupiscence stems from the disobedience of the first sin. It unsettles man's moral faculties and, without being in itself an offense, inclines man to commit sins" (2515).

8 "True patience" is an enduring of evil for the sake of preserving or enhancing friendship with God, while "false patience" is an enduring of evil for the sake of lesser goods such as fame, honor, money, or pleasure. Patience, as other virtues, admits of false imitators unconnected with true human flourishing and the final end.

9 This response implicitly seems to presuppose a distinction made earlier between two kinds of grace (I–II, q. 111, a. 1), distinguished by writers after Thomas as "sanctifying grace" and "actual grace." Sanctifying grace makes a person a child of God worthy of heaven, whereas those who may lack sanctifying grace can still do what is in external respects good. However, without the help of actual grace—that grace given by God for a particular act—they cannot do that good proportionate to human nature.

naturally has for his own flesh. Hence there is no comparison between this endurance and patience which proceeds from a supernatural love.

QUESTION 139

~~~~~~~~~~~~~~~~

THE GIFT OF COURAGE

ARTICLE 1 ⟿ **Is courage a gift?**

Yes, despite objections to the contrary, Courage is reckoned among the other gifts of the Holy Spirit (Is 11:2).

I answer that, Courage denotes a certain firmness of mind, as stated above (q. 123, a. 2; I–II, q. 61, a. 3); and this firmness of mind is required both in doing good and in enduring evil, especially with regard to goods or evils that are difficult. Now man, according to his proper and connatural mode, is able to have this firmness in both these respects, so as not to forsake the good on account of difficulties, whether in accomplishing an arduous work, or in enduring grievous evil. In this sense courage denotes a special or general virtue, as stated above (q. 123, a. 2).[1]

Yet furthermore man's mind is moved by the Holy Spirit, in order that he may attain the end of each work begun, and avoid whatever perils may threaten. This surpasses human nature: for sometimes it is not in a man's power to attain the end of his work, or to avoid evils or dangers, since these may happen to overwhelm him in death. But the Holy Spirit works this in man, by bringing him to everlasting life, which is

---

[1] Courage is a properly human virtue obtained through repeated human action, as Thomas makes clear in the first section of this article. However, in a related but different sense, courage is also a gift given by God, enabling us to endure dangers to salvation and accomplish difficult work related to the final end beyond the natural power of a human being.

the end of all good deeds, and the release from all perils. A certain confidence of this is infused into the mind by the Holy Spirit, Who expels
any fear of the contrary. It is in this sense that courage is reckoned a gift
of the Holy Spirit. For it has been stated above (I–II, q. 68, aa 1, 2) that
the gifts regard the motion of the mind by the Holy Spirit.

Objection 1. It seems that courage is not a gift. For the virtues differ
from the gifts, and courage is a virtue. Therefore it should not be reckoned a gift.

Reply to Objection 1. Courage, as a virtue, perfects the mind in the
endurance of all perils whatever; but it does not go so far as to give
confidence of overcoming all dangers: this belongs to the courage that
is a gift of the Holy Spirit.

TEMPERANCE

Temperance

JOINING practical wisdom, justice, and courage, the final cardinal virtue temperance enables us to moderate our desires, more particularly, our sense appetites in eating, drinking, and sexual activity, by keeping them in line with the order of right reason and the divine law. Sense appetite is the power by which we tend toward (or away from) and take delight in (or are pained by) particular things we sense as pleasurable (or painful). As you will recall, sense appetite is divided into the concupiscible and the irascible. The concupiscible appetite is the power by which we are inclined to seek what is sensibly pleasurable and to avoid what is sensibly painful, while the irascible appetite is that power by which we are inclined to resist what gets in the way of our seeking sensible pleasure and avoiding sensible pain. Just as courage is the cardinal virtue of the irascible sense appetite, so temperance is the cardinal virtue of the concupiscible.

We experience bodily pleasure in eating, drinking, and sexual activity. Bodily pleasure is the feeling that accompanies the proper functioning of our physical organism, and as it is proper for us to use food, drink, and sex for our individual species' health and preservation, it is natural and proper for us to feel pleasure in food, drink, and sexual activity—and the more so if we are physically healthy! But we are more than just physical organisms; we are human, and so the pleasure we feel in food, drink, and sexual activity must be proper to human beings living according to the rule of right reason and ultimately the rule of divine reason. Because the sense appetites we experience in eating, drinking, and sexual activity are powerful in themselves and can threaten our appetitive integrity and emotional stability, we need to humanize them by bringing them into line with right reason so that these sense appetites can work for us in our living well as human beings and children of God. For this we need the cardinal virtue of temperance.

St. Thomas sees temperance as a habit concerned with choosing both to act and to feel in accordance with the mean between two extremes of too little or too much eating, drinking, and sexual activity, as that mean is determined by our practical wisdom. As an infused virtue, temperance is the graced habit concerned with choosing that mean in accordance with practical wisdom as that virtue is ultimately in accordance with the rule of divine wisdom. The cardinal virtue of temperance is a habit of being rightly pleased in the use and enjoyment of food, drink, and sex as that use is in accord with right reason and divine law. With this virtue comes an experience of tranquility or serenity in our use of food, drink, and sex. Serenity describes the state of being free from distress and being pleased knowing that our appetites are in harmony with how we are supposed to live.

St. Thomas describes two virtues as "integral parts" of temperance: shamefacedness and honesty.

By "shamefacedness" St. Thomas means the healthy fear of doing what is wrong, or morally shameful, and being perceived by ourselves and others as being morally base and deserving of censure (q. 144, a. 1). The complementary integral part of temperance is that of "honesty." Honesty refers to a state of being worthy of honor principally on account of our moral rectitude with respect to our desires and emotions. Honesty is that state of being aware of the inner beauty of our appetites as they are in conformity with right reason. This awareness enables us to take joy in expressing with openness what is good and disposes us to be temperate, not out of disgrace, but out of love for the beauty of temperance (q. 143, a. 1).

Besides the integral parts of shamefacedness and honesty, St. Thomas understands the cardinal virtue of temperance as having a number of "subjective parts" or species. These subjective parts of temperance are abstinence, sobriety, and chastity, as each deals with one of the three sensible goods of food, drink, and sexual activity.

Abstinence is the subjective part of temperance that concerns the desire for and the use and enjoyment of food. Abstinence is the habit by which we respond to food with well-ordered desires and pleasures (q. 146, a. 1, ad 2). By this virtue our appetite for food is so ordered that all thoughts, feelings, and actions concerned with eating are governed by reason exercised through faith and love of God (q. 146, a. 1, ad 1) and with gladness of heart (q. 146, a. 1, ad 4). While abstinence is chiefly a habit of the internal affections (q. 146, a. 1, ad 2), it is expressed and cultivated by fasting (q. 147, a. 2). St. Thomas understands fasting as an act of abstaining in some measure from food for a reasonable purpose (q. 147, a. 1, ad 3), such as rooting out vicious habits of consumption in our lives, freeing ourselves from attachment to sensual things in general, or making satisfaction for sin—these are all ways of re-establishing a right relationship with God. We are to perform such acts of abstinence guided especially by reason, the exercise of infused virtue, the wisdom of sacred scripture, and the precepts of the Church (q. 147, a. 3).

Vices opposed to abstinence are, on the one hand, insensibility, that is, in desiring, using, and enjoying the good of food too little (q. 142, a. 1), and on the other hand, the much more common vice of gluttony, by which we knowingly exceed the right amount in eating from a desire for the pleasure of eating (q. 148, a.1, ad 2).

The subjective part of temperance that deals principally with the use and enjoyment of alcoholic beverages St. Thomas calls sobriety (q. 149, aa 1, 2). Sobriety is the virtue by which we respond appropriately to the pleasures of alcohol. By this virtue we are able to enjoy alcoholic beverages with their moderate use as we determine the mean by virtue of our practical wisdom. The two vices opposed to sobriety are insensibility as a habitually deficient desire, use, and enjoyment of alcohol, and drunkenness as the characteristic disposition to desire and use alcohol to become inebriated (q. 150, a. 2).

Chastity is the subjective part or species of temperance having to do with our sensible appetite for sexual relations. St. Thomas distinguishes chastity from purity, as the former virtue regards the desires and pleasures of sexual intercourse, while the latter regards what he calls the external signs of intercourse, such as looking, kissing, and touching (q. 151, a. 4). Even more than our sensible appetites for food and drink, the uncontrolled sensible appetite for sex can destroy our peace of mind, cloud our judgment, and so prevent us from living in the peace and freedom of the children of God. By the virtue of chastity we are able to chasten and restrain ourselves in our sense appetite for sexual intercourse in order to experience sexual desire and pleasure in the beautiful way of one who is a temple of the Holy Spirit (q. 153, a. 3, ad 2).

According to St. Thomas, right reason and divine law require that we understand sexual relations as having procreation and thus the preservation of the human race as their purpose (q. 153, a. 2). We are to form our sexual desires according to right reason and divine law by being open to the generation of new life.

As with the other subjective parts of temperance, there are two vices opposed to the virtue of chastity: the one, a vice of insensitivity occurring in those married couples who refuse each other their legitimate due in this regard (q. 152, a. 2); the other, the vice of lust as the habit of exceeding what is proper in the matter of sexual activity, that is, in the disposition to desire and enjoy sex with the wrong person or for the wrong reason (q. 153, aa 1, 3).

QUESTION **141**

TEMPERANCE

ARTICLE 1 ~~ **Is temperance a virtue?**

Yes, despite objections to the contrary, Augustine says (*Music.* vi, 15): "Temperance is the name of a virtue."

I answer that, As stated above (I–II, q. 55, a. 3), it is essential to virtue to incline man to good. Now the good of man is to be in accordance with reason, as Dionysius states (*Div. Nom.* iv).[1] Hence human virtue is that which inclines man to something in accordance with reason. Now temperance evidently inclines man to this, since its very name implies moderation or temperateness, which reason causes. Therefore temperance is a virtue.

Objection 1. It seems that temperance is not a virtue. For no virtue goes against the inclination of nature, since "there is in us a natural aptitude for virtue," as stated in *Ethic.* ii, 1. Now temperance withdraws us from pleasures to which nature inclines, according to *Ethic.* ii, 3, 8. Therefore temperance is not a virtue.

Reply to Objection 1. Nature inclines everything to whatever is becoming to it. Therefore man naturally desires pleasures that are becoming to

---

[1] The influence of (Pseudo) Dionysius on St. Thomas is deep and pervasive. Thomas had early contact with the thought of Dionysius through St. Albert the Great, who taught a course on the *Divine Names* in which Thomas himself took the official notes. On Thomas's own commentary on the *Divine Names*, see Jean Pierre Torrell, *Saint Thomas Aquinas: Vol. I, The Person and His Work* (Washington, DC: The Catholic University of America Press, 1996), 127–29.

him. Since, however, man as such is a rational being, it follows that those
pleasures are becoming to man which are in accordance with reason.
From such pleasures temperance does not withdraw him, but from those
which are contrary to reason.[2] Therefore it is clear that temperance is not
contrary to the inclination of human nature, but is in accord with it. It
is, however, contrary to the inclination of the animal nature that is not
subject to reason.[3]

Objection 2. Further, virtues are connected with one another, as
stated above (I–II, q. 65, a. 1). But some people have temperance
without having the other virtues: for we find many who are temperate, and yet covetous or timid. Therefore temperance is not a virtue.

Reply to Objection 2. The temperance which fulfils the conditions of
perfect virtue is not without prudence, while this is lacking to all who
are in sin. Hence those who lack other virtues, through being subject
to the opposite vices, have not the temperance which is a virtue,
though they do acts of temperance from a certain natural disposition,
in so far as certain imperfect virtues are either natural to man, as stated
above (I–II, q. 63, a. 1), or acquired by habituation, which virtues,
through lack of prudence, are not perfected by reason, as stated above
(I–II, q. 65, a. 1).

---

[2] Pleasure is not simply of one kind but rather of various kinds, based on various
kinds of activities. Certain pleasures are bodily and shared with animals such as
eating, drinking, and sexual activity. Other pleasures are what one might call
intellectual pleasures such as making conversation, kindling friendship, and
acting with integrity. Temperance, properly speaking, concerns not intellectual
pleasures, but rather bodily pleasures. For more on the nature of various kinds
of pleasures, see Thomas's *Commentary on the Nicomachean Ethics*, Books VII
and X.

[3] For example, a hungry father at dinner with his children may, according to
his animal nature, desire to eat as much food as will satisfy his hunger, but if
the food is in relative short supply, he knows according to his rational nature
that he should share the food with his children. It is not contrary to human
nature to share the food inasmuch as it is in accord with human nature to
look after one's own children. However, there is also an inclination, in accord
with the animal nature of the human being, that looks simply to what will
fulfill the body.

Objection 3. Further, to every virtue there is a corresponding gift, as appears from what we have said above (I–II, q. 68, a. 4). But seemingly no gift corresponds to temperance, since all the gifts have been already ascribed to the other virtues (qq. 8, 9, 19, 45, 52, 71, 139). Therefore temperance is not a virtue.

Reply to Objection 3. Temperance also has a corresponding gift, namely fear, whereby man is withheld from the pleasures of the flesh, according to Psalm 118:120: "Pierce my flesh with Your fear." The gift of fear has for its principal object God, Whom it avoids offending, and in this respect it corresponds to the virtue of hope, as stated above (q. 19, a. 9, ad 1). But it may have for its secondary object whatever a man shuns in order to avoid offending God. Now man stands in the greatest need of the fear of God in order to shun those things which are most seductive, and these are the matter of temperance. Therefore the gift of fear corresponds to temperance also.

ARTICLE 3 ⸺ **Is temperance only about desires and pleasures?**

Yes, despite objections to the contrary, Isidore says (*Etym.*) that "it is temperance whereby lust and desire are kept under control."[4]

I answer that, As stated above (q. 123, a. 12; q. 136, a. 1), it belongs to moral virtue to safeguard the good of reason against the passions that rebel against reason. Now the movement of the soul's passions is twofold, as stated above (I–II, q. 23, a. 2), when we were treating of the passions: the one, whereby the sensitive appetite pursues sensible and bodily goods; the other, whereby it flies from sensible and bodily evils.[5]

---

4 The editors of the Dominican translation note: "The words quoted do not occur in the work referred to; cf. his *De Summo Bono* xxxvii, xlii, and *De Different.* ii, 39."

5 The "passions," or emotions, incline us toward that which is delightful and repel us from that which is threatening. These passions, when habitually under the sway of reason, lead to virtuous behavior. When the passion to delight in pleasure is properly and habitually under the guidance of reason, we have the virtue of temperance. When the passion to avoid the physically painful or harmful is properly and habitually under the guidance of reason, we have the virtue of courage.

The first of these movements of the sensitive appetite rebels against reason chiefly by lack of moderation, because sensible and bodily goods, considered in their species, are not in opposition to reason, but are subject to it as instruments that reason employs in order to attain its proper end; and that they are opposed to reason is owing to the fact that the sensitive appetite fails to tend towards them in accord with the mode of reason.[6] Hence it belongs properly to moral virtue to moderate those passions which denote a pursuit of the good.

On the other hand, the movement of the sensitive appetite in flying from sensible evil is mostly in opposition to reason, not through being immoderate, but chiefly in respect of its flight, because when a man flies from sensible and bodily evils, which sometimes accompany the good of reason, the result is that he flies from the good of reason.[7] Hence it belongs to moral virtue to make man while flying from evil to remain firm in the good of reason.

Accordingly, just as the virtue of courage, which by its very nature bestows firmness, is chiefly concerned with the passion, viz. fear, which regards flight from bodily evils, and consequently with daring, which attacks the objects of fear in the hope of attaining some good, so too temperance, which denotes a kind of moderation, is chiefly concerned with those passions that tend towards sensible goods, viz. desire and pleasure, and consequently with the sorrows that arise from the absence of those pleasures. For just as daring presupposes objects of fear, so too such like sorrow arises from the absence of the aforesaid pleasures.

---

[6] Sensible and bodily goods are indeed goods for the human person. However, these goods are often sought in ways that exclude other goods that are also important. Thomas notes that these goods can be sought in the wrong way, at the wrong time, or in undue amount.

[7] No one chooses evil as evil or avoids good as good. However, it is often the case that to a particular good (say, preserving the life of one's family) a particular evil is attached (one must risk one's life to fend off an attack on one's family). On the other hand, there can be a good (bodily pleasure gained by alcohol) to which an evil is attached (the loss of reason, impaired judgment). In order to avoid the evil of impaired judgment when driving a car, a person may have to forgo the good of the enjoyment of drinking. The virtues enable a person to stand firm in the pursuit of good despite attached evils (courage) and to avoid pursuing certain goods of the body, the pursuit of which is contrary to the good of reason due to the attachment of some evil (temperance).

Objection 1. It would seem that temperance is not only about desires and pleasures. For Tully says (*De Invent. Rhet.* ii, 54) that "temperance is reason's firm and moderate mastery of lust and other wanton emotions of the mind." Now all the passions of the soul are called emotions of the mind. Therefore it seems that temperance is not only about desires and pleasures.

Reply to Objection 1. As stated above (I–II, q. 23, aa 1, 2; q. 25, a. 1), when we were treating of the passions, those passions which pertain to avoidance of evil presuppose the passions pertaining to the pursuit of good; and the passions of the irascible presuppose the passions of the concupiscible.[8] Hence while temperance directly moderates the passions of the concupiscible, which tend towards good, as a consequence, it moderates all the other passions, inasmuch as moderation of the passions that precede results in moderation of the passions that follow, since he that is not immoderate in desire is moderate in hope, and grieves moderately for the absence of the things he desires.

Objection 2. Further, "Virtue is about the difficult and the good" (*Ethic.* ii, 3). Now it seems more difficult to temper fear, especially with regard to dangers of death, than to moderate desires and pleasures, which are despised on account of deadly pains and dangers, according to Augustine (Q. 83, qu. 36). Therefore it seems that the virtue of temperance is not chiefly about desires and pleasures.

Reply to Objection 2. Desire denotes an impulse of the appetite towards the object of pleasure, and this impulse needs control, which

---

8 The avoidance of evil presupposes the pursuit of some good. Death would not be viewed as an evil were life not a good. This psychology of human action presupposes Thomas's metaphysics of goodness. Evil has no existence or substance of its own. Rather, an evil is always a lack of due perfection of some good. The desire for the good therefore motivates the desire to avoid evil. Implicitly we have here another argument for the unity of the virtues, for only through a right desiring of the goods of the body (temperance) will a person have a sound estimation of the evils involved in loss of the body and bodily pleasure. This sound estimation of the evils involved is critical to the virtue of courage. The person lacking in the virtue of temperance will not therefore have a correct estimation of the goods and evils involved in risking death and will be impaired with respect to the virtue of courage.

belongs to temperance. On the other hand, fear denotes a withdrawal of the mind from certain evils, against which man needs firmness of mind, which courage bestows. Hence temperance is properly about desires, and courage about fears.

Objection 3. Further, according to Ambrose (*De Offic.* i, 43), "the grace of moderation belongs to temperance"; and Tully says (*De Offic.* ii, 27) that "it is the concern of temperance to calm all disturbances of the mind and to enforce moderation." Now moderation is needed not only in desires and pleasures, but also in external acts and whatever pertains to the exterior. Therefore temperance is not only about desires and pleasures.

Reply to Objection 3. External acts proceed from the internal passions of the soul: therefore their moderation depends on the moderation of the internal passions.

ARTICLE 4 ⁓ **Is temperance only about desires and pleasures of touch?**

Yes, despite objections to the contrary, The Philosopher says (*Ethic.* iii, 10) that "temperance is properly about desires of pleasures of touch."

I answer that, As stated above (a. 3), temperance is about desires and pleasures in the same way as courage is about fear and daring. Now courage is about fear and daring with respect to the greatest evils whereby nature itself is dissolved; and such are dangers of death. Therefore, in like manner, temperance must be about desires for the greatest pleasures. And since pleasure results from a natural operation, it is so much the greater according as it results from a more natural operation. Now to animals the most natural operations are those which preserve the nature of the individual by means of food and drink, and the nature of the species by the union of the sexes. Hence temperance is properly about pleasures of food and drink and sexual pleasures.[9]

---

[9] In an extended sense, one could be temperate in seeking honors or other non-bodily goods, but properly speaking, temperance has to do with bodily pleasure.

Now these pleasures result from the sense of touch. Therefore it follows that temperance is about pleasures of touch.

Objection 1. It would seem that temperance is not only about desires and pleasures of touch. For Augustine says (*De Morib. Eccl.* xix) that "the function of temperance is to control and quell the desires which draw us to the things which withdraw us from the laws of God and from the fruit of His goodness"; and a little further on he adds that "it is the duty of temperance to spurn all bodily allurements and popular praise." Now we are withdrawn from God's laws not only by the desire for pleasures of touch, but also by the desire for pleasures of the other senses, for these, too, belong to the bodily allurements, and again by the desire for riches or for worldly glory. Therefore it is written (1 Tim 6:10): "Desire is the root of all evils." Therefore temperance is not only about desires of pleasures of touch.

Reply to Objection 1. In the passage quoted, Augustine apparently takes temperance not as a special virtue having a determinate matter, but as concerned with the moderation of reason in any matter whatever: and this is a general condition of every virtue.[10] We may also reply, however, that if a man can control the greatest pleasures, much more can he control lesser ones. Therefore it belongs chiefly and properly to temperance to moderate desires and pleasures of touch, and secondarily other pleasures.

Objection 4. Further, spiritual pleasures are greater than the pleasures of the body, as stated above (I–II, q. 31, a. 5) in the treatise on the passions. Now sometimes men forsake God's laws and the state of virtue through desire for spiritual pleasures, for instance, through curiosity in matters of knowledge. Therefore the devil promised man

---

10 In this passage, Thomas is making reference to Augustine's polemical work *On the Morals of the Catholic Church* (*De moribus ecclesiae catholicae*). In this fascinating treatise, Augustine proceeds using reason alone, arguing that God is the highest good and that love of God is the basis of all true virtues. He also strenuously argues against the Manichaeans and their conception of God and the good life.

knowledge, saying (Gen 3:5): "You shall be as Gods, knowing good and evil." Therefore temperance is not only about pleasures of touch.

Reply to Objection 4. Although spiritual pleasures are by their nature greater than bodily pleasures,[11] they are not so perceptible to the senses, and consequently they do not so strongly affect the sensitive appetite, against whose impulse the good of reason is safeguarded by moral virtue. We may also reply that spiritual pleasures, strictly speaking, are in accordance with reason; therefore they need no control, save accidentally, in so far as one spiritual pleasure is a hindrance to another greater and more binding.

ARTICLE 7 ~~ **Is temperance a cardinal virtue?**

Yes, despite objections to the contrary, Gregory reckons temperance among the principal virtues (*Moral.* ii, 49).

I answer that, As stated above (q. 123, a. 11; q. 61, a. 3), a principal or cardinal virtue is so called because it has a foremost claim to praise on account of one of those things that are requisite for the notion of virtue in general. Now moderation, which is requisite in every virtue, deserves praise principally in pleasures of touch, with which temperance is concerned, both because these pleasures are most natural to us, so that it is more difficult to abstain from them, and to control the desire for them,[12] and because their objects are more nec-

---

[11] Why does Thomas hold that spiritual pleasures are greater than bodily pleasures? Earlier in the *Summa* (I–II, q. 31, a. 5), Thomas points out that "there is no one who would not forfeit his bodily sight rather than his intellectual vision": we would rather have our mind and become blind, than retain eyesight and lose our mind, indicating that we prefer the pleasures of the intellect to the pleasures of sense. In I–II, q. 32, a. 8, Aquinas notes that "the greater the desire for the thing loved, the greater the pleasure when it is attained." Since God is perfect goodness, and therefore perfectly fulfilling of our will's desire for goodness, and since God is truth, perfectly fulfilling our intellect's desire for knowledge, human beings ultimately desire nothing more than God. In part because the goods of the body are more immediately evident to the senses, we tend to choose bodily goods over spiritual goods (*ST* I–II, q. 31, a. 5). For this very reason, we need the virtue of temperance to help moderate this tendency.

[12] The idea of "controlling desire" may at first glance seem impossible. Desire is sometimes understood as an impromptu response to a stimulus that one can

essary to the present life,[13] as stated above (a. 4). For this reason temperance is reckoned a principal or cardinal virtue.

Objection 1. It would seem that temperance is not a cardinal virtue. For the good of moral virtue depends on reason. But temperance is about those things that are furthest removed from reason, namely about pleasures common to us and the lower animals, as stated in *Ethic.* iii, 10. Therefore temperance, seemingly, is not a principal virtue.

Reply to Objection 1. The longer the range of its operation, the greater is the agent's power [*virtus*] shown to be. Therefore the very fact that the reason is able to moderate desires and pleasures that are furthest removed from it proves the greatness of reason's power. This is how temperance comes to be a principal virtue.

Objection 2. Further, the greater the impetus, the more difficult is it to control. Now anger, which is controlled by meekness, seems to be more impetuous than desire, which is controlled by temperance. For

---

not control. While direct control of desires, however, may not be possible (I either do or do not want to eat a steak, for example, and cannot choose otherwise), indirect control of desires is entirely possible. I can dampen my desire for steak by eating something else and by distracting myself with other desirable things, or I can heighten my desire for steak by dwelling on how great it would taste by savoring the aroma of the searing meat as it sits on the grill. Desires can also be manipulated by others, e.g., advertising.

13 Temperance is concerned with matters of everyday occurrence, such as eating and drinking. Unlike say, courage on the battlefield, opportunities to practice temperance abound and are as common as every meal. Through small, everyday acts of self-mastery, the excellence of temperance becomes second nature. Bishop Fulton J. Sheen recommends: "At least three times a day, deny yourself some tiny, legitimate pleasure, such as that . . . second drink, or the extra lump of sugar, in order to discipline your spirit and keep mastery over yourself for the love of God. These little 'deaths' are so many rehearsals for the final death. Dying is a masterpiece, and to do it well, we must die daily, 'If any man would come after me, let him . . . take up his cross daily' (Lk 9:23)." Fulton Sheen, *Wartime Prayer Book* (Manchester, NH: Sophia Press, 2003), p. 35. Indeed, each meal provides an occasion for growth in, for instance, skipping the butter or cheerfully eating what is not to your liking: "The day you leave the table without having done some small mortification you have eaten like a pagan." St. Josemaria Escrivá, *The Way* (New York: Scepter Publishers, mini edition, 1992), #681.

it is written (Prov 27:4): "Anger has no mercy, nor fury when it breaks forth; and who can bear the violence [*impetum*] of one provoked?" Therefore meekness is a principal virtue rather than temperance.

Reply to Objection 2. The impetuousness of anger is caused by an accident, for instance a painful hurt; therefore it soon passes, although its impetus be great. On the other hand, the impetuousness of the desire for pleasures of touch proceeds from a natural cause; therefore it is more lasting and more general, and consequently its control regards a more principal virtue.

ARTICLE 8 ⁓ **Is temperance the greatest of the virtues?**

No, despite objections to the contrary, The Philosopher says (*Rhet.* i, 9) that the "greatest virtues are those which are most profitable to others, for which reason we give the greatest honor to the brave and the just."[14]

I answer that, As the Philosopher declares (*Ethic.* i, 2), "the good of the many is more godlike than the good of the individual." Therefore the more a virtue regards the good of the many, the better it is. Now justice and courage regard the good of the many more than temperance does, since justice regards the relations between one man and another, while courage regards dangers of battle which are endured for the commonwealth, whereas temperance moderates only the desires and pleasures which affect man himself. Hence it is evident that justice and courage are more excellent virtues than temperance, while prudence and the theological virtues are more excellent still.[15]

Objection 1. It would seem that temperance is the greatest of the virtues. For Ambrose says (*De Offic.* i, 43) that "what we observe and seek most in temperance is the safeguarding of what is honorable, and the regard

---

[14] "The Philosopher," Aristotle, speaks only about the acquired virtues. The greatest moral virtue in the natural order is justice (as most beneficial to all and perfective of the highest faculty, rational appetite I–II, q. 66, a. 4), but, as Thomas notes, the greatest virtue without qualification is charity (*ST* II–II, q. 23, a. 6).

[15] Prudence is more excellent than any of the moral virtues because it perfects a higher potency (the practical intellect) in us than do the moral virtues, which are rational only by participation. The theological virtues are greater still because the object of faith, hope, and charity is the greatest of all things: God.

for what is beautiful." Now virtue deserves praise for being honorable and beautiful. Therefore temperance is the greatest of the virtues.

Reply to Objection 1. Honor and beauty are especially ascribed to temperance, not on account of the excellence of the good proper to temperance, but on account of the disgrace of the contrary evil from which it withdraws us, by moderating the pleasures common to us and the lower animals.

Objection 2. Further, the more difficult the deed, the greater the virtue. Now it is more difficult to control desires and pleasures of touch than to regulate external actions, the former pertaining to temperance and the latter to justice. Therefore temperance is a greater virtue than justice.

Reply to Objection 2. Since virtue is about the difficult and the good, the excellence of a virtue is considered more under the aspect of good, wherein justice excels, than under the aspect of difficult, wherein temperance excels.

Objection 3. Further, seemingly the more general a thing is, the more necessary and the better it is. Now courage is about dangers of death, which occur less frequently than pleasures of touch, for these occur every day, so that temperance is in more general use than courage. Therefore temperance is a more excellent virtue than courage.

Reply to Objection 3. That which is general because it regards the many conduces more to the excellence of goodness than that which is general because it occurs frequently: courage excels in the former way, temperance in the latter. Hence courage is greater simply, although in some respects temperance may be described as greater not only than courage but also than justice.[16]

---

16 In ranking the virtues, as in ranking the accomplishments of people, one may be better than another in a certain respect but not in another respect. Churchill was better *qua* politician than Mozart, but Mozart was better *qua* musician than Churchill. Similarly, one virtue may be "better" in one respect than in another. There is a certain excellence had in a stupendous feat of excellence (more typical of courage); there is another kind of excellence consisting in a steadfastness and dependability of ongoing, daily achievement (more typical of temperance). Each virtue excels the other in a certain respect.

QUESTION **142**

THE VICES OPPOSED TO TEMPERANCE

ARTICLE 1 ~ **Is insensibility a vice?**

Yes, despite objections to the contrary, Nothing save vice is opposed to virtue. Now insensibility is opposed to the virtue of temperance, according to the Philosopher (*Ethic.* ii, 7; iii, 11). Therefore insensibility is a vice.

I answer that, Whatever is contrary to the natural order is vicious. Now nature has introduced pleasure into the operations that are necessary for man's life. Therefore the natural order requires that man should make use of these pleasures, in so far as they are necessary for man's well-being, as regards the preservation either of the individual or of the species. Accordingly, if anyone were to reject pleasure to the extent of omitting things that are necessary for nature's preservation, he would sin, as acting counter to the order of nature. And this pertains to the vice of insensibility.[1]

It must, however, be observed that it is sometimes praiseworthy, and even necessary for the sake of an end, to abstain from such pleasures as result from these operations. Thus, for the sake of the body's health, certain persons refrain from pleasures of food, drink, and sex, as also for the fulfillment of certain engagements: thus athletes and soldiers have to

---

[1] Temperance, like other virtues, consists in a mean, in this case the mean between overindulging in bodily pleasures and under-indulging in bodily pleasures. What both the over- and under-indulgence have in common is that they are to the detriment of the well being of the person and the community.

deny themselves many pleasures, in order to fulfill their respective duties. In like manner penitents, in order to recover health of soul, have recourse to abstinence from pleasures, as a kind of diet, and those who are desirous of giving themselves up to contemplation and Divine things need much to refrain from carnal things. Nor do any of these things pertain to the vice of insensibility, because they are in accord with right reason.

Objection 1. It would seem that insensibility is not a vice. For those are called insensible who are deficient with regard to pleasures of touch. Now seemingly it is praiseworthy and virtuous to be altogether deficient in such matters: for it is written (Dan 10:2, 3): "In those days I, Daniel mourned the days of three weeks. I ate no desirable bread, and neither meat nor wine entered my mouth, neither was I anointed with ointment." Therefore insensibility is not a sin.

Reply to Objection 1. Daniel abstained thus from pleasures not through any horror of pleasure as though it were evil in itself, but for some praiseworthy end, in order, namely, to adapt himself to the heights of contemplation by abstaining from pleasures of the body. Hence the text goes on to tell of the revelation that he received immediately afterwards.

Objection 2. Further, "man's good is to be in accord with reason," according to Dionysius (*Div. Nom.* iv). Now abstinence from all pleasures of touch is most conducive to man's progress in the good of reason: for it is written (Dan 1:17) that "to the children" who took vegetables for their food (Dan 1:12), "God gave knowledge, and understanding in every book and wisdom." Therefore insensibility, which rejects these pleasures altogether, is not sinful.[2]

Reply to Objection 2. Since man cannot use his reason without his sensitive powers, which need a bodily organ, as stated in I, q. 84, aa 7, 8, man needs to sustain his body in order that he may use his reason. Now

---

[2] Thomas refers here to the first chapter of the book of Daniel in which God rewarded the children who turned down the pleasures of the king's rich food and wine and instead ate only vegetables and drank only water.

the body is sustained by means of operations that afford pleasure: therefore the good of reason cannot be in a man if he abstain from all pleasures. Yet this need for using pleasures of the body will be greater or less, according as man needs more or less the powers of his body in accomplishing the act of reason. Therefore it is commendable for those who undertake the duty of giving themselves to contemplation, and of imparting to others a spiritual good, by a kind of spiritual procreation, as it were, to abstain from many pleasures, but not for those who are in duty bound to bodily occupations and carnal procreation.

Objection 3. Further, that which is a very effective means of avoiding sin would seem not to be sinful. Now the most effective remedy in avoiding sin is to shun pleasures, and this pertains to insensibility. For the Philosopher says (*Ethic.* ii, 9) that "if we deny ourselves pleasures we are less liable to sin." Therefore there is nothing vicious in insensibility.

Reply to Objection 3. In order to avoid sin, pleasure must be shunned, not altogether, but so that it is not sought more than necessity requires.

ARTICLE 3 ⇀ **Is cowardice worse than intemperance?**

No, despite objections to the contrary, The Philosopher says (*Ethic.* iii, 12) that "intemperance seems more akin to voluntary action than cowardice." Therefore it is more sinful.

I answer that, One may be compared with another in two ways: first, with regard to the matter or object; secondly, on the part of the man who sins; and in both ways intemperance is a more grievous sin than cowardice.

First, as regards the matter. For cowardice shuns dangers of death, to avoid which the principal motive is the necessity of preserving life. On the other hand, intemperance is about pleasures, the desire of which is not so necessary for the preservation of life, because, as stated above (a. 2, ad 2), intemperance is more about certain annexed pleasures or desires than about natural desires or pleasures.[3] Now the more necessary the

---

[3] Natural desires, such as our appetite for nourishing food, are not intemperate in themselves. Intemperance has to do not with these natural desires and pleasures but rather with a distortion of what is reasonable in terms of natural

motive of sin the less grievous the sin. Therefore intemperance is a more grievous vice than cowardice, on the part of the object or motive matter.[4]

In like manner again, on the part of the man who sins, and this for three reasons. First, because the more sound-minded a man is, the more grievous his sin; therefore sins are not imputed to those who are demented. Now grave fear and sorrow, especially in dangers of death, stun the human mind, but not so pleasure, which is the motive of intemperance. Secondly, because the more voluntary a sin, the graver it is. Now intemperance has more of the voluntary in it than cowardice has, and this for two reasons. The first is because actions done through fear have their origin in the compulsion of an external agent, so that they are not simply voluntary but mixed, as stated in *Ethic.* iii, 1, whereas actions done for the sake of pleasure are simply voluntary. The second reason is because the actions of an intemperate man are more voluntary individually and less voluntary generically. For no one would wish to be intemperate, yet man is enticed by individual pleasures that make of him an intemperate man. Hence the most effective remedy against intemperance is not to dwell on the consideration of singulars.[5] It is the other way about in matters relating to cowardice, because the particular action that imposes itself on a man is less voluntary, for instance to cast aside his shield, and the like, whereas the general purpose is more voluntary, for instance to save himself by flight. Now that which is more voluntary in the particular circumstances in which the act takes place is simply more voluntary. Therefore intemperance, being

---

desire, such as an unreasonable insistence on having the food prepared "just so" or in overeating.

[4] Desire for pleasure, as great as it can be, is overcome by desire not to die. When a couple engaged in an adulterous act is interrupted by the ferocious anger of the cuckolded husband, the fear of attack overmasters the desire to continue the sexual act. Fear of death, at least imminent, violent death, deflates desires of the flesh. It is, Thomas reasons, therefore more difficult to practice the virtue of courage, having to do particularly with facing death in battle, than to practice the virtue of temperance. So it is more blameworthy to be intemperate than cowardly.

[5] Temperate living involves self-mastery of what one looks to see (purity of the eyes) and what one recalls in the memory and imagination. A person trying to live purely avoids looking at, remembering, or imagining things that will give rise to or reinforce desires for intemperate action.

simply more voluntary than cowardice, is a greater vice. Thirdly, because it is easier to find a remedy for intemperance than for cowardice, since pleasures of food and sex, which are the matter of intemperance, are of everyday occurrence, and it is possible for man without danger, by frequent practice in their regard, to become temperate, whereas dangers of death are of rare occurrence, and it is more dangerous for man to encounter them frequently in order to cease being a coward.

Objection 1. It would seem that cowardice is a greater vice than intemperance. For a vice deserves reproach through being opposed to the good of virtue. Now cowardice is opposed to courage, which is a more excellent virtue than temperance, as stated above (II–II, q. 141, a. 8). Therefore cowardice is a greater vice than intemperance.

Reply to Objection 1. The excellence of courage in comparison with temperance may be considered from two standpoints. First, with regard to the end, which has the aspect of good, because courage is directed to the common good more than temperance is. And from this point of view cowardice has a certain precedence over intemperance, since by cowardice some people forsake the defense of the common good. Secondly, with regard to the difficulty, because it is more difficult to endure dangers of death than to refrain from any pleasures whatever; and from this point of view there is no need for cowardice to take precedence of intemperance. For just as it is a greater strength that does not succumb to a stronger force, so on the other hand, to be overcome by a stronger force is proof of a lesser vice, and to succumb to a weaker force is the proof of a greater vice.[6]

Objection 2. Further, the greater the difficulty to be surmounted, the less is a man to be reproached for failure. Therefore the Philosopher says (*Ethic.* vii, 7) that "it is no wonder, in fact it is pardonable, if a

---

6 One might compare resistance to temptation to a fortress. If the fortress is breached by a weak force, that indicates the weakness of the fortress. If, on the other hand, only a very powerful force can overcome the defense of the fortress, this indicates the strength of the fortress. Since Thomas has already indicated that standing in the face of lethal danger is much more difficult than resisting bodily pleasure, it would follow that it shows a greater vice to be overcome by bodily pleasures than by fear of death.

man is mastered by strong and overwhelming pleasures or pains." Now seemingly it is more difficult to control pleasures than other passions; hence it is stated in *Ethic.* ii, 3 that "it is more difficult to contend against pleasure than against anger, which would seem to be stronger than fear." Therefore intemperance, which is overcome by pleasure, is a less grievous sin than cowardice, which is overcome by fear.

Reply to Objection 2. Love of self-preservation, for the sake of which one shuns perils of death, is much more connatural than any pleasures whatever of food and sex, which are directed to the preservation of life. Hence it is more difficult to overcome the fear of dangers of death than the desire of pleasure in matters of food and sex, although the latter is more difficult to resist than anger, sorrow, and fear, occasioned by certain other evils.

QUESTION 147

FASTING FROM FOOD

ARTICLE 1 ⟿ **Is fasting a virtue?**

Yes, despite objections to the contrary, It is written (2 Pet 1:5, 6): "Join with your faith virtue, and with virtue knowledge, and with knowledge fasting," where fasting is numbered among other virtues. Therefore fasting is a virtue.

I answer that, Abstinence by its very name denotes fasting from food. Hence the term abstinence may be taken in two ways: first, as denoting fasting from food absolutely, and in this way it signifies neither a virtue nor a virtuous act, but something indifferent.[1] Secondly, it may be taken as regulated by reason, and then it signifies either a virtuous habit or a virtuous act. This is the meaning of Peter's words quoted above, where he says that we ought "to join fasting with knowledge," namely that in abstaining from food a man should act with due regard for those among whom he lives, for his own person, and for the requirements of health.

---

[1] Not eating, considered simply as such, or in St. Thomas's terms "absolutely," does not have a moral character. One might be fasting simply because no food is available, an act that is neither morally good nor morally bad. In terms of the virtue of abstinence, Thomas is talking about minimizing food intake as regulated by reason, that is, done for an important spiritual purpose with due regard to maintaining the strength and health of the body. Abstaining from food could also be a morally evil act if done to an extreme or out of contempt for bodily health.

Objection 1. It seems that fasting is not a virtue. For the Apostle says (1 Cor 4:20): "The kingdom of God is not in speech but in power [*virtute*]." Now the kingdom of God does not consist in fasting, for the Apostle says (Rom 14:17): "The kingdom of God is not food and drink," where a gloss[2] observes that "justice consists neither in abstaining nor in eating." Therefore fasting is not a virtue.

Reply to Objection 1. The use of and abstinence from food, considered in themselves, do not pertain to the kingdom of God, since the Apostle[3] says (1 Cor 8:8): "Food does not commend us to God. For neither if we eat not [Vulg.: 'Neither if we eat . . . nor if we eat not'] shall we have the less, nor if we eat shall we have the more," i.e., spiritually. Nevertheless they both belong to the kingdom of God, in so far as they are done reasonably through faith and love of God.

Objection 2. Further, Augustine says (*Confess.* x, 11), addressing himself to God: "This have You taught me, that I should set myself to take food as medicine." Now it belongs not to virtue, but to the medical

---

2 A "gloss," as we have alreaady noted, is an interpretation of Scripture found in the margins alongside the biblical text. Here the Dominican editors note that this interpretation is originally found in St. Augustine's *Quaestiones evangeliorum*, ii, qu. 11.

3 As Thomas calls Aristotle "the Philosopher," so he calls St. Paul "the Apostle." Thomas devoted considerable time and energy to commenting on the writings of St. Paul, making efforts to show the unity and cohesion of Pauline thought. An anecdote about Thomas found in several early biographies, and related by Jean-Pierre Torrell, tells of a contemporary of Aquinas who had a dream: "Thomas was seated in his magisterial chair, in the process of commenting on the epistles, when, behold, the Apostle himself entered the lecture hall, which was already filled with a distinguished crowd. Thomas interrupted himself to give witness to his reverence for the Apostle and, after a few casual words of conversation, asked him if he was explaining Paul's text according to the meaning that he had wanted to give it. To this question the Apostle responded that Thomas indeed was teaching what could be understood from his epistles during this life; but a time would come when he would understand them according to their whole truth. Saying this, he took him by the cape and dragged him along with him. Three days later Thomas's death became known in Naples." Jean Pierre Torrell, O.P., *Saint Thomas Aquinas: Vol. I, The Person and His Work* (Washington DC: The Catholic University of America Press, 1996), 253.

art, to regulate medicine. Therefore, in like manner, to regulate one's food, which belongs to fasting, is an act not of virtue but of art.

Reply to Objection 2. The regulation of food, in the point of quantity and quality, belongs to the art of medicine as regards the health of the body, but in the point of internal affections with regard to the good of reason, it belongs to fasting. Hence Augustine says (QQ. *Evang.* ii, qu. 11): "It makes no difference whatever to virtue what or how much food a man takes, so long as he does it with due regard for the people among whom he lives, for his own person, and for the requirements of his health, but it matters how readily and uncomplainingly he does without food when bound by duty or necessity to abstain."

Objection 3. Further, every virtue "observes the mean," as stated in *Ethic.* ii, 6, 7. But fasting seemingly inclines not to the mean but to deficiency, since it denotes a minimalization of food intake. Therefore fasting is not a virtue.

Reply to Objection 3. It belongs to temperance to bridle the pleasures which are too alluring to the soul, just as it belongs to courage to strengthen the soul against fears that deter it from the good of reason. Therefore, just as courage is commended on account of a certain excess, from which all the parts of courage take their name, so temperance is commended for a kind of deficiency, from which all its parts are denominated. Hence fasting, since it is a part of temperance, is named from deficiency, and yet it observes the mean, in so far as it is in accord with right reason.[4]

Objection 4. Further, no virtue excludes another virtue. But fasting excludes patience: for Gregory says (*Pastor.* iii, 19) that "impatience not infrequently dislodges the abstainer's mind from its peaceful seclusion." Likewise he says (*Pastor.* iii, 19) that "sometimes the sin of pride

---

[4] In order to hit the moral mean, it is sometimes necessary to be "excessive" in comparison with the mathematical mean. If someone has a tendency to overeat, he or she may purposely have to eat less than the amount customarily eaten at times in order to correct a customary excess and thereby hit the moral mean.

pierces the thoughts of the abstainer," so that fasting excludes humility. Therefore fasting is not a virtue.

Reply to Objection 4. Those vices result from fasting in so far as it is not in accord with right reason. For right reason makes one abstain as one ought, i.e., with gladness of heart, and for the due end, i.e., for God's glory and not one's own.

ARTICLE 3 ～ **Is fasting a matter of obligation?**

Yes, despite objections to the contrary, Jerome (*Ad Lucin.*, Ep. lxxi), speaking of fasting, says: "Let each province keep to its own practice, and look upon the commands of the elders as though they were laws of the apostles." Therefore fasting is a matter of precept or obligation.[5]

I answer that, Just as it belongs to the secular authority to make legal precepts which apply the natural law to matters of commonweal in temporal affairs, so it belongs to ecclesiastical superiors to prescribe by statute those things that concern the commonweal of the faithful in spiritual goods.[6]

Now it has been stated above (a. 1) that fasting is useful as atoning for and preventing sin, and as raising the mind to spiritual things.

---

[5] Fasting is part of the life of a Christian disciple. Scripture records: "Then John's disciples came and asked him [Jesus], 'How is it that we and the Pharisees fast, but your disciples do not fast?' Jesus answered, 'How can the guests of the bridegroom mourn while he is with them? The time will come when the bridegroom will be taken from them; then they will fast'" (Mt 9:14–15; cf. Lk 5:35). Jesus gave example by fasting himself (Mt 4:2), by advising his disciples how to conduct themselves while fasting (Mt 6:17), and by teaching that fasting alone does not make a person righteous (Lk 18: 9–14). For an excellent treatment of the topic, see Slavko Barbaric, O.F.M., *Fasting* (Steubenville, OH: Franciscan University Press, 1988).

[6] It does not pertain to the natural law *per se* to drive on the right side of the street rather than on the left side. The natural law indicates that public order should be maintained by those who are responsible for the common good, and part of the public order are the regulations that pertain to road travel. The public authority makes a determination of the natural law and regulates that driving should be on one side of the street or another. Similarly, to fast pertains to the natural law, but to fast on this day rather than another day is a determination of the natural law by those with the responsibility for the common good of the Church, namely its pastors and bishops.

And everyone is bound by the natural dictate of reason to practice fasting as far as it is necessary for these purposes. Therefore fasting in general is a matter of precept of the natural law, while the fixing of the time and manner of fasting as becoming and profitable to the Christian people is a matter of precept of positive law established by ecclesiastical authority; the latter is the Church fast, the former is the fast prescribed by nature.

Objection 1. It would seem that fasting is not a matter of precept. For precepts are not given about works of supererogation, which are a matter of counsel. Now fasting is a work of supererogation, else it would have to be equally observed at all places and times.[7] Therefore fasting is not a matter of precept.

Reply to Objection 1. Fasting considered in itself denotes something not choiceworthy but penal; yet it becomes choiceworthy in so far as it is useful to some end. Therefore, considered absolutely, it is not binding under precept, but it is binding under precept to each one that stands in need of such a remedy. And since men, for the most part, need this remedy, both because "in many things we all offend" (Jas 3:2), and because "the flesh lusts against the spirit" (Gal 5:17), it was fitting that the Church should appoint certain fasts to be kept by all in common. In doing this, the Church does not make a precept of a matter of supererogation, but particularizes in detail that which is of general obligation.

Objection 2. Further, whoever infringes a precept commits a mortal sin. Therefore, if fasting were a matter of precept, all who do not fast would sin mortally, and a widespreading snare would be laid for men.

Reply to Objection 2. Those commandments which are given under the form of a general precept do not bind all persons in the same way, but according to the requirements of the end intended by the lawgiver. It will be a mortal sin to disobey a commandment through contempt of

---

7 In other words, the objection is that fasting is not a duty (precept) but rather an action above and beyond the call of duty (supererogation), done only in certain times and places. A duty, however, must always be done, so fasting must not be a duty commanded by the law (precept).

the lawgiver's authority, or to disobey it in such a way as to frustrate the end intended by him; but it is not a mortal sin if one fails to keep a commandment when there is a reasonable motive, and especially if the lawgiver would not insist on its observance if he were present. Hence it is that not all who do not keep the fasts of the Church sin mortally.[8]

Objection 3. Further, Augustine says (*De Vera Relig.* 17) that "the Wisdom of God having taken human nature, and called us to a state of freedom, instituted a few most salutary sacraments whereby the community of the Christian people, that is, of the free multitude, should be bound together in subjection to one God." Now the liberty of the Christian people seems to be hindered by a great number of observances no less than by a great number of sacraments. For Augustine says (*Ad inquis. Januar.,* Ep. lv) that "whereas God in His mercy wished our religion to be distinguished by its freedom and the evidence and small number of its solemn sacraments, some people render it oppressive with slavish burdens." Therefore it seems that the Church should not have made fasting a matter of precept.

Reply to Objection 3. Augustine is speaking there of those things that are neither contained in the authorities of Holy Scripture, nor found among the ordinances of bishops in council, nor sanctioned by the custom of the universal Church. On the other hand, the fasts that are of obligation are appointed by the councils of bishops and are sanctioned by the custom of the universal Church. Nor are they opposed to the

---

[8] According to Church guidelines, not all people are bound to fast. For example, many dioceses publish guidelines about fasting that indicated that people with medical conditions worsened by fasting or abstaining from meat are under no obligation to fast or abstain but instead should substitute another suitable act of penance or charity. These rules, meant to promote spiritual well being, may also not apply in a given case for other serious reasons. Currently in the United States, those 14 years of age and older are obliged not to eat meat on Ash Wednesday and all Fridays during Lent. On Ash Wednesday, those between 18 and 59 are obliged to eat only one full meal and two lighter meals and refrain from eating between meals. In addition, each Friday during the year is a day for special sacrifice and offering to God in memory of Good Friday, though the sacrifice need not be to abstain from eating meat. Of course, these absolutely minimal requirements can be exceeded.

freedom of the faithful;[9] rather are they of use in hindering the slavery of sin, which is opposed to spiritual freedom, of which it is written (Gal 5:13): "You, brethren, have been called unto liberty; only make not liberty an occasion for the flesh."

---

[9] Freedom is not simply the ability to do whatever one chooses. True freedom is the ability to attain one's good, and therefore sinning is not an exercise of true freedom but rather a form of slavery. Fasting, by restraining sinful impulses, helps a person to be more free. Thus the Church's norms on fasting empower and enhance authentic human freedom.

QUESTION **148**

GLUTTONY

ARTICLE 1 ～ **Is gluttony a sin?**

Yes, despite objections to the contrary, Gregory says (*Moral.* xxx, 18) that "unless we first tame the enemy dwelling within us, namely our gluttonous appetite, we have not even stood up to engage in the spiritual combat." But man's inward enemy is sin. Therefore gluttony is a sin.

I answer that, Gluttony denotes not any desire of eating and drinking, but an inordinate desire. Now desire is said to be inordinate through leaving the order of reason, wherein the good of moral virtue consists, and a thing is said to be a sin through being contrary to virtue. Therefore it is evident that gluttony is a sin.

Objection 1. It would seem that gluttony is not a sin. For our Lord said (Mt 15:11): "Not that which goes into the mouth defiles a man." Now gluttony regards food which goes into a man. Therefore, since every sin defiles a man, it seems that gluttony is not a sin.

Reply to Objection 1. That which goes into man by way of food, by reason of its substance and nature, does not defile a man spiritually. But the Jews, against whom our Lord is speaking, and the Manichees deemed certain foods to make a man unclean, not on account of their signification, but by reason of their nature.[1] It is the inordinate desire of food that defiles a man spiritually.

---

[1] See *ST* I–II, q. 102, a. 6, ad 1.

Objection 2. Further, "No man sins in what he cannot avoid" [Ep. lxxi, *ad Lucin.*]. Now gluttony is immoderation in food; and man cannot avoid this, for Gregory says (*Moral.* xxx, 18): "Since in eating pleasure and necessity go together, we fail to discern between the call of necessity and the seduction of pleasure," and Augustine says (*Confess.* x, 31): "Who is it, Lord, that does not eat a little more than necessary?" Therefore gluttony is not a sin.

Reply to Objection 2. As stated above, the vice of gluttony does not regard the substance of food, but the desire for food not being regulated by reason. Therefore, if a man exceed in quantity of food, not from desire of food, but through deeming it necessary to him, this pertains not to gluttony, but to some kind of inexperience. It is a case of gluttony only when a man knowingly exceeds the measure in eating, from a desire for the pleasures of the palate.

Objection 3. Further, in every kind of sin the first movement is a sin. But the first movement in taking food is not a sin, else hunger and thirst would be sinful. Therefore gluttony is not a sin.

Reply to Objection 3. The appetite is twofold. There is the natural appetite, which belongs to the powers of the vegetal soul. In these powers virtue and vice are impossible, since they cannot be subject to reason; therefore the appetitive power is differentiated from the powers of secretion, digestion, and excretion, and to it hunger and thirst are to be referred. Besides this there is another, the sensitive appetite, and it is in the concupiscence of this appetite that the vice of gluttony consists. Hence the first movement of gluttony denotes inordinateness in the sensitive appetite, and this is not without sin.[2]

ARTICLE 4 ⟿ Are the kinds of gluttony fittingly distinguished?

Yes, despite objections to the contrary, Stands the authority of Gregory.

---

[2] Simply to be hungry or thirsty is not in any way sinful. It pertains to our bodily nature (the power of the vegetal aspect of our soul) to desire these things. Eating and drinking, however, are not merely a matter of satisfying bodily needs but also of satisfying our appetites and "tastes." It is disordination of the sensitive appetite that is not without sin.

I answer that, As stated above (a. 1), gluttony denotes inordinate concupiscence in eating. Now two things are to be considered in eating, namely the food we eat, and the eating thereof. Accordingly, the inordinate concupiscence may be considered in two ways: first, with regard to the food consumed: and thus, as regards the substance or species of food a man seeks "sumptuous"—i.e., costly food; as regards its quality, he seeks food prepared too nicely—i.e., "daintily"; and as regards quantity, he exceeds by eating "excessively."

Secondly, the inordinate concupiscence is considered as to the consumption of food: either because one forestalls the proper time for eating, which is to eat "hastily," or one fails to observe the due manner of eating, by eating "greedily."

Isidore [*De Summo Bon.* ii, 42] comprises the first and second under one heading, when he says that the glutton exceeds in "what" he eats, or in "how much," "how," or "when he eats."

Objection 1. It seems that the species of gluttony are unfittingly distinguished by Gregory, who says (*Moral.* xxx, 18): "The vice of gluttony tempts us in five ways. Sometimes it forestalls the hour of need; sometimes it seeks costly food; sometimes it requires the food to be daintily cooked; sometimes it exceeds the measure of refreshment by taking too much; sometimes we sin by the very heat of an immoderate appetite"—which are contained in the following verse: "Hastily, sumptuously, excessively, greedily, daintily." For the above are distinguished according to diversity of circumstance. Now circumstances, being the accidents of an act, do not differentiate its species. Therefore the species of gluttony are not distinguished according to the aforesaid.

Reply to Objection 1. The corruption of various circumstances causes the various species of gluttony, on account of the various motives, by reason of which the species of moral things are differentiated.[3] For in

---

3 Thomas speaks here of what might be called "specifying circumstances," circumstances that change an act from being of one kind or species into another kind. What might otherwise be a good act can become wrong through addition of specifying circumstances. For example, a married couple having sex is one kind of act, but making love in public (circumstance of place) changes marital coitus into another kind of act (exhibitionism). For an

him that seeks sumptuous food, concupiscence is aroused by the very species of the food; in him that forestalls the time, concupiscence is disordered through impatience of delay, and so forth.

Objection 2. Further, as time is a circumstance, so is place. If, then, gluttony admits of one species in respect of time, it seems that there should likewise be others in respect of place and other circumstances.

Reply to Objection 2. Place and other circumstances include no special motive connected with eating that can cause a different species of gluttony.

Objection 3. Further, just as temperance observes due circumstances, so do the other moral virtues. Now the species of the vices opposed to the other moral virtues are not distinguished according to various circumstances. Neither, therefore, are the species of gluttony distinguished thus.

Reply to Objection 3. In all other vices, whenever different circumstances correspond to different motives, the difference of circumstances argues a specific difference of vice, but this does not apply to all circumstances, as stated above (I–II, q. 72, a. 9).[4]

ARTICLE 5 ❦ **Is gluttony a capital vice?**

Yes, despite objections to the contrary, Gregory (*Moral.* xxxi, 45) reckons gluttony among the capital vices.

---

act to be good, the act itself, the motive, and the circumstances must all be fitting (see *ST* I–II, q. 18; John Paul II, *Veritatis Splendor* 80).

[4] Special motives for sinning are one example of a specifying circumstance. Thomas says in the article cited, "wherever there is a special motive for sinning, there is a different species of sin, because the motive for sinning is the end and object of sin. Now it happens sometimes that although different circumstances are corrupted, there is but one motive: thus the illiberal man, for the same motive, takes when he ought not, where he ought not, and more than he ought, and so on with the circumstances, since he does this through an inordinate desire of hoarding money; and in such cases the corruption of different circumstances does not diversify the species of sins, but belongs to one and the same species. Sometimes, however, the corruption of different circumstances arises from different motives: for instance, that a man eat hastily may be due to the fact that he cannot brook the delay in taking food. . . ."

I answer that, As stated above (I–II, q. 84, a. 3), a capital vice denotes one from which, considered as final cause,[5] i.e., as having a most desirable end, other vices originate: therefore, through desiring that end, men are incited to sin in many ways.[6] Now an end is rendered most desirable through having one of the conditions of happiness, which is desirable by its very nature; and pleasure is essential to happiness, according to *Ethic.* i, 8; x, 3, 7, 8. Therefore the vice of gluttony, being about pleasures of touch, which stand foremost among other pleasures, is fittingly reckoned among the capital vices.

Objection 1. It would seem that gluttony is not a capital vice. For capital vices denote those whence, under the aspect of final cause, other vices originate.[7] Now food, which is the matter of gluttony, has not the aspect of end, since it is sought not for its own sake, but for the body's nourishment. Therefore gluttony is not a capital vice.

Reply to Objection 1. It is true that food itself is directed to something as its end; but since that end, namely the sustaining of life, is most desirable and whereas life cannot be sustained without food, it follows that food too is most desirable: indeed, nearly all the toil of man's life is directed thereto, according to Ecclesiastes 6:7: "All the labor of man is for his mouth." Yet gluttony seems to be about pleasures of food rather

---

[5] The final cause is that for the sake of which the action is performed or the product made. The final cause of a bicycle part is to enable the bicycle to work well; the final cause of the criminal investigation is to solve the crime. The most desirable end is the final cause of those things that are a means to that end.

[6] Only things that in fact are actually good, such as food, drink, sex, honor, praise, riches, freedom from toil, etc., could motivate a person to turn away from what is perfectly good, God. So the capital vices are various ways in which one seeks things that are good, but in a way that perverts their goodness, removing them from their proper ordering to the Absolute, Perfect Good (*ST* I–II, q. 84, a. 4). No one seeks evil for the sake of seeking evil, but rather seeks goods in ways that are inconsistent with love of neighbor and union with the highest Good.

[7] A capital vice is from the Latin *caput*, meaning "head." Thomas explains that the head of an animal is that which leads and directs it. Likewise, a capital vice is one that leads and directs a person to commit other sins (see *ST* I–II, q. 84, a. 3).

than about food itself; therefore, as Augustine says (*De Vera Relig.* liii), "with such food as is good for the worthless body, men desire to be fed," wherein namely the pleasure consists, "rather than to be filled, since the whole end of that desire is this—not to thirst and not to hunger."

Objection 2. Further, a capital vice would seem to have a certain pre-eminence in sinfulness. But this does not apply to gluttony, which, in respect of its genus, is apparently the least of sins, seeing that it is most akin to what is according to nature. Therefore, gluttony is not a capital vice.

Reply to Objection 2. In sin the end is ascertained with respect to the conversion, while the gravity of sin is determined with regard to the aversion.[8] Therefore it does not follow that the capital sin which has the most desirable end surpasses the others in gravity.

Objection 3. Further, sin results from a man forsaking the good of virtue on account of something useful to the present life, or pleasing to the senses. Now as regards goods having the aspect of utility, there is but one capital vice, namely covetousness. Therefore, seemingly, there would be but one capital vice in respect of pleasures, and this is lust, which is a greater vice than gluttony, and is about greater pleasures. Therefore gluttony is not a capital vice.

Reply to Objection 3. That which gives pleasure is desirable in itself, and consequently corresponding to its diversity there are two capital vices, namely gluttony and lust. On the other hand, that which is useful is desirable not in itself, but as directed to something else: therefore, seemingly in all useful things, there is one aspect of desirability. Hence there is but one capital vice, in respect of such things.

---

[8] In wrongdoing, the end is that which is sought, but the gravity of the wrongdoing is determined by that which is undermined or turned away from in the seeking of the end. What was sought determines the end; but what was turned away from in the process determines how bad the wrongdoing was. In the case of gluttony, what is sought is the pleasure of eating too hastily, sumptuously, excessively, greedily, or daintily. The seriousness or gravity of this wrongdoing is determined by what is set aside when the pleasure of eating is sought in this way. For in making bodily pleasure in terms of eating so important, the importance of love of God and neighbor is thereby diminished.

QUESTION 149

SOBRIETY

ARTICLE 3 — **Is it always wrong to drink wine?**

No, despite objections to the contrary, The Apostle says (1 Tim 5:23): "Do not still drink water, but use a little wine for your stomach's sake, and your frequent infirmities"; and it is written (Sir 31:36): "Wine drunken with moderation is the joy of the soul and the heart."

I answer that, No food or drink, considered in itself, is unlawful, according to Matthew 15:11, "Not that which goes into the mouth defiles a man." Therefore it is not unlawful to drink wine as such. Yet it may become unlawful accidentally. This is sometimes owing to a circumstance on the part of the drinker, either because he is easily the worse for taking wine, or because he is bound by a vow not to drink wine; sometimes it results from the mode of drinking, because, to wit, he exceeds the measure in drinking;[1] and sometimes it is on account of others who would be scandalized thereby.

Objection 1. It would seem that the use of wine is altogether unlawful. For without wisdom, a man cannot be in the state of salvation, since it is written (Wis 7:28): "God loves none but him that dwells with wisdom," and further on (Wis 9:19): "By wisdom they were healed, whosoever have pleased You, O Lord, from the beginning." Now the

---

[1] The proper "measure of drink" would depend upon physical factors, such as the body weight and tolerance of the person drinking, the responsibilities that the person has (e.g., driving), and other factors (e.g., alcoholism running in the family).

use of wine is a hindrance to wisdom, for it is written (Eccles 2:3): "I thought in my heart to withdraw my flesh from wine, that I might turn my mind to wisdom." Therefore wine-drinking is altogether unlawful.

Reply to Objection 1. A man may have wisdom in two ways: first, in a general way, according as it is sufficient for salvation; and in this way it is required, in order to have wisdom, not that a man abstain altogether from wine, but that he abstain from its immoderate use. Secondly, a man may have wisdom in some degree of perfection; and in this way, in order to receive wisdom perfectly, it is requisite for certain persons that they abstain altogether from wine, and this depends on circumstances of certain persons and places.

Objection 2. Further, the Apostle says (Rom 14:21): "It is good not to eat flesh, and not to drink wine, nor anything whereby your brother is offended or scandalized, or made weak." Now it is sinful to forsake the good of virtue, as likewise to scandalize one's brethren. Therefore it is unlawful to make use of wine.

Reply to Objection 2. The Apostle does not declare simply that it is good to abstain from wine, but that it is good in the case where this would give scandal to certain people.

Objection 3. Further, Jerome says [*Contra Jovin.* I] that "after the deluge wine and flesh were sanctioned, but Christ came in the last of the ages and brought back the end into line with the beginning." Therefore it seems unlawful to use wine under the Christian law.

Reply to Objection 3. Christ withdraws us from some things as being altogether unlawful, and from others as being obstacles to perfection. It is in the latter way that he withdraws some from the use of wine, that they may aim at perfection, even as from riches and the like.

QUESTION **150**

DRUNKENNESS

ARTICLE 1 ∼ **Is it wrong to get drunk?**

Yes, despite objections to the contrary, The Apostle says (Rom 13:13): "Not in rioting and drunkenness."

I answer that, Drunkenness may be understood in two ways. First, it may signify the defect itself of a man resulting from his drinking much wine, the consequence being that he loses the use of reason. In this sense drunkenness denotes not a sin, but a penal defect resulting from a fault. Secondly, drunkenness may denote the act by which a man incurs this defect. This act may cause drunkenness in two ways. In one way, through the wine being too strong, without the drinker being cognizant of this, and in this way, too, drunkenness may occur without sin, especially if it is not through his negligence, and thus we believe that Noah was made drunk as related in Genesis 9.[1] In another way drunkenness

---

[1] The example Thomas gives of Noah brings to mind his treatment of the question: "Is ignorance a sin?" He answers, "Therefore all are bound in common to know the articles of faith, and the universal principles of right, and each individual is bound to know matters regarding his duty or state. Meanwhile there are other things which a man may have a natural aptitude to know, yet he is not bound to know them, such as the geometrical theorems, and contingent particulars, except in some individual case. Now it is evident that whoever neglects to have or do what he ought to have or do commits a sin of omission. Therefore, through negligence, ignorance of what one is bound to know is a sin, whereas it is not imputed as a sin to man if he fails to know what he is unable to know. Consequently ignorance of such like things is called 'invincible,' because it cannot be overcome by study. For this

may result from inordinate concupiscence and use of wine: in this way it is accounted a sin, and is comprised under gluttony as a species under its genus. For gluttony is divided into "rioting and drunkenness," which are forbidden by the Apostle (Rom 13:13).

Objection 1. It would seem that drunkenness is not a sin. For every sin has a corresponding contrary sin, thus timidity is opposed to daring, and presumption to pusillanimity. But no sin is opposed to drunkenness. Therefore drunkenness is not a sin.

Reply to Objection 1. As the Philosopher says (*Ethic.* iii, 11), insensibility which is opposed to temperance "is not very common," so that like its species, which are opposed to the species of intemperance, it has no name. Hence the vice opposed to drunkenness is unnamed; and yet if a man were knowingly to abstain from wine to the extent of molesting nature grievously, he would not be free from sin.[2]

Objection 2. Further, every sin is voluntary [Augustine, *De Vera Relig.* xiv]. But no man wishes to be drunk, since no man wishes to be deprived of the use of reason. Therefore drunkenness is not a sin.

Reply to Objection 2. This objection regards the resulting defect which is involuntary, whereas immoderate use of wine is voluntary, and it is in this that the sin consists.

Objection 3. Further, whoever causes another to sin sins himself. Therefore, if drunkenness were a sin, it would follow that it is a sin to

---

reason such like ignorance, not being voluntary, since it is not in our power to be rid of it, is not a sin. Therefore it is evident that no invincible ignorance is a sin. On the other hand, vincible ignorance is a sin, if it be about matters one is bound to know, but not, if it be about things one is not bound to know" (I–II, q. 76, a. 2). Ignorance about what you could not have known or had no obligation to know excuses; ignorance about what you can and should know does not. So, in terms of drinking, the person inexperienced with drinking having too many beers and finding himself drunk may be excused. The person who knows that six beers gets him drunk and proceeds to drink six cannot claim ignorance.

2 Perhaps Thomas had in mind this passage from 1Timothy 5:23 in which Paul advises Timothy to drink: "Stop drinking only water, and use a little wine because of your stomach and your frequent illnesses."

ask a man to drink that which makes him drunk, which would seem very hard.

Reply to Objection 3. Even as he that is drunk is excused if he knows not the strength of the wine, so too is he that invites another to drink excused from sin if he be unaware that the drinker is the kind of person to be made drunk by the drink offered. But if ignorance be lacking, neither is excused from sin.

Objection 4. Further, every sin calls for correction. But correction is not applied to drunkards: for Gregory says that "we must forbear with their ways, lest they become worse if they be compelled to give up the habit."[3] Therefore drunkenness is not a sin.

Reply to Objection 4. Sometimes the correction of a sinner is to be foregone, as stated above (q. 33, a. 6). Hence Augustine says in a letter (*Ad Aurel. Episc.* Ep. xxii), "It seems to me that such things are cured not by bitterness, severity, harshness, but by teaching rather than commanding, by advice rather than threats. Such is the course to be followed with the majority of sinners: few are they whose sins should be treated with severity."

ARTICLE 2 ⤳ **Is drunkenness a mortal sin?**

Yes, despite objections to the contrary.

I answer that, The sin of drunkenness, as stated in the foregoing article, consists in the immoderate use and concupiscence of wine. Now this may happen to a man in three ways: first, so that he does not realize that the drink is immoderate and intoxicating, and then drunkenness may be without sin, as stated above (a. 1);[4] secondly, so that he perceives the drink to be immoderate, but without knowing it

---

[3] The Dominican edition adds the reference, "Canon *Denique*, dist. 4 where Gratian refers to a letter of St. Gregory to St. Augustine of Canterbury."

[4] For an act to be a human act (as opposed to an act of a human being) the act must be voluntary. So if someone were to unknowingly (and therefore non-willingly) drink alcohol or be drugged, that person would not have performed a human act, an act that can be assessed as ethically meritorious or blameworthy.

to be intoxicating, and then drunkenness may involve a venial sin.[5] Thirdly, it may happen that a man is well aware that the drink is immoderate and intoxicating, and yet he would rather be drunk than abstain from drink. Such a man is a drunkard properly speaking, because morals take their species not from things that occur accidentally and beside the intention, but from that which is directly intended.[6] In this way drunkenness is a mortal sin, because then a man willingly and knowingly deprives himself of the use of reason, whereby he performs virtuous deeds and avoids sin, and thus he sins mortally by running the risk of falling into sin.[7] For Ambrose says (*De Patriarch.* [*De Abraham* i.]): "We learn that we should shun drunken-

---

[5] Drinking too much, like eating too much, is sinful. So if someone were to drink too much, not knowing that the drink was alcoholic, that person would have voluntarily exceeded the reasonable quantity of fluid, and since the liquid contained alcohol, drunkenness would ensue. The act in question, however, though gluttonous, is not properly speaking the act of getting drunk.

[6] This important principle of ethics, that what is intended determines the kind of act that is performed, morally speaking, is explored in terms of the issue of self-defense earlier in this volume in *ST* II–II, q. 64, a. 7. This emphasis on intention is not a lapse into mere subjectivism, but a recognition that ethics is properly about what a human being knowingly and freely does. Pope John Paul II explores this issue at some length in *Veritatis Splendor*. One such passage is the following: "*The morality of the human act depends primarily and fundamentally on the 'object' rationally chosen by the deliberate will,* as is borne out by the insightful analysis, still valid today, made by Saint Thomas. In order to be able to grasp the object of an act which specifies that act morally, it is therefore necessary to place oneself *in the perspective of the acting person.* The object of the act of willing is in fact a freely chosen kind of behavior. To the extent that it is in conformity with the order of reason, it is the cause of the goodness of the will; it perfects us morally, and disposes us to recognize our ultimate end in the perfect good, primordial love. By the object of a given moral act, then, one cannot mean a process or an event of the merely physical order, to be assessed on the basis of its ability to bring about a given state of affairs in the outside world. Rather, that object is the proximate end of a deliberate decision which determines the act of willing on the part of the acting person" (John Paul II, *Veritatis Splendor* 78).

[7] The principle at work here seems to be that it is wrong to risk doing evil, and that a drunk person risks doing evil. Needlessly risking the well-being of oneself and others is morally problematic. In this regard, one could also appeal to the damage that alcohol and drug abuse inflicts on the bodily well-being and health of those who abuse them.

ness, which prevents us from avoiding grievous sins. For the things we avoid when sober we unknowingly commit through drunkenness." Therefore drunkenness, properly speaking, is a mortal sin.

Objection 1. It would seem that drunkenness is not a mortal sin. For Augustine says in a sermon on Purgatory [*Serm.* civ in the Appendix to St. Augustine's works] that "drunkenness, if indulged in assiduously, is a mortal sin." Now assiduity denotes a circumstance which does not change the species of a sin, so that it cannot aggravate a sin infinitely, and make a mortal sin of a venial sin, as shown above (I–II, q. 88, a. 5). Therefore, if drunkenness is not a mortal sin for some other reason, neither is it for this.

Reply to Objection 1. Assiduity makes drunkenness a mortal sin, not on account of the mere repetition of the act, but because it is impossible for a man to become drunk assiduously, without exposing himself to drunkenness knowingly and willingly, since he has many times experienced the strength of wine and his own liability to drunkenness.

Objection 2. Further, Augustine says [*Serm.* civ in the Appendix to St. Augustine's works]: "Whenever a man takes more food and drink than is necessary, he should know that this is one of the lesser sins." Now the lesser sins are called venial. Therefore drunkenness, which is caused by immoderate drink, is a venial sin.

Reply to Objection 2. To take more food or drink than is necessary belongs to the vice of gluttony, which is not always a mortal sin, but knowingly to take too much drink to the point of being drunk is a mortal sin. Hence Augustine says (*Confess.* x, 31): "Drunkenness is far from me: You will have mercy, that it come not near me. But full feeding sometimes has crept upon Your servant."

Objection 3. Further, no mortal sin should be committed on the score of medicine. Now some drink too much at the advice of the physician, that they may be purged by vomiting; and from this excessive drink drunkenness ensues. Therefore drunkenness is not a mortal sin.

Reply to Objection 3. As stated above (q. 141, a. 6), food and drink should be moderate in accordance with the demands of the body's health. Therefore, just as it happens sometimes that the food and drink which are moderate for a healthy man are immoderate for a sick man, so too it may happen conversely, that what is excessive for a healthy man is moderate for one that is ailing. In this way, when a man eats or drinks much at the physician's advice in order to provoke vomiting, he is not to be deemed to have taken excessive food or drink.

ARTICLE 4 ~~ Does drunkenness excuse from sin?

Yes, despite objections to the contrary, According to Augustine (*Contra Faust.* xxii, 43), Lot was to be excused from incest on account of drunkenness.

I answer that, Two things are to be observed in drunkenness, as stated above (a. 1), namely the resulting defect and the preceding act. On the part of the resulting defect whereby the use of reason is fettered, drunkenness may be an excuse for sin, in so far as it causes an act to be involuntary through ignorance. But on the part of the preceding act, a distinction would seem necessary, because, if the drunkenness that results from that act be without sin,[8] the subsequent sin is entirely excused from fault, as perhaps in the case of Lot. If, however, the preceding act was sinful, the person is not altogether excused from the subsequent sin, because the latter is rendered voluntary through the voluntariness of the preceding act, inasmuch as it was through doing something unlawful that he fell into the subsequent sin.[9] Nevertheless, the resulting sin is diminished, even as the character of voluntariness is diminished. Therefore Augustine says (*Contra Faust.* xxii, 44) that "Lot's guilt is to be measured, not by the incest, but by his drunkenness."

---

[8] Although perhaps unusual, people can get drunk involuntarily. Perhaps they did drink alcohol but they did not know how powerful the alcohol would be. In such cases, the loss of control was not voluntary, and the subsequent bad acts that they may perform would also not be fully voluntary.

[9] If people voluntarily diminish their capacity to reason through alcohol (or drug abuse), then what they subsequently do, even in a drunken state, is to a degree voluntarily done. As Thomas makes clear, however, in the next sentence, it is nevertheless still less voluntary than if they had done the same acts completely sober.

Objection 1. It would seem that drunkenness does not excuse from sin. For the Philosopher says (*Ethic.* iii, 5) that "the drunkard deserves double punishment." Therefore drunkenness aggravates a sin instead of excusing from it.

Reply to Objection 1. The Philosopher does not say that the drunkard deserves more severe punishment, but that he deserves double punishment for his twofold sin. Or we may reply that he is speaking in view of the law of a certain Pittacus, who, as stated in *Polit.* ii, 9, ordered "those guilty of assault while drunk to be more severely punished than if they had been sober, because they do wrong in more ways than one." In this, as Aristotle observes (*Polit.* ii, 9), "he seems to have considered the advantage," namely of the prevention of wrong, "rather than the leniency which one should have for drunkards," seeing that they are not in possession of their faculties.

Objection 2. Further, one sin does not excuse another, but increases it. Now drunkenness is a sin. Therefore it is not an excuse for sin.

Reply to Objection 2. Drunkenness may be an excuse for sin, not in the point of its being itself a sin, but in the point of the defect that results from it, as stated above.

Objection 3. Further, the Philosopher says (*Ethic.* vii, 3) that just as man's reason is tied by drunkenness, so is it by concupiscence. But concupiscence is not an excuse for sin; neither therefore is drunkenness.

Reply to Objection 3. Concupiscence does not altogether fetter the reason, as drunkenness does, unless perchance it be so vehement as to make a man insane. Yet the passion of concupiscence diminishes sin, because it is less grievous to sin through weakness than through malice.

QUESTION 151

CHASTITY

ARTICLE 1 ⌁ **Is chastity a virtue?**

Yes, despite objections to the contrary, Augustine says (*De Decem Chord.* [*Serm.* ix, *de Tempore*]): "Whereas you should excel your wife in virtue, since chastity is a virtue, you give in to the first onslaught of lust, while you wish your wife to be victorious."

I answer that, Chastity takes its name from the fact that reason "chastises" concupiscence, which, like a child, needs curbing, as the Philosopher states (*Ethic.* iii, 12). Now the essence of human virtue consists in being something moderated by reason, as shown above (I–II, q. 64, a. 1). Therefore it is evident that chastity is a virtue.

Objection 1. It would seem that chastity is not a virtue. For here we are treating of virtues of the soul. But chastity, seemingly, belongs to the body: for a person is said to be chaste because he behaves in a certain way as regards the use of certain parts of the body. Therefore chastity is not a virtue.

Reply to Objection 1. Chastity does indeed reside in the soul as its subject, though its matter is in the body. For it belongs to chastity that a man make moderate use of bodily members in accordance with the judgment of his reason and the choice of his will.[1]

---

[1] In a similar way, justice is a virtue in the soul and yet relates to matters outside the soul, such as monetary exchange. Courage is a virtue of the soul, but it too relates to matters outside the soul, such as fighting in battle. Chastity

Objection 2. Further, virtue is "a voluntary habit," as stated in *Ethic.* ii, 6. But chastity, apparently, is not voluntary, since it can be taken away by force from a woman to whom violence is done. Therefore it seems that chastity is not a virtue.

Reply to Objection 2. As Augustine says (*De Civ. Dei* i, 18), "so long as her mind holds to its purpose, whereby she has merited to be holy even in body, not even the violence of another's lust can deprive her body of its holiness, which is safeguarded by her persevering continency." He also says (*De Civ. Dei* i, 18) that "in the mind there is a virtue which is the companion of courage, whereby it is resolved to suffer any evil whatsoever rather than consent to evil."[2]

Objection 3. Further, there is no virtue in unbelievers. Yet some unbelievers are chaste. Therefore chastity is not a virtue.

Reply to Objection 3. As Augustine says (*Contra Julian.* iv, 3), "it is impossible to have any true virtue unless one be truly just; nor is it possible to be just unless one live by faith." Whence he argues that in unbelievers there is neither true chastity, nor any other virtue, because, to wit, they are not referred to the due end, and as he adds (*Contra Julian.* iv, 3) "virtues are distinguished from vices not by their functions," i.e., their acts, "but by their ends."[3]

---

does not involve a denial of the existence of sexual desires, but rather moderates the actions of a person so that they accord with right reason, rather than simply with whatever a person happens at that moment to desire.

[2] Chastity, like every other virtue, cannot be taken away by any external force. Another can tempt one to act against virtue, but in order for the agent to act truly against virtue the act must be free, and if free, it must not be the result of external physical force against the will of the agent. Just as no one is guilty of murder whose hand is forced to pull the trigger against his will, and just as persons would not be guilty of drunkenness if drinks were literally poured down their throat against their will, so too a sexual act against a woman's will (or for that matter, a man's will) does not in the least actually constitute an act of unchastity on her part. She is the victim of wrongdoing, not a wrongdoer.

[3] Augustine defends the same view in his work *On the Morals of the Catholic Church* (*De moribus ecclesiae catholicae*). The fullness of true virtue is a perfection that leads a person to the Ultimate Perfection, God. Of course, a person can exercise virtue to a certain degree without the theological virtues. Not every courageous soldier is a believer. But true courage, as true chastity,

Objection 4. Further, the fruits are distinct from the virtues. But chastity is reckoned among the fruits (Gal 5:23). Therefore chastity is not a virtue.

Reply to Objection 4. Chastity is a virtue in so far as it works in accordance with reason, but in so far as it delights in its act, it is reckoned among the fruits.

ARTICLE 2 ⇢ **Is chastity a general virtue?**

No, despite objections to the contrary, Macrobius [*Commentary on the Dream of Scipio* i, 8] reckons it to be a part of temperance.[4]

I answer that, The word "chastity" is employed in two ways: first, properly; and thus it is a special virtue having a special matter, namely concupiscence relating to sexual pleasures. Secondly, the word "chastity" is employed metaphorically: for just as a mingling of bodies conduces to sexual pleasure, which is the proper matter of chastity and of lust its contrary vice, so too the spiritual union of the mind with certain things conduces to a pleasure that is the matter of a spiritual chastity, metaphorically speaking, as well as of a spiritual fornication, likewise metaphorically so called. For if the human mind delights in the spiritual union with that to which it behooves it to be united, namely God, and refrains from delighting in union with other things against the requirements of the order established by God, this may be called a spiritual chastity, according to 2 Corinthians 11:2, "I have espoused you to one husband, that I may present you as a chaste virgin to Christ." If, on the other hand, the mind be united to any other

---

must be pursued for the right reason. Simply "doing what duty demands" is less than full virtue unless this is done for the right reason. The most perfect reason for all human action is measured by Ultimate Goodness and Ultimate Wisdom. So agents whose life and actions are not ordered to this end, however much they may approach perfect virtue (and this may be a great deal indeed!), nevertheless could be made more perfect still by approaching the Perfection only to be found in God.

4 Macrobius (395–423) wrote a commentary on Cicero's *Dream of Scipio* that was important throughout the Middle Ages, influencing many authors from Aquinas to Chaucer. The text is a dialogue between a dead man and another man still living that addresses Platonic themes of the importance of virtue, the soul's immortality, and the body's frailty.

things whatsoever, against the prescription of the Divine order, it will be called spiritual fornication, according to Jeremiah 3:1, "But you have prostituted yourself to many lovers." Taking chastity in this sense, it is a general virtue, because every virtue withdraws the human mind from delighting in a union with unlawful things. Nevertheless, the essence of this chastity consists principally in charity and the other theological virtues, whereby the human mind is united to God.[5]

Objection 1. It would seem that chastity is a general virtue. For Augustine says (*De Mendacio* xx) that "chastity of the mind is the well-ordered movement of the mind that does not prefer the lesser to the greater things." But this belongs to every virtue. Therefore chastity is a general virtue.

Reply to Objection 1. This argument takes chastity in the metaphorical sense.

Objection 2. Further, "chastity" takes its name from "chastisement" [cf. a. 1]. Now every movement of the appetitive part should be chastised by reason. Since, then, every moral virtue curbs some movement of the appetite, it seems that every moral virtue is chastity.

Reply to Objection 2. As stated above (a. 1; q. 142, a. 2), the concupiscence of that which gives pleasure is especially likened to a child, because the desire of pleasure is connatural to us, especially of pleasures of touch, which are directed to the maintenance of nature. Hence it is that if the concupiscence of such pleasures be fostered by consenting to it, it will wax very strong, as in the case of a child left to his own will.

---

[5] The contrast between "special virtue" and "general virtue" applies to all the cardinal virtues, and here it is also applied to the virtue of chastity. The "general virtue" of justice relates to any just ordering, including an ordering among parts of one's soul. Thus the person with the individual virtues has the "general virtue" of justice. The "special virtue" or "particular virtue" of justice has to do only with exchange among persons. The "general virtue" of courage has to do with facing obstacles and threats; the "special" or "particular" virtue of courage has to do with facing the threat of death. Chastity as a special virtue orders sexual desires in accordance with reason; chastity considered more generally, in a metaphorical sense, "chastises" or properly orders any desire to be in accord with fidelity to God's will.

Therefore the concupiscence of these pleasures stands in very great need of being chastised: and consequently chastity is applied antonomastically[6] to such like concupiscences, even as courage is about those matters wherein we stand in the greatest need of strength of mind.

Objection 3. Further, chastity is opposed to fornication. But fornication seems to belong to every kind of sin: for it is written (Ps 72:27): "You shall destroy all them that are disloyal to You." Therefore chastity is a general virtue.

Reply to Objection 3. This argument considers spiritual fornication, metaphorically so called, which is opposed to spiritual chastity, as stated.

---

6 "Antonomasia" is the figure of speech whereby we substitute the general for the individual term, e.g., substituting "the philosopher" for "Aristotle" (cf. p. 177, n. 35).

QUESTION 152

VIRGINITY

ARTICLE 2 — **Is it wrong to remain a virgin?**

No, despite objections to the contrary, No sin is a matter of direct counsel. But virginity is a matter of direct counsel: for it is written (1 Cor 7:25): "Concerning virgins I have no commandment of the Lord, but I give counsel." Therefore virginity is not an unlawful thing.

I answer that, In human acts, those are sinful which are against right reason. Now right reason requires that things directed to an end should be used in a measure proportionate to that end. Again, man's good is threefold, as stated in *Ethic.* i, 8: one consisting in external things, for instance riches; another consisting in bodily goods; the third consisting in the goods of the soul, among which the goods of the contemplative life take precedence of the goods of the active life, as the Philosopher shows (*Ethic.* x, 7), and as our Lord declared (Lk 10:42): "Mary has chosen the better part."[1] Of these goods, those that are

---

[1] Aristotle argues that the contemplative life is superior to the active life of politics for a number of reasons (cf. Aristotle's *Nicomachean Ethics*, Book 10, Chapters 7 and 8, and Thomas's summary in *ST* II–II, q. 182, a. 1). Contemplation, he argues, is the best activity of man's highest faculty. Our mind is the most divine aspect of us, not shared with lower animals, and the highest activity of the mind is contemplation, unlike practical activities such as looking for food, which are shared with lower animals. So human happiness, *as distinctly human*, must consist in this aspect of us. Secondly, contemplation is the most pleasant because unlike pleasures that rely on a previous privation, such as the pleasure of eating relying on the pain of being hungry, the pleasures of contemplation are "pure" pleasures not requiring a previous pain to be enjoyable.

external are directed to those that belong to the body, and those that belong to the body are directed to those that belong to the soul; and furthermore those that belong to the active life are directed to those that belong to the life of contemplation. Accordingly, right reason directs that one use external goods in a measure proportionate to the body, and in like manner as regards the rest. Therefore, if a man refrain from possessing certain things (which otherwise it were good for him to possess), for the sake of his body's good, or of the contemplation of truth, this is not sinful, but in accord with right reason. In like manner, if a man abstain from bodily pleasure in order more freely to give himself to the contemplation of truth, this is in accordance with the rectitude of reason. Now holy virginity refrains from all sexual pleasure in order more freely to have leisure for Divine contemplation: for the Apostle says (1 Cor 7:34): "The unmarried woman, and the virgin, thinks on the things of the Lord: that she may be holy in both body and in spirit. But she that is married thinks on the things of the world, how she may please her husband." Therefore it follows that virginity, instead of being sinful, is worthy of praise.[2]

The contemplative life is also to be preferred to the active life because it is the most self-sufficient. In the active life of politics, the agent must rely on the contributions of others, whereas in contemplation, while other people (especially friends) may be very helpful and desirable in aid of contemplation, strictly speaking they are not necessary. In addition, contemplation aims at no end beyond itself; but the active life is a means to some other end. Finally, contemplation is most akin to the divine and therefore most worthy of imitation. Although contemplation has a supremacy over activity (both considered simply as such), Thomas himself sees what might be called a "mixed life," a life of both contemplation and action, as actually the best, all things considered (cf. II–II, q. 188, a. 6). Members of the Society of Jesus (Jesuits) speak of their ideal in a similar way. They strive to be "contemplatives in action."

[2] This view of virginity has always been controversial but for very different reasons. In the ancient world, childlessness, in particular for women, was seen as a curse and sign of disfavor. A woman was viewed as incomplete unless married. Today, virginity is held in disfavor on account of the view that sexual pleasure is a necessary condition for a life worth living. To abstain from sexual pleasure entirely, as Paul indicates here, is not a call for everyone. Such voluntary abstention for the sake of the Kingdom of God, however, is a living witness and testimony to the sovereignty of God and to God's ultimate plan for all of us to see Him face to face like the angels as sons and daughters

Objection 1. It would seem that virginity is unlawful. For whatever is contrary to a precept of the natural law is unlawful. Now just as the words of Genesis 2:16—"Of every tree" that is in "paradise, you shall eat"—indicate a precept of the natural law, in reference to the preservation of the individual, so also the words of Genesis 1:28—"Increase and multiply, and fill the earth"—express a precept of the natural law, in reference to the preservation of the species. Therefore, just as it would be a sin to abstain from all food, as this would be to act counter to the good of the individual, so too it is a sin to abstain altogether from the act of procreation, for this is to act against the good of the species.

Reply to Objection 1. A precept implies a duty, as stated above (q. 122, a. 1). Now there are two kinds of duty. There is the duty that has to be fulfilled by one person, and a duty of this kind cannot be set aside without sin. The other duty has to be fulfilled by the multitude, and the fulfillment of this kind of duty is not binding on each one of the multitude. For the multitude has many obligations which cannot be discharged by the individual, but are fulfilled by one person doing this, and another doing that. Accordingly the precept of natural law which binds man to eat must be fulfilled by each individual; otherwise the individual cannot be sustained. On the other hand, the precept of procreation regards the whole multitude of men, which needs not only to multiply in body, but also to advance spiritually. Therefore sufficient provision is made for the human multitude, if some undertake the work of human procreation, while others, abstaining from this, should have leisure for the contemplation of Divine things, for the beauty and welfare of the whole human race. Thus too in an army, some take sentry duty, others are standard-bearers, and others fight with the sword; yet all these things are necessary for the multitude, although they cannot be done by one person.

Objection 2. Further, whatever declines from the mean of virtue is apparently sinful. Now virginity declines from the mean of virtue, since it abstains from all sexual pleasures: for the Philosopher says (*Ethic.* ii, 2) that "he who revels in every pleasure, and abstains from not even one, is

---

of God, sons and daughters of the Resurrection (Lk 20: 34–40). See also the *Catechism of the Catholic Church* (1618–20).

intemperate, but he who refrains from all is loutish and insensible."
Therefore virginity is something sinful.

Reply to Objection 2. The person who, beside the dictate of right
reason, abstains from all pleasures through aversion, as it were, for
pleasure as such is insensible. But a virgin does not refrain from every
pleasure, but only from that which is sexual, and abstains from these
according to right reason, as stated above. Now the mean of virtue is
fixed with reference not to quantity but to right reason, as stated in
Ethic. ii, 6: therefore it is said of the magnanimous (*Ethic.* iv, 3) that
"in point of quantity he goes to the extreme, but in point of becomingness he follows the mean."[3]

ARTICLE 3 ~~ **Is virginity a virtue?**

Yes, despite objections to the contrary, Ambrose says (*De Virgin.* i,
3): "Love of virginity moves us to say something about virginity, lest
by passing it over we should seem to cast a slight on what is a virtue of
high degree."[4]

　　I answer that, As stated above (a. 1), the formal and completive
element in virginity is the purpose of abstaining from sexual pleasure,

---

　　[3] The mean of virtue, in other words, is not a mathematical mean. The number
　　five is the mathematical mean between zero and ten, but it does not follow that
　　one ought to drink five drinks before driving, rather than having no drinks or
　　having ten drinks. The mean is determined according to reason, and in some
　　cases having even a single drink would be unreasonable. So too, for those who
　　are not married and for those who have taken vows as a priest, religious brother
　　or sister, performing even a single sexual act is contrary to reason.
　　[4] The Second Vatican Council echoed the words of Ambrose: "The chastity
　　'for the sake of the kingdom of heaven' (Mt 19:12) which religious profess
　　should be counted an outstanding gift of grace. It frees the heart of man in a
　　unique fashion (cf. 1 Cor 7:32–35) so that it may be more inflamed with
　　love for God and for all people. Thus it not only symbolizes in a singular
　　way the heavenly goods but also the most suitable means by which religious
　　dedicate themselves with undivided heart to the service of God and the
　　works of the apostolate. In this way they recall to the minds of all the faith-
　　ful that wondrous marriage decreed by God and which is to be fully revealed
　　in the future age in which the Church takes Christ as its only spouse. Reli-
　　gious [priests, brothers, and sisters], therefore, who are striving faithfully to
　　observe the chastity they have professed must have faith in the words of the

which purpose is rendered praiseworthy by its end, in so far, to wit, as this is done in order to have leisure for Divine things, while the material element in virginity is integrity of the flesh free of all experience of sexual pleasure. Now it is manifest that where a good action has a special matter through having a special excellence, there is a special kind of virtue: for example, magnificence which is about great expenditure is for this reason a special virtue distinct from liberality, which is about all uses of money in general. Now keeping oneself free from the experience of sexual pleasure has an excellence of its own deserving of greater praise than keeping oneself free from inordinate sexual pleasure. Therefore virginity is a special virtue being related to chastity as magnificence to liberality.[5]

Objection 1. It would seem that virginity is not a virtue. For "no virtue is in us by nature," as the Philosopher says (*Ethic.* ii, 1). Now virginity is in us by nature, since all are virgins when born. Therefore virginity is not a virtue.

Reply to Objection 1. Men have from their birth that which is material in virginity, namely integrity of the flesh and freedom from sexual experience. But they have not that which is formal in virginity, namely

Lord, and trusting in God's help not overestimate their own strength but practice mortification and custody of the senses. Neither should they neglect the natural means which promote health of mind and body. As a result they will not be influenced by those false doctrines which scorn perfect continence as being impossible or harmful to human development and they will repudiate by a certain spiritual instinct everything which endangers chastity. In addition let all, especially superiors, remember that chastity is guarded more securely when true brotherly love flourishes in the common life of the community" (Vatican II, *Perfectae Caritatis*, 12).

5 Before becoming Pope Benedict XVI, Joseph Cardinal Ratzinger had this to say about the meaning of religious celibacy: "The renunciation of marriage and family is thus to be understood in terms of this vision: I renounce what, humanly speaking, is not only the most normal but also the most important thing. I forego bringing forth further life on the tree of life, and I live in the faith that my land is really God—and so I make it easier for others, also, to believe that there is a kingdom of heaven. I bear witness to Jesus Christ, to the gospel, not only with words, but also with a specific mode of existence, and I place my life in this form at his disposal." *Salt of the Earth: The Church at the End of the Millennium* (San Francisco: Ignatius Press, 1997), 195.

the purpose of safeguarding this integrity for God's sake, which purpose gives virginity its character of virtue. Hence Augustine says (*De
Virgin.* xi): "Nor do we praise virgins for being virgins, but because
their virginity is consecrated to God by holy continence."

Objection 2. Further, whoever has one virtue has all virtues, as stated
above (I–II, q. 65, a. 1). Yet some have other virtues without having
virginity: else, since none can go to the heavenly kingdom without
virtue, no one could go there without virginity, which would involve
the condemnation of marriage. Therefore virginity is not a virtue.

Reply to Objection 2. Virtues are connected together by reason of that
which is formal in them, namely charity, or by reason of prudence, as
stated above (q. 129, a. 3, ad 2), but not by reason of that which is
material in them. For nothing hinders a virtuous man from providing
the matter of one virtue, and not the matter of another virtue: thus a
poor man has the matter of temperance, but not that of magnificence.[6]
It is in this way that one who has the other virtues lacks the matter of
virginity, namely the aforesaid integrity of the flesh. Nevertheless he can
have that which is formal in virginity, his mind being so prepared that
he has the purpose of safeguarding this same integrity of the flesh,
should it be fitting for him to do so, even as a poor man may be so prepared in mind as to have the purpose of being magnificent in his expenditure, were he in a position to do so, or again, as a prosperous man is
so prepared in mind as to purpose bearing misfortune with equanimity,
without which preparedness of the mind no man can be virtuous.

Objection 3. Further, every virtue is recovered by penance. But virginity
is not recovered by penance; therefore Jerome says [Ep. *xxii ad Eustoch.*]:

---

6 *Magnificence* comes from two Latin words, *magna,* or "great," and *facere,*
meaning "to do" or "to make." The word really means to make a great monetary expenditure, to engage in philanthropy. Since not all people have the
wealth to make lavish donations, not all people can exercise the virtue of mag-
nificience, although they can still be prepared to do so should the opportunity
arise (say, from winning the lottery). In similar manner, all people who are
not married can make the "lavish expenditure" of committing themselves to
celibacy for the sake of the kingdom of God.

"Other things God can do, but He cannot restore the virgin after her downfall." Therefore, seemingly, virginity is not a virtue.

Reply to Objection 3. Virtue can be recovered by penance as regards that which is formal in virtue, but not as to that which is material therein. For if a magnificent man has squandered all his wealth, he does not recover his riches by repenting of his sin. In like manner, a person who has lost virginity by sin recovers by repenting not the matter of virginity but the purpose of virginity.

As regards the matter of virginity, there is that which can be miraculously restored by God, namely the integrity of the organ, which we hold to be accidental to virginity, while there is something else which cannot be restored even by miracle, to wit, that one who has experienced sexual lust should cease to have had that experience. For God cannot make that which is done not to have been done, as stated in I, q. 25, a. 4.[7]

Objection 4. Further, no virtue is lost without sin. Yet virginity is lost without sin, namely by marriage. Therefore virginity is not a virtue.

---

[7] The article mentioned by Thomas states that "there does not fall under the scope of God's omnipotence anything that implies a contradiction. Now that the past should not have been implies a contradiction. For as it implies a contradiction to say that Socrates is sitting, and is not sitting, so does it to say that he sat, and did not sit. But to say that he did sit is to say that it happened in the past. To say that he did not sit is to say that it did not happen. Whence that the past should not have been does not come under the scope of divine power." Now, one may ask, why can God not do that which implies a contradiction? In *Summa contra Gentiles*, Book one, Chapter 84, Thomas treats this very question. Certain things, namely those that imply a contradiction, would contradict the divine will could they be willed (e.g. God wills that man be rational; hence He would contradict His own will were He also to will that man be irrational), and obviously God does not and cannot oppose Himself. Thus God cannot will a contradiction. It is also true that God cannot will that which is opposed to being as such (for He is the cause of being as such), but the impossible is opposed to being as such, and since a contradiction is opposed to being as such, God cannot will a contradiction, for it contradicts His own Being. Since He is perfectly good, God also can only will that which is good. For a thing to be and not to be at the same time and in the same respect is a non-being. But non-being is not good, and therefore God's perfectly good will cannot will it. God is not ruled by a logic book, but God's action always reflects His wisdom, love, and existence.

Reply to Objection 4. Virginity as a virtue denotes the purpose, confirmed by vow, of observing perpetual integrity. For Augustine says (*De Virgin.* viii) that "by virginity, integrity of the flesh is vowed, consecrated and observed in honor of the Creator of both soul and flesh." Hence virginity, as a virtue, is never lost without sin.

Objection 5. Further, virginity is condivided with widowhood and conjugal purity. But neither of these is a virtue. Therefore virginity is not a virtue.

Reply to Objection 5. Conjugal chastity is deserving of praise merely because it abstains from unlawful pleasures: hence no excellence attaches to it above that of chastity in general. Widowhood, however, adds something to chastity in general; but it does not attain to that which is perfect in this matter, namely to entire freedom from sexual pleasure; virginity alone achieves this. Therefore virginity alone is accounted a virtue above chastity, even as magnificence is reckoned above liberality.

ARTICLE 4～～**Is virginity more excellent than marriage?**

Yes, despite objections to the contrary, Augustine says (*De Virgin.* xix): "Both solid reason and the authority of Holy Writ show that neither is marriage sinful, nor is it to be equaled to the good of virginal continence or even to that of widowhood."[8]

I answer that, According to Jerome (*Contra Jovin.* i), the error of Jovinian consisted in holding virginity not to be preferable to marriage. This error is refuted above all by the example of Christ, Who both chose a virgin for His mother and remained Himself a virgin, and by the teaching of the Apostle, who (1 Cor 7) counsels virginity as the greater good.[9] It is also refuted by reason, both because a Divine

---

[8] Interestingly, Thomas cites Augustine of Hippo, who was not, we know from his *Confessions*, himself a virgin. Although Augustine and Thomas give a priority to consecrated virginity, neither denigrates marriage. Indeed, Augustine is forceful in his condemnation of the Manichaean view that marriage is incompatible with godly living.

[9] This passage reads: "I wish that all men were as I am. But each man has his own gift from God; one has this gift, another has that. Now to the unmarried and the widows I say: It is good for them to stay unmarried, as I am."

good takes precedence of a human good, and because the good of the soul is preferable to the good of the body, and again because the good of the contemplative life is better than that of the active life. Now virginity is directed to the good of the soul in respect of the contemplative life, which consists in thinking "on the things of God" [Vulg.: 'the Lord'], whereas marriage is directed to the good of the body, namely the bodily increase of the human race, and belongs to the active life, since the man and woman who embrace the married life have to think "on the things of the world," as the Apostle says (1 Cor 7:34). Without doubt, therefore, virginity is preferable to conjugal continence.

Objection 1. It would seem that virginity is not more excellent than marriage. For Augustine says (*De Bono Conjug.* xxi): "Continence was equally meritorious in John who remained unmarried and Abraham who begot children." Now a greater virtue has greater merit. Therefore virginity is not a greater virtue than conjugal chastity.

Reply to Objection 1. Merit is measured not only by the kind of action, but still more by the mind of the agent. Now Abraham had a mind so disposed that he was prepared to observe virginity, if it were in keeping with the times for him to do so. Therefore in him conjugal continence was equally meritorious with the virginal continence of John, as regards the essential reward, but not as regards the accidental reward. Hence Augustine says (*De Bono Conjug.* xxi) that both "the celibacy of John and the marriage of Abraham fought Christ's battle in keeping with the difference of the times; but John was continent even in deed, whereas Abraham was continent only in habit."

Objection 2. Further, the praise accorded a virtuous man depends on his virtue. If, then, virginity were preferable to conjugal continence, it would seem to follow that every virgin is to be praised more than any married woman. But this is untrue. Therefore virginity is not preferable to marriage.

Reply to Objection 2. Though virginity is better than conjugal continence, a married person may be better than a virgin for two reasons: first, on the part of chastity itself, if, to wit, the married person is more prepared in mind to observe virginity, if it should be expedient, than the one who is actually a virgin. Hence Augustine (*De Bono Conjug.* xxii) charges the virgin to say: "I am no better than Abraham, although the chastity of celibacy is better than the chastity of marriage." Further on he gives the reason for this: "For what I do now, he would have done better, if it were fitting for him to do it then; and what they did I would even do now if it were advantageous for me now to do it." Secondly, because perhaps the person who is not a virgin has some more excellent virtue. Therefore Augustine says (*De Virgin.* xliv): "Whence does a virgin know the things that belong to the Lord, however solicitous she be about them, if perchance on account of some mental fault she be not yet ripe for martyrdom, whereas this woman to whom she delighted in preferring herself is already able to drink the chalice of the Lord?"[10]

Objection 3. Further, the common good takes precedence of the private good, according to the Philosopher (*Ethic.* i, 2). Now marriage is directed to the common good: for Augustine says (*De Bono Conjug.* xvi): "What food is to a man's well being, such is sexual intercourse to the welfare of the human race." On the other hand, virginity is ordered to the individual good, namely in order to avoid what the Apostle calls the "tribulation of the flesh," to which married people are subject (1 Cor 7:28). Therefore virginity is not greater than conjugal continence.

Reply to Objection 3. The common good takes precedence of the private good, if it be of the same genus, but it may be that the private good is better generically. It is thus that the virginity that is consecrated to God is preferable to carnal fruitfulness. Hence Augustine

---

[10] Marriage, like consecrated virginity, is a virtuous state established by God. As the *Catechism of the Catholic Church* notes: "Both the sacrament of Matrimony and virginity for the Kingdom of God come from the Lord himself. It is he who gives them meaning and grants them the grace which is indispensable for living them out in conformity with his will. Esteem of virginity for the sake of the kingdom and the Christian understanding of marriage are inseparable, and they reinforce each other: "Whoever denigrates marriage also diminishes the glory of virginity. Whoever praises it makes virginity more admirable and resplendent. What appears good only in comparison with evil would not be truly good. The most excellent good is something even better than what is admitted to be good" (*CCC* 1620).

says (*De Virgin.* ix): "It must be confessed that the fruitfulness of the flesh, even of those women who in these times seek naught else from marriage but children in order to make them servants of Christ, cannot compensate for lost virginity."

QUESTION **153**

LUST

ARTICLE 2 ～ Is every sexual act a sin?

No, despite objections to the contrary, Augustine says (*De Bono Conjug.* xxv): "This is a sufficient answer to heretics, if only they will understand that no sin is committed in that which is against neither nature, nor morals, nor a commandment"; and he refers to the act of sexual intercourse between the patriarchs of old and their several wives. Therefore not every sexual act is a sin.

I answer that, A sin, in human acts, is that which is against the order of reason. Now the order of reason consists in its ordering everything to its end in a fitting manner. Therefore it is no sin if one, by the dictate of reason, makes use of certain things in a fitting manner and order for the end to which they are adapted, provided this end be something truly good. Now just as the preservation of the bodily nature of one individual is a true good, so too is the preservation of the nature of the human species a very great good. And just as the use of food is directed to the preservation of life in the individual, so is the use of sexual acts directed to the preservation of the whole human race. Hence Augustine says (*De Bono Conjug.* xvi): "What food is to a man's well being, such is sexual intercourse to the welfare of the whole human race." Therefore, just as the use of food can be without sin, if it be taken in due manner and order, as required for the welfare of the body, so also the use of sexual acts can be without sin, provided they be performed in due manner and order, in keeping with the end of human procreation.[1]

Objection 1. It would seem that no sexual act can be without sin. For nothing but sin would seem to hinder virtue. Now every sexual act is a great hindrance to virtue. For Augustine says (*Soliloq.* i, 10): "I consider that nothing so casts down the manly mind from its height as the fondling of a woman, and those bodily contacts." Therefore, seemingly, no sexual act is without sin.

Reply to Objection 1. A thing may be a hindrance to virtue in two ways: first, as regards the ordinary degree of virtue, and as to this, nothing but sin is an obstacle to virtue; secondly, as regards the perfect degree of virtue, and as to this, virtue may be hindered by that which is not a sin, but a lesser good. In this way sexual intercourse casts down the mind not from virtue, but from the height, i.e., the perfection of virtue. Hence Augustine says (*De Bono Conjug.* viii): "Just as that was good which Martha did when busy about serving holy men, yet better still that which Mary did in hearing the word of God, so too we praise the good of Susanna's conjugal chastity, yet we prefer the good of the widow Anna, and much more that of the Virgin Mary."[2]

Objection 2. Further, any excess that makes one forsake the good of reason is sinful, because virtue is corrupted by "excess" and "deficiency,"

---

[1] "[I]n keeping with the end of human procreation" does not mean that every sexual act must actually lead to conception, but rather that every sexual act should be open to the possibility, not contrary to the end, of human procreation. Married couples who for various physical reasons are unable to procreate may still engage in marital acts.

[2] Just as wealth and the freedom to do what one wills are not wrong or evil in themselves but indeed great goods, so too sexual acts. It is sometimes fitting, however, to put aside even great goods, which can become distractions to the Greatest Good, so that one can focus on what really matters most. Many people are so focused on wealth, sexual pleasure, and liberty that their relationship with God suffers. (It is, as Thomas notes, possible to maintain focus on God and still have these things. This is, however, difficult.) Some people take vows, or promises, of poverty, chastity, and obedience in order to free themselves, to the extent possible, to serve God without these potential distractions and hindrances.

as stated in *Ethic.* ii, 2. Now in every sexual act there is excess of pleasure, since it so absorbs the mind that "it is incompatible with the act of understanding," as the Philosopher observes (*Ethic.* vii, 11), and as Jerome [Origen, *Hom. vi in Num.*; Cf. Jerome, Ep. cxxiii, *ad Ageruch*] states, rendered the hearts of the prophets, for the moment, insensible to the spirit of prophecy. Therefore no sexual act can be without sin.

Reply to Objection 2. As stated above (q. 152, a. 2, ad 2; I–II, q. 64, a. 2), the mean of virtue depends not on quantity but on conformity with right reason,[3] and consequently the exceeding pleasure attaching to a sexual act directed according to reason is not opposed to the mean of virtue. Moreover, virtue is not concerned with the amount of pleasure experienced by the external sense, as this depends on the disposition of the body; what matters is how much the interior appetite is affected by that pleasure. Nor does it follow that the act in question is contrary to virtue from the fact that the free act of reason in considering spiritual things is incompatible with the aforesaid pleasure. For it is not contrary to virtue if the act of reason be sometimes interrupted for something that is done in accordance with reason, else it would be against virtue for a person to set himself to sleep. That sexual concupiscence and pleasure are not subject to the command and moderation of reason is due to the punishment of the first sin, inasmuch as the reason, for rebelling against God, deserved that its body should rebel against it, as Augustine says (*De Civ. Dei* xiii, 13).

Objection 3. Further, the cause is more powerful than its effect. Now original sin is transmitted to children by concupiscence, without which no sexual act is possible, as Augustine declares (*De Nup. et Concup.* i, 24). Therefore no sexual act can be without sin.

Reply to Objection 3. As Augustine says (*De Civ. Dei* xiii, 13), "the child, shackled with original sin, is born of fleshly concupiscence

---

3 The mean of virtue is not a mathematical averaging. In terms of consumption of food, the small, inactive person may eat very little and a large athlete might eat a great deal, but in these two different quantities of food may nevertheless both be a mean. Aristotle speaks of virtue as a state that decides, consisting in a mean, *a mean relative to us,* as the reason of a wise person determines.

(which is not imputed as sin to the regenerate) as of a daughter of sin." Hence it does not follow that the act in question is a sin, but that it contains something penal resulting from the first sin.

ARTICLE 3 ~~ **Is the lust that is brought about by sexual acts a sin?**

Yes, despite objections to the contrary, The cause is more powerful than its effect. Now wine is forbidden on account of lust, according to the saying of the Apostle (Eph 5:18), "Be not drunk with wine wherein is lust." Therefore lust is forbidden. Further, it is numbered among the works of the flesh (Gal 5:19).

I answer that, The more necessary a thing is, the more it behooves one to observe the order of reason in its regard; therefore the more sinful it becomes if the order of reason be forsaken. Now the use of sexual acts, as stated in the foregoing article, is most necessary for the common good, namely the preservation of the human race. Therefore there is the greatest necessity for observing the order of reason in this matter, so that if anything be done in this connection against the dictate of reason's ordering, it will be a sin. Now lust consists essentially in exceeding the order and mode of reason in the matter of sexual acts.[4] Therefore without any doubt lust is a sin.

Objection 1. It would seem that lust brought about by sexual acts cannot be a sin. For the sexual act consists in the emission of semen which is the surplus from food, according to the Philosopher (*De Gener. Anim.* i, 18). But there is no sin attaching to the emission of other superfluities. Therefore neither can there be any sin in sexual acts.

Reply to Objection 1. As the Philosopher says in the same book (*De Gener. Anim.* i, 18), "the semen is a surplus that is needed." For it is said to be superfluous because it is the residue from the action of the

---

4 Thomas is not claiming that all sexual acts are lustful but rather that some could be. Put in more contemporary terms, for example, it is possible for someone moved by lust to treat his or her spouse as less than fully human, to use him or her *merely* as an object to satisfy desire. Such treatment is wrongful, exceeding "the order and mode of reason in the matter of sexual acts." Sexual pleasure in itself is not at all sinful; indeed, Thomas says that had Adam and Eve not sinned, sexual pleasure would have been greater than it now is. *ST* I, q. 98, a. 2, Reply 63.

nutritive power, yet it is needed for the work of the generative power. But the other superfluities of the human body are such as not to be needed, so that it matters not how they are emitted, provided one observe the decencies of social life. It is different with the emission of semen, which should be accomplished in a manner befitting the end for which it is needed.

Objection 2. Further, everyone can lawfully make what use he pleases of what is his. But in the sexual act a man uses only what is his own, except perhaps in adultery or rape. Therefore there can be no sin in sexual acts, and consequently lust is no sin.

Reply to Objection 2. As the Apostle says (1 Cor 6:20) in speaking against lust, "You are bought with a great price: glorify and bear God in your body." Therefore, by inordinately using the body through lust a man wrongs God, Who is the Supreme Lord of our body. Hence Augustine says (*De Decem. Chord.* 10 [*Serm.* ix (xcvi *de Temp.*)]): "God, Who thus governs His servants for their good, not for His, made this order and commandment, lest unlawful pleasures should destroy His temple which you have begun to be."

Objection 3. Further, every sin has an opposite vice. But, seemingly, no vice is opposed to lust. Therefore lust is not a sin.

Reply to Objection 3. The opposite of lust is not found in many, since men are more inclined to pleasure. Yet the contrary vice is comprised under insensibility, and occurs in him who has such a dislike for sexual intercourse with a woman as not to pay the marriage debt to his wife.[5]

---

[5] Husbands and wives have a duty to "render the marital debt," which means they ought not to refuse reasonable requests for sexual intercourse. As St. Paul puts it: "Let the husband render the debt to his wife, and the wife also in like manner to the husband. The wife has not power of her own body, but the husband. And in like manner the husband also has not power of his own body, but the wife" (1 Cor 7:3, 4). "Rendering the marital debt" is among the duties that spouses have to one another, such as mutual support and kindness. It can do great damage to the relationship of husband and wife for either party to refuse reasonable requests for marital intimacy. Of course, there are situations in which it is unreasonable to request sexual intercourse from a spouse, for example in times of illness.

QUESTION 154

THE PARTS OF LUST

ARTICLE 2 ~~ **Is premarital sex (simple fornication) a mortal sin?**[1]

Yes, despite objections to the contrary, It is written (Tob 4:13): "Take heed to keep yourself . . . from all fornication, and beside your wife never endure to know a crime." Now crime denotes a mortal sin. Therefore fornication (premarital sex) and all intercourse with someone other than one's wife is a mortal sin.

Further, nothing but mortal sin debars a man from God's kingdom. But fornication debars him, as shown by the words of the Apostle (Gal 5:21), who, after mentioning fornication and certain other vices, adds: "They who do such things shall not obtain the kingdom of God." Therefore simple fornication is a mortal sin.

Further, it is written in the Decretals (XXII, qu. i, can. *Praedicandum*): "They should know that the same penance is to be enjoined for perjury as for adultery, fornication, and willful murder and other criminal offenses." Therefore simple fornication is a criminal or mortal sin.

I answer that, Without any doubt we must hold simple fornication to be a mortal sin, notwithstanding that a gloss [St. Augustine, QQ. *in Deut.,* qu. 37] on Dt. 23:17 says: "This is a prohibition against going with whores, whose vileness is venial." For instead of "venial" it

---

[1] By "simple fornication," Thomas means sexual intercourse between an unmarried man and an unmarried woman. If one or both are married to someone else, the act is "adultery." Fornication is another way to speak of "premarital sex."

should be "venal"[2] since such is the wanton's trade. In order to make this evident, we must take note that every sin committed directly against human life is a mortal sin. Now simple fornication implies an inordinateness that tends to injure the life of the offspring to be born of this union. For we find in all animals where the upbringing of the offspring needs care of both male and female that these come together not indeterminately, but the male with a certain female, whether one or several (such is the case with all birds), while on the other hand, among those animals where the female alone suffices for the offspring's upbringing, the union is indeterminate, as in the case of dogs and like animals. Now it is evident that the upbringing of a human child requires not only the mother's care for his nourishment, but much more the care of his father as guide and guardian, and under whom he progresses in goods both internal and external.[3] Hence human nature rebels against an indeterminate union of the sexes and demands that a man should be united to a determinate woman and should abide with her a long time or even for a whole lifetime. Hence it is that in the

2 Venal here meaning "obtained by a price."

3 Contemporary empirical research supports Thomas's claim. Although there are exceptions to the rule, single parenthood greatly increases the chances that the child will have a disadvantaged life. In an April 1993 *Atlantic Monthly* article, Barbara Dafoe Whitehead concludes her vast survey of social science research as follows: "Single parent families are not able to do well economically. . . . In fact, most teeter on the economic brink, and many fall into poverty and welfare dependency. Growing up in a disrupted family does not enrich a child's life or expand the number of adults committed to the child's well-being. In fact, disrupted families threaten the psychological well-being of the children and diminish the investment of adult time and money in them. Family diversity in the form of increasing numbers of single-parent and stepparent families does not strengthen the social fabric. It dramatically weakens and undermines society, placing new burdens on schools, courts, and prisons, and the welfare system. These new families are not an improvement on the nuclear family, nor are they even just as good, whether you look at outcomes for children or outcomes for society as a whole." Whitehead notes that children from single-parent families typically have more trouble in school, are more likely to get on welfare, and have a greater chance of spending time in prison. "The relationship is so strong that controlling for family configuration erases the relationship between race and crime and between low income and crime." Single-parenthood risks putting both single parents and children at a severe disadvantage. (Barbara Dafoe Whitehead, "Dan Quayle Was Right," *The Atlantic Monthly* [April 1993]: 47.)

human race the male has a natural solicitude for the certainty of off-spring, because on him devolves the upbringing of the child, and this certainly would cease if the union of sexes were indeterminate.

This union with a certain definite woman is called matrimony, which for the above reason is said to belong to the natural law. Since, however, the union of the sexes is directed to the common good of the whole human race, and common goods depend on the law for their determination, as stated above (I–II, q. 90, a. 2), it follows that this union of man and woman, which is called matrimony, is determined by some law.[4] Therefore, since fornication is an indeterminate union of the sexes, as something incompatible with matrimony, it is opposed to the good of the child's upbringing,[5] and consequently it is a mortal sin.

Nor does it matter if a man having knowledge of a woman by forni-cation make sufficient provision for the upbringing of the child because a matter that comes under the determination of the law is judged accord-ing to what happens in general, and not according to what may happen in a particular case.

Objection 2. Further, no mortal sin is the matter of a Divine precept. But the Lord commanded (Hos 1:2): "Go take a wife of fornications, and have of her children of fornications." Therefore fornication is not a mortal sin.

---

[4] In the third part of the *Summa* (*Supp.*, q. 50 and following), Thomas writes about the sacrament of matrimony.

[5] Every act of premarital sex risks premarital pregnancy. Use of contraception, which Thomas argues in article 11 of this question is itself sinful, does not eliminate possible conception. Even a "one percent risk taken monthly over ten years, accumulates a 70% probability that an unwanted pregnancy will occur during that period." John A. Ross, "Contraception: Short-Term vs. Long-Term Failure Rates," *Family Planning Perspectives* 21:6 (1989): 275. It is a simple matter of justice that a person should not risk someone else's well-being without a serious reason. This is precisely what takes place in premarital sex. Premarital sex risks premarital pregnancy, and each response to premarital pregnancy—(1) single parenthood, (2) abortion, (3) cohabitation, (4) adop-tion, or (5) shot-gun marriage—risks the well-being of the offspring to a greater (abortion, single parenthood, cohabitation) or a lesser degree (adop-tion, shot-gun marriage). For more on this argument, see Christopher Kaczor, "Marital Acts without Marital Vows: Social Justice and Premarital Sex," *Josephinum Journal of Theology* 9:2 (Summer/Fall 2002): 310–19.

Reply to Objection 2. Fornication is said to be a sin because it is contrary to right reason. Now man's reason is right in so far as it is ruled by the Divine Will, the first and supreme rule. Therefore that which a man does by God's will and in obedience to His command is not contrary to right reason, though it may seem contrary to the general order of reason: even so, that which is done miraculously by the Divine power is not contrary to nature, though it be contrary to the usual course of nature. Therefore, just as Abraham did not sin in being willing to slay his innocent son, because he obeyed God, although considered in itself it was contrary to right human reason in general, so too Hosea did not sin in committing fornication by God's command. Nor should such a copulation be strictly called fornication, though it be so called in reference to the general course of things. Hence Augustine says (*Confess.* iii, 8): "When God commands a thing to be done against the customs or agreement of any people, though it were never done by them heretofore, it is to be done"; and afterwards he adds: "For as among the powers of human society, the greater authority is obeyed in preference to the lesser, so must God in preference to all."[6]

---

[6] God reveals in the Ten Commandments laws that help human beings achieve that which they want—happiness. Without obeying these commandments, happiness is thwarted; for our happiness is found in loving God and neighbor, and these rules forbid behavior that is contrary to proper love of God and neighbor. Things are right and wrong, it would seem, by nature. Nature itself is a creation of God, however, and so God ultimately rules even over nature. Thus it is possible for God to make what appears to be "exceptions" to certain precepts of the natural law. These exceptions, however, retain the essence of the entire purpose of the law, which is to keep a person in fellowship with God. As Thomas explains elsewhere: "All men alike, both guilty and innocent, die the death of nature, which death of nature is inflicted by the power of God on account of original sin, according to 1 Kings 2:6, 'The Lord kills and makes alive.' Consequently, by the command of God, death can be inflicted on any man, guilty or innocent, without any injustice whatever. In like manner adultery is intercourse with another's wife, who is allotted to him by the law emanating from God. Consequently intercourse with any woman, by the command of God, is neither adultery nor fornication. The same applies to theft, which is the taking of another's property. For whatever is taken by the command of God, to Whom all things belong, is not taken against the will of its owner, whereas it is in this that theft consists. Nor is it only in human things that whatever is commanded by God is right; but also

Objection 3. Further, no mortal sin is mentioned in Holy Writ without disapprobation. Yet simple fornication is mentioned without disapprobation by Holy Writ in connection with the patriarchs. Thus we read (Gen 16:4) that Abraham slept with his handmaid Agar, and further on (Gen 30:5, 9) that Jacob slept with Bala and Zelpha, the handmaids of his wives, and again (Gen 38:18), that Juda slept with Thamar, whom he thought to be a harlot. Therefore simple fornication is not a mortal sin.

Reply to Objection 3. Abraham and Jacob went in to their handmaidens with no purpose of fornication, as we shall show further on when we treat of matrimony (*Supp.*, q. 65, a. 5, ad 2). As to Juda, there is no need to excuse him, for he also caused Joseph to be sold.

Objection 4. Further, every mortal sin is contrary to charity. But simple fornication is not contrary to charity, neither as regards the love of God, since it is not a sin directly against God, nor as regards the love of our neighbor, since thereby no one is injured. Therefore simple fornication is not a mortal sin.

Reply to Objection 4. Simple fornication is contrary to the love of our neighbor because it is opposed to the good of the child to be born, as we have shown, since it is an act of generation accomplished in a manner disadvantageous to the future child.[7]

---

in natural things, whatever is done by God is, in some way, natural" (*ST* I–II, q. 94, a. 5, ad 2). If I lend my car to my son, and then later tell my daughter that she may use my car, my daughter does not steal from my son when she takes the car out of his possession. The car belongs to me, and I may dispose of it as I see fit. In like manner, human life, human marriage, and human property in the most ultimate sense "belong" to God as part of his creation, and so God may dispose of these things according to the Divine Wisdom (if God pleases through the use of agents).

7 There is, indeed, a considerable amount of empirical data to back up this claim. See, for example, the numerous studies cited by Glenn Stanton in *Why Marriage Matters: Reasons to Believe in Marriage in Postmodern Society* (Colorado Springs, CO: Navpress Publishing Group, Sept. 1997).

Objection 5. Further, every mortal sin leads to eternal perdition. But simple fornication has not this result, because a gloss of Ambrose[8] on 1 Timothy 4:8, "Godliness is profitable to all things," says: "The whole of Christian teaching is summed up in mercy and godliness; if a man conforms to this, even though he gives way to the inconstancy of the flesh, doubtless he will be punished, but he will not perish." Therefore simple fornication is not a mortal sin.

Reply to Objection 5. A person who, while given to works of piety, yields to the inconstancy of the flesh is freed from eternal loss, in so far as these works dispose him to receive the grace to repent, and because by such works he makes satisfaction for his past inconstancy, but not so as to be freed by pious works if he persist in carnal inconstancy impenitent until death.

Objection 6. Further, Augustine says (*De Bono Conjug.* xvi) that "what food is to the well-being of the body, such is sexual intercourse to the welfare of the human race." But inordinate use of food is not always a mortal sin. Therefore neither is all inordinate sexual intercourse; and this would seem to apply especially to simple fornication, which is the least grievous of the aforesaid species.

Reply to Objection 6. One copulation may result in the begetting of a man. Therefore inordinate copulation, which hinders the good of the future child, is a mortal sin as to the very genus of the act, and not only as to the inordinateness of concupiscence. On the other hand, one meal does not hinder the good of a man's whole life. Therefore the act of gluttony is not a mortal sin by reason of its genus. It would, however, be a mortal sin, if a man were knowingly to partake of a food that would alter the whole condition of his life, as was the case with Adam.

Nor is it true that fornication is the least of the sins comprised under lust, for the marriage act that is done out of sensuous pleasure is a lesser sin.

---

[8] The Dominican translators note: "The quotation is from the Gloss of Peter Lombard, who refers it to St. Ambrose: whereas it is from Hilary the deacon".

ARTICLE 3 ~ Is premarital sex the most grievous of sins?

No, despite objections to the contrary, Gregory says (*Moral.* xxxiii, 12) that the sins of the flesh are less grievous than spiritual sins.

I answer that, The gravity of a sin may be measured in two ways: first with regard to the sin in itself, secondly with regard to some accident. The gravity of a sin is measured with regard to the sin itself by reason of its species, which is determined according to the good to which that sin is opposed.[9] Now fornication is contrary to the good of the child to be born. Therefore it is a graver sin, as to its species, than those sins which are contrary to external goods, such as theft and the like, while it is less grievous than those which are directly against God, and sins that are injurious to the life of one already born, such as murder.

Objection 1. It would seem that fornication is the most grievous of sins. For seemingly a sin is the more grievous according as it proceeds from a greater sensuous pleasure. Now the greatest sensuous pleasure is in fornication, for a gloss on 1 Corinthians 7:9 says that the "flame of sensuous pleasure is most fierce in lust." Therefore it seems that fornication is the gravest of sins.

Reply to Objection 1. The sensual pleasure that aggravates a sin is that which is in the inclination of the will. But the sensual pleasure that is in the sensitive appetite lessens sin, because a sin is the less grievous according as it is committed under the impulse of a greater passion. It is in this way that the greatest sensual pleasure is in fornication. Hence Augustine says (*De Agone Christiano* [*Serm.* ccxciii; ccl *de Temp.*; see Appendix to St. Augustine's works]) that of all a Christian's conflicts, the most difficult combats are those of chastity, wherein the fight is a daily one, but victory rare; and Isidore declares (*De Summo Bono* ii, 39) that "mankind is subjected to the devil by carnal

---

[9] The greater the good damaged by the wrongdoing, the greater the sin itself. Accidentally, however, various sins can lead to greater or lesser damage. So any given act of fornication might lead to unlikely but disastrous consequences, whereas a sin that is worse in its genus might not lead to such consequences. An unkind word can accidentally lead to someone's death; a robbery may not; but in terms of genus, a robbery is a worse kind of sin than simply an unkind word.

lust more than by anything else," because, to wit, the vehemence of this passion is more difficult to overcome.

Objection 2. Further, a sin is the more grievous that is committed against a person more closely united to the sinner: thus he sins more grievously who strikes his father than one who strikes a stranger. Now according to 1 Corinthians 6:18, "He that commits fornication sins against his own body," which is most intimately connected with a man. Therefore it seems that fornication is the most grievous of sins.

Reply to Objection 2. The fornicator is said to sin against his own body, not merely because the pleasure of fornication is consummated in the flesh, which is also the case in gluttony, but also because he acts against the good of his own body by an undue resolution and defilement thereof, and an undue association with another. Nor does it follow from this that fornication is the most grievous sin, because in man reason is of greater value than the body. Therefore, if there be a sin more opposed to reason, it will be more grievous.[10]

Objection 3. Further, the greater a good is, the graver would seem to be the sin committed against it. Now the sin of fornication is seemingly opposed to the good of the whole human race, as appears from what was said in the foregoing article. It is also against Christ, according to 1 Corinthians 6:15, "Shall I . . . take the members of Christ, and make them the members of a harlot?" Therefore fornication is the most grievous of sins.

Reply to Objection 3. The sin of fornication is contrary to the good of the human race, in so far as it is disadvantageous to the one who may be born. Now one who is already an actual member of the human species attains to the perfection of the species more than one who is a man potentially, and from this point of view murder is a

---

[10] Germain Grisez notes: "By violating their own bodies in committing sexual sins, Christians, paradoxically, violate what is not their own. By Jesus' redemptive act and their baptism into it, Christians are consecrated and incorporated into Christ. Forming one body in him, they are the temple of the Holy Spirit. Rather than profane that temple, Christians must glorify God in their bodies." "Sin, Grace, and Zero Tolerance," *First Things* 151 (March 2005): 27–36.

more grievous sin than fornication and every kind of lust, through being more opposed to the good of the human species. Again, a Divine good is greater than the good of the human race, and therefore those sins also that are against God are more grievous. Moreover, fornication is a sin against God, not directly, as though the fornicator intended to offend God, but consequently, in the same way as all mortal sins. And just as the members of our body are Christ's members, so too our spirit is one with Christ, according to 1 Corinthians 6:17, "He who is joined to the Lord is one spirit." Therefore also spiritual sins are more against Christ than fornication is.

ARTICLE 8 ～ **Is adultery a special kind of lust?**

Yes, despite objections to the contrary, Pope Leo [St. Augustine, *De Bono Conjug.* iv; Cf. Append. Grat. ad can. *Ille autem.* xxxii, qu. 5] says that "adultery is sexual intercourse with another man or woman in contravention of the marriage compact, whether through the impulse of one's own lust, or with the consent of the other party." Now this implies a special deformity of lust. Therefore adultery is a determinate species of lust.

I answer that, Adultery, as its name implies, "is access to another's marriage-bed [*ad alienum torum*]" [Cf. Append. Gratian, ad can. *Ille autem.* xxxii, qu. 1.] By so doing a man is guilty of a twofold offense against chastity and the good of human procreation: first, by accession to a woman who is not joined to him in marriage, which is contrary to the good of the upbringing of his own children; secondly, by accession to a woman who is united to another in marriage, and thus he hinders the good of another's children. The same applies to the married woman who is corrupted by adultery. Therefore it is written (Sir 23:32, 33): "Every woman . . . that leaves her husband . . . shall be guilty of sin. For first she has been unfaithful to the law of the Most High," since there it is commanded: "You shall not commit adultery"; "and secondly, she has offended against her husband," by making it uncertain that the children are his; "thirdly, she has fornicated in adultery, and has gotten children of another man," which is contrary to the good of her offspring. The first of these, however, is common to all mortal sins, while the two others belong especially to the deformity of adultery. Hence it is manifest that adultery is a determinate species of lust, through having a special deformity in sexual acts.[11]

Objection 1. It would seem that adultery is not a determinate species of lust, distinct from the other species. For adultery takes its name from a man having intercourse "with a woman who is not his own [*ad alteram*]," according to a gloss [St. Augustine: *Serm.* li, 13 (*de Divers.* lxiii)] on Exodus 20:14. Now a woman who is not one's own may be of various conditions, namely either a virgin, or under her father's care, or a harlot, or of any other description. Therefore it seems that adultery is not a species of lust distinct from the others.

Reply to Objection 1. If a married man has intercourse with another woman, his sin may be denominated either with regard to him, and thus it is always adultery, since his action is contrary to the fidelity of marriage, or with regard to the woman with whom he has intercourse; and thus sometimes it is adultery, as when a married man has intercourse with another's wife; and sometimes it has the character of seduction, or of some other sin, according to various conditions affecting the woman with whom he has intercourse; and it has been stated above (a. 1) that the species of lust correspond to the various conditions of women.

Objection 2. Further, Jerome says [*Contra Jovin.* i]: "It matters not for what reason a man behaves as one demented. Hence Sixtus the Pythagorean says in his Maxims: He that is insatiable of his wife is an adulterer," and in like manner one who is unduly enamored of any woman. Now every kind of lust includes a too ardent love. Therefore adultery is in every kind of lust; and consequently it should not be reckoned a species of lust.

---

[11] Like many kinds of wrongdoing, adultery is wrong for a number of reasons. Like premarital sex, adultery risks creating a child outside of the stability of a marriage relationship between the child's parents. In addition, adultery violates the vows of the one who has promised fidelity to another. Often, of course, it is also the case that adultery brings emotional devastation for the one cheated against. For good reason, then, adultery is explicitly mentioned in the Ten Commandments.

Reply to Objection 2. Matrimony is specially ordained for the good of human offspring, as stated above (a. 2). But adultery is specially opposed to matrimony, in the point of breaking the marriage faith that is due between husband and wife. And since the man who is too ardent a lover of his wife acts counter to the good of marriage if he use her indecently, although he be not unfaithful, he may in a sense be called an adulterer; and even more so than he that is too ardent a lover of another woman.

Objection 3. Further, where there is the same kind of deformity, there would seem to be the same species of sin. Now, apparently, there is the same kind of deformity in seduction and adultery, since in either case a woman is violated who is under another person's authority. Therefore adultery is not a determinate species of lust, distinct from the others.

Reply to Objection 3. The wife is under her husband's authority, as united to him in marriage,[12] whereas the maid is under her father's

---

[12] Various "subordination" passages are found throughout the text of Thomas. At times, however, Thomas also speaks of the equality between husband and wife: "[J]ust as in both the marriage act and in the management of the house-hold the husband is bound to the wife in all things pertaining to the husband, so is the wife bound to the husband in all things pertaining to the wife. It is in this sense that it is stated in the text (*Sent.* iv, D. 32) that they are equal in paying and demanding the debt" (*ST Supp.*, q. 64, a. 5). Even more strikingly he says in the *Summa contra Gentiles*: "[T]he greater a friendship is, the more solid and long lasting will it be. Now there seems to be *the greatest friendship between husband and wife*, for they are united not only in the act of fleshly union, which produces a certain gentle association even among beasts, but also in the partnership of the whole range of domestic activity" (*ScG* III, ch. 123, #6, trans. Vernon J. Bourke [Notre Dame, IN: University of Notre Dame Press, 1975], 148). On the basis of this equality between husband and wife, Thomas rejects the ancient custom that a husband could divorce his wife but the wife could not divorce her husband: "[I]f a husband were permitted to abandon his wife, the society of husband and wife would not be an association of equals, but, instead, a sort of slavery on the part of the wife" (*ScG* III, ch. 123, #4 [Notre Dame, IN: University of Notre Dame Press, 1975], 148). Instead, marriage for Thomas involves the pledge of unconditional love on the part of both husband and wife.

authority, as one who is to be married by that authority. Hence the sin of adultery is contrary to the good of marriage in one way, and the sin of seduction in another; therefore they are reckoned to differ specifically. Of other matters concerning adultery we shall speak in the Third Part [*Supp.*, q. 59, a. 3; *Supp.*, qq. 60, 62], when we treat of matrimony.[13]

ARTICLE 11 ~~ Is the unnatural vice a species of lust?

Yes, despite objections to the contrary, It is reckoned together with the other species of lust (2 Cor 12:21) where we read: "And have not done penance for the uncleanness, and fornication, and lasciviousness," where a gloss says: "Lasciviousness, i.e., unnatural lust."

I answer that, As stated above (aa 6, 9), wherever there occurs a special kind of deformity whereby the sexual act is rendered unbecoming, there is a determinate species of lust. This may occur in two ways: first, through being contrary to right reason, and this is common to all lustful vices; secondly, because, in addition, it is contrary to the natural order of the sexual act as becoming to the human race, and this is called "the unnatural vice."[14] This may happen in several ways: first, by procuring orgasm via masturbation, without any copulation, for the sake of sexual pleasure: this pertains to the sin of "uncleanness" which some call "effeminacy;" secondly, by copulation with a thing of undue species, and this is called "bestiality;" thirdly, by copulation with an undue sex, male with male, or female with female, as the Apostle states (Rom 1:27), and this is called the "vice of sodomy;" fourthly, by not observing the natural manner of copulation, either as to undue means, or as to other monstrous and bestial manners of copulation.[15]

---

13 Thomas did not finish the *Summa theologiae*, so later editors created a supplement made of Thomas's earlier writings to address the subjects Thomas had planned to explore in the unfinished portion of the *Summa*.

14 In the next article, omitted here, Thomas notes: "Just as the ordering of right reason proceeds from man, so the order of nature is from God Himself. Therefore in sins contrary to nature, whereby the very order of nature is violated, an injury is done to God, the Author of nature" (*ST* II–II, a. 12, ad 1).

15 The last sentence here may refer to oral or anal sex between a man and a woman or two people of the same sex. As Thomas notes later, these sins are not all of equal gravity. "Gravity of a sin depends more on the abuse of a

Objection 3. Further, lust regards acts directed to human generation, as stated above (q. 153, a. 2), whereas the unnatural vice concerns acts from which generation cannot follow. Therefore the unnatural vice is not a species of lust.

Reply to Objection 3. The lustful man intends not human generation but sexual pleasures. It is possible to have this without those acts from which human generation follows, and it is that which is sought in the unnatural vice.

---

thing than on the omission of the right use. Therefore, among sins against nature, the lowest place belongs to the sin of uncleanness, which consists in the mere omission of copulation with another. The most grievous is the sin of bestiality because use of the due species is not observed. Hence a gloss on Genesis 37:2, 'He accused his brethren of a most wicked crime,' says that 'they copulated with cattle.' After this comes the sin of sodomy, because use of the right sex is not observed. Lastly comes the sin of not observing the right manner of copulation, which is more grievous if the abuse regards the due vessel than if it affects the manner of copulation in respect of other circumstances" (a. 12, ad 3).

CONTINENCE (SELF-CONTROL)

ARTICLE 1 ~ Is continence a virtue?

Yes, despite objections to the contrary, Every praiseworthy habit would seem to be a virtue. Now such is continence, for Andronicus[1] says [*De Affectibus*] that "continence is a habit unconquered by pleasure." Therefore continence is a virtue.

I answer that, The word "continence" is taken by various people in two ways. For some understand continence to denote abstention from all sexual pleasure: thus the Apostle joins continence to chastity (Gal 5:23). In this sense perfect continence is virginity in the first place, and widowhood in the second. Therefore the same applies to continence understood thus as to virginity, which we have stated above (q. 152, a. 3) to be a virtue. Others, however, understand continence as signifying that whereby a man resists evil desires, which in him are vehement. In this sense the Philosopher takes continence (*Ethic.* vii, 7), and thus also it is used in the *Conferences of the Fathers* (*Collat.* xii, 10, 11). In this way continence has something of the nature of a virtue, in so far, to wit, as the reason stands firm in opposition to the passions, lest it be led astray by them; yet it does not attain to the perfect nature of a moral virtue, by which even the sensitive appetite is subject to reason so that vehement passions contrary to

---

[1] Andronicus of Rhodes is known to history as the tenth successor (ca. 58 B.C.) to Aristotle in the Peripatetic school. Plutarch wrote that Andronicus published a new edition of the works of Aristotle as well as works about Aristotle.

reason do not arise in the sensitive appetite. Hence the Philosopher says (*Ethic.* iv, 9) that "continence is not a virtue but a mixture," inasmuch as it has something of virtue, and somewhat falls short of virtue.

If, however, we take virtue in a broad sense, for any principle of commendable actions, we may say that continence is a virtue.

Objection 1. It would seem that continence is not a virtue. For species and genus are not co-ordinate members of the same division. But continence is coordinated with virtue, according to the Philosopher (*Ethic.* vii, 1, 9). Therefore continence is not a virtue.

Reply to Objection 1. The Philosopher includes continence in the same division with virtue in so far as the former falls short of virtue.[2]

Objection 2. Further, no one sins by using a virtue, since, according to Augustine (*De Lib. Arb.* ii, 18, 19), "a virtue is a thing that no one makes ill use of." Yet one may sin by containing oneself: for instance, if one desire to do a good, and contain oneself from doing it. Therefore continence is not a virtue.

Reply to Objection 2. Properly speaking, man is that which is according to reason. Therefore from the very fact that a man holds [*tenet se*] to that which is in accord with reason, he is said to contain himself. Now whatever pertains to perversion of reason is not according to reason. Hence he alone is truly said to be continent who stands to that which is in accord with right reason, and not to that which is in accord with perverse reason. Now evil desires are opposed to right reason, even as good desires are opposed to perverse reason. Therefore he is properly and truly continent who holds to right reason, by abstaining from evil desires, and not he who holds to perverse reason, by abstaining from good desires: indeed, the latter should rather be said to be obstinate in evil.

Objection 3. Further, no virtue withdraws man from that which is lawful, but only from unlawful things: for a gloss on Galatians 5:23,

---

[2] Aristotle notes an order of character development whose lowest level is the vicious person, who takes pleasure in doing wrong. Next comes the incontinent person, who does wrong but does not take pleasure in it. More advanced is the continent person, who does what is right but does not yet enjoy doing it. Finally, the virtuous person does what is right and enjoys doing it.

"Faith, modesty," etc., says that by continence a man refrains even from things that are lawful. Therefore continence is not a virtue.

Reply to Objection 3. The gloss quoted takes continence in the first sense, as denoting a perfect virtue, which refrains not merely from unlawful goods, but also from certain lawful things that are lesser goods, in order to give its whole attention to the more perfect goods.

ARTICLE 4 ⟶ **Is continence better than temperance?**

No, despite objections to the contrary, Tully (*De Invent. Rhet.* ii, 54) and Andronicus [*De Affectibus*] reckon continence to be annexed to temperance, as to a principal virtue.

I answer that, As stated above (a. 1), continence has a twofold signification. In one way it denotes cessation from all sexual pleasures; and if continence be taken in this sense, it is greater than temperance considered absolutely, as may be gathered from what we said above (q. 152, a. 5) concerning the preeminence of virginity over chastity considered absolutely. In another way continence may be taken as denoting the resistance of the reason to evil desires when they are vehement in a man, and in this sense temperance is far greater than continence, because the good of a virtue derives its praise from that which is in accord with reason. Now the good of reason flourishes more in the temperate man than in the continent man, because in the former even the sensitive appetite is obedient to reason, being tamed by reason so to speak, whereas in the continent man the sensitive appetite strongly resists reason by its evil desires. Hence continence is compared to temperance, as the imperfect to the perfect.[3]

---

[3] The reasonableness of a person admits of many degrees. The virtuous person does what is right and enjoys doing it, for it accords with the passions, which have been informed by reason. The continent person does what is right, but faces a struggle to do what is right because the passions have not been fully informed by reason. The incontinent person does what is wrong but feels guilty about doing wrong and knows what is right. The vicious person does what is wrong and rejoices in so doing. Through our repeated acts we all move ourselves toward becoming virtuous or toward becoming bestial. As in Oscar Wilde's *Portrait of Dorian Gray*, each person paints his own ethical self-portrait in each choice—becoming more and more beautiful or horribly disfigured.

Objection 2. Further, the greater the reward a virtue merits, the greater the virtue. Now continence apparently merits the greater reward; for it is written (2 Tim 2:5): "He . . . is not crowned, except he strive lawfully," and the continent man, since he is subject to vehement evil desires, strives more than the temperate man, in whom these things are not vehement. Therefore continence is a greater virtue than temperance.

Reply to Objection 2. The strength or weakness of concupiscence may proceed from two causes. For sometimes it is owing to a bodily cause, because some people by their natural temperament are more prone to concupiscence than others; and again opportunities for pleasure which inflame the concupiscence are nearer at hand for some people than for others. Such like weakness of concupiscence diminishes merit, whereas strength of concupiscence increases it. On the other hand, weakness or strength of concupiscence arises from a praiseworthy spiritual cause, for instance the vehemence of charity, or the strength of reason, as in the case of a temperate man. In this way weakness of concupiscence, by reason of its cause, increases merit, whereas strength of concupiscence diminishes it.[4]

---

[4] Here Thomas takes a nuanced approach to the relationship between moral worth and inclination. If by nature or circumstances beyond the person's control, a man has vehement desires to do what is not right but pursues what is right despite his desires, this act has great moral worth. If, on the other hand, his desires are tamed because of his own overwhelming charity (which, for example, might lead him to diminish as much as possible occasions of sin) then a lesser concupiscence is meritorious. Hence, the relationship between inclination and moral worth must take into account what gave rise to the inclination. If the inclination is for something bad, but this inclination was not given rise to through a person's voluntary action, then the more intense the inclination, the more meritorious it is to resist the inclination. If the inclination is for something bad, but the inclination was "fed" and not hindered by the person, then the greater inclination does not increase the merit of acting against the inclination. However, other things being equal, to have an inclination to do good and to act upon it is for Thomas much better than not to have an inclination to do good but to do good anyway. In this, Thomas follows Aristotle in that the virtuous person not only does what is right but enjoys doing it. Indeed, the virtuous person is pained at the very thought of doing evil. This reflects a greater degree of perfection than is present in the merely continent or self-restrained person and therefore a greater moral worth.

Objection 3. Further, the will is a more excellent power than the concupiscible power. But continence is in the will, whereas temperance is in the concupiscible power (Latin: *vis concupiscibilis*), as stated above (a. 3). Therefore continence is a greater virtue than temperance.

Reply to Objection 3. The will is more akin to the reason than the concupiscible power is. Therefore the good of reason—on account of which virtue is praised, by the very fact that it reaches not only to the will but also to the concupiscible power, as happens in the temperate man—is shown to be greater than if it reach only to the will, as in the case of one who is continent.[5]

---

[5] To be more perfect as a human being is to have even more of oneself brought under what is distinctly human, namely reason. Thus a virtuous person whose desires are moderated by what is truly reasonable is better than a person whose desires are not yet fully "humanized" by the influence of virtue.

QUESTION 156

INCONTINENCE[1]

ARTICLE 2 ~ Is incontinence a sin?

Yes, despite objections to the contrary, It is numbered together with other sins (2 Tim 3:3) where it is written: "Slanderers, incontinent, unmerciful," etc. Therefore incontinence is a sin.

I answer that, Incontinence about a matter may be considered in two ways. First, it may be considered properly and simply: and thus incontinence is about concupiscences of pleasures of touch, even as intemperance is, as we have said in reference to continence (q. 155, a. 2). In this way incontinence is a sin for two reasons: first, because the incontinent man goes astray from that which is in accord with reason; secondly, because he plunges into shameful pleasures. Hence the Philosopher says (*Ethic.* vii, 4) that "incontinence is censurable not only because it is wrong," that is, by straying from reason, "but also because it is wicked," that is, by following evil desires. Secondly, incontinence about a matter is considered properly—inasmuch as it is a straying from reason—but not simply, for instance when a man does not observe the mode of reason in his desire for honor, riches, and so forth, which seem to be good in themselves. About such things there

---

[1] Incontinence, in its most common contemporary sense, refers to loss of physical control of the bowels. In the moral sense used here by Thomas, incontinence is a moral disability in which a person disregards a sound ethical judgment and pursues a morally wrong goal. Incontinence in this sense is sometimes also called "weakness of will."

is incontinence, not simply but relatively, even as we have said above in reference to continence (q. 155, a. 2, ad 3). In this way incontinence is a sin, not from the fact that one gives way to wicked desires, but because one fails to observe the mode of reason, even in the desire for things that are of themselves desirable.

Thirdly, incontinence is said to be about a matter, not properly, but metaphorically, for instance about the desires for things of which one cannot make an evil use, such as the desire for virtue. A man may be said to be incontinent in these matters metaphorically, because just as the incontinent man is entirely led by his evil desire, even so is a man entirely led by his good desire, which is in accord with reason. Such like incontinence is no sin, but pertains to the perfection of virtue.[2]

Objection 1. It would seem that incontinence is not a sin. For as Augustine says (*De Lib. Arb.* iii, 18): "No man sins in what he cannot avoid." Now no man can by himself avoid incontinence, according to Wisdom 8:21, "I know [Vulg.: 'knew'] that I could not . . . be continent, except God gave it." Therefore incontinence is not a sin.

Reply to Objection 1. Man can avoid sin and do good, yet not without God's help, according to John 15:5: "Without Me you can do nothing." Therefore the fact that man needs God's help in order to be continent does not show incontinence to be no sin, for, as stated in *Ethic.* iii, 3, "what we can do by means of a friend we do, in a way, ourselves."[3]

---

2 There are, in other words, three different senses of continence: continence considered (1) properly and simply, (2) properly but not simply, and (3) not properly, but rather metaphorically. Properly and simply, incontinence involves straying from reason (properly) and indulging in shameful bodily pleasures (simply). Properly, but not simply, incontinence strays from reason in misguided pursuit of something that is otherwise good, such as honor. Not properly, but metaphorically, incontinence is a passionate pursuit of the good in accordance with reason, such as virtue. The first two senses of incontinence are always sinful, as departing from the order of reason, but the last sense is not sinful but rather virtuous.

3 Some people might conclude that we can therefore blame God for our own wrongdoing. Following Augustine, Pope John Paul II notes: "[T]emptations can be overcome, sins can be avoided, because together with the commandments the Lord gives us the possibility of keeping them: 'His eyes are on those who fear him, and he knows every deed of man. He has not commanded any

Objection 2. Further, apparently every sin originates in the reason. But the judgment of reason is overcome in the incontinent man. Therefore incontinence is not a sin.

Reply to Objection 2. The judgment of reason is overcome in the incontinent man, not necessarily, for then he would commit no sin, but through a certain negligence on account of his not standing firm in resisting the passion by holding to the judgment formed by his reason.

Objection 3. Further, no one sins in loving God vehemently. Now a man becomes incontinent through the vehemence of divine love: for Dionysius says (*Div. Nom.* iv) that "Paul, through incontinence of divine love, exclaimed: I live, now not I" (Gal 2:20). Therefore incontinence is not a sin.

Reply to Objection 3. This argument takes incontinence metaphorically and not properly.

ARTICLE 3 ⁓ **Does the incontinent person sin more gravely than the intemperate person?**

No, despite objections to the contrary, Impenitence aggravates every sin: therefore Augustine says (*De Verb. Dom. serm.* xi, 12, 13) that "impenitence is a sin against the Holy Spirit." Now according to the

one to be ungodly, and he has not given any one permission to sin' (Sir 15:19–20). Keeping God's law in particular situations can be difficult, extremely difficult, but it is never impossible. This is the constant teaching of the Church's tradition, and was expressed by the Council of Trent: 'But no one, however much justified, ought to consider himself exempt from the observance of the commandments, nor should he employ that rash statement, forbidden by the Fathers under anathema, that the commandments of God are impossible of observance by one who is justified. For God does not command the impossible, but in commanding he admonishes you to do what you can and to pray for what you cannot, and he gives his aid to enable you. His commandments are not burdensome (cf. 1 Jn 5:3); his yoke is easy and his burden light (cf. Mt 11:30)'. . . . And if redeemed man still sins, this is not due to an imperfection of Christ's redemptive act, but to man's will not to avail himself of the grace which flows from that act. God's command is of course proportioned to man's capabilities; but to the capabilities of the man to whom the Holy Spirit has been given; of the man who, though he has fallen into sin, can always obtain pardon and enjoy the presence of the Holy Spirit" (*Veritatis Splendor* 102, 103).

Philosopher (*Ethic.* vii, 8), "the intemperate man is not inclined to be penitent, for he holds on to his choice, but every incontinent man is inclined to repentance." Therefore the intemperate man sins more gravely than the incontinent.

I answer that, According to Augustine [*De Duab. Anim.* x, xi], sin is chiefly an act of the will, because "by the will we sin and live aright" [*Retract.* i, 9]. Consequently where there is a greater inclination of the will to sin, there is a graver sin. Now in the intemperate man, the will is inclined to sin in virtue of its own choice, which proceeds from a habit acquired through repeated choices, whereas in the incontinent man, the will is inclined to sin through a passion. And since passion soon passes, whereas a habit is "a disposition difficult to remove," the result is that the incontinent man repents at once, as soon as the passion has passed; but not so the intemperate man; in fact he rejoices in having sinned, because the sinful act has become connatural to him by reason of his habit.[4] Therefore in reference to such persons it is written (Prov 2:14) that "they are glad when they have done evil, and rejoice in most wicked things." Hence it follows that "the intemperate man is much worse than the incontinent," as also the Philosopher declares (*Ethic.* vii, 7).[5]

---

[4] That which is "connatural" to us is what might be called "second nature." Although we may not be born with this nature, second nature becomes natural to us and is deeply ingrained. When an action proceeds from "first nature," like eyesight, or from the "second nature" of habit, the action is enjoyable. The intemperate person's vice leads to an enjoyment of what would not be enjoyable for a virtuous person. The person who acts merely from passion soon loses desire for the object of passion after having acquired it through some act; the agent acting from habit retains the habit even after the act is done.

[5] Like Aristotle, Thomas believes in the possibility of moral development as well as moral devolution. So long as a person continues to make certain self-shaping free choices, progress continues toward saintly virtue or toward bestial vice. In terms of moral development, both the intemperate person and the incontinent person do what is wrong. They differ, however, in that the intemperate person takes pleasure in doing wrong, whereas the incontinent person regrets having done wrong and wishes to be able to do the opposite. The incontinent person reflects the experience of St. Paul, "For the good that I would I do not, but the evil which I would not, that I do" (Rom 7:19).

Objection 1. It would seem that the incontinent man sins more gravely than the intemperate. For, seemingly, the more a man acts against his conscience, the more gravely he sins, according to Luke 12:47, "That servant who knew the will of his lord . . . and did not . . . shall be beaten with many stripes." Now the incontinent man would seem to act against his conscience more than the intemperate because, according to *Ethic.* vii, 3, the incontinent man, though knowing how wicked are the things he desires, nevertheless acts through passion, whereas the intemperate man judges what he desires to be good. Therefore the incontinent man sins more gravely than the intemperate.

Reply to Objection 1. Ignorance in the intellect sometimes precedes the inclination of the appetite and causes it, and then the greater the ignorance, the more does it diminish or entirely excuse the sin, in so far as it renders it involuntary. On the other hand, ignorance in the reason sometimes follows the inclination of the appetite, and then such like ignorance, the greater it is, the graver the sin, because the inclination of the appetite is shown thereby to be greater. Now in both the incontinent and the intemperate man, ignorance arises from the appetite being inclined to something, either by passion, as in the incontinent, or by habit, as in the intemperate. Nevertheless greater ignorance results thus in the intemperate than in the incontinent. In one respect as regards duration, since in the incontinent man this ignorance lasts only while the passion endures, just as an attack of intermittent fever lasts as long as the humor is disturbed, whereas the ignorance of the intemperate man endures without ceasing, on account of the endurance of the habit. Therefore it is likened to phthisis[6] or any chronic disease, as the Philosopher says (*Ethic.* vii, 8). In another respect, the ignorance of the intemperate man is greater as regards the thing ignored. For the ignorance of the incontinent man regards some particular detail of choice (in so far as he deems that he must choose this particular thing now), whereas the intemperate man's ignorance is about the end itself, inasmuch as he judges this thing good, in order that he may follow his desires without being curbed. Hence the Philosopher says (*Ethic.* vii, 7, 8) that "the

---

6 "Phthisis" is an archaic term for pulmonary tuberculosis, severe asthma, or any other severe lung or throat infection.

incontinent man is better than the intemperate, because he retains the best principle [*to beltiston, e arche,* 'the best thing, i.e., the principle']," to wit, the right estimate of the end.

Objection 2. Further, apparently, the graver a sin is, the more incurable it is: therefore the sins against the Holy Spirit, being most grave, are declared to be unpardonable. Now the sin of incontinence would appear to be more incurable than the sin of intemperance. For a person's sin is cured by admonishment and correction, which seemingly are no good to the incontinent man, since he knows he is doing wrong, and does wrong notwithstanding, whereas it seems to the intemperate man that he is doing well, so that it were good for him to be admonished. Therefore it would appear that the incontinent man sins more gravely than the intemperate.

Reply to Objection 2. Mere knowledge does not suffice to cure the incontinent man, for he needs the inward assistance of grace, which quenches concupiscence, besides the application of the external remedy of admonishment and correction, which induce him to begin to resist his desires, so that concupiscence is weakened, as stated above (q. 142, a. 2). By these same means the intemperate man can be cured. But his curing is more difficult, for two reasons. The first is on the part of reason, which is corrupt as regards the estimate of the last end, which holds the same position as the principle in demonstrations.[7] Now it is more difficult to bring back to the truth one who errs as to the princi-

---

[7] Thomas frequently notes the similarities of practical and theoretical reasoning. Indeed, practical reasoning is an extension of theoretical reasoning (*ST* I, q. 79, a. 11, *sed contra*). The first principles of theoretical reason, the most primary and fundamental principles, find their analogue in the first principles of practical reason. Since all practical reasoning has to do with achieving an end, or goal, if a person is mistaken about the goal, practical reason will have gone more wrong than if a person has the proper end but is mistaken about how to reach that end. But the intemperate person, due to his vices, mistakes the very nature of the end. He desires that which, if he were not vicious, he would know is not really desirable. Like an addict who has come to think that taking heroin is the most important goal in life, the intemperate person does not properly understand and desire with respect to the final end. On the other hand, an incontinent person retains this desire and understanding of the final end but has passions that temporarily "cloud" this vision.

ple; and it is the same in practical matters with one who errs in regard to the end. The other reason is on the part of the inclination of the appetite: for in the intemperate man this proceeds from a habit, which is difficult to remove, whereas the inclination of the incontinent man proceeds from a passion, which is more easily suppressed.

Objection 3. Further, the more eagerly man sins, the more grievous his sin. Now the incontinent sins more eagerly than the intemperate, since the incontinent man has vehement passions and desires, which the intemperate man does not always have. Therefore the incontinent man sins more gravely than the intemperate.

Reply to Objection 3. The eagerness of the will, which increases a sin, is greater in the intemperate man than in the incontinent, as explained above. But the eagerness of concupiscence in the sensitive appetite is sometimes greater in the incontinent man, because he does not sin except through vehement concupiscence, whereas the intemperate man sins even through slight concupiscence and sometimes forestalls it. Hence the Philosopher says (*Ethic.* vii, 7) that we blame more the intemperate man, "because he pursues pleasure without desiring it or with calm," i.e., slight desire. "For what would he have done if he had desired it with passion?"[8]

ARTICLE 4 ∼ **Is the incontinent in anger worse than the incontinent in desire?**

No, despite objections to the contrary, The Philosopher says (*Ethic.* vii, 6) that "incontinence of anger is less disgraceful than incontinence of desire."

I answer that, The sin of incontinence may be considered in two ways. First, on the part of the passion which occasions the downfall of reason. In this way incontinence of desire is worse than incontinence of

---

8 Other things being equal, a person who is overcome by vehement passion is less blameworthy than a person who does wrong not through a vehement passion. In the comparison of the intemperate and the incontinent person, other things are not equal. For unlike the incontinent person, the intemperate person has a fixed disposition to do evil, and again, unlike the incontinent person, the intemperate person takes an evil end as good and so does not regret doing evil.

anger, because the movement of desire is more inordinate than the movement of anger. There are four reasons for this, and the Philosopher indicates them (*Ethic.* vii, 6): first, because the movement of anger partakes
somewhat of reason, since the angry man tends to avenge the injury
done to him, and reason guides this in a certain degree. Yet he does not
tend thereto perfectly, because he does not intend the due mode of
vengeance. On the other hand, the movement of desire is altogether in
accord with sense and nowise in accord with reason.[9] Secondly, because
the movement of anger results more from the bodily temperament
owing to the quickness of the movement of the bile which tends to
anger. Hence one who by bodily temperament is disposed to anger is
more readily angry than one who is disposed to concupiscence is liable to
be concupiscent. Therefore also it happens more often that the children
of those who are disposed to anger are themselves disposed to anger than
that the children of those who are disposed to concupiscence are also disposed to concupiscence. Now that which results from the natural disposition of the body is deemed more deserving of pardon.[10] Thirdly,
because anger seeks to work openly, whereas concupiscence is fain to dis-

---

[9] Anger arises from a judgment that a person has been wronged by another.
Consider the case of a baby who pulls her mother's hair. Although this pulling
may be painful, the (normal) mother is not angry, for she knows that the baby
is not trying to hurt her. On the other hand, if an adult pulls her hair, even if
the pulling is less painful, she may very well be angry. Unlike anger, sensuous
desires do not arise from a judgment of reason. If one sees an attractive person,
one finds the person attractive without need of consideration of further circumstances. This "instantaneous" quality of sense perception is obviously in a
certain sense governed by intelligence, but its immediacy and "closeness" to
animal instinct makes it different from anger. As Aristotle notes: "Indeed the
man incontinent in anger is prevailed upon to a degree by reason but this is
not so of one incontinent in sensual desire" (*Nicomachean Ethics,* vii, 6).

[10] In his *Commentary on the Ethics,* Thomas makes his point somewhat differently: "[T]olerance is more readily extended toward the common appetites, for
example, of food and drink—since they are natural—if they are taken precisely
as common. The desire for food but not for delicate food is natural and common. But anger is more natural and more difficult to resist than desires (not
the common ones which are necessary and natural, and less frequently the
matter of sin) but those desires that seek superfluous and unnecessary things—
those which temperance and intemperance treat" (*Commentary on the Ethics,*
book 7, lecture 6, #1390).

guise itself and creeps in by stealth.[11] Fourthly, because he who is subject to concupiscence works with pleasure, whereas the angry man works as though forced by a certain previous displeasure.[12]

Secondly, the sin of incontinence may be considered with regard to the evil into which one falls through forsaking reason; and thus incontinence of anger is, for the most part, more grievous, because it leads to things that are harmful to one's neighbor.[13]

Objection 1. It would seem that the incontinent in anger is worse than the incontinent in desire. For the more difficult it is to resist the passion, the less grievous, apparently, is incontinence; therefore the Philosopher says (*Ethic.* vii, 7): "It is not wonderful, indeed it is pardonable if a person is overcome by strong and overwhelming pleasures or pains." Now, "as Heraclitus says,[14] it is more difficult to resist desire than anger" [*Ethic.* ii. 3]. Therefore incontinence of desire is less grievous than incontinence of anger.

Reply to Objection 1. It is more difficult to resist pleasure perseveringly than anger, because concupiscence is enduring. But for the moment it is more difficult to resist anger, on account of its impetuousness.

---

[11] Given that people try to hide what is shameful, the fact that people often try to disguise or conceal their intemperance but openly display anger indicates that intemperance is considered more shameful.

[12] As Thomas notes in his *Commentary on the Ethics* (book 7, lecture 6, #1396), that which is done out of sadness has less the character of being voluntary than that which is done with pleasure. But the person acting from anger is acting out of sadness at the injury received, whereas the intemperate person is acting on account of pleasure. The intemperate person's act is thus more fully voluntary than the angry person's act, and as more voluntary and freely done, more blameworthy.

[13] In other words, with respect to the results, anger may be worse than intemperance because more injury to persons may take place. An act is not morally characterized simply in terms of results, however, for often times a good act might lead to bad results (one pays a just wage and a person uses it to buy drugs) or a bad act might lead to good results (for example, an act of adultery leads to the conception of someone who becomes a great saint).

[14] Heraclitus (540–480 B.C.) is one of the most important of the so-called "pre-Socratic" philosophers. According to Heraclitus, the universe, constituted primarily by fire, is ever changing, ever in flux, but behind it all lies the "Logos," the reason or word that orders the entire cosmos.

Objection 2. Further, one is altogether excused from sin if the passion be so vehement as to deprive one of the judgment of reason, as in the case of one who becomes demented through passion. Now he that is incontinent in anger retains more of the judgment of reason than one who is incontinent in desire, since "anger listens to reason somewhat, but desire does not," as the Philosopher states (*Ethic.* vii, 6). Therefore the incontinent in anger is worse than the incontinent in desire.

Reply to Objection 2. Concupiscence is stated to be without reason, not as though it destroyed altogether the judgment of reason, but because in no way does it follow the judgment of reason: and for this reason it is more disgraceful.

Objection 3. Further, the more dangerous a sin, the more grievous it is. Now incontinence of anger would seem to be more dangerous, since it leads a man to a greater sin, namely murder, for this is a more grievous sin than adultery, to which incontinence of desire leads. Therefore incontinence of anger is graver than incontinence of desire.

Reply to Objection 3. This argument considers incontinence with regard to its result.

QUESTION 158

ANGER

ARTICLE 1 ⟿ Is it ethically permissible to be angry?

Yes, despite objections to the contrary, Chrysostom [*Hom.* xi, in the *Opus Imperfectum*, falsely ascribed to St. John Chrysostom] says: "He that is angry without cause shall be in danger; but he that is angry with cause shall not be in danger: for without anger, teaching will be useless, judgments unstable, crimes unchecked." Therefore to be angry is not always an evil.[1]

I answer that, Properly speaking anger is a passion of the sensitive appetite, and gives its name to the irascible power, as stated above (I–II, q. 46, a. 1) when we were treating of the passions. Now with regard to the passions of the soul, it is to be observed that evil may be found in them in two ways: first by reason of the passion's very species, which is derived from the passion's object. Thus envy, in respect of its species, denotes an evil, since it is displeasure at another's good, and such displeasure is in itself contrary to reason; therefore, as the Philosopher remarks (*Ethic.* ii, 6), "the very mention of envy denotes something evil." Now this does not apply to anger, which is the desire for revenge, since revenge may be desired both well and ill. Secondly, evil is found in a passion in respect of the passion's quantity, that is, in respect of its excess or deficiency; and thus evil may be found in anger, when, to wit, one is angry more or less than right reason demands. But

---

[1] Indeed, in q. 158, a. 8, Thomas notes that sometimes failing to become angry when the circumstances are due is wrong.

if one is angry in accordance with right reason, one's anger is deserving of praise.

Objection 1. It would seem that it cannot be lawful to be angry. For Jerome in his exposition on Matthew 5:22, "Whosoever is angry with his brother," etc., says: "Some codices[2] add 'without cause.' However, in the genuine codices the sentence is unqualified, and anger is forbidden altogether." Therefore it is nowise lawful to be angry.

Reply to Objection 1. The Stoics designated anger and all the other passions as emotions opposed to the order of reason; and accordingly they deemed anger and all other passions to be evil, as stated above (I–II, q. 24, a. 2) when we were treating of the passions. It is in this sense that Jerome considers anger; for he speaks of the anger whereby one is angry with one's neighbor with the intent of doing him a wrong. But, according to the Peripatetics,[3] to whose opinion Augustine inclines (*De Civ. Dei* ix, 4), anger and the other passions of the soul are movements of the sensitive appetite, whether they be moderated or not according to reason; and in this sense anger is not always evil.

Objection 2. Further, according to Dionysius (*Div. Nom.* iv): "The soul's evil is to be without reason." Now anger is always without reason: for the Philosopher says (*Ethic.* vii, 6) that "anger does not listen perfectly to reason"; and Gregory says (*Moral.* v, 45) that "when anger sunders the tranquil surface of the soul, it mangles and rends it by its riot"; and Cassian[4] says (*De Inst. Caenob.* viii, 6): "From whatever cause

---

  2 "The usual form of book in late antiquity and in the middle ages was the codex [in the plural codices], which consisted of simple sheets of papyrus or parchment folded once and sewn together to form quires or gatherings. In origin it was an imitation of wax tablet diptychs and it had a predecessor in the parchment notebook." Bernhard Bischoff, *Latin Paleography: Antiquity and the Middle Ages* (Cambridge: Cambridge University Press, 1990), 20. Codices were written by hand, and so it often happened that scribal errors were introduced into manuscripts, leading over the centuries to various versions of the text that were not in accord with one another. Jerome sought to establish the "genuine" version of the text as opposed to the corruptions, sometimes a very difficult task indeed.

  3 The Peripatetics were inspired by the teachings of Aristotle.

  4 St. John Cassian (b. ca. 360; d. ca. 435) was a monk who, after having spent time with the desert monks in Bethlehem and Egypt, wrote two works that

it arises, the angry passion boils over and blinds the eye of the mind." Therefore it is always evil to be angry.

Reply to Objection 2. Anger may stand in a twofold relation to reason: first, antecedently; in this way it withdraws reason from its rectitude, and has therefore the character of evil; secondly, consequently, inasmuch as the movement of the sensitive appetite is directed against vice and in accordance with reason; this anger is good, and is called "zealous anger." Therefore Gregory says (*Moral.* v, 45): "We must beware lest, when we use anger as an instrument of virtue, it overrule the mind, and go before it as its mistress, instead of following in reason's train, ever ready, as its handmaid, to obey." This latter anger, although it hinder somewhat the judgment of reason in the execution of the act, does not destroy the rectitude of reason. Hence Gregory says (*Moral.* v, 45) that "zealous anger troubles the eye of reason, whereas sinful anger blinds it." Nor is it incompatible with virtue that the deliberation of reason be interrupted in the execution of what reason has deliberated, since art also would be hindered in its act if it were to deliberate about what has to be done, while having to act.[5]

Objection 3. Further, anger is "desire for vengeance" [Aristotle, *Rhet.* ii, 2]. According to a gloss on Levitcus 19:17, "You shall not hate your brother in your heart." Now it would seem unlawful to desire vengeance, since this should be left to God, according to Deuteronomy 32:35, "Revenge is Mine." Therefore it would seem that to be angry is always an evil.

---

became well known in the Middle Ages, namely the *Institutes* (mentioned here by Thomas), which treats the monastic life, and the *Conferences*, a work concerning inner spiritual perfection.

5 Although it is always wrong to act *against reason*, it is not always wrong to act without the concurrent deliberations of reason. We need not, indeed should not, deliberate or "reason" at all times. As Thomas notes in I–II, q. 34, a. 1, ad 1: "[I]n conjugal intercourse, though the pleasure be in accord with reason, yet it hinders the use of reason, on account of the accompanying bodily change. But in this case the pleasure is not morally evil, as neither is sleep, whereby the reason is fettered, morally evil, if it be taken according to reason: *for reason itself demands that the use of reason be interrupted at times*" (emphasis added).

Reply to Objection 3. It is unlawful to desire vengeance considered as evil to the man who is to be punished, but it is praiseworthy to desire vengeance as a corrective of vice and for the good of justice; and to this the sensitive appetite can tend, in so far as it is moved thereto by the reason, and when revenge is taken in accordance with the order of judgment, it is God's work, since he who has power to punish "is God's minister," as stated in Romans 13:4.

Objection 4. Further, all that makes us depart from likeness to God is evil. Now anger always makes us depart from likeness to God, since God judges with tranquility according to Wisdom 12:18. Therefore to be angry is always an evil.

Reply to Objection 4. We can and ought to be like to God in the desire for good; but we cannot be altogether likened to Him in the mode of our desire, since in God there is no sensitive appetite, as in us, the movement of which has to obey reason. Therefore Gregory says (*Moral.* v, 45) that "anger is more firmly erect in withstanding vice when it bows to the command of reason."

ARTICLE 2 ～ **Is anger a sin?**

Yes, despite objections to the contrary, The Apostle says (Eph 4:31): "Let all indignation and anger [Vulg.: 'anger and indignation'] . . . be put away from you."

I answer that, Anger, as stated above (a. 1), is properly the name of a passion. A passion of the sensitive appetite is good in so far as it is regulated by reason, whereas it is evil if it set the order of reason aside. Now the order of reason, in regard to anger, may be considered in relation to two things: first, in relation to the appetible object to which anger tends, and that is revenge. Therefore, if one desire revenge to be taken in accordance with the order of reason, the desire of anger is praiseworthy, and is called "zealous anger" [Cf. Gregory, *Moral.* v, 45]. On the other hand, if one desire the taking of vengeance in any way whatever contrary to the order of reason, for instance if he desire the punishment of one who has not deserved it, or beyond his deserts, or again contrary to the order prescribed by law, or not for the due end, namely the maintaining of justice and the correction of faults, then the desire of anger will be sinful, and this is called sinful anger.

Secondly, the order of reason in regard to anger may be considered in relation to the mode of being angry, namely that the movement of anger should not be immoderately fierce, neither internally nor externally; and if this condition be disregarded, anger will not lack sin, even though just vengeance be desired.

Objection 1. It would seem that anger is not a sin. For we are made blameworthy by sinning. But "we are not praiseworthy through the passions, even as neither do we incur blame thereby," as stated in *Ethic.* ii, 5. Consequently no passion is a sin. Now anger is a passion as stated above (I–II, q. 46, a. 1) in the treatise on the passions. Therefore anger is not a sin.

Reply to Objection 1. Since passion may be either regulated or not regulated by reason, it follows that a passion considered absolutely does not include the notion of merit or demerit, of praise or blame.[6] But as regulated by reason, it may be something meritorious and deserving of praise, while on the other hand, as not regulated by reason, it may be demeritorious and blameworthy. Therefore the Philosopher says (*Ethic.* ii, 5) that "it is he who is angry in a certain way that is praised or blamed."

Objection 2. Further, in every sin there is conversion to some mutable good. But in anger there is conversion not to a mutable good, but to a person's evil. Therefore anger is not a sin.

Reply to Objection 2. The angry man desires the evil of another, not for its own sake but for the sake of revenge, towards which his appetite turns as to a mutable good.

Objection 3. Further, "No man sins in what he cannot avoid," as Augustine asserts [*De Lib. Arb.* iii, 18]. But man cannot avoid anger,

---

[6] In other words, merely to have an emotion is not as such morally good or evil, but rather morally neutral. We simply have emotional reactions much like we simply have physical desire for food. As Thomas goes on to note, however, to the extent that our emotions can be and are informed by reason, to that extent we may form them (or deform them) in a way that merits praise or blame.

for a gloss on Psalm 4:5, "Be angry, but sin not," says: "The movement of anger is not in our power." Again, the Philosopher asserts (*Ethic.* vii, 6) that "the angry man acts with displeasure." Now displeasure is contrary to the will. Therefore anger is not a sin.

Reply to Objection 3. Man is master of his actions through the judgment of his reason. Therefore, as to the movements that forestall that judgment, it is not in man's power to prevent them as a whole, i.e., so that none of them arise, although his reason is able to check each one, if it arise. Accordingly it is stated that the movement of anger is not in man's power, to the extent, namely, that no such movement arise. Yet since this movement is somewhat in his power, it is not entirely sinless if it be inordinate. The statement of the Philosopher that "the angry man acts with displeasure" means that he is displeased, not with his being angry, but with the injury which he deems done to himself, and through this displeasure he is moved to seek vengeance.

Objection 4. Further, sin is contrary to nature, according to Damascene [*De Fide Orth.* ii, 4, 30]. But it is not contrary to man's nature to be angry, and it is the natural act of a power, namely the irascible; therefore Jerome says in a letter [Ep. xii, *ad Anton. Monach.*] that "to be angry is the property of man." Therefore it is not a sin to be angry.

Reply to Objection 4. The irascible power in man is naturally subject to his reason. Therefore its act is natural to man, in so far as it is in accord with reason, and in so far as it is against reason, it is contrary to man's nature.

QUESTION 161

~~~~~~~~~~~~

HUMILITY

ARTICLE 1 ~~ **Is humility a virtue?**

Yes, despite objections to the contrary, Origen, commenting on Luke 1:48, "He has regarded the humility of His handmaid," says (*Hom.* viii, *in Luc.*): "One of the virtues, humility, is particularly commended in Holy Scripture; for our Savior said: 'Learn from Me, because I am meek, and humble of heart.'"[1]

---

[1] One may wonder why humility is treated under the rubric of temperance, rather than, for example, under justice or courage. In II–II, q. 161, a. 4, Thomas answers: "[I]n assigning parts to a virtue we consider chiefly the likeness that results from the mode of the virtue. Now the mode of temperance, whence it chiefly derives its praise, is the restraint or suppression of the impetuosity of a passion. Hence whatever virtues restrain or suppress, and the actions which moderate the impetuosity of the emotions, are reckoned parts of temperance. Now just as meekness suppresses the movement of anger, so does humility suppress the movement of hope, which is the movement of a spirit aiming at great things. Therefore, like meekness, humility is accounted a part of temperance. For this reason the Philosopher (*Ethic.* iv, 3) says that a man who aims at small things in proportion to his mode is not magnanimous but 'temperate,' and such a man we may call humble. Moreover, for the reason given above (q. 160, a. 2), among the various parts of temperance, the one under which humility is comprised is modesty as understood by Tully (*De Invent. Rhet.* ii, 54), inasmuch as humility is nothing else than a moderation of spirit; therefore it is written (1 Pt 3:4): 'In the incorruptibility of a quiet and meek spirit.'" The "mode" of a virtue classifies the virtue as belonging to one of four general categories of ethical excellence. As Thomas notes in I–II, q. 61, a. 3: "[A]ny virtue that causes good in reason's act of consideration may be called prudence; every virtue that causes

I answer that, As stated above (I–II, q. 23, a. 2) when we were treating of the passions, the difficult good has something attractive to the appetite, namely the aspect of good, and likewise something repulsive to the appetite, namely the difficulty of obtaining it.[2] In respect of the former there arises the movement of hope, and in respect of the latter, the movement of despair. Now it has been stated above (I–II, q. 61, a. 2) that for those appetitive movements which are a kind of impulse towards an object, there is need of a moderating and restraining moral virtue, while for those which are a kind of recoil, there is need, on the part of the appetite, of a moral virtue to strengthen it and urge it on. Therefore a twofold virtue is necessary with regard to the difficult good: one to temper and restrain the mind, lest it tend to high things immoderately; and this belongs to the virtue

---

the good of right and due in operation, be called justice; every virtue that curbs and represses the passions, be called temperance; and every virtue that strengthens the mind against any passions whatever, be called courage. Many, both holy doctors, as also philosophers, speak about these virtues in this sense; and in this way the other virtues are contained under them." Although prudence, justice, temperance, and courage have their own proper matter, and as such are distinctive or "special virtues," these fundamental characteristics or modes of virtue are considered apart from what makes them distinctive from the general characterization of various other distinctive or special virtues. In this case, humility restrains the passion of hope (not the theological virtue of hope!) that would lead one to seek that which is too exalted for one's capacity. As such, humility is a potential part or secondary virtue of temperance, even though temperance itself, considered as a special virtue, treats bodily pleasures that are not an integral part of humility.

2 Thomas also expands on this idea in I–II, q. 23, a. 1: "In order, therefore, to discern which passions are in the irascible, and which in the concupiscible, we must take the object of each of these powers. For we have stated (in I, q. 81, a. 2), that the object of the concupiscible power is sensible good or evil, simply apprehended as such, which causes pleasure or pain. But, since the soul must, of necessity, experience difficulty or struggle at times, in acquiring some such good, or in avoiding some such evil, in so far as such good or evil is more than our animal nature can easily acquire or avoid, therefore this very good or evil, inasmuch as it is of an arduous or difficult nature, is the object of the irascible faculty. Therefore whatever passions regard good or evil absolutely belong to the concupiscible power: for instance joy, sorrow, love, hatred, and such like, whereas those passions which regard good or bad as arduous, through being difficult to obtain or avoid, belong to the irascible faculty; such are daring, fear, hope, and the like."

of humility; and another to strengthen the mind against despair, and urge it on to the pursuit of great things according to right reason; and this is magnanimity. Therefore it is evident that humility is a virtue.[3]

Objection 1. It would seem that humility is not a virtue. For virtue conveys the notion of a penal evil, according to Psalm 104:18, "They humbled his feet in fetters." Therefore humility is not a virtue.

Reply to Objection 1. As Isidore observes (*Etym.* x), "a humble man is so called because he is, as it were, '*homo acclinis*' [literally, 'a man bent to the ground']," i.e., inclined to the lowest place. This may happen in two ways: first, through an extrinsic principle, for instance when one is cast down by another, and thus humility is a punishment; secondly, through an intrinsic principle, and this may be done sometimes well, for instance when a man, considering his own failings, assumes the lowest place according to his mode: thus Abraham said to the Lord (Gen 18:27), "I will speak to my Lord, whereas I am dust and ashes." In this way humility is a virtue. Sometimes, however, this may be ill-done, for instance when man, "not understanding his honor, compares himself to senseless beasts, and becomes like to them" (Ps 48:13).

Objection 2. Further, virtue and vice are mutually opposed. Now humility seemingly denotes a vice, for it is written (Sir 19:23): "There is one that humbles himself wickedly." Therefore humility is not a virtue.

Reply to Objection 2. As stated (ad 1), humility, in so far as it is a virtue, conveys the notion of a praiseworthy self-abasement to the lowest place. Now this is sometimes done merely as to outward signs and pretense: therefore this is "false humility," of which Augustine says in a letter (Ep. cxlix) that it is "grievous pride," since, to wit, it would seem to aim at excellence of glory. Sometimes, however, this is done by an inward

---

3 St. Bernard describes humility as "a virtue by which a man knowing himself as he truly is, abases himself" (Arthur Devine, "Humility" *The Catholic Encyclopedia*, 1914 [San Diego: Catholic Answers, 2007] p. 543).This description is in accord with the definition of St. Thomas: "The virtue of humility," he says, "consists in keeping oneself within one's own bounds, not reaching out to things above one, but submitting to one's superior" (*Summa contra Gentiles*, Bk. IV, Ch. lv, trans. Rickaby).

movement of the soul, and in this way, properly speaking, humility is reckoned a virtue, because virtue does not consist in externals, but chiefly in the inward choice of the mind, as the Philosopher states (*Ethic.* ii, 5).

Objection 3. Further, no virtue is opposed to another virtue. But humility is apparently opposed to the virtue of magnanimity, which aims at great things, whereas humility shuns them. Therefore it would seem that humility is not a virtue.

Reply to Objection 3. Humility restrains the appetite from aiming at great things against right reason, while magnanimity urges the mind to great things in accord with right reason. Hence it is clear that magnanimity is not opposed to humility; indeed they concur in this, that each is according to right reason.[4]

Objection 4. Further, virtue is "the disposition of that which is perfect" (Aristotle, *Phys.* vii, text. 17). But humility seemingly belongs to the imperfect. Therefore it becomes not God to be humble, since He can be subject to none. Therefore it seems that humility is not a virtue.

Reply to Objection 4. A thing is said to be perfect in two ways: first absolutely; such a thing contains no defect, neither in its nature nor in respect of anything else, and thus God alone is perfect. To Him humility is fitting, not as regards His Divine nature, but only as regards His assumed nature. Secondly, a thing may be said to be perfect in a restricted sense, for instance in respect of its nature or state or time. Thus a virtuous man is perfect, although in comparison with God his perfection is found wanting, according to the word of Isaiah 40:17, "All nations are before Him as if they had no being at all." In this way humility may be competent to every man.[5]

---

[4] Virtue helps us attain the mean. The virtue of humility restrains us lest we seek that which is beyond our capacity, overreaching the limits of our potential; the virtue of magnanimity restrains us lest we seek only that which is beneath our capacity, not reaching for that which we can achieve. Although these virtues appear at first glance to be opposites, Thomas sees them in harmonious operation in the pursuit of great things.

[5] "Perfect" therefore has two distinct meanings. Perfect can mean enjoying every good, without any limitation, in every respect having the fullness of all that is

Objection 5. Further, every moral virtue is about actions and passions, according to *Ethic.* ii, 3. But humility is not reckoned by the Philosopher among the virtues that are about passions; nor is it comprised under justice, which is about actions. Therefore it would seem not to be a virtue.

Reply to Objection 5. The Philosopher intended to treat of virtues as directed to civic life, wherein the subjection of one man to another is defined according to the ordinance of the law, and consequently is a matter of legal justice. But humility, considered as a special virtue, regards chiefly the subjection of man to God, for Whose sake he humbles himself by subjecting himself to others.

---

desirable. In this sense, no one but God alone is perfect. Perfect can, however, also mean, as it literally does in Latin, "thoroughly made," *per-factum.* In this sense, a coffee cup, radio, or human being may be "perfect" as having all the due perfections a coffee cup, radio, or human being should have.

QUESTION 162

PRIDE

ARTICLE 1 ⮞ **Is pride a sin?**

Yes, despite objections to the contrary, It is written (Tob 4:14): "Never suffer pride to reign in your mind or in your words."

I answer that, Pride [*superbia*] is so called because a man thereby aims higher [*supra*] than he is; therefore Isidore says (*Etym.* x): "A man is said to be proud because he wishes to appear above [*super*] what he really is"; for he who wishes to overstep beyond what he is, is proud.[1] Now right reason requires that every man's will should tend to that which is proportionate to him. Therefore it is evident that pride denotes something opposed to right reason, and this shows it to have the character of sin, because according to Dionysius (*Div. Nom.* iv, 4), "the soul's evil is to be opposed to reason." Therefore it is evident that pride is a sin.[2]

Objection 1. It would seem that pride is not a sin. For no sin is the object of God's promise. For God's promises refer to what He will do;

---

1 Pride and humility are therefore closely related to self-knowledge and the truth. It is not pride to recognize and appreciate the gifts and talents one has received from God. It is not humility to pretend that one is less than one really is. The sin of pride is a failure of self-knowledge through an overestimation of one's own powers, but the virtue of humility does not underestimate what one has been given by God.

2 It is also evident how pride and humility have a relationship of contrariety, a vice and a virtue. The proud person lacks the virtue of humility and so "overreaches" for that which cannot be achieved.

and He is not the author of sin. Now pride is numbered among the
Divine promises: for it is written (Is 60:15): "I will make you to be an
everlasting pride, a joy from generation to generation." Therefore pride
is not a sin.

Reply to Objection 1. Pride [*superbia*] may be understood in two
ways; first, as overpassing [*supergreditur*] the rule of reason, and in this
sense we say that it is a sin. Secondly, it may simply denominate "superabundance"; in which sense any super-abundant thing may be called
pride, and it is thus that God promises pride as significant of super-
abundant good. Hence a gloss of Jerome on the same passage (Is 61:6)
says that "there is a good and an evil pride," or "a sinful pride which
God resists, and a pride that denotes the glory which He bestows."

It may also be replied that pride there signifies abundance of those
things in which men may take pride.

Objection 2. Further, it is not a sin to wish to be like God: for every
creature has a natural desire for this; and especially does this become the
rational creature which is made to God's image and likeness. Now it is
said in Prosper's *Lib. Sent., Sent.* 294 that "pride is love of one's own
excellence, whereby one is likened to God who is supremely excellent."
Hence Augustine says (*Confess.* ii, 6): "Pride imitates exaltedness, whereas
You alone are God exalted over all." Therefore pride is not a sin.

Reply to Objection 2. Reason has the direction of those things for
which man has a natural appetite, so that if the appetite wander from the
rule of reason, whether by excess or by defect, it will be sinful, as is the
case with the appetite for food which man desires naturally. Now pride is
the appetite for excellence in excess of right reason. Therefore Augustine
says (*De Civ. Dei* xiv, 13) that pride is the "desire for inordinate exalta-
tion"; and hence it is that, as he asserts (*De Civ. Dei* xiv, 13; xix, 12),
"pride imitates God inordinately: for it has equality of fellowship under
Him, and wishes to usurp His dominion over our fellow-creatures."[3]

---

[3] As understood by Augustine, pride is a form of idolatry, self-idolatry. In the
place of God, a human being puts himself at the center of the universe, as the
most important of all things, as that which takes first place. In every sin, there
is at least a bit of pride, for in every sin desire for self-satisfaction overrides the

Objection 3. Further, a sin is opposed not only to a virtue but also to a contrary vice, as the Philosopher states (*Ethic.* ii, 8). But no vice is found to be opposed to pride. Therefore pride is not a sin.

Reply to Objection 3. Pride is directly opposed to the virtue of humility, which, in a way, is concerned about the same matter as magnanimity, as stated above (q. 161, a. 1, ad 3). Hence the vice opposed to pride by defect is akin to the vice of pusillanimity, which is opposed by defect to magnanimity. For just as it belongs to magnanimity to urge the mind to great things against despair, so it belongs to humility to withdraw the mind from the inordinate desire of great things against presumption. Now pusillanimity, if we take it for a deficiency in pursuing great things, is properly opposed to magnanimity by defect; but if we take it for the mind's attachment to things beneath what is becoming to a man, it is opposed to humility by defect, since each proceeds from a smallness of mind. In the same way, on the other hand, pride may be opposed by excess, both to magnanimity and humility, from different points of view: to humility, inasmuch as it scorns subjection; to magnanimity, inasmuch as it tends to great things inordinately. Since, however, pride implies a certain elation, it is more directly opposed to humility, even as pusillanimity, which denotes littleness of soul in tending towards great things, is more directly opposed to magnanimity.

---

will to choose that which is in accord with the will of God. For more, see John Cavadini, "The Structure and Intention of Augustine's *De Trinitate*," *Augustinian Studies* 23 (1992): 103–23; for a wonderful resource on Augustine, see the book edited by Cavadini and Allan Fitzgerald, *Augustine Through the Ages: An Encyclopedia* (Grand Rapids, MI: W. B. Eerdmans, 1999).

General Index

Scripture Index

439